The publisher gratefully acknowledges the generous support of the Simpson Humanities Endowment Fund of the University of California Press Foundation.

MUSIC AFTER THE FALL

MUSIC AFTER THE FALL

Modern Composition and
Culture since 1989

———

Tim Rutherford-Johnson

UNIVERSITY OF CALIFORNIA PRESS

University of California Press, one of the most distinguished university presses in the United States, enriches lives around the world by advancing scholarship in the humanities, social sciences, and natural sciences. Its activities are supported by the UC Press Foundation and by philanthropic contributions from individuals and institutions. For more information, visit www.ucpress.edu.

University of California Press
Oakland, California

Library of Congress Cataloging-in-Publication Data

Names: Rutherford-Johnson, Tim, author.
Title: Music after the fall : modern composition and culture since 1989 / Tim Rutherford-Johnson.
Description: Oakland, California : University of California Press, [2017] | Includes bibliographical references and index.
Identifiers: LCCN 2016040711 | ISBN 9780520283145 (cloth : alk. paper) | ISBN 9780520283152 (pbk. : alk. paper) | ISBN 9780520959040 (ePub)
Subjects: LCSH: Music—20th century—History and criticism. | Music—21st century—History and criticism. | Music—Social aspects—History—20th century. | Music—Social aspects—History—21st century.
Classification: LCC ML197 .R94 2017 | DDC 780.9/04—dc23
LC record available at https://lccn.loc.gov/2016040711

Manufactured in the United States of America

26 25 24 23 22 21 20 19 18 17
10 9 8 7 6 5 4 3 2 1

This one's for Liz, Mizzle, and Conks.

CONTENTS

ILLUSTRATIONS

ACKNOWLEDGMENTS

Throughout this book's gestation and creation, many people gave generously of their time, ideas, and materials, both in formal interviews and informal conversations, virtually and in meatspace. I hope I can catch at least the most important ones here.

Among the composers, Richard Barrett, Aaron Cassidy, Evan Johnson, and Liza Lim have provided endless conversations, materials, and inspirations. Chaya Czernowin, Cassandra Miller, Alwynne Pritchard, James Saunders, Charlie Sdraulig, and Carl Stone were all generous with time, conversations, and materials. Philipp Blume, Daniel James Wolf, and Alistair Zaldua have proved excellent online companions, introducing me to more revelatory musical experiences than I thought possible. Michel van der Aa provided opportunities to write. Among the performers, I owe a particular debt of thanks for conversations, perspectives, and kickass musicianship to Daryl Buckley and the players of ELISION, as well as to Mark Knoop, Anton Lukoszevieze, Ian Pace, Heather Roche, Carl Rosman, and Philip Thomas.

Among the writers and scholars, Paul Griffiths and Alex Ross have provided both inspiration and encouragement. As a mentor, Keith Potter has provided support and direction for nearly two decades. An early conversation with Adrian Thomas strengthened my resolve to turn my ideas into a book. Seth Brodsky, Roddy Hawkins, and Lauren Redhead generously shared unpublished research. I have had invaluable conversations with Lawrence Dunn, John Fallas, Stephen Graham, Martin Iddon, and Tom Perchard. Andreas Engström, Larry Goves, and Nick Reyland all provided opportunities to present some of my work in public. Jennie Gottschalk bravely read my early drafts and has been an invaluable co-conspirator throughout. Christopher Fox, Will Robin, Chris Swithinbank, and Jennifer Walshe also read chapters and saved me from embarrassment on several occasions. (Any remaining errors are all mine.) David Mendoza made valuable criticisms of articles I published on *NewMusicBox*, and which I later incorporated into chapter 5 of this book. Vincenzo Donato suggested some architectural examples for chapter 8. Finally, I am grateful to the various reviewers of this book's proposal and manuscript, whose comments have improved the book immeasurably.

Among the editors, the enthusiasm and support of Mary Francis at University of California Press from this book's formal beginning and into its afterness has been awe-inspiring. I am indebted also to Mary's successor at UC Press, Raina Polivka, who guided the book over the finishing line, and to my copyeditor, Genevieve Thurston, who seemed to improve almost every line. Laura Macy, John Tyrrell, and Charles Wilson, as editors at the *New Grove,* gave me an old-fashioned and irreplaceable education in the written word and an unrivalled opportunity to learn about living composers. Molly Sheridan of *NewMusicBox* never turned down a pitch. Edward Bhesania at the BBC gave me opportunities to write about countless works in the form of program notes, many elements of which have found their way into the present text. Malcolm MacDonald and Bob Gilmore were supportive editors at *Tempo* and great servants to new music writing in the United Kingdom. Both passed away while this book was being written; both are very sadly missed.

I will be forever grateful to John and Sue for providing writing sanctuaries, in both Sussex and Suffolk, and to my White Crane instructor, Richard Wagstaff, for keeping my mind and body on track. A generous grant from the Hinrichsen Foundation helped see the book through its final few months. And nothing would have been possible without the limitless support and encouragement of my parents, Linda and Martin Johnson.

Finally, with endless love, I thank Elizabeth for throwing down this particular gauntlet and being my ideal reader ever since.

1989 AND AFTER

BEGINNINGS

It begins with a string quartet: two violins, a viola, and a cello pumping notes up and down like pistons. An image of the American machine age, hallucinated through the sound of the European Enlightenment. The image is strengthened as a voice—mature, female, American—intones an itinerary: "From Chicago . . . to New York." The sound is prerecorded, digitally sampled and amplified through speakers beside the ensemble. More samples are added: more voices; the whistles and bells of trains; one, two, three, or even more string quartets. Rapidly the musical space far exceeds what we see on stage. This is a string quartet for the media age, as much recordings and amplification as it is the four musicians in front of us. Yet everything extends from it and back into it, whether the quartet of quartets, which mirror and echo each other; the voices, which seem to blend seamlessly with the instrumental rhythms and melodies; or the whistles, which mesh so clearly with the harmonic changes that it seems certain they come from an unseen wind instrument and not a concrete recording.

· · ·

It begins with thumping and hammering, small clusters struck on the piano keyboard with the side of the palm or with three fingers pressed together, jabbing like a beak. The sound recalls a malevolent dinosaur or perhaps a furious child, but it isn't random; a melody of sorts, or an identifiable series of pitches at least, hangs over the tumult. After twenty seconds or so the thunder halts abruptly for a two-note rising motif played by the right hand, which is then imitated (slightly altered) by the left. It is a simple gesture, refusing, with that delicate variation on the repeat, to do as expected, and expressed with the utmost clarity and efficiency. We have jumped from breezeblocks to water, but the expressive force remains. At every turn the music—on paper just a short sonata for piano—seems about to burst its own edges. Distortion is applied in every dimension, from the blurring of the melodic line with those cluster chords, to the extremities of force and volume required from instrument and performer (for the majority of the piece, every note is marked to be played very loud, except those marked even louder), to the extremes of range, from the very highest to the very lowest notes of the piano that stretch any sense of sonic unity or middle ground to its limit. Even at just seven minutes long, it is a shattering experience for both performer and listener, only heightened by the few moments of quiet contemplation that occur toward the end of the piece.

. . .

It begins with water, gently lapping, close miked. In the distance, the hum of a city. The occasional calls of a gull suggest we are on the coast. A woman's voice enters, softly describing the location and where she is standing, where we are listening: "It's a calm morning. I'm on Kits Beach in Vancouver. It's slightly overcast—and very mild for January." She is very close, almost *inside* our ears, but the place she describes and what we can hear is far away. An aircraft passes overhead. A car sounds its horn in the distance, and it echoes against buildings and around the bay. This is Kitsilano Beach, on the south shore of Vancouver's English Bay, a popular spot in summer for sunbathing and beach sports. The narration is straightforward at first, but it soon moves from describing the sounds to reflecting on their acoustic properties: "The tiny clicking sounds that you hear are the meeting of the water and the barnacles. It trickles and clicks and sucks and . . . The city is roaring around these tiny sounds. But it's not masking them." Just as we start to internalize those sounds, hearing them in the same abstract headspace as the narrator's voice, the recording levels are suddenly turned up: "I could shock you or fool you by saying that the soundscape is this loud." And then: "The view is beautiful—in fact it is spectacular. So the sound level seems more like this." The levels drop again, now quieter than they were before, and our perceptions of what is real and what is artificial, out in the world and inside the recording, are completely subverted. "It doesn't seem that loud."

. . .

It is loud, and it begins instantly. We hear what is probably feedback, controlled in some way to create different pitches. Blank, artificial, but somehow also animal (fleshy at least)—overdriven and very distorted. After a few seconds it is intercut with something like the sound of tape spooling backward—high-pitched, an almost glistening sound. Then sudden, violent splices of what sound like fragments of orchestral music. Again, lots of distortion, electric screams. Sounds continue to snap in and out of the frame. Passing connections can be made as some noises return, but really the only constant is change. There is something concrete, something like material underneath it all, but it is crushed by layer upon layer of distortion, warping, splicing, and reconstitution. It's not that this isn't music, it's that it seems opposed to form itself, as anything resembling the sort of patterning and resemblance that creates meaning is smashed into oblivion.

. . .

It begins with a percussive crash. For an instant it is unnamable, then a brief flurry of woodwind and a dissonant string chord set us firmly in the sound of the twentieth-century orchestra. The winds cut short, accelerating slashes over the strings, before xylophone and double basses strike a menacing three-note motif. The strings shiver in response. As fragments from the rest of the orchestra coalesce into larger and larger stabs, the strings swell dissonantly and cinematically. Decades of Hollywood film scores have imbued the language of midcentury modernism with unmistakable meaning, and now that is being projected back into the concert hall with clear and forceful intent.

DIVERSITY

These five pieces are *Different Trains,* by Steve Reich (b. 1936); Piano Sonata No. 6, by Galina Ustvolskaya (1919–2006); *Kits Beach Soundwalk,* by Hildegard Westerkamp (b. 1946); "Brain Forest—For Acoustic Metal Concrete" from the album *Cloud Cock OO Grand,* by Merzbow (Masami Akita, b. 1956); and *H'un (Lacerations),* by Bright Sheng (b. 1955). With the possible exception of "Brain Forest," they were all created within what we might (for now) call the contemporary Western art music tradition. That is, they are all pieces that were composed or preplanned reflectively, fixed in some sort of notation for a performer or creator to interpret or execute, and intended to be listened to by an attentive, informed, and critical audience. We might add that it is a style of music that traces its primary lineage back to the courts and churches of pre-Renaissance Europe, and although those courts and churches are today mostly long defunct or culturally marginal, contemporary art music maintains an important relationship with their modern-day descendants and the structures of production and listening that they represent.

Yet even this definition, as broad as it is, barely captures the range of artistic production in these five examples. We might intuitively group most or all of these pieces according to some set of "contemporary art music" family resemblances, but each represents a distinct set of challenges to that model. In many important respects—style, technique, materials, media, and even audience—they are utterly remote from one another. *Different Trains,* for example, may on the surface be a conventionally "classical" work, yet its reception history depends far more on late twentieth-century models of patronage such as the entrepreneurial ensemble and the recording company than it does on the old institutions of church and court. The piece was commissioned by the Kronos Quartet (formed in 1973), one of the world's leading contemporary music groups, and is exemplary of a form of entrepreneurial new music practice that relies on the creation, identification, and fostering of market niches, as well as a media-conscious reinvention of the image and of the function of the string quartet itself.

Ustvolskaya's sonata looks and feels quite like conventional classical music. It even aligns itself with that tradition in its choice of title. Yet in codifying or enacting pain as a compositional parameter—the very real physical pain of the pianist, who is required to contort his or her hands awkwardly and strike the keyboard with punishing, repetitive force—Ustvolskaya disturbs the conventional image of the performer as a more or less impassive transmitter of the composer's vision, instead having him or her dramatize the work in an act of physical theater that is as close to the performance art of Antonin Artaud or Marina Abramović as it is to a classical piano sonata.

As works of electroacoustic music, both Westerkamp's *Kits Beach Soundwalk* and Merzbow's "Brain Forest" fundamentally challenge the score-based requirement of my outline definition of contemporary Western art music. The Reich and Ustvolskaya pieces may be said to exist as much in their scores as in their recordings (although Reich's use of tape stretches this definition), but no scores for the Westerkamp or Merzbow works exist, except perhaps as private studio notes by their creators. Yet this does not make the two pieces alike in how they were created. *Kits Beach Soundwalk* was produced in the studio over a period of time through a painstaking and reflexive period of composition, with Westerkamp selecting, manipulating, and organizing materials with extraordinary skill and technical finesse in much the same way as one would go about creating a conventionally notated piece of music. (Note the way in which features such as bird calls or swishes of water always counterpoint or fall between spaces in the narration rather than masking each other.) "Brain Forest," however, while executed with no less skill in terms of the selection, arrangement, and manipulation of materials, was created primarily in a live, semi-improvised setting and subjected to further postproduction manipulation during mastering.

Sheng's *H'un* is, in many respects, the most conventional of all the works presented, as it was written for a typical orchestra, fully notated, and intended for performance in the live setting of a concert hall. It is a work that audibly traces its lineage back to the European Renaissance, through Bartók, Shostakovich, and the Romantic symphonic tradition. And yet Sheng's biography as a Chinese-

American, who studied Western music at the Beijing Conservatory before moving to New York in 1982, renders this analysis problematic: this journey is one marked by patterns of adoption, negotiation, and accommodation within a series of colonial and postcolonial frameworks. Moreover, as I intimated above, geography is not the only mediating factor involved in the creation of Sheng's musical language: the repertory of affect from Hollywood cinema, itself derived from late nineteenth- to mid-twentieth-century orchestral music, has also played its part.

These five works were all composed within a year or so of each other, between 1988 and 1990. Capturing and explaining this sort of diversity presents obvious difficulties for the historian. Yet it also presents an opportunity. If we want to be able to discuss recent music history in any sort of collective sense (and let's assume that some of us still find it useful to do so), many of the usual ways of writing such a history fall short. This book hopes, in a small way, to contribute to that historical analysis by reconsidering how we tell the history of late twentieth-century music and by looking ahead to what the twenty-first century holds.

UNITY

Histories of contemporary Western art music usually begin in 1945. Its story has been told enough times, with expeditious changes of emphasis along the way, to be familiar: at the end of the Second World War, Europe, the home of post-Enlightenment Western culture, was devastated and in desperate need of reconstruction.[1] America had finally achieved the financial dominance that had been expected of it since the 1920s, thus initiating its dominance over the second half of the century. The postwar settlements with Soviet Russia had set the stage for the Cold War. New technologies and sciences, many of which had been developed in wartime, such as tape recording and information theory, were finding wide peacetime application, and the postwar industrial boom—as well as the increasing importance of cultural soft power as a weapon in the Cold War—began to fuel a rise in the public's consumption of the arts.

This story helps us understand how and why the musical innovations of the postwar decades, from *musique concrète* to minimalism, came about. However, by the end of the century this narrative begins to unravel, not least because of the rapidly changing scope of what "art music" could be. These histories struggle to accommodate the diversity of musical activity at the end of the twentieth century and the beginning of the twenty-first. Worse still, they cannot set the music of that period within the same contextual depth as, say, the serial music composed in the early 1950s (a product of wartime technologies, postwar rebuilding efforts, and the desires of a young generation to start again) or the early minimalist music of the mid-1960s (a product of jazz and non-Western influences, counterculture, and influences from the visual arts).

The first contention of this book, then, is that to understand the music of our present day and recent years, we need to reboot that story, to begin from a new date. Many of the precepts on which the post-1945 narrative is based were no longer applicable by the start of the twenty-first century: Europe had rebuilt itself and emerged as the European Union, becoming one of the world's largest economies; the fall of the Berlin Wall and the subsequent collapse of the Soviet Union had brought an end to the Cold War; and even the United States' claim to global dominance had begun to be threatened after China's opening to the global trading market at the end of the 1970s, the terrorist attacks of 9/11 and the wars in Afghanistan and Iraq that followed, and the global financial crisis of 2008. By the end of the century the social democratic consensus that had steered the West through postwar reconstruction had been replaced by market-led neoliberalism. Finally, the birth of the Internet and World Wide Web in the early 1990s, as well as the widespread popularization of digital technologies, transformed the production and consumption of culture in every sphere.

Admittedly, slicing history up like this is a somewhat arbitrary exercise. Any date, once it has been chosen, starts to look important simply from receiving special attention: enough events happen in any given year to make all years look significant. The wider the international focus, the more arbitrary a choice becomes. Most events have only a local significance; very few are truly global in importance. Even then, how can we claim that they are significant across all spheres of human activity? Nevertheless, lines are still useful, no matter how fuzzy, shallow, and semipermeable. They are useful in a teaching sense, in that they help frame, structure, and limit the period of study. From the point of view of relating history to today, divisions also enable us to present a sense of before and after, and therefore a sense of *now*, and how it is different from *then*.

There are several dates where a division could be made. The year 2000 is numerically neat, although relatively undistinguished in terms of global events. The year 2001, particularly after September 11, is a more obvious choice, and it seems likely that historians, in the near future at least, will often date the true beginning of the twenty-first century to the terrorist attacks on New York and Washington. Both dates, however, are too recent to leave room for historical depth or an exploration of patterns of continuity and change. They also arguably leave too much of a gap between the petering out of the post-1945 narrative and the beginning of the narrative that encompasses today.

Looking further back, 1968 presents itself as a strong candidate, and indeed several recent studies have taken this year of revolutions and protest as a starting or focal point.[2] The late 1970s were possibly even more significant for music, including as they did not only the rise and fall of punk, the pinnacle of disco, and the birth of hip-hop but also the premieres of Philip Glass's *Music in Twelve Parts*, Steve Reich's *Music for Eighteen Musicians*, and Gérard Grisey's *Partiels*; the start of Karlheinz Stockhausen's work on *LICHT*; and the founding of IRCAM in Paris. As has been argued elsewhere, the events of 1979—the year of the Islamic Revolution in Iran, the election of Margaret Thatcher as prime minister in Great Britain, the beginning of market reforms in China, and the Soviet Union's invasion of Afghanistan—had a major effect on the realities of the twenty-first century.[3] The events of 1968 can be read as a hangover from the war years, the reaction of the first postwar generation to the legacy of their parents' generation, but a decade later there was the sense of a clear distance from the midcentury, of events that were projecting into the future rather responding to the past.

A music history that began with either of these dates would certainly shine a light on aspects of late twentieth-century music that are often overlooked, such as the role of ensembles like L'Itinéraire in Paris and Stockhausen's ensemble in Cologne and important collectives like Feedback in Germany, ONCE in the United States, and the New Music Studio in Budapest, Hungary. However, despite the appeal and strong credentials of these dates, they are both trumped by a third, which signaled global changes of significance not seen since 1945, and which is the point where this book begins its survey.

Clearly, 1989 was a momentous year. Not only because of the fall of the Berlin Wall on November 9 and the events across Central and Eastern Europe and Russia that followed but also because of the pro-democracy protests in Tiananmen Square in China and the state-sponsored massacre that ensued and the beginning of a process that would see an end to apartheid in South Africa. The subsequent rapid ascent of a neoliberal political and economic orthodoxy across much of the globe in the 1990s was not a direct consequence of the fall of the wall; many of neoliberalism's structures had been in place for a decade or more. Lots of the geopolitical changes across Europe that came after were neither anticipated nor expected—the protesters in East Berlin were calling for more open borders, not for the end of the GDR. The descent of Russia into asset-stripping oligarchy could not have been predicted in 1989 (although it may have been feared), and neither could the extent to which China would embrace the markets of the West. Nevertheless, 1989 was the tipping point for the forces that shaped much of the economics, politics, and, one might say, psychology of our modern world.

The late 1980s and early 1990s also saw other important developments. The World Wide Web was first proposed by British computer scientist Tim Berners-Lee in March 1989 in the paper "Information Management: A Proposal"[4] and officially launched in 1991. Although initially the preserve of science institutions, the Web rapidly grew in significance and reach, and within a decade it had around half a billion users. At the same time as Berners-Lee was considering his proposal for a web of interlinked hypertext documents, Mark Weiser coined the term "ubiquitous computing" to describe what he believed would be the immediate future for computers; that is, that they would become highly networked devices that would be "so imbedded, so fitting, so natural"[5]—and so common—that we would hardly think of them as computers at all but simply as part of the environment. With the creation of the Internet and the development of wireless, mobile technologies, that prediction has pretty much proved true.

Taken together, the Internet and the rise of neoliberal global politics enabled a new phase of cultural and economic globalization. This in turn became the driver for many of the more significant events around the world in the years to come, from 9/11 to the 2008 credit crunch. Music, like any art form, is not immune to events around it, and although one cannot precisely key developments in culture to changes in the wider world, the past twenty-five years seem interestingly different enough to what has gone before to deserve examination.

CHANGE: ENABLEMENT AND INSPIRATION

What might unite the five examples given above, then, apart from the coincidence of when they were created? Does their diversity tell us something about the end of the 1980s, or does the turn of the decade provide clues as to how to consider all five works alongside each other? A bit of both, I think. This is not meant to be the fudge it sounds like. Cultural history works in two directions: works of music, or any other art, are both products of their time and contributions toward it. That is to say, artists invent new things as much as they respond to existing ones.

The late 1980s were a period of dramatic change across many fields, and these five works reflect and respond to changes of different kinds in different ways. Many of these shifts are personal, technical, or aesthetic developments in the individual composers' lives or ways of working, but just as the personal and the creative cannot always be easily teased apart from one another, so the changes articulated in these works cannot be separated completely from external influences.

The samples of speech that run through *Different Trains* mark the entry of a new element in Reich's style: speech melody. Although speech had been an important component of Reich's music from his earliest tape pieces—most notably *It's Gonna Rain* (1965) and *Come Out* (1966)—with *Different Trains* it enters the musical discourse as an equal partner with the instruments and not as an element in isolation. What made this possible was the digital sampler, versions of which had been commercially available since the mid-1970s, but which rose greatly in popularity from the mid-1980s. For the first time, Reich could arrange and collage his speech recordings with metrical precision to create a layer of speech that meshed perfectly with the performing instruments. In later works (such as *City Life*, 1994), Reich would use keyboards to trigger samples live, but in *Different Trains* they were all recorded to tape.

Reich noted the significance of this new element to his music in the following terms: "The piece thus presents both a documentary and a musical reality, and

FIGURE 1. CD cover for Steve Reich's *Different Trains*, 1989. Elektra Nonesuch 79176-2.

begins a new musical direction. It is a direction that I expect will lead to a new kind of documentary music video theater in the not too distant future."[6] *Different Trains* is documentary music not only in the sense that it tells a story that is based on real events—the transporting of European Jews by train during the Holocaust—but also in the particular way in which it tells that story. The speech samples don't tell a continuous story, like the libretto of an opera, but jump quickly between times and points of view, as in a film. As they accumulate, it becomes possible to imagine how the parts all relate.

Different Trains is unmistakably a product of the late twentieth-century media age, and in particular the cultural form of the television documentary, a mode that Reich developed after *Different Trains* in the video operas *The Cave* (1990–93) and *Three Tales* (1997–2001). It is also music that works well in recordings: Reich's strategy of overlaying live musicians with multiple prerecorded versions of themselves puts the works closer in aesthetic to pop studio productions, in which a solo artist will often sing over a prerecorded backing track, than concert hall shows.

Elektra Nonesuch's recording of *Different Trains* (see figure 1) reaches beyond the classical sphere in other ways too. It was another label, ECM, that in the late 1970s accidentally discovered a new music audience when it released Reich's *Music for 18 Musicians,* one that was educated, curious, young(er), and spiritually and/or socially conscious—not necessarily the same as the audience for the staple eighteenth- and nineteenth-century repertory. This new audience—if it may be said to exist as a homogenous unit—was attracted to influences from pop and rock, world music, and exotica, as well as minimalism and noise: the vestiges of the avant garde, but in a digestible format. By the time of *Different Trains,* Nonesuch had been catering to this audience for several years, releasing recordings of the Kronos Quartet, John Zorn, David Fanshawe, and others, as well as putting out pioneering recordings of world music on the Nonesuch Explorer series.[7] Works that challenged a "stuffy" modernist and/or classical hegemony through the use of formal simplicity, emotional directness, amplification, multimedia, and non-Western elements were valued. *Different Trains* was something of a breakthrough in this respect, and it marked the arrival not only of a new direction in Reich's music but also of the viability of a new intersection of classical prestige, emotional profundity, and pop appeal. As Christopher Fox noted:

> The combination of [Reich's] (so called) "crossover" credentials with those of the Kronos (and the pairing on record of *Different Trains* with Reich's *Electric Counterpoint,* written for the equally cultish Pat Metheny) is the stuff of record company executives' wilder dreams. If one assumes that the meaning of any musical work owes as much to the means of production and dissemination as to the sounds themselves, then *Different Trains* is a contemporary cultural phenomenon whose significance is quite different from that of most new music and almost certainly unique amongst new works for string quartet.[8]

Different Trains speaks of and to America in the 1990s: it is redeemed, technologically ascendant, media friendly, culturally dehierarchized, and postmodernistically optimistic. The world of Ustvolskaya's Piano Sonata No. 6 could not be more different. Written during the years of glasnost, the gradual opening up of government institutions in the Soviet Union initiated by Mikhail Gorbachev, it marks an ending much more than a beginning, not just politically but also personally: although Ustvolskaya went on to live for another seventeen years, physical debilitation meant that she wrote only one more piece, her equally bleak and magnificent Symphony No. 5, "Amen" (1989–90).

Ustvolskaya was a remarkable and unique figure within late twentieth-century composition. She is often remembered first for the relationship she had in her youth with her teacher Dmitri Shostakovich, but she firmly rejected that association and considered herself a follower of her own path. Although she began composing in the 1940s, and despite the admiration of her former teacher, who occasionally quoted her work in his own, she languished in obscurity until the late 1980s, and she lived in poverty until her last days. She led a hermetic life and rarely ventured outside of St. Petersburg. By chance, her music was heard in concert by

Jürgen Köchel, the director of the Sikorski publishing house, and the Dutch musicologist Elmer Schönberger. They introduced Ustvolskaya's work to the wider world, and in the second half of the 1980s it began to receive occasional performances in Europe. Yet even as her recognition grew, she firmly dismissed suggestions that she should emigrate from Russia, which in its late-Soviet years had become stagnant.

The Piano Sonata No. 6 is the last of a series of pieces that goes back to 1947. All six are blunt and bald, but none more than this. Indeed, the first is playful in its evocations of Bach, featuring two-voice counterpoint, a walking melody, cadential trill figures, and a structure made from terraced changes in tempo and texture. And if, in the later sonatas, this archetypal vocabulary is further distilled—into short scales, unrelieved quarter-note rhythms, pedal tones, alternating chords, and so on—it is always accompanied by a kind of (controlled? frustrated?) lyricism effected by Ustvolskaya's masterful use of light and shade. Yet not even listening to the sonatas in sequence really prepares the listener for the visceral force of the sixth.

And for the performer, it really is visceral. The clusters used and the work's exceedingly loud volume, requiring uncomfortable hand positions and extreme physical force, make learning and performing the work a genuinely painful experience. Most musical performance demands a certain level of physical discomfort, due to awkward hand positions, repetitive stress injuries, and the like, but Ustvolskaya's sonata intensifies this to the extent that pain, embodied and enacted, becomes part of the work's expressive language.[9] The fact that such a work was written under glasnost is not insignificant. The glasnost reforms were gradually making possible public discussion of traumatic events in Russia's recent past, and by creating a space where pain can be enacted, Ustvolskaya's piece explicitly engages with that conversation, which includes "the redemptive possibilities of addressing pain; and the struggle to express and know another's suffering."[10]

Discomfort and pain also feature in Merzbow's music, although generally in a more ecstatic and/or erotic context. His early works, released in small runs of homemade cassettes, were wrapped in pages from pornographic magazines, and bondage—particularly the rope-based erotic art of *kinbaku*—has continued to inform his aesthetic. The music itself, with its extremes of volume and harsh sounds, is frequently uncomfortable to listen to, although this discomfort is laced with an ecstatic/erotic charge rather than suffering.

Merzbow's output is enormous, numbering more than four hundred releases.[11] Such an exceptional, even surreal, prolixity makes it almost impossible to identify turning points.[12] And what would a turning point even look like? Do oceans turn? In many ways, *Cloud Cock OO Grand* can stand in for dozens of other Merzbow albums, and the same points about aesthetic and method might be made. However, the consensus is that it was soon after the release of this album that the genre Japanoise (Japanese noise music) broke out of the local underground and figured on the international scene. Noise music, whether in a general sense or its Japanese species, predated 1989, but it is only after this point that it began to have a significant impact on the aesthetics of global contemporary music.

Cloud Cock OO Grand is special because it marks the arrival of digital technology in Merzbow's output; it is the first of his records to be recorded to DAT (digital audio tape), and, after more than a decade of releases on cassette and vinyl, it was the first Merzbow album to be issued on CD. Although the initial outlay was expensive, the ease of recording onto and duplicating CDs undoubtedly helped with the logistics of distribution, facilitating the massive growth of his output. When the composer John Zorn and influential alternative rock artists like Nirvana's Kurt Cobain and Sonic Youth's Thurston Moore began drawing attention to Japanoise, Merzbow's international profile was raised dramatically. He toured the United States for the first time in 1990, shortly after *Cloud Cock OO Grand's* release, and he began to release albums straight to the US market in 1994, starting with *Venereology,* by which time his name was well established among audiences for experimental music on both sides of the Pacific. Since the early 1990s, noise music has been characterized as an underground globalized network, operating in resistance to the dominant transnationalism of global corporations and a homogenized global culture that is largely Anglo-American in origin. The models of circulation, reception, and feedback that began shortly after the release of *Cloud Cock OO Grand* are a substantial contributor to this alternative positioning.[13]

Merzbow toured Europe for the first time in 1989, and his experiences there fed into the making of *Cloud Cock OO Grand.* On the track "Modular," recordings from those live shows were used as raw material. Until this point, Merzbow had worked extensively with tape recordings and a variety of sound sources to create complex, many-layered collages. However, the practicalities of flying outside Japan necessitated a reduction in the amount of gear he could travel with and, in turn, a switch to more portable electronic tools such as simple mixer consoles and guitar effects pedals (and, later, laptops) (see figure 2). This change in method had a profound effect on Merzbow's style, leading to the development of what came to be known as a "harsh noise" aesthetic, characterized by high frequencies and abrasive, highly distorted sounds. The switch to CDs had artistic benefits too, removing the unwanted background noise of tape and extending the playing time of vinyl. These two benefits allowed for a fuller, more immersive experience. On later releases, Merzbow exploited the conditions of CD mastering as a further opportunity for noise and distortion, pushing the levels right up to maximize the sound's "presence."[14] "Masami Akita was, it seems," writes Paul Hegarty, "just waiting for CD to come along to expand the range and potential for loudness that he felt records lacked."[15]

Merzbow's sound and his overproduction both share a principle of excess, an aesthetic of saturation. Yet this is not excess in the creation of the fantastical or the ornate, but rather as a model of obsessive and empty consumption, an endless

FIGURE 2. Merzbow on stage at the Boiler Room, Tokyo, June 24, 2014. Still from performance video, www.youtube.com/watch?v=fR_8gpJCT4I.

pursuit of meaning that undoes itself with every new step. Each new release adds volume or mass to Merzbow's body of work, like the piles of rubbish in Kurt Schwitters's Merzbau house, from which the musician takes his name. But the proliferation of recordings makes it impossible to grasp the whole, to make sense of any of it. The same is true of the music itself, in its endless displacements of repetition and structure, its perpetual dismantling of meaning. It is, as Hegarty vividly describes Japanoise in general, "noise all the way down."[16]

Japanoise challenged the established relationship between the listener and what they were listening to. Yet it wasn't the only branch of experimental music to do so around the turn of the decade. Until the late 1980s, Hildegard Westerkamp's music had been motivated by a resistance to noise pollution and might be thought of as standing in complete opposition to Merzbow's noisy interventions. Born in Osnabrück, Germany, in 1946, Westerkamp immigrated to Vancouver in 1968 with her partner, Norbert Ruebsaat. She studied at Simon Fraser University, where she met R. Murray Schafer, inventor of the discipline of "acoustic ecology" and founder of the World Soundscape Project (WSP), and her interest in noise abatement began. After completing her degree, she joined the WSP as a research assistant.

Acoustic ecology and the WSP were reactions to the intrusion of man-made noise into the everyday soundscape, and a distaste for manufactured and artificial sonic ambiences continued to inform Westerkamp's work through the 1980s. One early piece, *A Walk through the City* (1981), is based around a text written and read by Ruebsaat and describes urban noise in terms of violence, fear, and threat—a world away from Merzbow's ecstatic digitalism. In 1988 Westerkamp completed a master's degree at Simon Fraser University with a thesis entitled "Listening and Soundmaking: A Study of Music-as-Environment," a critical investigation of the role of Muzak within the urban soundscape.

Yet within that thesis are the seeds of a new, more complex relationship to noise. In 1989 Westerkamp composed *Kits Beach Soundwalk,* the first indication of a new direction in her music, and one of her best-known works. Soundwalking is a genre of music making, or participative listening, that Westerkamp would come to develop very much as her own, and which, as early as 1974, she described as "any excursion whose main purpose is listening to the environment."[17] *Kits Beach Soundwalk* is different from soundwalking as normally conceived, however, in that the journey is recorded to tape; the listener is not required to leave her seat or do any aural exploration of her own. (The idea grew out of a radio program, called *Soundwalking,* that Westerkamp hosted on Vancouver Co-operative Radio, in which she "took the listener to different locations in and around the city and explored them acoustically."[18]) The idea of a walk, or a journey, encoded and artic-ulated purely through sound, structures the piece, and one of its key effects is the tension created between the fixed physical location of the listener and the dynamic aural space of the music. This is captured in the description at the start of this chapter of the work's opening minute or so, but it is expanded throughout the work as the listening location becomes increasingly fabricated. Immediately after the point described above, Westerkamp confirms the mediated, fabricated nature of what we are hearing: "I'm trying to listen to those tiny sounds in more detail now. Suddenly the background sound of the city seems louder again. . . . Luckily we have bandpass filters and equalizers. We can just go into the studio and get rid of the city, pretend it's not there. Pretend we are somewhere far away." At this point, Westerkamp's accompanying tape does exactly that: the city's low roar is filtered away, leaving only the click and suck of the barnacles. This is the key moment in the piece: until now, everything we heard seemed believable. Those sounds could be heard, like that, on Kits Beach (see figure 3). Westerkamp could have been there, exactly as she described. Now, she takes us on a fantastical jour-ney through dreams and memories (of insects and tinkling bullets and Xenakis and Mozart) before returning us to the beach.

From her study of Muzak, Westerkamp reached the conclusion that, since music designed not to be listened to was an agent of commerce, then listening itself must be a political act. Moreover, the self-actualization that comes about through listening could be tied to (feminist) arguments for the politicization of the personal:

> I found the courage for self-analysis, as well as for *articulating and expressing* my experiences, making the personal public. With this I joined with many other women who had to learn to understand that our concerns—which have always seemed "too" personal and private, and therefore not fit for public exposure—are *shared* concerns

FIGURE 3. Kits Beach, Vancouver, December 2008. Photo by James Sherrett.

and must therefore be voiced. It is this voicing of the personal (the "inner world") which constitutes a political act, the raising of a voice that traditionally has not been raised, has been shrouded in silence.[19]

After *Kits Beach Soundwalk*, Westerkamp's construction of the political within the activity of listening became explicit in *Breathing Room* (1990) and, especially, *École Polytechnique* (1990), a response to the mass shooting of fourteen women at the École Polytechnique in Montreal, Canada, by a gunman motivated by misogynistic revenge at what he perceived as the unfair advancement of women at the college.[20] In Westerkamp's work, listening is no longer an act of passive consumption but one of politically active production—a site of resistance, if a radically private one. Environmentalism and industrial critique align with the creation of a modern subjectivity that is aware of its endlessly fluid relationship to perceived reality.

A very different kind of environmentally formed subjectivity is expressed in Bright Sheng's *H'un (Lacerations): In memoriam 1966–1976*. Sheng (born Sheng Zong Liang) was a teenager during the years of the Chinese Cultural Revolution. As a middle-class, urban youth, he was sent via the so-called Down to the Countryside initiative from his home in Shanghai to live with and learn from rural workers in Qinghai, on the Tibetan border. A talented musician, he was saved from compulsory farm labor and was instead allowed to perform with a local folk music and dance troupe. When China's universities reopened in 1978, he passed the entrance exam for the Shanghai Conservatory. In 1982 he immigrated to New York to study at Columbia University with fellow émigré Chou Wen-chung, and in 1985 he became a student of and assistant to Leonard Bernstein. Sheng has since figured prominently as a de facto cultural ambassador for Chinese–American relations: in 1999 he was commissioned by President Clinton to compose a work to honor the state visit of the Chinese Premiere Zhu Rongji, and in 2008 he was invited to compose for the Beijing Olympics.

H'un was Sheng's first major orchestral work and one of the first pieces to establish his reputation in the West. Coincidentally, its first performance, by the New York Chamber Symphony, took place a few months before the Tiananmen Square massacre. Composed in memory of the victims of the Cultural Revolution, it evoked one of modern China's darkest periods, just as the country was about to enter a new one.

H'un is a powerful and evocative work, but it is striking how un-Chinese—or, at least, how *Western*—it sounds. Sheng's orchestra incorporates a few Chinese percussion instruments (Chinese tom-toms, a temple block, a Peking Opera gong) but makes few other concessions toward Chinese music. At the Shanghai Conservatory, Sheng was instructed in Western models of classical composition before being taught in the United States by Chou and Bernstein. If that instruction was relatively conservative, it shows in Sheng's own descriptions of composing the piece:

> Perhaps the most challenging aspect in this composition for the composer is that there is no melodic line (or "tune"). Instead, it is built upon a spare two-note motive of a semitone. . . . Yet thematic melody remains one of the most crucial elements (if not *the* most crucial) for the construction of a musical composition. A work without a melody therefore must take full advantage of other musical elements in order for the listener to perceive the logic of the structure—beginning, development, climax, and end.[21]

Toward the end of the same analysis, Sheng emphasizes the mimetic quality of his work in a brief description of the second half of the piece, intended as a solemn meditation on the lives lost during the Cultural Revolution:

> The entire section has a very subdued manner, as if the world has just gone through a devastating catastrophe and everyone is too exhausted even to weep or to make a sound. Gradually, through a circuitous line of crescendo and an expansion toward the extreme registers of the string orchestra, it reaches a passage of tutti *fff*, where the upper three strings are against the lower two. The strings remain muted, however, to produce a sound evoking the painful crying out of millions of people when strangled.[22]

If we consider Sheng's piece in terms of the global context from which it emerged, we can see quite clearly the power and influence of a common, transnational aesthetic that is based on a Western model of taste, prestige, and meaning-making.

. . .

In their different ways, all five of these works connect with the wider political, social, economic, and technological changes of the time, whether late Cold War geopolitics, the emergence of digital technology, the conditions of modern-day globalization, or the politicization of the personal. Associations like these suggest the first component of my methodological framework: enablement and inspiration.

Technological, social, and political developments can and do influence developments in art in two ways: they either enable them, or they inspire them. That is, a new development can make certain artistic aims possible (through the creation of new technical means, for example), or it can inspire new aesthetic propositions, not necessarily by making use of the new technology, but by pursuing some of its wider implications. In the Reich example, digital sampling enabled the development of speech melody as a technical device; in the Westerkamp, the possibilities of recording inspired a new conception of sound as a means of creating private narratives. Often both forces are present. This can be seen in the example of Merzbow: digitization was initially of practical value to Merzbow, as it enabled greater portability of his on-stage setup. What it inspired, however, was the creation of the harsh noise aesthetic.

The architectural critic Douglas Murphy has drawn a similar division with respect to the impact of digitization on architectural practice since the 1980s, which serves as an example for the wider distinction that I am making.[23] Initially, Murphy writes, architects saw the computer as a tool for achieving greater efficiency and accuracy. The slow and imprecise paper, pen, and set square were replaced by the keyboard, mouse, and screen. By the late 1980s, however, we can identify "a genuine methodological shift in the way architecture is produced,"[24] exemplified by the deconstructivist (or "decon") buildings of Frank Gehry, Peter Eisenman, and others (see figure 4). In Murphy's description, digital modeling allowed Gehry (using software from the aerospace industry) to create engineering solutions for the warped and twisted architectural shapes that he was already imagining; this is my paradigm of *enabling*. The resulting buildings may have been radical in design, but still, the computer remained a tool. Eisenman, however, took a more "'theoretical' approach" that was "far more experimental and self-consciously avant-garde,"[25] drawing on the theories of Gilles Deleuze and Félix Guattari in particular to reimagine the possibilities of architectural space. Although computers were still used, it was the new concepts of knowledge, connection, and transformation to which digitization gave rise that inspired Eisenman's designs.

A similar trajectory can be traced in music. On the most pragmatic level, computers have functioned as a tool for composers. Digital draftsmanship, in theory, enables

FIGURE 4. Weisman Art Museum, designed by Frank Gehry, 1993. Photo by Joel Nilsson, www.flickr.com/photos/joel_nilsson/15209464949, licensed under CC Attribution-ShareAlike 2.0.

greater productivity (removing the need, for example, for external copyists to create individual instrumental parts from a complete score). It has transformed the way in which scores are disseminated, and its most significant impact may yet prove to be enabling patterns of self-publication and self-promotion, indeed a new ecosystem of composition and performance, outside the traditional institutions of production, promotion, and distribution. Digitization, in the form of sound sampling, also enabled the creation of works like *Different Trains*, which in these terms is perhaps the musical equivalent of a Gehry building. And of course digitization created whole new kinds of material and ways of working in electronic music, for which the architectural parallel might be more akin to the invention of reinforced concrete, for example. However, digitization also had a profound impact on the aesthetics of music, as it gave rise to new ways of thinking about material, process, and form.

CONNECTIONS: FORCES THAT CAN ENABLE OR INSPIRE

External forces may enable or inspire changes in musical aesthetics, but what in fact are those forces? Looking back to our five examples, they might all be described in relation to trauma. In the Reich and Ustvolskaya pieces, this relationship is clear: in *Different Trains,* a large-scale historical trauma is approached and to some extent assuaged (through aesthetics, technical intervention, and the narrative of the work); in Ustvolskaya's sonata, a more personal trauma, the relationship of the individual to the totalitarian state, is presented raw through genuine pain and discomfort. In Sheng's *H'un,* another historical trauma is described and partially resolved, similarly to the Reich, although by different stylistic means. *Kits Beach Soundwalk* is less specifically about trauma, although it does stem from a personal sense of anguish about the dehumanizing impact of the modern sound environment. However, the work did define a mode of musical subjectivity that enabled Westerkamp, a year later, to tackle the much more harrowing topic of the École Polytechnique killings. Merzbow's work (at least at the time of *Cloud Cock OO Grand*) does not thematize trauma in the same way as these other pieces do, and it emphatically renounces any programmatic connection to real world events.[26] Nevertheless, the experience of listening to the music, in its harshness, its disorienting, dizzying formlessness, and the aggression of its surrounding discourse, at least imitates trauma, if only to sublimate it or subvert it. This shared ground may suggest a connecting force.

Trauma is certainly a common theme in contemporary art and has grown particularly in response to the increased presence of groups in mainstream culture that had hitherto been marginalized (and hence traumatized) on the basis of gender, sexuality, ethnicity, or class. Yet it may also be argued that trauma is not a force in itself but rather a symptom of external forces, such as, for example, gender or race discrimination, globalization, technological alienation, and economic inequality. Already, some of the forces that shape contemporary culture, the status of individuals within it, and the ways in which they might respond through music, are starting to surface.

With all this in mind, I suggest that the main developments of the last twenty-five years that might enable or inspire the stylistic development of new music are social liberalization, globalization, digitization, the Internet, late capitalist economics, and the green movement. There may be others, of course, and some will appear at points in this book. But these six provide a useful set of vectors along which much of the musical activity of the last twenty-five years, to say nothing of the wider cultural and political landscape, might be understood.

None of them stand in isolation, and some have themselves been enabled or inspired by others. The form taken by modern-day globalization, for example, is unthinkable without the Internet; so too is the virtuality of late capitalist finance. Green politics, in turn, acquire their urgency because of the necessity of consumption demanded by late capitalism and the energy demands created by the Internet and our increasingly electronic way of life. Some vectors, such as environmentalism or social liberalism, have origins that predate 1989. However, it is clear that the new world order precipitated by the fall of the Berlin Wall brought many of them into the cultural forefront and created the particular pattern of intersections between them that characterizes and shapes much of our contemporary lives. The emergence of a neoliberal political consensus that emerged after the "victory" of capitalism in 1989–91 itself stands in complex relation to each of the six forces listed above.

That said, these forces do not serve as simple chapter headings. Instead, I have taken a further step toward abstraction, at least on the highest organizational level, and chosen a series of quasi-psychological states that reflect the intersections between these techno-socioeconomic axes. There are five of these: permission, fluidity, mobility, excess, and loss. After this introduction and a second chapter describing some of the structural changes that have taken place around new music after 1989, these make up the largest part of this book. A final chapter focuses on what I am calling "afterness," that is, the approaches to the past (or pasts) that emerge from the changed conditions of the post-1989 world.

My initial reason for this layout was straightforward: I wanted to avoid any single composer who might be listed under a heading such as "the green movement" or "social liberalization" coming to be understood and labeled as, solely, a "green" or "liberal" composer. This is not because I think that politics and music do not mix—quite the opposite—but because such a categorization would force composers' works to be understood as a series of thematically connected slogans rather than as artistically and aesthetically nuanced statements in their own right. As much as I have talked about the need to read new music through its social context, it is important also to consider its aesthetics. Not to do so means to fall into the simplistic, marketing-led instrumentalization of musical works that I and some of the composers I discuss critique at various points in this book.

A second reason emerged as a consequence of my early experiments with such an organization. I found that it allowed me to discuss in close proximity music by composers very remote from one another stylistically. This does not just allow me the pleasure of overturning expectations but it also better reflects the reality of how musicians actually operate. They talk to one another, they have respect for each other's work, they attend each other's concerts, they discuss professional and aesthetic matters, and they disagree. A history that can reflect such friendships and conversations will better capture the reality of the contemporary music ecosystem than one that is organized by artificially determined technical correspondences (which sometimes conceal personal antagonisms), such as minimalism or New Complexity. It will also, I suggest, lead to a more interesting analysis of the works themselves that is based on comparison and difference rather than similarity and taxonomy.

LIMITS: THE SCOPE OF THIS BOOK

However, as we have already seen, any examination of what might qualify as Western art music in the twenty-first century shows that the borders of this definition have become highly permeable and fuzzy. Clearly it can accommodate scored works for (predominantly) acoustic performers, like the Ustvolskaya and Reich examples. But what about Japanoise, which is created for recording and employs many of the facts of recording, such as overload and distortion, as part of its aesthetic? Can it include Westerkamp's soundwalks, which involve no performers at all and do not take place in anything we might recognize as a conventional concert space? What about Richard Barrett's (b. 1959) *Codex* series (2001–), which is a set of guided instructions for group improvisation, or Amnon Wolman's (b. 1955) text pieces, which do away with the performer-audience divide and even raise questions as to the way in which they are listened to. And what about Ludovico Einaudi (b. 1955), who, in albums such as *Le Onde* (1996) and *Nightbook* (2009), combines aspects of eighteenth-century classical style with minimalism and sentimental pop balladry to appeal to a mass audience?

So much for the "art" and "music" elements of the term. But what about the "Western"? As globalization is one of the main forces to have influenced music of the last two and half decades, what is meant by the "Western" in Western art music deserves some consideration. First of all, it no longer means quite what it used to. At one time, before the Internet, before satellite communications, before the explosion in commercial recording, before global organizations like the World Bank and the United Nations, the West of Western art music was much the same as the West of geography: Europe and North America. Now, as can be seen in the examples of Bright Sheng and Merzbow presented in this chapter, as well as many hundreds of other composers from South America, Africa, Asia, and Oceania, it is something more complicated than that. One can compose Western art music without necessarily coming from or living in the geographical West.

Here, "Western" is as much a historical construct as it is a geographical or geopolitical one. It refers to a kind of music making that belongs to a tradition originating in the West (and propagating many of its values) and maintains certain continuities with that tradition (especially in its modes of production and consumption, and perhaps also in some of its formal properties), but it need not be physically situated there. Those who write Western art music enter a particular sphere of connected approaches, styles, chains of prestige, and flows of cultural and financial capital, just as an Algerian rapper enters the different sphere of approaches, styles, chains of prestige, and flows of cultural and financial capital that define hip-hop. Likewise, to be accepted into that sphere, musicians must meet certain conditions. Regrettably, Western art music's close associations in the past with colonial power and aristocratic patronage have meant that those conditions have included tightly policed definitions of race, gender, sexuality, and class. Those legacies are still, slowly, being cleared out today. Yet even as they are, something indefinable about Western art music remains that goes beyond this and continues to attract musicians from all over the world.

In this book, I am choosing to deal with a set of familial resemblances rather than a single, hard and fast definition. So while the core of my repertory is notated composition for some form of concert-like realization, examples from the fringes of this definition—where it shades into pop, improvisation, sound art, and electronic music—are included throughout to give an idea of the overall fluid situation and nature of cross-pollination. Merzbow, for example, lies at an extreme edge of this field; but Westerkamp is not far behind, even though we might more easily recognize her work as belonging to the "classical tradition." Even the pieces by Ustvolskaya and Reich, self-identifying composers in the most old-fashioned sense of the term, raise issues about our conventional understanding of what a work of musical composition actually is.

In spite of all this, this book is not a definitive or comprehensive history of Western art music since 1989. Such a book would be much longer, for a start. Nor is it an attempt to establish a canon of the "best" works composed since that date. Even if we are prepared to accept canons as a necessary evil for making sense of the world, it is too early for much of the music discussed here to be considered in such a way. In any case, the rationales that I use here—based as they are not on chains of influence and accumulations of prestige but on responses to questions from outside the world of musical exchange value—challenge the very idea of a canon. This book provides a few useful routes into the appreciation and study of contemporary music, but it is no substitute for listening to and exploring that world for oneself.

New music has something of an image problem, to say the least. For whatever reason—whether the radicalism of the postwar modernists or the conservatism of their more reactionary counterparts—a wedge was driven between the Western art music audience and its contemporary manifestations. Since roughly the early 1970s, composers and institutions have sought ways to mitigate this situation, each taking an approach of their own. Some have devised musical aesthetics—like minimalism—that explicitly set out to simplify the listening experience. Others have devised means of greater audience participation or have incorporated spectacular elements like site specificity or multimedia to relieve the burden of interpretation from the ears alone. Others have more or less accepted the status quo and have written within an identifiable if updated extension of late-Romantic idioms. Others have turned away from the concert hall and set out to find an entirely new audience. Still others have chosen not to concentrate on audiences at all but rather to focus their attention on creating communities and collectives in which the boundaries between listeners, performers, and composers are less well defined.

A history of contemporary music could be written around approaches to this challenge alone. What those approaches have led to is a fragmentation of musical styles, a diversity that is extremely difficult to contain within a single narrative. This book doesn't attempt to describe every one of those approaches or to offer a comprehensive catalogue of the most important works or composers of the period.

However, it does attempt to show the full spectrum. My aim is to present a map of the forest and (some of) its outermost edges rather than portraits of every tree.

More useful than a complete survey or a genealogy of techniques and styles, I believe, are suggestions for how to read contemporary music. Composers and their works are important to this book's story, but so too are performers, promoters, publishers, record executives, and even listeners. *Music after the Fall* looks at the whole ecosystem of new music within the technological, social, and political technological conditions of its time and, from there, suggests a few ways to proceed.

MEDIATION AND THE MARKETPLACE

A NEW DECADE: SPIRITUAL MINIMALISM
AND THE EARLY 1990S

"Even at one minute past midnight on 1 January 1990, we already knew that this would be a formative decade in Europe. A forty-year-old European order had just collapsed with the Berlin Wall. Everything seemed possible. Everyone was hailing 'a new Europe.' But no one knew what it would look like."[1] The historian Timothy Garton Ash is referring here specifically to political and social circumstances within Europe—and, by extension, the United States and Soviet Union—at the start of the 1990s, as the Cold War drew to an end. But a sense of the auspicious and the uncertain permeated all aspects of life at this time. The works discussed in the previous chapter all relate to some extent to the tensions that were in the air at the turn of the decade. Yet it was the music of three other composers that most immediately captured the preoccupations of the moment. The Pole Henryk Górecki (1933–2010), the Estonian Arvo Pärt (b. 1935), and the Briton John Tavener (1944–2013) were fortuitous and largely unwitting benefactors of the upheavals taking place around them.

Although all three were in their prime in the 1980s, they all languished to some extent during that decade on the margins of contemporary music's mainstream. By the start of the 1990s this situation had changed dramatically, however, and all three had become box office and recording successes on a scale unprecedented for contemporary music. For want of a better term, critics soon dubbed the trio "holy" or "spiritual" minimalists, highlighting the simple approachability that their styles shared, as well as their common reference to Christian texts, symbols, and themes.

("Holy minimalism" was used first, initially often in a somewhat derogatory sense; "spiritual minimalism" is a more recent, more neutral, coinage.) Connections—more or less spurious—were also drawn with others who appeared to be doing similar things. Mostly, but not exclusively, these were composers from Eastern Europe and the former Soviet Union, such as the Russian Sofia Gubaidulina (b. 1931), the Estonian Erkki-Sven Tüür (b. 1959), and the Latvian Pēteris Vasks (b. 1946). The term stuck, and spiritual minimalism became enshrined as one of the last musical "-isms" of the twentieth century.[2] Despite significant shortcomings, it remains a convenient way to describe what was a definable phenomenon.

Yet was something happening, or was this mere coincidence? Besides spiritual minimalism's sheer popularity, what makes the genre interesting is the way it was promoted. Other descriptors, such as minimalism or serialism, may be applied more or less completely according to widely agreed upon technical features, shared stylistic reference points, a bounded period of time, and an identifiable group of practitioners. Reich and Glass may have rejected the term "minimalism," and Stockhausen, Boulez, Luigi Nono, and Bruno Maderna swiftly discarded the term "Darmstadt school" (first used by Nono), but at least these composers shared common backgrounds, had spent parts of their lives in close company, had collaborated on ideas and music, and could point to a shared ancestry of teachers and models. Spiritual minimalism, however, possessed none of these. Its composers had worked independently of one another, in different countries and even on different sides of the Iron Curtain. They did not correspond with each other or formulate shared goals. They did not share teachers or stylistic touchstones. As far as technique is concerned, there is little that connects Górecki, Pärt, and Tavener apart from a general taste for forms of extended tonality, slow tempi, and static harmonies. Even designating them as minimalists in the manner of Reich, Glass, or La Monte Young remains a subject of debate.[3] Strictly speaking, only Pärt's music for strings and voices of the late 1970s and the 1980s, plus one or two works by Tavener and Górecki, really support the comparison. The term was a critics' invention, a branding convenience devised wholly separately from the authentic musical work of the composers concerned.

What synchronicity there was around spiritual minimalism was driven not by compositional output or relationships, but by record releases. This has long been commonplace for popular music, whose home is recording: records are the defining moments of pop; no one notes the live debut of a new song. For classical music, however, the live premiere is the primary moment in a work's lifecycle. Any reception history that it may have begins then. If it is to find a place as part of a wider movement, it is with works that were first performed at around the same time and usually in roughly the same place.

Yet the defining moments of spiritual minimalism were recordings, especially Pärt's *Tabula rasa* on ECM, Tavener's *The Protecting Veil* on Virgin, and Górecki's

Symphony No. 3 on Elektra Nonesuch. This may have been a first for a movement within contemporary music. There had been important recordings before this date—Philips' releases of Stockhausen in the 1960s, for example, or ECM's recording of Reich's *Music for Eighteen Musicians* (1978)—but these served more as confirmation of the importance of a particular style or composer. In contrast, the spiritual minimalist recordings from the late 1980s to the mid-1990s launched a particular historical formulation.

Moreover, these recordings made a mark that few others could match. In 1996, the journalist Norman Lebrecht even suggested that the way in which Górecki's symphony in particular was marketed—which he claims revealed the record industry to be godless, starless, and sexless—contributed to the industry's subsequent downfall as a culturally and economically viable entity.[4] One does not need to subscribe to Lebrecht's messianic pronouncements, however, to agree that there was something new about how the music industry had started to market classical music in the early 1990s. The music of Górecki, Pärt, Tavener, and others played a significant part in this. In this chapter I offer a detailed history and analysis of the spiritual minimalist phenomenon and then discuss the implications the movement had for the ways in which contemporary music was presented, promoted, disseminated, and listened to in the 1990s and after. I do this by looking at two mechanisms within the music industry that came to the forefront at around the same time: mediation and the marketplace.

After the 1980s, state funding for new music was cut in many countries, the result of the end of the Cold War and with it the justification for supporting cultural soft power, and of a general shift toward neoliberal policies that favored market-led dynamics over state intervention. This led to a turn toward ways of support, creation, and dissemination that were in tune with free market ideology, putting new music in the marketplace to help it survive under less generous financial conditions. Performers, promoters, and even composers began to develop entrepreneurial skills, identifying or creating market niches, developing audiences and brands, and so on.

Mediation—as in the transmission of music from originator to listener via one form of media or another—has been a factor in Western art music since the invention of musical notation itself. More recently it can refer to the various apparatuses and institutions that surround the printing, performance, and recording of music. These might be found within the concert hall (in the form of video backdrops, for example) or they can refer to new ways of listening to music outside the concert hall (such as through personal music players, in TV or film, or online).

As we will see, both mechanisms are deeply intertwined. Mediation often greatly increases the profile and sales of a musical work—think about what happens when a piece of music is used in a TV commercial, for example. Some works or styles of music are better suited to mediation than others, and the most appropriate form of mediation may differ between works. The verse-chorus song structure works well for the three minutes of a seven-inch record, for example, whereas video game music requires something more flexible to meet the unpredictable demands of duration and changes of scene. This appropriateness may even be written into the music itself. The clearest examples here are house or garage tracks, which often begin with long buildups of layered percussion and end with similar breakdowns to make it easier to sequence overlapping tracks within a DJ set. Music that is more susceptible to mediation will generally be easier to market across a range of channels. Similarly, music that makes use of multimedia strategies as part of its conception—site-specific work, work with video, staged work, and so on—may benefit in terms of profile and ticket sales because of its more "spectacular" nature (although it may equally be swamped and rendered relatively anonymous by those strategies).

AN INTRODUCTION TO SPIRITUAL MINIMALISM

On April 2, 1989, seven months before the Berlin Wall fell, Bob Hurwitz, senior vice president of New York's Elektra Nonesuch Records, was in London to attend a performance by the London Sinfonietta of Górecki's Symphony No. 3 (1976), with Margeret Field singing. It was, by all available accounts, a remarkable event. Górecki's symphony is a masterpiece of slow piano and string chords that slide like ice sheets, crested by a serene, prayerful soprano lament, and it made a striking impression. Reviewing the concert in the *Observer* newspaper, Nicholas Kenyon (a future controller of BBC Radio 3) wrote: "It was as if a spark had been lit . . . the evening had all the signs of an event which could change the course of our musical taste."[5] Hurwitz evidently saw the same spark. Górecki's symphony had already been recorded twice (for Polskie Nagrania in 1978 and Schwann in 1982), with both recordings available on CD (Schwann issued CDs in 1986 and 1988, and Polskie Nagrania's recording was issued as a CD by Olympia in 1989); a third recording, obscurely marketed as a film soundtrack, was released by Erato in 1985. The Schwann recording in particular had received several favorable press notices and was a modest success in its own right. Hurwitz already knew the Polskie Nagrania release,[6] yet after hearing the Sinfonietta's performance he was convinced that the market could support a fourth recording, and he began the process of putting one together.[7]

Hurwitz was taking a risk: four recordings of any contemporary work was unusual. Yet Górecki's symphony already had something of a cult following, particularly among artists working on the borders between art and popular music. The official UK premiere of Górecki's symphony had taken place on September 20, 1988, given by the City of Birmingham Symphony Orchestra. Yet taped excerpts of the piece had been played in concert venues long before this, starting around 1983, at the start of gigs by the group Test Dept, which was part of the post-punk industrial music scene that also included Throbbing Gristle and Whitehouse. The group's core members were Jonathan Toby Burdon, Graham Cunnington, Angus Farquhar, Paul Hines, and Paul Jamrozy. It was Jamrozy, the son of a Polish émigré, who introduced Górecki's music into their sets. On a visit to Poland with his father in 1982, Jamrozy stopped at a Warsaw record shop and was attracted to the sleeve of the Polskie Nagrania LP (another form of mediation), which had been released in Poland in 1978, a "dot matrix graphic of density and shade" that recalled the Op Art paintings of Bridget Riley and was characteristic of the abstract graphical style of many Polskie Nagrania releases of the time.

Jamrozy bought two copies of the record, and soon extracts from the LP were incorporated into the barrage of light, film, and sound that opened Test Dept concerts. Part of the appeal of these intros lay in the jarring juxtaposition of Górecki's delicate simplicity and Test Dept's harsh electronics and metallic percussion, which Jamrozy says "triggered a sensory meltdown in the audience." Yet Jamrozy was also attracted to the political and social undertones he could hear in the symphony, and although the composer himself denied them, they became an important part of the work's subsequent reception. Jamrozy's father was born in the same mining area of Poland as Górecki and was forced into manual labor by the Nazis when he was fourteen. Jamrozy describes how Górecki's music "spoke of both suffering and transcendence in its harmony and dissonance. The soaring spiritual overtones were shafts of light, stoking the burning embers that were bound to the earth, submerged in the industry of totalitarianism."[8]

While Test Dept's multimedia collages were introducing Górecki to industrial music fans, the symphony appeared in another audio-visual format, this time excerpted for the soundtrack of Maurice Pialat's 1985 film, Police, starring Gérard Depardieu and Sophie Marceau. For Elektra Nonesuch (home of the Kronos Quartet, and the label that released the first recording of Reich's Different Trains), this sort of between-the-gaps crossover was familiar territory, and Górecki's symphony seemed well suited to it.

By the end of the decade, when Hurwitz attended the London Sinfonietta's performance, a distinct and definite buzz had built up around the symphony.[9] The work's appearances in a variety of mediated forms, from the intriguing design of the Polskie Nagrania sleeve to its inclusion in Test Dept's preshow collages to the Police soundtrack, had created an audience and a market for performances and recordings of the complete work. The US premiere took place in November 1990, and in April 1992 the new Elektra Nonesuch recording, sung by Dawn Upshaw, played by the London Sinfonietta, and conducted by David Zinman, was released in the United States.

At first it performed only modestly and continued to do so two months later when it was released in the United Kingdom. However, things started to change at the beginning of autumn. In September the first British commercial radio station dedicated to classical music, Classic FM, was launched. Among its DJs was the former rock critic Paul Gambaccini, another operator in the gaps between popular and art music. From the station's first week he began to feature the symphony on his *Classical Countdown* show. Frequently requested by listeners, the work soon went into heavy rotation. The response prompted Warner Brothers, Elektra Nonesuch's parent company, to review its marketing strategy. It began sending copies to their list of so-called tastemakers, which incongruously included Mick Jagger and Tori Amos alongside Cardinal Basil Hume and the prime minister's wife, Norma Major. Warners also began promoting the record as an ideal Christmas gift, alongside albums by Enya, Mike Oldfield, Madonna, and REM. The strategy worked, and the symphony quickly rose to the top of the classical recording charts. This was already a better performance than anyone had expected, yet sales continued to grow through Christmas. In January 1993 Górecki's Symphony No. 3 entered the unprecedented territory of the UK pop charts.

At its height, the Elektra Nonesuch recording is reported to have sold somewhere between six thousand and ten thousand copies per day—respectable *all-time* figures for most recordings of contemporary music—and in February 1993 it reached number six on the popular album charts in Britain. At around the same time it reached number one on *Billboard*'s classical album charts, staying there until November. The album continued to sell strongly for the next two or three years, and final sales figures are reckoned to be in excess of one million copies, exceptional territory for a classical recording and unique for one of contemporary music.

The scale of the success of Górecki's Symphony No. 3 may have taken all by surprise, but there was a recent precedent. Two months before the US release of the Elektra Nonesuch recording of the piece, Virgin Records released its own recording of slow, string-dominated, spiritual music: John Tavener's *The Protecting Veil*. A quasi-concerto for solo cello and string orchestra, *The Protecting Veil* was a huge success, at least on pre-Górecki terms, going to the top of the classical charts. It won the *Gramophone* Award for Best Contemporary Recording and was classical music's representative on the shortlist for the inaugural Mercury Music Prize.[10]

The Protecting Veil was composed in 1987 after a request from the cellist Stephen Isserlis. At this time Tavener, who had first made his name with his oratorio *The Whale* (1968), famously recorded on the Beatles' Apple label, was writing only vocal music: meditative, chant-like settings of texts based on the liturgy and music of the Greek Orthodox Church, into which he was received in 1977. Yet something about Isserlis's request appealed to him, and within a few months he had completed the work. Subsequently commissioned by the BBC, it received its first performance at the BBC Proms on September 4, 1989. This was the culmination of several months of Tavener-related activity. First, the work was recorded by the BBC SO at Maida Vale in early summer. Then, in July, Channel 4 broadcast the television documentary *Sounding Icons*, part of the series Art, Faith and Vision by the Oxford professor of poetry Peter Levi, which presented a portrait of Tavener's life and work. Again, processes of mediation were paving the way for the work's reception, although in Tavener's case they were less dramatic at this stage than they would be for Górecki. Compared to the private, tender ecstasies of Tavener's recent choral music—works such as *Funeral Ikos* (1981), *The Lamb* (1982), and 2 *Hymns to the Mother of God* (1985)—*The Protecting Veil* was quite a contrast. Using a wide range of textural effects that pit the solo cello against a wall of massed strings, from subterranean bass drones to stratospheric chatter, Tavener vividly dramatizes the life of the Virgin Mary as portrayed in Orthodox iconography (The Protecting Veil is the name of one of the most important feasts in the Orthodox Church calendar, celebrated on October 1). In a preview discussion broadcast before the Proms concert, the composer Steve Martland (1954–2013), already an admirer of Górecki's Symphony No. 3, proclaimed *The Protecting Veil* "one of the most unbelievably beautiful and moving pieces I have ever heard."[11] The audience and the critics agreed, and the work had a sensational reception. Nicholas Kenyon, who had responded so enthusiastically to the London Sinfonietta's Górecki performance earlier in the year, declared *The Protecting Veil* a masterpiece of contemporary religious music to sit alongside the Górecki, Olivier Messiaen's opera *Saint François d'Assise* (1983), and Arvo Pärt's *St. John Passion* (1982).

Kenyon's grouping is revealing. His inclusion of Messiaen (1908–92)—a devout Catholic whose music was closely and explicitly connected to his personal faith—clearly indicates that Kenyon made these connections on the basis of spiritual perspective rather than stylistic similarity; Messiaen's rhythmically and harmonically intricate music belongs to an entirely different mode of expression. As spiritual minimalism subsequently took hold as an idea in the early 1990s, Messiaen's name was rarely invoked. And while it was Tavener and Górecki who were having all the success at this stage—at least on London's concert stages—it was in many ways Pärt who established the spiritual minimalist template that they and their promoters were able to take advantage of.

Pärt's role in this story goes back to 1980, when the record producer Manfred Eicher, driving between Stuttgart and Zürich, happened upon a broadcast (recorded in 1977) of the first performance of Pärt's *Tabula rasa*. He was so captivated that he had to leave the Autobahn and find a quiet hilltop in order to listen properly and with clear reception.[12] It was a chance moment, but it ensured that Pärt's future as a composer would run in close parallel with a process of mediation that at that time was almost unique among living composers in its extent and careful management. Eicher ran ECM records, a jazz label that was already known for its high artistry and unusual tastes. After hearing *Tabula rasa*, he decided that he had to record Pärt's music, and that to do so he was going to launch an ECM offshoot, the ECM New Series. In 1984 that new label was born. Named after *Tabula rasa*, its first release was a collection of Pärt's works that closed with a reedited version of the Westdeutscher Rundfunk recording that had captivated Eicher in the first place.

Before it came *Cantus in memoriam Benjamin Britten* (1977), placed between two arrangements of *Fratres* (the original work of which was composed 1977, with arrangements made in 1980 and 1983), now one of Pärt's best-known pieces.

Many things were unusual about the *Tabula rasa* disc, and they each contributed to the template for Pärt's subsequent recordings for ECM (of which there are now more than fifteen) and shaped the reception of what would become known as spiritual minimalism. For a start, this was more than simply a portrait or recital disc, a more or less random anthology of a composer's works, a tacitly second-rate substitute for hearing them live in concert. This was a release that was conceived from the start as a recording, an album designed to be heard in one sitting, in conjunction with its supplementary materials—liner notes, illustrations, and cover art.

The first clue is the track listing itself and the fact that there are two versions of *Fratres* (albeit in different arrangements). Eicher has spoken of the importance of these in creating a "dramaturgical line" for the disc as a whole. Eicher's production—as with any ECM CD—is carefully considered so that it is not only well suited to domestic listening but also in line with general ECM house style. The choice of musicians is also significant. The Westdeutscher Rundfunk recording featured the violinists Gidon Kremer and Tatiana Grindenko, the Lithuanian Chamber Orchestra, and the composer Alfred Schnittke playing the prepared piano part. Twelve cellists from the Berlin Philharmonic recorded the cello ensemble version of *Fratres,* and *Cantus* was performed by the Staatsorchester Stuttgart, conducted by Dennis Russell Davies, who would go on to conduct many works by Philip Glass, as well as other recordings for ECM. Kremer was brought back for the second version of *Fratres,* for violin and piano, to maintain a continuity between this work and *Tabula rasa.* Yet it is the presence of the jazz pianist Keith Jarrett as his duo partner that really stands out. This was Eicher's suggestion. Jarrett was already one of ECM's most prominent artists (his *Köln Concert* recording released on ECM in 1975 remains the best-selling jazz solo album of all time), and Pärt, who by this stage had left Estonia and was living in Vienna, already knew his work. More significantly, Jarrett had previously recorded for ECM in 1980 an album of sacred hymns by the Armenian spiritualist George Ivanovich Gurdjieff (1866–1949) that occupy a similar soundworld—although from a rather more esoteric impulse—to Pärt's own music. If the Berlin Philharmonic's cellists give the recording classical prestige, Jarrett's presence provides a link with the worlds of jazz, experimental music, and even new age music. This was a package designed to have an appeal beyond the typical contemporary music recording and to set an agenda for the composer's reception in the West.

A Model to Follow?

One of the consequences of musical modernism, it is sometimes argued, has been a reduction in the audience for classical music. The argument goes that, as new music became increasingly abstract and alienating, particularly after World War II, Western art music ceased to be a living art and became instead a museum culture with no viable contemporary form.[13] This had a consequent impact on audience numbers, which in turn threatened music's financial viability. Spiritual minimalism was perceived by some to have vanquished this modernist demon. This idea extended far beyond exclusively musical spheres. In 1995, for example, the conservative American commentator Robert Reilly wrote in the Catholic magazine *Crisis* that Górecki, Pärt, and Tavener could be thanked for the "recovery" of music from modernism's spiritual sickness.[14]

Yet new music has always been difficult to market, a fact acknowledged early on when Arnold Schoenberg set up his Society for Private Musical Performances in 1918 in order to build a stable audience for his music (and even earlier still, if one goes back to Schubert). Whether one regards this problem of marketing as a failure of composers (for having pursued abstract, alienating musical forms, such as atonality) or a failure of music's supporting infrastructure of promotion, performance, and education—or whether one regards it as a failure at all—depends on what one considers the responsibility of the contemporary artist to be: to challenge or to console, to ask questions or to provide answers.

At the end of the twentieth century, new music's difficult financial straits were compounded by the spread of neoliberal cultural policies, which were based on the principle that artworks should succeed or fail according to the rules of the free market. This meant reductions in state funding in many Western countries for all the arts, including contemporary music. One effect of this has been that institutions have increasingly had to seek new audiences or expand their existing ones in order to stay afloat. Just as the Cold War had encouraged spending on soft power and hence on the avant garde, so neoliberalism encouraged the production of more accessible, populist forms of music.

Spiritual minimalism became a poster child for the principle of letting the market determine the direction of new music, exemplified in a two-page newspaper advertisement for Górecki's Symphony No. 3 run by Warners in 1993. In a clear suggestion of the moral superiority of consumer power over critical opinion, the first page listed only negative press quotes; the second listed its record-breaking sales achievements. However, it should not be forgotten that even this music wasn't supported entirely by the market: state funding played a significant role in its development. Górecki composed his symphony under Communism; the recording that attracted the notice of musicians like Paul Jamrozy was released on the Polish state record label, Polskie Nagrania, and the score was published by the state music publishers, Polskie Wydawnictwo Muzyczne (PWM). Moreover, his Symphony No. 3 was commissioned by the German public broadcaster Sudwestrundfunk. Tavener's *The Protecting Veil* was commissioned by the BBC and benefitted from the broadcaster's promotion of its first performance within the

BBC Proms. Even Pärt's ECM release benefitted from the licensed use of a live recording of *Tabula rasa* made by another German public broadcaster, Westdeutscher Rundfunk.

Two decades on it is easy to forget the impact spiritual minimalism had. Many composers, from the Russian Alfred Schnittke (1934–98) to the Scot James Mac-Millan (b. 1959) to the popular English church music composer John Rutter (b. 1945), were reconsidered within its paradigm. Living composers started to appear on television with an unusual frequency. Pärt, Tavener, and Górecki all became internationally famous, to a degree previously experienced by very few composers and at a speed shared by almost none. Pärt's releases for ECM helped his music cross over into popular music and film. Tavener's *The Protecting Veil* was an instant bestseller, but even this success was beaten when his *Song for Athene* (1993) was chosen for the funeral service of Diana, Princess of Wales, in 1997—which was broadcast to a reported (although surely exaggerated) global television audience of two billion—and featured on countless subsequent compilation albums. And then there was the epoch-defining success of Górecki's Symphony No. 3.

Spiritual minimalism demonstrated in the clearest terms to those with a financial stake in contemporary music—particularly venue managers, record executives, and ensemble directors—that there was a potentially large and hitherto untapped audience for new music, as long as that music fulfilled certain criteria. As this idea gained strength, spiritual minimalism helped create an entirely new market niche, or collection of niches, that came to define a large proportion of subsequent practice in new music marketing. These were listeners who wanted music that was exotic yet unthreatening; music that spoke directly to their contemporary, day-to-day mood (and could be used to soundtrack it through domestic and mobile listening); music that contributed to a chic, design-oriented, aspirational lifestyle; and music that could transition easily between popular and more art-oriented formats. Spiritual minimalism, like other popular musical genres of the early 1990s, such as IDM (intelligent dance music), ambient music, world music, and progressive forms of alternative rock (Radiohead, for example), ticked all these boxes and therefore found a wide audience. In addition to creating new niches and identifying new audiences, the spiritual minimalist phenomenon helped clarify new channels for marketing contemporary music to a wider audience.

There are many reasons for the popular appeal of spiritual minimalism. Part of it was timing. With the fading of the European avant garde and the dominance of American minimalism, which had reached a popular and artistic zenith in the mid-to late 1980s with works like Philip Glass's *Koyaanisqatsi* (1983), John Adams's *Nixon in China* (1987), and Reich's *Different Trains* (1988), there was room for a European response. The fact that, Tavener's work aside, much of this music was coming out of the newly liberated East gave it an appealing story: its appearance appeared to reflect the new European landscape that had come suddenly into being.

More than this, however, spiritual minimalism was cathartic for a world that had passed through the Cold War and the threat of thermonuclear annihilation. Luke Howard notes that Górecki's Symphony No. 3 was received "in the aftermath of the Cold War, the collapse of Communism, and the freshly rekindled guilt of Nazi atrocities."[15] Perhaps the most notorious example of this was a documentary on the symphony made by Tony Palmer for the British TV program *The South Bank Show* and broadcast in the run-up to Easter in 1993, which intercut interviews with Górecki and footage of Dawn Upshaw and the London Sinfonietta with graphic scenes from the concentration camps at Auschwitz and Birkenau and further footage of contemporary horrors such as neo-Nazi marches, warfare in Bosnia, and famine in Africa. Palmer's film was widely condemned for its crassness and insensitivity—Górecki was apparently "appalled."[16] Nevertheless, when viewed in a considerably more benign light, the simplicity of spiritual minimalism was taken by some to give it a pan-cultural global resonance. Eicher explicitly connected Pärt to the new globalized landscape: "Now you can hear the music of Arvo Pärt not only in Berlin but in Alaska and Rawalpindi, Pakistan."[17] Wilfrid Mellers, in a review of another ECM release of Pärt written in the same year as Palmer's documentary was broadcast, writes of Górecki, Pärt, and Tavener: "Presumably their fame must mean that although we the people cannot for the most part embrace their Christian faith, we recognise its potential solace the more the criminal imbecilities of the world—for which we are in part responsible—induce dismay or despair."[18]

Related to both of these features was the music's spiritual dimension. This not only helped with its redemptive, cathartic nature but also gave it an exotic tang, particularly in the wake of the fanatically secular 1980s. Spiritual minimalism keyed into a vaguely spiritualist trend that passed through 1990s music; for example, samples of music by the twelfth-century Abbess Hildegard of Bingen appeared in rave songs such as The Beloved's "The Sun Rising" (1990), and the monks of the Abbey of Santa Domingo de Silos released the triple platinum album *Chant* (1994). Spiritual minimalism, in its simplicity of form and expression, also acted as therapy (or soma) against the "unremitting influx of signs" that characterized contemporary life.[19]

With its turn toward ancient stylistic references, spiritual minimalism was also in tune with postmodernism, giving it critical respectability and middlebrow appeal. Some writers even conceived of it as representing a new avant garde in its radical break from modernist procedures and values. With modernism having grown stale, the argument goes that the rediscovery of pure tones, triads, repetition, and even melody is avant garde. Indeed, like most trailblazing work, Górecki's Symphony No. 3 was poorly received at its premiere, at the Royan International Festival of Contemporary Art and Music in 1977. One "prominent French musician"[20] was reported to have shouted "Merde!" during the third movement, and it was widely dismissed in many subsequent reviews. Yet, in a rhetorical move that was common within the postmodern era, Górecki much later described it as "the most avant-garde piece I heard there."[21]

Although none of these factors is exclusive to spiritual minimalism, the combination of them was significant to the music's popular reception. More important still was the role of recording and broadcasting, which was almost unprecedented for contemporary classical music. This pointed to the most important and more universal factor, which is the importance of mediation in the reception and marketing of contemporary music. Public forms of mediation, such as film soundtracks and recording presentations, weren't the only factor here; also crucial were the increasing significance of private, domestic listening spheres and the changing landscape for musical consumption that had followed the invention of the CD and would soon accelerate with the arrival of the Internet and the iPod.

It was also important that the music's style suited the kinds of mediation that had enabled it to become popular. Those modes helped situate the music within particular marketing streams, highlighting—in spectacular fashion—the sales potential for new music. Models for how this could be done were subsequently established and continued by other performers, promoters, and composers.

Processes of mediation were crucial to the reception of spiritual minimalism. The music of Pärt and Górecki especially became known outside the traditional Western concert hall format and the idealized presentation of absolute music. Pärt's music became known through the design and production qualities of his ECM CDs. Górecki's symphony was heard in live performances from the late 1970s through the 1980s, but it was his music's presentation through Test Dept's work (itself a consequence of the work's mediated form as a Polskie Nagrania LP with a strikingly designed sleeve) and Pialat's film that helped set its path toward success, followed by Tony Palmer's *South Bank Show* documentary and the symphony's adoption by Classic FM. Pärt's and Górecki's music later became a popular choice for film and TV soundtracks—to the point of being cliché—emphasizing still further the genre's suitability for mediated presentation.[22]

This suggests that two elements were present: an appetite for classical (and/or contemporary) music in such mediated forms and a musical style that was easily susceptible to such forms of mediation. Both were present in spiritual minimalism, and it was their almost uniquely strong combination that was crucial to its popular reception. Classical music has recently become a permanent soundtrack not only to film and television but also to people's lives, through domestic and mobile listening.[23] There are plenty of earlier examples of its mediation through film and television (the most famous being the use of Rachmaninov in David Lean's *Brief Encounter*, 1945; of Wagner in Francis Ford Coppola's *Apocalypse Now*, 1979; and of Johann Strauss, Richard Strauss, and György Ligeti in Stanley Kubrick's *2001: A Space Odyssey*, 1968), but by the end of the century examples like these were the norm rather than the exception.

Spiritual minimalism was simply slipping into this wider trend. Yet it has proved especially accommodating of such treatment. While it is often emotionally direct, using strings and voices to astringent effect, music by Górecki, Pärt, and Tavener appeals to filmmakers for other reasons too. Most importantly, it is generally non-narrative. That is, the meaning of one section does not depend on having heard what has come before. Large chunks of it—Pärt's *Cantus*, Tavener's *Hymn to the Mother of God*, and the second movement of Górecki's Symphony No. 3—are mostly textural. This means that they can easily be extracted, cut to shot length, or faded in or out as required by the director. These features not only make spiritual minimalism suitable for use on TV or film soundtracks but also mean that it works well on personal music players or as background music in the home, via CD or radio.

With the invention of the Walkman personal cassette player by Sony in the early 1980s, it became possible to "soundtrack" one's own life as though it were a film by enhancing mood, aurally coloring the environment, or adding a fantastical or dramatic dimension to one's day-to-day business. The Walkman enabled the experience of music as a wholly private, mobile phenomenon, and in turn realized new modes of listening and of relating musical experience to day-to-day life and the environment. Shuhei Hosokawa, in one of the first analyses of what he termed "the Walkman effect,"[24] outlined four features that are specific to the Walkman and its contribution to a new practice of mobile musical listening. These are: *miniaturization*, that is, the small size of the Walkman, which makes "an experience which had only been feasible indoors" possible on foot; *singularization,* that is, that the portability of the Walkman "enables our musical listening to be more occasional, more incidental, more contingent," creating unique and singular musical events at the intersection of where we are listening and what we are listening to in that moment; *autonomy,* by which Hosokawa (drawing on Deleuze) means a process of "self-unification" with the reality of a particular moment; and *the construction/deconstruction of meanings,* whereby the three previous features emphasize the "surface-ness" of the music.[25] The Walkman therefore makes it possible to mix listening with other nonmusical acts, such as walking or eating, opposed to the exclusive act of listening to music in a concert. The private experience of music can be overlapped with one's daily activities, each bleeding into the other.

A decade and a half later the Walkman was eclipsed by the invention of the portable MP3 player, first in the form of the short-lived SaeHan MPMan, and more definitively with Apple Computers' iPod. Although the Walkman had enabled a kind of listening that hadn't been possible before, it was the MP3 player that fully realized the potential of that rupture. Despite its portability, the Walkman still remained what Michael Bull calls a "door-to-door" device: you put it on when you left the house, and you switched it off when you arrived at your destination. As Bull points out, however, the vastly extended playing time of the iPod's library (a 64GB iPod can hold more than one thousand hours of music encoded in MP3 format at 128kbps, versus the sixty to ninety minutes that can fit on a cassette tape), plus its seamless integration with docking stations and computer ports, means that the user's soundtrack can stay with them at home, in the car, or at their desk at work, giving them "unprecedented ability to weave the disparate threads of the day into one uniform soundtrack."[26] Furthermore, the sheer scale of an iPod's database, as well as the various ways in which it can be categorized, tagged, searched, and queried, makes finding the appropriate music for a particular mood, moment, or space trivially easy. "The development of MP3 players," Bull says, "has now provided a technological fix to the management of the contingency of aural desire."[27]

However, there are limits to this technology. Storage and selection may be virtually infinite on an iPod, but certain musics are better suited than others to this sort of listening. The acoustic instability of the environment and the nature of headphones mean that music of a relatively narrow and consistent volume (dynamic range) sounds best. So too is music that is not formally too complex—that is, music that is comprised of too much essential sonic detail that might be lost in the event of external distractions or variations in attentiveness. In his own discussion of urban iPod use, Brandon LaBelle suggests that a regular rhythm or beat is important.[28] Length, too, is a consideration; works that are very long, and unlikely to be completed within a bus journey, say, may be overlooked. Likewise, works that are very short and may lead to a kind of listening that is too piecemeal may get avoided. Popular music—largely by design—fits these parameters well, but lots of contemporary art music falls outside them, and there are reasons to be grateful for a kind of music making that resists these constraints in the face of technological and social transformation, if only in the interest of preserving a diversity in possible human experience.

Yet changes in listening create changes in demand. Spiritual minimalism fit those demands well. Other musics that have proved similarly successful—Gregorian chant and Vivaldi, for example—fit this profile too. Commercial classical music stations like Classic FM that emerged in the 1990s further respond to and contribute to this demand. Playlists on stations like these are selected as much for how suitable they are for broadcast as for any other factor: the music must be able to play a functional role and suit the medium of its presentation. With commercial pop, records are produced precisely to fit these parameters. Works of art music, however, have been composed for the very different presentational requirements of the concert hall. This means that the music on a commercial station—if it is to succeed and therefore attract listeners, advertisers, and revenue—must be more carefully selected for factors such as length, dynamic range (narrower dynamic spectra work better on radio), mood, back story, and so on. A work like Górecki's Symphony No. 3, with its texts from World War II internment camps, static textures and dynamics, and broad brush emotional palette, fits these requirements well, and the same might be said of many works by Pärt and Tavener. These factors are much less of a consideration for public service broadcasters like BBC Radio 3 or Westdeutscher Rundfunk, whose broadcast choices are weighted more heavily toward artistic merit and cultural significance (however these are defined). Although few contemporary composers have had their recordings broadcast or embraced by film and TV directors as soundtrack music to the same extent as Górecki, Pärt, or Tavener, many have responded—positively or negatively, consciously or unknowingly—to the new pressures of mediation and the marketplace.

NEW MUSIC, NEW ECOSYSTEMS

In the wake of spiritual minimalism, new niches and previously unexploited audience segments were eagerly sought by new music's promoters. Mediation also played a part. By incorporating multimedia elements in their concerts, whether stipulated in the original composition or not, ensembles were able both to present music in a manner more familiar to consumers of films and music videos and users of mobile music devices and to create a reason for attending concerts by making them events that recordings could not replicate.

One effect of the new economic framework of neoliberalism has been the emergence of an entrepreneurial spirit among composers. At the simpler end of this scale, many act as their own promoters and publicists. Much of this work now takes place online, with many composers maintaining websites where they offer samples of their work to prospective performers and listeners. Others supplement these activities with a strong social media presence. The way they go about doing this can be more or less formal and professional. John Adams (b. 1947) writes his own, often provocative, blog, *Hellmouth*. Michel van der Aa (b. 1970) maintains a businesslike web presence that exists separately from the "official" pages on his publisher's website and helps effectively control his "brand."[29] Nico Muhly (b. 1981) is one of many younger composers to maintain an active social media presence on Twitter and Facebook and through his blog at nicomuhly.com. In the mid-2000s the music of many younger composers and contemporary music performers could also be found through the social networking site Myspace. Although Myspace has since been overtaken as a social network by Facebook, Twitter, and others, it remains an important platform for accessing music online, and many established musicians have profiles there.

The online presence of contemporary music, like that of anything else, has grown almost exponentially over the past decade. Some examples from my own experience may illustrate those changes. When I began blogging about new music in summer 2003, blogs themselves had just started to become a mainstream phenomenon, but cultural blogging was still relatively marginal. Music blogs existed, principal among them Matthew Perpetua's *Fluxblog* and *New York London Paris Munich*, by Tom Ewing and others, as well as webzines like *Pitchfork* and *Tiny Mix*

Tapes, but similar sites on contemporary music, or even just classical music per se, were almost nonexistent. In 2003 it was simple to link to every blog there was about new music—there were only three or four of us blogging about the topic. After the *New Yorker's* Alex Ross launched his own blog, named for his then forthcoming book *The Rest Is Noise,* in April 2004, the landscape began to change, and increasing numbers of classical critics, performers, and even composers began to blog. For two or three years after that, this online community grew, but it remained of mappable size. However, by 2008 or so the field had become so large it was no longer possible to keep track of every blog.

Similarly, in 2006 it was feasible to collect links to all the live performances of contemporary and late twentieth-century music available on YouTube (as in fact I did); within a couple of years, however, sheer volume made this impossible. New music found other uses for YouTube too. Lectures by composers, from events such as the Darmstadt Summer School, began to appear, as did television and film documentaries, archive footage, and uploads of recordings themselves. Most original of all has been the phenomenon of "score-follower" videos, produced and uploaded by a small group of dedicated new music enthusiasts.[30] These feature recordings of contemporary works—often not yet commercially available—with slides of the score, synchronized so that they follow the music as it sounds. Before such videos, this kind of insight into contemporary music making was only accessible to a very limited number of insiders. The existence of these videos is only possible because of the particular blend of amateur enthusiasm and global dissemination that the Web encourages.

In 2016, information about young composers, as well as many older ones, is more easily found by visiting their own webpages and by searching sites such as YouTube and Soundcloud, where composers and ensembles upload many live recordings, than by consulting official channels, such as the websites of publishers. Several composers, and not only the younger ones, have added a more overtly commercial dimension to their online presence. Between 1996 and 2007, Sir Peter Maxwell Davies (1934–2016) sold MP3 downloads of his music directly through his website, MaxOpus. Van der Aa runs a small record label, Disquiet Media, on which he releases his own music. Increasing numbers of younger composers are releasing their music through channels like Bandcamp.

Ensembles have adopted similar behaviors. The London Sinfonietta releases CDs under its own imprint. Cologne's Musikfabrik sells downloads of single works from its recorded catalogue. Even some venerable institutions like Ensemble Intercontemporain have a substantial presence on YouTube, and it has become standard practice for younger ensembles to upload videos of their performances as part archive, part promotional materials. Practices like these are not limited to smaller ensembles or new music specialists. Major orchestras like the London Symphony Orchestra and the Chicago Symphony Orchestra have been releasing recordings on their own labels for some time (one of the earliest, the London Symphony Orchestra's label LSO Live, was launched in 1999). Others, most notably the Berlin Philharmonic through their Digital Concert Hall,[31] have created lavish online repositories of concert footage. In these instances, orchestras are not only producing archives of their own work and expanding their brand footprint but also creating entirely new income streams, which slumps in public funding and conventional record sales have made more urgent.

At the most entrepreneurial end of the scale are those groups or individuals who have developed completely independent frameworks for the promotion and dissemination of their music and that of sympathetic colleagues. Whereas most of the activities I have just mentioned might be described as means of expanding the audience for existing products, these musicians are taking the much harder tack, which is to create an entirely new market niche.

Bang on a Can was founded in 1987 by composers Michael Gordon (b. 1956), David Lang (b. 1957), and Julia Wolfe (b. 1958). It was originally set up as a music festival, the Bang on a Can Marathon, but as that grew, the group diversified into two performing ensembles (the Asphalt Orchestra and Bang on a Can All-Stars), a commissioning fund (the People's Commissioning Fund), a summer school for young musicians (the Bang on a Can Summer Institute), and a high school educational program (Found Sound Nation). The three composers have also founded a publishing house for their own music (Red Poppy) and a record label (Cantaloupe Music). Based as it is around the musical styles and preferences of its three founder composers, Bang on a Can has an instantly recognizable "house style" characterized by amplification, groove-based rhythms and musical structures, and a direct and powerful sound, influenced by De Volharding and Hoketus, the ensembles founded by Louis Andriessen (b. 1939) in the 1970s. For Andriessen, the development of that style was related to his leftist politics, but for the founders of Bang on a Can, it was related to their desire to change the format of new music presentation.

This is exemplified by the Bang on a Can Marathon, held annually since 1987. Although it varies year by year, the basic format has remained much the same. Ensembles play one after the other in the same space, creating a more or less continuous concert over ten or twelve hours (see figure 5).[32] The emphasis is on serendipity: audiences are free to come and go as they please; musicians and repertoire are selected not on the basis of style or genre but on the basis of "innovation."[33] Wolfe writes of the first festival: "We did not want to simply produce a concert, but wanted to create an event. To accomplish this we made curatorial and marketing decisions that were unusual at the time."[34] She explained that the decision to change the format of new music presentation was made deliberately and analytically, and prioritized a shift in the event's center of gravity, from the authority and autonomy of the performers and composers toward the experience and freedom of the audience: "What was unsatisfying about the new music scene? New music

FIGURE 5. Bang on a Can Marathon, World Trade Center, New York, 2007. Photo by Jason Bergman.

concerts had the aura of academic lectures. The audience was select and serious, the programme notes were lengthy and the composers' biographies filled with accolades. The performers looked like they had spent their lives in practice rooms. The 19th-century classical music conventions they employed were formal and distancing."[35]

In 1987, Bang on a Can's approach was unusual. As Wolfe notes, nineteenth-century conventions, which enforced a barrier between performers and audience, were very much the norm. They have become less prevalent now, and new music has proved adaptable to more flexible and more interactive performance contexts. The London-based club night and record label Nonclassical, founded in 2003 by composer and producer Gabriel Prokofiev (b. 1975), for example, presents evenings in bars and club spaces that combine live music with DJ sets. The settings are relaxed, more like jazz clubs than concert halls, and the music played is a mix of pieces by artists on Nonclassical's roster,[36] leftfield electronica and dance tracks, and modernist and experimental classics—all specially chosen for their suitability to the informal context. Works with a strong rhythmic profile and a loud dynamic (such as some of Iannis Xenakis's percussion music) work well, as do those that do not require concentrated listening in service of a continuous musical narrative (such as certain works by John Cage). Releases on the Nonclassical label—mostly new works by young composers or recital discs by up-and-coming performers—always include specially commissioned remixes, many of which subsequently appear in DJ sets at the club nights.

Nonclassical's aesthetic—and to a degree that of Bang on a Can before it—tends toward the accessible, using the sounds and rhythms of contemporary popular music to lower the barriers between audience and performers. But this is not the only available approach. The Australian ensemble ELISION (founded in 1986), who perform music that is in many ways at the opposite end of the spectrum in terms of accessibility—dense, complex, strange, and disorienting—have developed a practice of creating evening-length works in unusual settings, often in conjunction with installation artworks and with a ritualistic dimension, that the audience can walk around and experience visually and spatially as well as aurally. *DARK MATTER* (1990–2002) and *Opening of the Mouth* (1992–7), by Richard Barrett (b. 1959), were both performed within and around installation works (by the artists Per Inge Bjørlo and Richard Crow, respectively), with the latter distributed throughout several rooms. *Opening* was first performed in a disused railway foundry on the edge of the Australian desert outside Perth, in stifling heat. The smell of rotting fish carcasses—specially cooled to keep the bacteria alive—filled the confined space. The installation also used the foundry's rusting machinery, bottles of putrid milk, and other surreal detritus. John Rodgers's *Inferno* (2000) and *TULP: The Body Public* (2003–4) are immersive works of music theater that surround their audiences with moments of extraordinary multimedia spectacle. In *TULP,* the audience becomes part of the spectacle through the use of roving video cameras and onstage projection screens. In *Inferno,* listeners were located even more viscerally within the action, seated on the second tier of a four-tier structure of concentric circles (with one ring of performers below and a second ring, plus a ring of speakers, above) that mimicked Dante's multilevel Hell; the amplification of all the instruments, which was then redistributed across the surrounding speaker system, was intended to disrupt the audience's sense of spatial familiarity.[37]

The most extended example of such a piece is Liza Lim's (b. 1966) *Bardo'i-thosgrol* (1994–5), based on the Tibetan Book of the Dead and written for performance at a New South Wales wrecking yard. Comprising seven sections of two hours each, it was performed over seven days, starting at 6pm on the first day (a Sunday) and moving progressively through the night so that the final performance began at 5am the following Sunday.[38] Each day's performance was given in a different part of the yard, tracing a circular route over the week, with a unique performance on each day. Each performance space was further enhanced by a particular colored light that corresponded to one of the seven chakras of the body, from the root chakra (red, representing reproductive organs) to the crown chakra (white, representing the top of the head), designed by the artist Domenico de Clario (see figure 6). During the week the piece therefore traced a movement from evening to morning, a circuit around a defined space, the colors of the rainbow, and the parts of the

FIGURE 6. ELISION Ensemble performing Liza Lim's
Bardo'i-thos-grol, fourth chakra, Midland Railway Workshops,
Perth, Western Australia, March 9, 1995. Tim O'Dwyer,
saxophone (foreground); Carl Rosman, clarinet (background).
Photo courtesy of ELISION Ensemble.

body. Audiences coming on any night were led progressively through the areas of the previous performances, with lighting still in place, so that the sense of an ongoing journey was clear.

Although few audience members attended all seven parts, the work was designed to incorporate also the times between performances, when listeners were not attending. These periods are the bardos, or "betweens," which, in Tibetan Buddhism, mark the soul's transitional states between death and rebirth; there are six of these, corresponding in *Bardo'i-thos-grol* to the six periods between sections of the piece. The audience is thus invited to continue experiencing the piece during their daily lives over the work's week-long duration—as though these periods were long pauses between movements. As de Clario describes it, "By extending the inclusive framing as widely as each of us can, the 'work' allows us an opportunity to re-define the seamlessness of the art-experience/life-experience landscape. The 'work's' potential is not activated until the moment the audience participates by walking through the chakra-sites and, later, by venturing back into each life-frame."[39]

Other musicians have worked hard to resist forms of mediation and thereby prevent their music's exploitation in the marketplace. Attempts have taken different forms, including the exceptionally quiet music of Jakob Ullmann (b. 1958) and the spatialized works of Henry Brant (1913–2008). Benedict Mason (b. 1955) works particularly hard in this regard. To begin with, Mason carefully controls the release of information about his pieces before they are performed, thereby minimizing the preconditioning of his audience. However, his primary strategy is the use of site-specificity. Works such as the *Music for Concert Halls* series (1993–7) are composed in line with the features of a particular building and are exclusive to that venue. The building itself becomes a performer in the work, with doors, layout, and so on all being brought into use. In *Meld*, written for the 2014 BBC Proms, the circular galleries of the Royal Albert Hall, its arena, the organ, and the aisles between seats were all brought into the work's conception, with musicians appearing and parading between different locations throughout the piece. The arena at the bottom of the hall was used to stage an elaborate round dance. In another section, each box around the circle was occupied by a violinist, who passed notes between one another in great curved sweeps of sound. Even the corridors behind seats, outside the hall itself, took part, as players could be glimpsed running between doorways, rather like horses between the slits on a spinning zoetrope.

In practice, however, it is rare that an artist is solely resisting or embracing the media or the market. Many composers who reject mediation are in the happy position, whether by fortunes of funding or senior teaching positions, of not being obliged to engage with it in order to support themselves financially. Mediation and marketing have permeated so deeply into contemporary culture that it is almost impossible to make any sort of public music that does not engage with both at some level; even Mason's music, in its use of mystery, intrigue, and spectacle, is employing market-friendly strategies of a sort. A rare exception may be the text scores of Amnon Wolman. These feature no musical notation at all, but are instead short narratives describing a sound; one reads these and reenacts them in the mind. They require no performer, except the reader, and no audience, except the reader, and as such are almost entirely unmediated, taking place in an entirely private sphere of the imagination.[40]

Nevertheless, Wolman's pieces are clearly an extreme case. Although fascinating, they have limited potential as a more general approach to music making. In the remainder of this chapter, I look at one example of contemporary musical practice that shows elements of both resistance to and embrace of the media/market nexus.

Experimental Boutique: Edition Wandelweiser

A dozen or so performers are spread around the space, on all sides of the audience. In front of each of them is a small table, on which are placed two bowls, one containing dried leaves, the other very small stones. One by one the performers start dropping these items on the floor, in small collections: two leaves together, one leaf and one stone, one leaf, one stone, and so on. What is heard is the delicately percussive sound of stones striking and bouncing on the floor and the still more delicate sound of leaves settling on the ground. After a while, the dropping sounds are replaced with very quiet whistling ("more like air on the lips than a clear pitch," says the score). Finally, we return to a new sequence of stone and leaf dropping. The impression over the course of more than twenty minutes is of incredible intensity and gentleness of sound (can those falling leaves even be heard at all?), combined with a starkly formal juxtaposition of vertical and horizontal: vertical drops onto a horizontal floor; vertical percussive strikes and horizontal sustained whistles. The piece ends before all the stones and leaves have been dropped, but they litter the floor in every direction.

This is *Un champ de tendresse parsemé d'adieux (4)* (2012), by Jürg Frey (b. 1953). Frey is a prominent member of the Wandelweiser group, a collective of composers and performers centered around Edition Wandelweiser, an independent publishing house and record label founded in 1992 by Antoine Beuger (b. 1955) and Burkhard Schlothauer (b. 1957). Although nominally based in Haan, Germany, where Beuger administrates the recording and publishing operations, Wandelweiser is an international, largely decentered network. It currently numbers more than twenty composers, including Frey and Manfred Werder (b. 1965) from Switzerland; Radu Malfatti (b. 1943) from Austria; Michael Pisaro (b. 1961) and Craig Shepard (b. 1975) from the United States; and Eva-Maria Houben (b. 1955), Carlo Inderhees (b. 1955), and Marcus Kaiser (b. 1967) from Germany. Previous members include Chico Mello (b. 1956) from Brazil, Kunsu Shim (b. 1958) from Korea, and Makiko Nishikaze (b. 1968) from Japan. Alongside Edition Wandelweiser, and helping to reinforce the sense of a collective aesthetic identity, is the Wandelweiser Composers Ensemble, which plays many works written by the collective's members.

Edition Wandelweiser was founded and grew in significance in line with the growth in CD production, desktop publishing, and latterly online sales and distribution. While such self-publishing enterprises were unusual at the start of the 1990s, they have become common, particularly among composers working outside the core aesthetic of contemporary art music. This description certainly fits the Wandelweiser composers. Some of their works are concerned with specific places or times; some with the condition of being in *a place,* or *a time,* even if it is not specified. Some works are concerned with very long durations; some works are composed in extensive series. Some works are closely related to works of visual art; some to text. Some are written for conventional instruments; some for nontraditional instruments or objects. Yet most, like *Un champ de trendresse,* are experimental in nature, taking Cage's *4'33"* as a key reference; they are often very quiet, if not largely silent; and they frequently sit on the border between music and performance art.

Other works produced by members of the group are not like this at all. Frey has written string quartets, for example, that in many ways are quite conventional in their presentation; Kaiser's works accumulate many layers of sound; and Pisaro's *White Metal* (2013) and *Ricefall 2* (2007) are positively noisy. Members downplay any sense of a centralized aesthetic. Pisaro has written: "Wandelweiser does not embody, as far as I'm concerned, a single aesthetic stance."[41] Indeed the group's identity has grown contingently and organically as an accumulation of shared preoccupations among individuals (like, perhaps, Fluxus) rather than the collective realization of a core manifesto (like the Futurists). Yet none of this is to claim that family characteristics, even a brand, cannot be perceived from the outside. Like the Second Viennese School, the Wandelweiser name has become both a designation of certain composers and a stylistic descriptor, and this is happily exploited by some composers. At the very least, Wandelweiser composers are comfortable with the label, in a way that minimalist composers or serialist composers never have been. The Edition Wandelweiser website prominently lists confirmed members, and composers in the group frequently identify themselves as belonging to it.

Wandelweiser is a significant feature of art music in the twenty-first century for a number of reasons, including the size of its audience and the breadth of its influence; its contribution to and extension of aesthetic debates begun in the postwar years; and the quality of its work. Works by individual composers will be covered at points throughout this book. Here, however, I want to focus on Edition Wandelweiser Records, the group's record label.

Edition Wandelweiser Records was begun in 1996 and today lies close to the heart of the group's operations. The recordings serve as aural documentation of the group's work, a revenue stream, and a means of dissemination. Yet the way in which they are presented indicates that they are meant to perform much more than these basic functions. Edition Wandelweiser recordings are attractive, collectable objects in their own right and go far beyond serving as simple objects of documentation. Since 2003 the label has used a uniform design, which builds and strengthens the visual aspects of the Wandelweiser aesthetic, transmuting it into a brand image. Rather than using the standard jewel case or even digipak formats, Wandelweiser discs are attached to a flexible paper-like sheet that is folded to resemble a pamphlet or greetings card. The design is striking, unusual, and seductive to the touch, but it

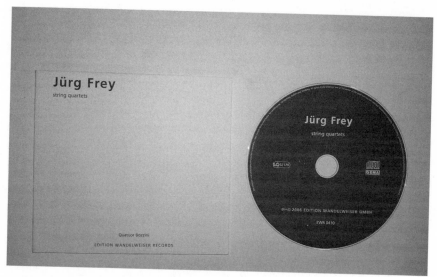

FIGURE 7. Wandelweiser CD and packaging for Jürg Frey's String Quartets, 2006. Edition Wandelweiser Records EWR0410. Photo by the author.

also emphasizes fragility and creates an air of exclusivity, almost as though each disc was made by hand. Crucially, however, the quality of the materials, the precision of the design, the clarity of the printing, and the selection of fonts remind you at the same time that these are products of a technological process, not purely artisanal, and very much of the present day. The materials have been considered for their touch and feel as much as for their durability or appearance: the flimsiness of the sleeve in your hands and the slightly rough texture of the material itself both restore something of the haptic communication that vinyl once had, which has largely been lost in the CD era (and which has been completely lost with online downloading and streaming). Like artists' edition prints and other luxury goods, Wandelweiser recordings thus appeal to many aesthetic levels; they also exploit the aesthetics of both high-quality manufacturing and handmade artistry. The only disappointment when unwrapping one is that the CD inside is of the usual generic size, weight, and shape (see figure 7).

These features have helped make Wandelweiser recordings successful within the circles of contemporary composition and experimental music. Like other boutique labels dedicated to contemporary music (including ECM), Edition Wandelweiser uses look and feel to distinguish its CDs as desirable objects.[42] The Austrian label KAIROS was founded in 1999 by producers Peter Oswald—who was also a former director of the ensemble Klangforum Wien (founded in 1985)—and Barbara Fränzen. As well as having a focus on exceptionally high quality of sound and performance, its releases, mostly of European late modernist ensemble music, are characterized by a consistent and instantly recognizable sleeve design. CDs are held in unique SmartPac sleeves within chunky digipak packaging made to resemble a small hardback book. The covers feature original paintings by artists such as Jakob Gasteiger and Erwin Bohatsch. Every release is accompanied by a detailed booklet, typically featuring two essays and/or interviews, translated into English, French, and German, as well as short excerpts from the scores in question. innova, the label of the American Composers Forum, founded in 1982, occasionally produces releases in unusual packaging as well: the Ethel string quartet's 2012 album *Heavy* came in a heavily embossed card sleeve styled as a 7" record, for example; and every copy of Alexander Berne's *Self-Referentials Volumes I and II* (2012) came with a small, original painting by the composer. Where Wandelweiser succeeds even further, however, is the ease with which the music can be co-opted into the sort of mediated listening that is characteristic of the late recording era, something that can rarely be said of the music released by many other new music labels.[43]

This is not purely accidental, as it was in the case of spiritual minimalism. Wandelweiser music has been conceived and composed within the era of ubiquitous recordings and is written (just as it is presented and distributed) in full awareness of the nature of mediation that comes from the CD. The London Sinfonietta's performance of Górecki's Symphony No. 3 and Pärt's recordings for ECM suggested the potential of the album as an artwork in its own right for classical music, but Edition Wandelweiser takes it much further. Pisaro captures this awareness:

> With recording [as opposed to live performance], sound is stored for use. How do you use a recording like [Christian Wolff's] *Stones* [recorded as EWR 9604]? Do you just listen to it like anything else (perfectly possible in this case) or do you find ways of listening to it that suit the recording in other ways: say playing it all day at low volume (so that it can be forgotten, except for those very few moments when a sound rises to the surface, reminding you it's still there). Or play it so loud that you hear everything.
>
> In other words, the recording can be viewed as open, something like an instrument—a particular instrument that makes a limited set of sounds that can nonetheless have a variable relationship in the environment in which they are played.[44]

At first glance, Wandelweiser music would appear well suited for headphones and an—albeit idealized—form of domestic listening of quiet solitary contemplation. Yet, unexpectedly, it also works even better as mobile or soundtrack music. Although the music is quiet, putting it at risk of being masked by external noise, it meets many of the conditions of successful mobile or soundtrack music: its dynamic range may be low, but it is consistent and narrow; the level of formal complexity is low; and the musical continuity can be interrupted at any point without the need for resolution. The long duration of many of the works, as well as their passive nature, minimally encroaching on their surroundings, also serves the sort of extended soundtrack listening that Bull describes. The nondialectical nature of the music, which encourages changing degrees of listener engagement, also fits well with the sorts of mediated modes of listening that Bull discusses in relation to iPod users. The kind of soundtrack that a Wandelweiser work might create is very different from that of a piece of high energy techno or a melancholy pop ballad, for example, but the kind of musical consistency it often presents over long durations can create different effects as one journeys from place to place or carries out different tasks within the span of a single piece. Pisaro suggests that the kind of mediated interaction that certain Wandelweiser recordings invite, particularly those that present more or less unvarying *states* of music rather than musical journeys or narratives as such, might encourage the listener to experiment with their own mediation of recordings of more traditional concert music.[45]

Yet the success of Wandelweiser's recordings conceals a profound tension at the heart of the project, since much Wandelweiser output equally *resists* recording. This is not to say that it doesn't work on disc—it clearly does—but that it is unusually aware of that mediated function. The fact that so much of it is extremely quiet makes it hard to record and reproduce effectively on disc and play through a domestic hi-fi.[46] Much of it is also site- and/or time-specific, meaning that it does not transfer well to recordings or that it only does so on the understanding that some important quality of its original conception and presentation will be lost. This may be in the sense of Cage's *4'33"*, in which the incidental sounds of the surrounding environment enter and participate in the space framed by the music; or it may be in a more pragmatic yet still unrecordable sense that certain works have been written for a specific time or a specific place. An example of the former would be Shim's . . . *floating, song, feminine* . . . (1992), a twenty-three-minute piece for solo marimba almost entirely made up of silence, punctuated only by the very occasional sound of a beater being dropped onto the marimba from the top of a ladder. An example of the latter would be *3 Jahre—156 musikalische Ereignisse—eine Skulptur* (1997–9), conceived and realized by Inderhees and the artist Christoph Nicolaus, in which 156 consecutive weekly concerts of just ten minutes each were given at the Zionskirche in the Mitte district of Berlin alongside a stone sculpture whose components were slightly rearranged before each concert.

The extreme duration of many Wandelweiser works—Beuger's *calme étendue* (1996–7), for solo instrument, may last up to nine hours, for example, and Frey's *One Instrument, Series (1)* (1999) for one to ten days—also mitigates against recording. In 1995 Beuger, in collaboration with the artist Mauser, began producing daylong concerts, often featuring only a single work. The production of Wandelweiser works in series, often in very large quantities, also makes faithful recording difficult. There is an aesthetic of surplus at work in the output of, for example, Frey and Beuger, both of whom have well over a hundred compositions in their catalogs, the superabundance seeming to mimic and/or critique modern production line technology. In critical contrast to the particular, spectacular practice of much contemporary music, which is commissioned and composed for one-off occasions and premieres, the music of these composers is just *written,* as part of a continuum of practice and identity-formation whose flow cannot be captured except in isolated, decontextualized moments. To borrow a different recording metaphor, it is the difference between film and photography.

Edition Wandelweiser Records represents a particularly contemporary marriage of style and mediation. The aesthetics of the works that are released, and of the label itself, are complementary and inseparable. By so thoroughly blurring the line between musical and nonmusical sound, between music and life, Wandelweiser music can often eliminate the question of mediation altogether. When one walks through the city listening to Wandelweiser, it's not that the music soundtracks the city, it's the other way around. The city enters the music. There is no mediation because there are not two distinct states to mediate between. Or, seen another way, the question of mediation becomes absolutely primary; as in Pisaro's field recordings or in the occasional sounds that Werder's date pieces introduce into a space, the content of the musical sound is almost beside the point. What we hear primarily is the *otherness* of a (musical) sound in relation to our (nonmusical) surroundings. Like a veil over our eyes, it is not the particular qualities of the veil that we see (the pattern or density of the weave, the thickness of the threads), but the general state of "veil-ness" that it casts on what we see through it.

PERMISSION

Freedom, Choice, and the Body

SEX AT THE OPERA

The pneumatically enhanced Playboy bunny turns drowsily toward the audience, a salacious grin passing over her lips. "I want to blow you all," she sings, ". . . a kiss." The closing moments of *Anna Nicole* (2010), by Mark-Anthony Turnage, may be some of the most naughtily suggestive in operatic history. A contemporary fable of sex, money, exploitation, and the media, it portrays the Playboy model and media personality Anna Nicole Smith, who was equally notorious for her surgically enhanced body and her marriage to a billionaire sixty-three years her senior. Its fictionalized account follows her life from her beginnings as a waitress and single mother in the small town of Mexia, Texas, through her career as a model, her marriage to the octogenarian oil magnate J. Howard Marshall II, the death of her son, Daniel, and finally her own death from an accidental overdose of sedatives and painkillers in a Florida hotel room in 2007.

Turnage's work proved an easy fit with the new mediation of contemporary music. The story alone was press bait: Smith epitomized a new form of celebrity—people who were famous for being famous—that has become ubiquitous in the twenty-first century but was, in her 1990s heyday, still relatively new. Then there was the fact that the opera came with a libretto by the acclaimed comedian Richard Thomas, fresh from the success of his musical *Jerry Springer: The Opera* (2001–2), which he cowrote with another well-known comic, Stewart Lee. Finally, there was Turnage's own reputation as a brash yet accessible talent. The music for *Anna Nicole* included parts for an onstage band made up of jazz guitarist John Parricelli, Led Zeppelin's John Paul Jones, and drummer Peter Erskine, and the score is full

FIGURE 8. Still from the video trailer for Mark-Anthony Turnage's opera *Anna Nicole*, 2010.

of sounds and inflections from Broadway and sleazy lounges that tint (or taint, depending on how you look at it) the grand operatic setting.

For its part, the show's venue, Covent Garden, made the most of the attention. Few new operas get the sort of preshow hype that *Anna Nicole* received before its premiere in February 2011. For a full year preceding the opening, a press campaign highlighted the attractions—especially for audiences who had never been to an opera before—of this contemporary story of sex and celebrity. Part of this campaign was a YouTube video trailer (see figure 8). Featuring lap dancing, drug taking, and glamour, it was shot from a claustrophobic point of view that recalled the graphic and controversial music video for the Prodigy's 1997 techno hit "Smack My Bitch Up." Strikingly, the video's soundtrack was not Turnage's music at all but the song "Heartbreak" (2012), by the British gothic-pop act Age of Consent, an interesting statement on the relative functions and importance of imagery, story, and music in the marketing of contemporary opera, as well as a clue as to the type of audience Covent Garden were hoping to attract. (Both Covent Garden and London's other grand opera, English National Opera, have since used similar tactics in their promotional videos for other new productions, such as Nico Muhly's *Two Boys*, which premiered in 2011.) The fact that Smith herself was a figure of mediation and market placement only made the story more appropriate to such attention.

Anna Nicole wasn't the first opera to tell a real-life story about sex and the media. Nor was it even the first by a British composer. Thomas Adès (b. 1971) had been the first to do so with his 1995 opera *Powder Her Face,* the story of Margaret Campbell, Duchess of Argyll, who was infamous for a series of sexually explicit photographs that emerged during her 1963 divorce trial. However, whereas Adès's story was history when it came out, as it was about events three decades earlier, Turnage's was defiantly of the present; Nicole Smith's death had come only a few years before the premiere, and her estate apparently even considered a legal challenge against the production.[1] Other composers have made operas about the recent past—notably John Adams's *The Death of Klinghoffer* (1991), Christopher Theofanidis's *Heart of a Soldier* (2011), and Tansy Davies's *Between Worlds* (2015)—but only Turnage has turned to a figure as inherently not noble as Smith.

Turnage's blend of high and low culture is something of a hallmark. Just months before *Anna Nicole* opened, he surprised the BBC Proms audience at the Royal Albert Hall with *Hammered Out* (2010), an orchestral commission from BBC Radio 3 and the Los Angeles Philharmonic that was heavily indebted to Beyoncé's hit "Single Ladies" (2008). Previous works have kept their points of reference more carefully hidden, but noticeable elements of funk, soul, and rock run throughout Turnage's output.

It may have been a talking point, but this sort of intergenre referencing was no longer new. Turnage himself had been at it since the late 1980s, most notably in his first opera, *Greek* (1986–8), which combined Berg-like expressionism with football chants, swing jazz, and even the rhythm from a TV sports theme tune. In fact, criticisms were made of both *Anna Nicole* and *Hammered Out* that, if their intent was to shock or shake up a stuffy establishment, they didn't go nearly far enough. Indeed, had the establishment—certainly shakable at the time of *Greek*—become a straw man? Was a porn star opera really that shocking? Or was it inevitable, not only because of a wider cultural fascination with celebrity but also because of new music's increasing comfort with popular cultural references? The postwar decades are frequently caricatured for their inwardness, their prioritization of cerebral over physical pleasure, and a turning away of audiences, but by the 1980s composers had begun to discover they could compose without ideological constraints and with a new sense of permission. By the twenty-first century that degree of permissibility, in which everything—and in every combination—was possible, had become the new norm.

POSTMODERNISM

It is often said of John Cage that he gave composers "permission" to pursue their ideas without fear of ideology. While Cage certainly enabled many stylistic and technical possibilities, including the use of noise, silence, and a host of "unmusical" materials, we can still register enough of a change between the 1960s and the early twenty-first century—between, say, Cage's *HPSCHD* (1969) and Turnage's *Anna Nicole*—to suggest that, after Cage, there were still many more permissions to be won and changes to come to the nature of permissiveness itself (although some age-old conventions and constraints would continue to be perpetuated).

A lot of this has to do with postmodernism, and Cage himself was a wellspring of inspiration and ideas for the postmodernists who came after him. Defining postmodernism is a treacherous business, not least because of its own skeptical attitude toward fixed meanings, grand narratives, and historicist logic.[2] However, at its heart is a turn (or return) to the freedom of the individual subject and away from objective authority, in whatever form that may take. This is captured most succinctly in Jonathan Kramer's observation that postmodernist music "locates meaning and even structure in listeners, more than in scores, performances, or composers."[3]

This leads to a different form of permission than is the one usually referred to when referring to Cage. In spite of his use of chance procedures, Cage still maintained the agency and will of the composer; the permission he granted was to composers to assert that agency without fear of reproach. Postmodernism, on the other hand—or at least the various phenomena that came to define it—opened up the agency of the listener. This, in turn, led to a reconsideration of the nature and value of musical pleasure and of the composer's responsibility toward satisfying the listener's needs. Just as third-wave feminism—another postmodern phenomenon—turned feminism's focus away from structural paradigms for all women and toward matters of individual female identity (recognizing differences in ethnicity, religion, or sexuality) and pleasure, so too did music, and the discourse surrounding it, turn to the subjective listener as an individual participant, consumer, and pleasure seeker.

In line with postmodernism's wider turn toward the body, pleasure was often determined in physical and/or erotic terms, and the body, as a performing or listening subject, has become central to a number of trends within recent music, from "relaxing" minimalism to highly determined forms of embodiment. The civil rights victories during the 1990s and early 2000s, from the end of apartheid in South Africa in the early 1990s to the progressive legalization of gay marriage in many countries around the world in the twenty-first century, made the body a focus of political attention—leading to the emergence of so-called identity politics. Likewise, the genocides in the former Yugoslavia and Rwanda, the suppression of female rights in parts of the Middle East, the often violent debates around abortion in the United States, and the continuing oppression of homosexuals in many countries highlight the importance of identity and the body in contemporary politics around the world. The real-life Anna Nicole Smith was an extreme manifestation of the primacy of the body in identity-formation—the subject reduced to practically nothing more than a body, identity a matter of image and physical augmentation—and part of her appeal as a subject for opera lies in the attempt to claim something more for her than that. Yet postmodernism's turn toward the subject was encouraged not only by politics but also by the increasing importance of consumer choice (and of choice as a means of identity construction) that arose through the logic of neoliberal economics. Modernism was defined by an active utopianism, often demanding a high cost along the way. Its primary impulse was to create and move forward. Postmodernism encouraged different—perhaps more passive—modes of consumption. Its primary impulse was to select and combine.

This chapter is not about postmodernism as such. It was simply the path by which pleasure was brought to the forefront of contemporary music. In looking at how permission and pleasure were manifest in music after 1989, I consider four fundamental categories of musical material: harmony, meter, noise, and silence. I examine them not only from the point of view of creation but also—and just as importantly—from the point of view of reception, so as to emphasize the changing status of the listener in the postmodern era and after. Although some of these categories suggest tendencies toward either the radical (noise, silence) or the conservative (harmony, meter), the fact is that, in the wake of postmodernism, such delineations are no longer possible. Every type of material has become equally available to every composer; triadic harmony or regular pulse can be just as radical as the gestures of the historical avant garde. (And, conversely, noise and silence can be just as prosaic as an age-old chord sequence.) This is Cage's "permission" turned not only outward to nonmusical sounds but also inward to the most simple and naively musical.

The guiding ethic is choice rather than innovation. No longer tasked with forging, in modernist fashion, a path toward a shared future, musicians are free to choose, from the available possibilities, what best expresses their subjective tastes and desires, or perhaps what they believe best communicates their ideas to an audience. The dilemma this raised was expressed well by guitarist and composer Rhys Chatham (b. 1952) at the very start of the 1990s: "Now that we are liberated from the academy and from asking whether what we do is art or not, what are we going to do with this freedom?"[4] Expressed, too, are the political and ethical complexities that come with embracing liberation. Chatham's question includes both the language of rebellion ("liberated from the academy") and that of market-led economic orthodoxy (choice and "freedom"). In the chapter's final section, I look at how this duality has led to opportunities for crossover and intermixing between musical styles and genres. I start, however, with the body—in particular that of the listener.

RESTORING THE BODY

The impulse to reinstate the listener (as two ears and a responsive body) as the site of meaning making and pleasure came from studies of music as well as from music itself. Inspired by postmodern theory and the identity politics of the 1970s and '80s, scholars like Philip Brett, Nicholas Cook, Richard Leppert, Susan

McClary, and Gary Tomlinson sought to place the listener at the center of musical analysis.

Among the so-called new musicologists, McClary has done the most to reconsider music in terms of our bodily, rather than intellectual, responses. Her primary motive has been to establish a mode of feminist musicology, and her collection *Feminine Endings* (1991) did much to set out the landscape and language of this methodology.[5] Related to this is a desire to break from the supposed dominance within the academy of high modernism of the 1950s and '60s (itself not unrelated to certain masculinist tropes). Like other writers (and many composers) of the time, McClary felt that music like that of Boulez, Stockhausen, and Cage had fallen short not only aesthetically but also ethically by not sufficiently engaging the body.[6] McClary reasoned that, by not doing so, these composers had made their work incomprehensible. She contended that music that does re-engage the body might once more connect with "the social functions and values" she claimed had been renounced by modernism's intellectual turn.[7]

The relationship between musical pleasure and physical response is often articulated through repetitive rhythms ("cycles of kinetic pleasure"[8]), climactic or wavelike structures, and sensual harmonies. In an essay on Janika Vandervelde's *Genesis II* (1983), for piano trio, McClary maps the repetitive, slowly changing textures of Vandervelde's piece to the multiclimactic form of the female orgasm. These, she argues, are opposed to "the neotonality of John Adams and David Del Tredici [that] has promoted its unembarrassed reassertion [of the musical climax that ends in "a spasm of ejaculatory release"] in compositions that once again give concert audiences what they want to hear."[9] In an analysis of the mid-1970s minimalism of Steve Reich and Philip Glass, Robert Fink draws further on the erotic potential of musical form, suggesting a link between the twenty-two simulated orgasms in Donna Summer and Giorgio Moroder's disco epic "Love to Love You Baby" (1975) and the repetitive surfaces of Reich's *Music for 18 Musicians* (1974–6) or Glass's *Einstein on the Beach* (1975).[10]

The growing importance of physical response—affect—was not limited to musicological analysis, however. Since the 1980s, affect has played an increasing role in the way in which classical music—and by extension contemporary composition—has been marketed and distributed. This is reflected in the reception of spiritual minimalism, described in the previous chapter. Marketing strategies drawn from popular music have led to an increase in what Freya Jarman calls "a logic of affect" that prioritizes listener responses (this music is energizing, relaxing, somber, and joyful), rather than obeisance to old-fashioned notions of historical greatness, in how it assigns value.[11] The way that Classic FM's daily schedule is organized—around music for waking up and preparing for work, getting through the day, driving home, and then relaxing in the evening—is a reflection of this.[12] So too is the rise of classical compilation albums, which are often branded as doses of pure affect or function: "chill out," "feel good," "music for driving," "music for babies."

The embodied, erotic musicology of McClary and others represents a socially progressive stance. Perhaps not coincidentally, it was formulated and developed alongside a reinvigoration of the so-called culture wars—the particularly American struggle between conservative and liberal social values. In the Nixon era this had been fought over influences from the counterculture, such as drugs and popular music, as well as the identity politics of the civil rights and women's liberation movements. In the early 1990s, however, inspired by a speech given by Pat Buchanan at the 1992 Republican National Convention, the focus turned to attitudes toward the body, particularly in regards to abortion, gay rights, and sexual promiscuity. Yet there is an irony that, by emphasizing the value of physical pleasure in musical listening, the new musicology might unwittingly support a more conservative economics, in which music is valued (and therefore commodified) purely for its functional ability to elicit affect. "Useful" affects might include familiarity, comfort, and consolation, leading to music that relies on gestures, styles, and idioms from the past that have already achieved cultural acceptance.

When the importance of physical response and pleasure in determining musical value is over-emphasized, the risk is a race to the bottom for the most easily accessed pleasure. In some instances this has proved to be the case. However, musical pleasure is also more complex than this, and it is not always easy to align the conservative with the physical, easy, and pleasant and the radical with the cerebral, difficult, and unpleasant.

HARMONY AND METER

As my examples so far suggest, musical minimalism played an important role in reinserting the body into contemporary music. Works such as Reich's *Music for 18 Musicians* and Glass's *Music in Twelve Parts* not only featured rhythmic grooves and pungent harmonic changes but could also accommodate the "relaxed, feel good, chilled out" impulse behind the logic of affect. Minimalism's emphasis on beat and groove also enabled crossovers with popular, dance, and electronic music, some of which will be discussed later. Something of this connection can be seen in Fink's juxtaposition of minimalist and disco grooves; McClary also drew a line between the repetitive beats of minimalism and rap.[13]

Yet, although the 1980s and '90s saw an increase in the importance of harmonic stability,[14] its expressions varied greatly in their origins and intentions. Gérard Grisey created glittering acoustic tableaux from computer analyses of sound spectra; Arvo Pärt turned his studies of medieval chant into delicately dancing scales and arpeggios; and Rhys Chatham pursued the logic of the rock power chord into massed choirs of electric guitars. At the same time, other composers of a more experimental mind—among them Lou Harrison (1917–2003), Ben Johnston (b. 1926), James Tenney (1934–2006), and La Monte Young (b. 1935)—were exploring the implications of just intonation tuning systems that rejected the compromised, equally tempered tuning of Western instruments (exemplified by the equal note spacing of the piano) in search of a "purer," more "natural" harmony based on simpler mathematical proportions. All were united in a general wish to restore a certain legibility to contemporary music, which could be articulated to a greater or lesser extent through the body.

The harmonic-metrical turn began in earnest in the mid-1970s: Grisey began working with spectral analysis in 1974, Pärt revealed his new "tintinnabular" style in 1976, and Chatham's hypnotic, one-chord *Guitar Trio* was introduced to downtown New York in 1977. By the end of the 1980s, therefore, to compose with triads or other vestiges of tonality was no longer an unusual or confrontational choice. In many places it had become commonplace. Pärt, Branca, Grisey, Johnston, and others began their experiments in tonality not from the point of view of market placement but as personal explorations of the expressive and formal limits of musical materials. Yet tonality has also enabled commercially minded composers—among them Carl Vine (b. 1954) in Australia, Eric Whitacre (b. 1970) in Great Britain, and Ludovico Einaudi in Italy—to access large audiences.

Neo-tonality has been described as an "antimodernist" tendency,[15] an attempt to restore the language and idiom—and presumably prestige and popularity—of nineteenth-century symphonism. Along with the more commercial works described above, other examples of antimodernist works are David Del Tredici's (b. 1937) *Gotham Glory* for piano (2004), Lowell Liebermann's (b. 1961) Symphony No. 2 (1999), and Ellen Taaffe Zwilich's (b. 1939) Violin Concerto (1997). These works all use techniques—such as extended tonality and melodic variation—and rhetorical figures from the nineteenth century within a more contemporary idiom. Antimodernism also includes earlier pieces such as George Rochberg's *Ricordanza* (1972) and movements like Neue Einfachheit ("new simplicity") among German composers in the late 1970s and early 1980s. Not related directly to minimalism, these movements nevertheless contributed, together with minimalism, to a general tendency toward tonal or tonal-derived thinking at the end of the twentieth century.

The desire of the Neue Einfachheit composers—among them Wolfgang Rihm (b. 1952), Detlev Müller-Siemens (b. 1957), and Manfred Trojahn (b. 1949)—to seek out "a more immediate relationship, unmediated by complex pre-compositional planning, between their creative impulse and its musical expression and, by extension, between their music and its listeners"[16] is undoubtedly a nod toward the listening subject. Rihm and his colleagues were, like any generation of young composers before or since, seeking to establish a difference between themselves and their predecessors; they decided the way to do so was to liberate the listener and place the communicative responsibility onto the composer. Much the same can be said of the later generation of (largely American) antimodernists: their turn to the idioms of the past is in large part driven by a desire to draw on their residual communicative power.[17] Context, however, is important: the difference between social democratic West Germany, with its generous state funding of contemporary music, and neoliberal America, without this kind of support, alters the motivations for why composers would want to strengthen their music's immediate connection to its audience. In the United States, the listeners are privileged at least in part because they pay the bills.

A curious example, sometimes held up as an example of antimodernism, is *Ash* (1988), by Michael Torke (b. 1961). Its model is heroic Beethoven, placing it very definitely in the antimodernist stream. Yet its entire fifteen minutes is effectively a collage of gestures from the last movements of imagined Beethoven symphonies. It's a somewhat unrelenting stream, in fact; endless variations on the same triumphalist tonic-dominant gesture, never quite developing or concluding—as Beethoven would have—but simply maintaining a state of suspension. It's hard to know how to respond—which at least makes it intriguing on some level. However, at least one critic, Jonathan Bernard, is damning, claiming that Torke has "latched onto the style" of minimalism, but "the conventional tonal-harmonic aspects of most of his compositions are so blatant that they reduce this (in the end) pseudominimalist rhythmic activity to, effectively, a backdrop." Ultimately, he argues, works like Torke's represent "a true triumph of manner over substance."[18]

I suggest that *Ash* is more perplexing than that and that it asks awkward questions about the nature of musical pleasure. Bernard's criticism stems from a view that minimalism, while it was one of the great innovations of the late twentieth century, has become weakened and made meaningless in recent years by the encroaching of tonal and metrical conventions. Certainly, as minimalism gave way to postminimalism in the 1980s, still simpler iterations of tonal harmony and metrical rhythm began to appear. By the end of the decade, exemplified in works such as Glass's *Solo Piano* (1988), Adams's *Fearful Symmetries* (1988), and Torke's *Bright Blue Music* (1985),[19] the consonance of some early minimalism had morphed into a restoration of quasi-functional tonality, and pulse become little more than a steady beat. What Torke appears to be doing with *Ash,* however, goes beyond a casual watering-down of historical idioms. Bernard speaks in more general terms of a "reverse-chronological alchemy" in which the devices of minimalism, such as pulse and ostinato, have morphed into earlier devices "such as *moto perpetuo* and ostinato."[20]

Minimalism has proved adept at such transformations, creating discomfiting hybrids of high and low, past and present, familiar and strange. Michael Nyman (b. 1944), for example, has exploited the trans-epochal connection between the late twentieth century and the early eighteenth century in film scores such as those for Peter Greenaway's *The Cook, the Thief, His Wife and Her Lover* (1989) and *The Draughtsman's Contract* (1982). Before him, the Russian Valentin Silvestrov

(b. 1937) was creating minimalistic collages of nineteenth-century pianism in his *Kitsch Music* (1977), while in the Netherlands Andriessen was composing pounding, amplified scores—*De Staat* (1972–6), *Hoketus* (1976), *De Tijd* (1980–81)—that combined the tight ensemble playing, coarse timbres, and legible harmonies and rhythms of pop and jazz with the confrontational edge of the 1968 generation. Later, Steve Martland, a student of Andriessen's, drew his own links between minimalism and the baroque, as well as with punk and funk, finding in pieces like *Dance Works* (1993) musical compatibilities where social ones did not exist. On the American West Coast, John Adams was making even more unexpected connections between art and popular culture in his anarchic Chamber Symphony (1992), which combines nods to Arnold Schoenberg's modernist masterwork of 1906 with the "hyperactive, insistently aggressive, and acrobatic" cartoon scores of Carl Stalling and Scott Bradley.[21] All of these works use the broadly tonal and metrical backdrop of minimalism to soften their shocking or bizarre effects.

In the United States, where serialism's perceived stranglehold on the sources of funding, prestige, and employment from the 1950s to the 1970s was challenged most polemically, neo-tonal composition of one form or another appeared to have become dominant, even normative, by the end of the twentieth century.[22] Between 1989 and 2014, the Pulitzer Prize for Music was awarded almost exclusively for works in a neo-tonal or advanced tonal idiom; recent examples include Steven Stucky's Second Concerto for Orchestra (the 2005 prizewinner) and Jennifer Higdon's Violin Concerto (the 2010 prizewinner).[23] The same can also be said of the seven American-born winners of the Grawemeyer Award for Music,[24] given by the University of Louisville "in recognition of outstanding achievement by a living composer in a large musical genre." Indeed, here the observation is more acute, since the non-American winners (among them Tōru Takemitsu, Pierre Boulez, Unsuk Chin, and György Kurtág) represent a range of less tonally bound approaches to harmony.

In 1992 the scholarly journal *Contemporary Music Review* published its first issue dedicated to new American music, and in particular what it described as "The New Tonality." Unusually, this issue, edited by Paul Moravec and Robert Beaser, focused not on analytical, theoretical, or critical texts but on source materials from composers themselves. It includes artist statements from George Rochberg (1918–2005), Kamran Ince (b. 1960), Moravec (b. 1957) himself, and others, as well as a long interview with Del Tredici. The editors' introduction sets out the reasons for publication: "From the perspective of the early 1990s, the tonal tradition, in particular the common practice period (ca. 1600 to ca. 1910), appears to be the headstream from which countless springs continue to flow."[25]

Several contributors make explicit the connection between tonal composition and affect. Rochberg writes that "the *Zeitgeist* [the compulsion to return to tonal means that he detected around the end of the 1970s] was real, it ran deep, and it clamored for and demanded concreteness again, i.e., concreteness in human expression, warmth, and passion of feeling, working from an emotional, living core in the making, projection, and response to art."[26] John Anthony Lennon (b. 1950), echoing McClary, writes that "music, in seeking its newly evolved form, has entered a maze of confounding complexity, one that has limited its *immediacy, its accessibility, and its humanity.*" Later, he makes explicit the link he draws between tonal harmony and metered rhythm, physical affect, and audience appeal: "The intellectual process has too often come before the aural. When the sensual was abandoned, the audience exited the halls, leaving us to ask one another why, or worse, not noticing its exodus. . . . We sat staring at empty chairs, while the audience decamped to jazz clubs and rock 'n' roll auditoriums, where triadic harmony prevailed over chromatic excess, where rhythmic pulse was wonderfully developed."[27] Such applications of tonality as these are invariably read as either a welcome restoration of time-honored values or a naïve regression into consolation and base entertainment. In a highly critical review, James Boros describes the collection as "a grotesquely distorted throwback to premodernist outlooks."[28] This is a strident response, but it was not untypical.

Reading such polemics, it can seem as though the tonal triad has become so loaded with ideological baggage that it is impossible to write one without first engaging in this debate. Regardless of the rights or wrongs of the arguments, which draw liberally for support on theories of cognition, psychoacoustics, aesthetics, and music history, the fact is that tonality—whether viewed as a return, rediscovery, regression, or relapse—has played a significant part in the discourse around contemporary music and its self-identity around the turn of the twenty-first century. And using tonal, consonant materials needs not necessarily indicate a conservative position. Some composers have managed to go beyond the polemics—or simply ignore them altogether—and use triads and other elements of functional tonality in ways that are entirely individual and original.

Peter Garland (b. 1952), a student of Lou Harrison (1917–2003), who was known for his syntheses of Asian and Western styles of music, has found a path to writing consonant and/or tonal music that maintains its experimental edge through extensive contact with non-Western traditions.[29] This is exemplified in pieces such as *Another Sunrise* (1995), inspired by music found in Mexico and around the Caribbean, and his String Quartet No. 2 "Crazy Cloud" (1994), which combines inspirations from the fifteenth-century Japanese poet Ikkyu with influences from Mexican songs, the blues, and Native American ceremonial music.

Another Harrison student, Mamoru Fujieda (b. 1955), followed his teacher in rejecting equal temperament, the twelve-note tuning system that has been at the heart of Western art music since the seventeenth century. In the early 1990s he formed a small group focused on alternative-tuned music, the Monophony Consort, with *koto* players Yoko Nishi and Miki Maruta and *shō* player Ko Ishikawa. In

1995, in need of music for the group, he began composing *Patterns of Plants* (1995–
2007), a project that has since yielded dozens of short pieces across eighteen collections of music. Despite the charming lyricism of the pieces, however, their origins
are in scientific experiment rather than musical sentimentalism. The "patterns" of
the title are the minute electrical impulses given off by plants as they respond to
changes in their environment. For some time at this stage, the Japanese botanist and
artist Yuji Dogane had been using a machine he called the Plantron to detect these
impulses and convert them to sound using a synthesizer.[30] It was while listening to
these sounds that Fujieda realized there were melodies that could be extracted and
used musically: "I patiently listened to the sonic result over and over again. . . . I
found and picked out melodies that I liked one by one, relying on my own ears. The
behavior of 'finding out melodies' is similar to going into a deep forest . . . in search
of beautiful flowers and rare butterflies."[31] As Fujieda describes it, therefore, although
the source material for his music (the sonified electrical impulses of plants) was
distinctly nonmusical in origin, it was his own intuition and taste that ultimately
selected what parts of that source he was going to use. Thus, the pieces themselves
are tasteful, with a hint of Japanese delicacy about them, while maintaining an odd
unpredictability.

One of the most remarkable "tonal" composers today is the Briton Laurence
Crane (b. 1961). Crane writes mostly short pieces for small numbers of instruments. As a rule, their harmony is tonally based (although it admits "sweeter"
dissonances like added ninths). Rhythms are metered, regular, and simple. Timbre
is uncomplicated; only rarely are extended techniques or auxiliary instruments
employed, although Crane has started to use the latter in recent works such as
Come back to the old specimen cabinet, John Vigani, John Vigani, part 1 (2007). In
these respects, Crane has an obvious forebear in his compatriot Howard Skempton
(b. 1947).[32] Yet while Skempton's music has a relatively straightforward (yet immac-
ulately crafted) attractiveness, Crane's music is far odder.

Crane's "quietly crazy"[33] rehabilitation of tonality, in which familiar sounds and
gestures are emptied almost entirely of content, formed part of a wider and older
trend within English so-called experimental music, which has roots in the music
of Cornelius Cardew and the Scratch Orchestra in the 1960s. Crane is too young to
have been a member of the Scratch Orchestra himself, but his work shares features
with that of several former Scratchers: not only Skempton but also Gavin Bryars
(b. 1943), Michael Parsons (b. 1938), Dave Smith (b. 1949), and John White (b.
1936). The fact that their work, as well as his, found a wider audience and acceptance in the 1990s and early twenty-first century was partially thanks to the postmodern narrative, which gave legitimacy and even radical status to works rooted
in consonance and rhythmic regularity, in contrast to the dissonance and aperio-
dicity of postwar modernism. Connections may also be drawn to the reception of
works such as Skempton's *Lento* (1990) and Bryars's *Jesus' Blood Never Failed Me*

Yet (1971, rev. 1993), both of which were accidentally hitched to the spiritual mini-malism fervor of the early 1990s and thus became unexpected popular successes. A final contributing factor is the rise, in the 1990s and after, of a generation of ensembles committed to performing and building repertories of often tonally ori-ented music. These include not only composer-led groups like the Steve Martland, Michael Nyman, and Graham Fitkin bands but also ensembles like Icebreaker (founded in 1989), which has focused on music related to the Hague school of Andriessen and others, and Apartment House (founded in 1995 by cellist Anton Lukoszevieze), which has concentrated on mostly American and British experi-mental composers and has championed Crane's music since it began.

Sparling (1992), which exists in several versions for solo clarinet and accompa-niment, is among Crane's early works, yet it has become something of a calling card. It was written for the clarinetist Andrew Sparling, now a member of Apart-ment House. The clarinet part is limited to two notes: a rising major second; a short note followed by a very long one. The accompaniment is limited to three-chord cadential sequences (short–short–long) played underneath the long note. After four repetitions (with changes only in the chord sequences) the clarinet sud-denly stops, leaving just the accompaniment for two repetitions. Two repetitions with clarinet and accompaniment follow, then four of just accompaniment. The piece ends with seven repetitions of clarinet and accompaniment together.

For all its radical simplicity, *Sparling* established a template for many of Crane's subsequent works. Its form is unexpectedly asymmetrical: despite its unchanging four-four meter, evenly divided into quarter notes and half notes, and its overall grouping into sets of four repetitions (the second set divided into two pairs), the perfectly square four-by-four cycles are extended in the final section for clarinet and accompaniment. And this last set of repetitions breaks the square pattern again, running for just three cycles instead of the expected four. The change is sub-tle, and if the listener does not count throughout the work, it may only be felt sub-liminally, but it is there nevertheless. Similar twists and gentle ambiguities can be found in the accompaniment's cadential sequences. And then there is the clarinet part itself: those two notes can easily be heard as the outline of either an upbeat or a concluding cadence, but in fact they are neither. They form a free-floating musical unit, unmoored from its usual contexts and creating new meaning of its own.

Crane's deployment of standard, even archetypal, tonal building blocks invites comparison with Torke's similar use of simple harmonic materials. Yet there is a large difference between the two composers' approaches, which we might consider as the difference between tonality as a pool of available sounds and tonality as a form of rhetoric.[34] Torke uses not only the sounds and/or objects of tonality but also its rhetoric to create musical structures that build narratives and climaxes in (or perhaps through) the language of common practice tonality. In most of his works, this is disguised by his use of updated (i.e., pop-inspired) rhythms and contemporary orchestration, but in *Ash* the style of the Classical era is also borrowed, even as the harmonic material is simplified and abstracted. By contrast Crane, through a radical simplification of his style, removes any trace of historical rhetoric from his music and focuses instead on tonal objects—chords, simple harmonic progressions—as sounds in themselves, such as the two clarinet notes of *Sparling* that hint at, but never realize, a range of rhetorical implications. This creates great challenges for the performer, in spite of the outward simplicity of Crane's scores—it's not easy to play with such a lack of inflection or interpretation.[35] By different means, Fujieda, Garland, and Crane all succeed in approaching tonal materials with an experimentalist's ear, outside of the ideological attachments that drove the use of tonality elsewhere.

NOISE AND SILENCE

If triadic harmony and metered rhythm do, regardless of the exceptions just noted, represent a pole of maximal accessibility and therefore acquiescence to the desires of the listener and of the market, noise is surely their opposite. If one pole is welcoming, the other is a site of resistance. Yet noise music itself is not immune to the marketplace. Nick Smith and David Novak have both described the complex relationship between scarcity value and commodification in regards to releases by Merzbow and other Japanese noise artists, for example.[36] Commodification entails not only the transformation of musical material into marketable units but also the separation of material from context, in which noise—as much as Crane's tonal triads—may function as a free-floating signifier, separate from the grand narratives of musical meaning making.

Noise also, and perhaps even more than harmony and meter, invokes the body. Exposure to undesired noise, in the commonplace sense of the word, elicits direct physical responses, such as a raised heartbeat, hands over the ears, and an urge to escape the noisy space itself. "At its most intense," writes Marie Thompson, "noise music disorganizes the body, it disrupts the organization of the organs. It transforms the organs into a thousand ears, the ears into a vibrating, fluttering drum skin. Noise music addresses me as matter, rendering the body porous. I can feel it in my lungs, my stomach, my throat; it can turn me inside out."[37] Noise can also serve a powerful cathartic function for the private listener and can act as a powerful bonding agent for the public body—witness, for example, the communal ecstasy of the heavy metal mosh pit.

Reasons for the prevalence of noise within contemporary music are many, as indeed are definitions and descriptions of noise itself. However, the physical connection is important. Undoubtedly an important precursor to current noise practices is Krzysztof Penderecki's (b. 1933) *Threnody (To the Victims of Hiroshima)* (1960), for fifty-two string instruments, a collage of harsh noise effects produced by playing the instruments in unusual ways, which seemingly evokes the force and terror of a nuclear detonation. Yet when he composed it, Penderecki hadn't intuited the visceral potential of noise—the title was an afterthought, suggested to him after the work's first performance. However, the reception of *Threnody* by artists from Frank Zappa to the members of Slovenian industrial group Laibach suggests that this potential was never far beneath the surface. Penderecki himself later linked noise to physical torment in two of his finest works, *St Luke Passion* (1963–6) and *Dies Irae* (1967), which was composed in memory of those who died at Auschwitz.

Despite—or perhaps even because of—its oppositional character, noise has helped restore the outside world to music. Distant reflections of Penderecki's association of pain and noise can be seen in the bondage imagery that accompanied the early releases of Merzbow, for example. Those reflections are given greater political focus in Merzbow's more recent releases, such as his anti-whaling protest record *Bloody Sea*, 2006. Connections between noise, anguish, and protest can also be heard in the orchestral works of the Israeli-Swedish composer and activist Dror Feiler (b. 1951), particularly pieces such as *Ember* (1997), dedicated to Che Guevara and the struggle against imperialism; and *Halat Hisar* (State of siege, 2008), a response to the Israeli-Palestinian conflict, which the Bavarian Radio Symphony Orchestra initially refused to play because of its extreme volume.

The voice has proved a particularly fruitful source of noise. In a sense, all vocal utterances are noisy,[38] and in the figure of the composer-cum-vocal performer, body and noise generator become one. Pioneered by artists such as Antonin Artaud and the German dancer and cabaret artist Valeska Gert (1892–1978), and having its origins in early twentieth-century Dadaist and expressionist experiments, the figure of the singular noise vocalist matured in the later twentieth century and into the twenty-first through performers such as Jaap Blonk (b. 1953), Diamanda Galás (b. 1955), Christian Kesten (b. 1966), Chris Mann (b. 1949), Maja S. K. Ratkje (b. 1973), Masonna (Maso [Takushi] Yamakazi, b. 1966), and Amanda Stewart (b. 1959), to name only a few. These artists draw on the tendency of speech to slip into noise, whether fragmented into its phonemes (Blonk and Mann) or intercut with differing speech or song styles (Galás and Stewart); or simply make use of and magnify the inherently noisy properties of the voice itself (Galás, Kesten, Masonna, and Ratkje).

While many of these artists work within and derive their aesthetic largely from a Western history of experimental music, poetry, and sound art, Masonna comes instead from the Japanese noise scene. One of Japanoise's most charismatic performers, Masonna is famed for his ultra-intense live performances. These are often extremely short, with entire appearances rarely lasting more than a minute or two. Whereas other Japanoise musicians, such as Boredoms or Merzbow, use external objects like metal plates, electric cables, tape loops, and laptops as sound generators, Masonna's main instrument is his voice, which he uses to emit screams, howls,

FIGURE 9. Masonna live at Fandango, Osaka, August 3, 2012. Photo by Simon Torssell Lerin and Bettina Hvidevold Hystad.

and blasts of indecipherable text, as though parodying the macho rock archetype of Mick Jagger or Roger Daltrey. He does not sit impassively behind a table of wires and switches but rather hurls his body about the stage without fear or restraint, colliding with speakers, mike stands, audience members, the floor—whatever interrupts his body's particular trajectory at any given moment. Often he injures himself in the process. This, and the extreme stress he places on his vocal cords, accounts for the brevity of his sets. Like other noise artists, however, Masonna also relies on the noise-generating properties of guitar effects pedals wired together to create loops of feedback and distortion. He therefore wears a belt specially fitted with some basic controllers for his equipment (see figure 9). Sometimes he uses this to manipulate the noise around him; at other times he simply crashes down onto the pedals themselves, his fall randomly flicking switches and breaking connections. The body is both movement and noise; the two become inseparable.

Masonna's vocal extremes speak to the anarchic, nihilistic state of noise. Although they emanate from a body, they are to a degree fashioned to erase that body's specific identity as a person. Masonna noise is extrahuman, avowedly nonlinguistic. It shatters all possibilities of meaning making; it just, supremely, *is*. Diamanda Galás also works with the extremities of her voice, at the same time foregrounding its physicality. Yet her work retains a distinct relationship to musical meaning systems—even as it strives in every moment to exceed them.

Using extremes of register, dynamic, and vocal production techniques, Galás highlights the flaws, breakages, imperfections, and limits of her voice. Yet instead of subsuming it to pure noise, like Masonna, she withdraws just enough to stress (and distress) its human, fleshly qualities. We can hear, for example, the tension in her vocal chords, the mucus in her throat. Her style borrows widely from the range of vocal genres, from blues to operatic bel canto. Each of them—like her voice itself—is stretched and distorted to draw out the imperfections hidden within: the extreme registers or wobbling vibrato of the opera singer (as in "Swing Low Sweet Chariot," which appears on *You Must Be Certain of the Devil*, 1988); the slow pitch bends of the blues (as in "Let My People Go," which concludes her *Plague Mass*, 1990); the overt expressionism of gospel (as in her version of "Amazing Grace," on *Vena Cava*, 1993). In this way, Galás uses noise, or the pursuit of noise—the noisification of the otherwise familiar—to tear her music away from itself, like a soul departing the body. This splitting effect is emphasized through further, electronic extensions of her voice—multitracking, delays, and so on—which highlight the multiperspectival, multivocal nature of her work ("a polyrhythmic, schizophrenic space," she has called it[39]). The image is appropriate: an important reference point for Galás is the Maniot Greek tradition of mourning laments (this is the culture in which she grew up; her parents are Turkish-Armenian-Syrian). The lament—the singing of which is one of few public roles permitted Maniot women—serves as a kind of ventriloquy of the deceased between death and passing on. It is often used to articulate the grievances of the dead against those who remain, who "are concerned not only with the pain of loss, but with revenge and retribution."[40]

Galás frequently turns to tragedies in her work. These often have both personal and wider cultural resonances—*Defixiones, Will and Testament: Orders from the Dead* (2004), for example, is a memorial to the victims of the Armenian Genocide carried out by the Ottoman Empire in 1915—that allow her to exploit noise's capacity to be both intensely intimate and socially disturbing. Since the mid-1980s, AIDS has been a particular theme for her. She began writing and performing on the subject in 1984, when living in San Francisco, and the result was the three-album trilogy *Masque of the Red Death: The Divine Punishment* (1986), *Saint of the Pit* (1986), and *You Must Be Certain of the Devil* (1988). Shortly after she began recording in 1986, her brother, Philip-Dimitri, a playwright, contracted the disease, and he died later that year. In 1988 Galás joined the direct action advocacy group ACT UP (AIDS Coalition to Unleash Power), and in December 1989 she was arrested inside St Patrick's Cathedral in New York as part of an ACT UP–supported protest against Cardinal John Joseph O'Connor.

The following year, Galás appeared inside New York's other cathedral, the Anglican St. John the Divine, for two performances of *Plague Mass*, one of her most powerful statements on the ongoing tragedy of AIDS. By this time, public awareness of AIDS in the United States, if not yet complete, was growing rapidly: the

"NAMES" AIDS Memorial Quilt, a giant patchwork quilt of forty-eight thousand panels sewn by the friends, lovers, and family members of individuals who had died of AIDS, was well underway; the story of Ryan White, a hemophiliac teenager who had become infected through a contaminated blood transfusion, had been a national news story for some time; the lists of victims had begun to include celebrity names like Rock Hudson; and December 1, 1988, saw the first World AIDS Day. Nevertheless, Galás's work, a twelve-part song cycle based on texts she wrote herself and texts taken from the Bible, the Latin Mass, and the French Decadent poet Tristan Corbière, is an uncompromising howl of accusation. Although she is supported by keyboards, percussion, and electronics, Galás and her voice dominate: she sang almost unbroken for the work's ninety-five-minute duration, the sounds echoing back from every corner of one of the world's largest cathedrals.[41] Stripped to the waist and dripping in sacrificial blood, she performed in front of a giant crucifix. The stage was lit with candles, the apse red and filled with smoke. In its range— from denunciations, declaimed as though from a pulpit, to a closing warped blues, with every kind of vocal noise in between—the music strikes, unmistakably, chillingly, shamingly, with all the retributive grief of a Maniot lament.

If noise has one opposite in harmony and rhythm, it has another in silence. At the same time as some artists were exploring the outer limits of noise, others were reaching into different extremes. As with noise music, examples of this style are wide in variety and can be found around the world. They include the improvisational sparseness of the Japanese *onkyō* movement, epitomized by Sachiko M (b. 1973) and Otomo Yoshihide (b. 1959); the environmentally oriented sound art of the Canadian Robin Minard (b. 1953); and the work of the American Steve Roden (b. 1964), whose focus on tiny sounds—such as those of paper being handled, as in *Forms of Paper* (2001)—has earned it the moniker "lowercase music."

The premises for composing with silence, pseudo-silence, or extreme quiet are similar to those for composing with noise; Valeska Gert's most notorious performance, *Pause* (1920), consisted only of her standing on stage, still and silent, a gesture at least as disruptive as any of her noisier vocal works. Again, Cage is an important source of inspiration. 4'33" was a piece of noise music as much as it was anything else, and many of the artists already mentioned may be equally associated with both noise and silence. And as those artists working with noise had done, musicians in the 1990s and after went far beyond Cage in exploring silence or near silence. For all their diversity, one characteristic that unites these musicians is a denial of the idea of silence as a fixed condition. Cage made a musical virtue of the fact that true silence is not possible, but his artistic descendants have explored with great invention the variety of possible silences.

The most formal explorations of these many potential states of silence have been carried out by the composers of the Wandelweiser group. Jürg Frey has articulated a simple taxonomy of different types of silence: "Silence between sounds, before you hear a sound and after you've heard a sound. Silence which never comes into contact with the sounds, but which is omnipresent and exists only because sound exists."[42] The distinctions are more than rhetorical, and the result is a large and diverse body of music at which 4′33″ could only hint. Beuger's *etwas (lied)* (1995), for mezzo-soprano and piano, fractures the word "etwas" into its component letters. In the second section, "t," the two performers simply repeat the letter "t" every five seconds, in unison. The twist is that they shouldn't look at each other, so there is no possibility of visual cueing. The silence between each pair of plosive attacks is unpredictable and tense, both for the performers and the audience. Pisaro's *Fade* (2000), for solo piano, asks for single notes to be played in even pulses, each pulse quieter than the one before. As the notes disappear from audibility, the ear is drawn in closer and closer. What appears at first a way of marking the precise boundary between sound and silence instead only serves to dissolve that border entirely, until the two states become indistinguishable. Beginning with *2005¹*, the score of which reads simply "place / time / (sounds)," Manfred Werder's "year/number" pieces—whose titles are also their dates of composition—offer a series of subtle and progressive colorations of the 4′33″ premise. Subsequent scores in this series first elaborate on the situational premise of *2005¹* (*2006¹* reads, "a place, natural light, where the performer, performers, like to be / a time / [sounds]"); then introduce specific sounding objects, such as "spider / air / eucalyptus / wasp / petals / rain" (*2008⁶*); and finally shift fully into the realm of text, providing just evocative quotations that are presumably intended to instigate some sort of musical act (*2012³* supplies a line from Alain Badiou's *Logique des Mondes,* for example). Whether the works in this final group are to be rendered as publically audited sound at all is open to question; Werder provides no other guidance in his scores, and realizations of them that take place entirely in the mind of a single reader are conceivable.

The spaces Wandelweiser composers have opened up within and around 4′33″ are certainly large, and they are often beautiful and interesting. Yet they are not the only silences. At the more cerebral end of the scale is *Metamusica* (2001), by Sergei Zagny (b. 1960), a transcription of Webern's Variations for Piano, Op. 27 (1935–6), with all the noteheads removed, leaving just the rests, dynamics, and articulation marks.[43] Other works use silence in more overtly political ways; *mehr als 4:33* (2003), for speaking pianist, by Hermann Keller (b. 1945), for example, makes use of proportionally determined blocks of silence punctuated by isolated piano chords to commemorate "victims of reactionary politics."[44] Still others are private listening performances that do not themselves create any sound; *oehr* (2006), for solo listener, by Robin Hoffmann (b. 1970), for example, composes an auditory situation by means of different hand positions around, over, or inside the performer's and listener's ears.

The most comprehensive exploration of Cage's legacy may come from Peter Ablinger (b. 1959). Although not a formal member of the Wandelweiser group, he has been a sympathetic colleague, and his reputation in Europe and North America followed a similar upward trajectory through the 1990s and 2000s. His profile has been additionally enhanced by works like *A Letter From Schoenberg* (after 1996), in which a computer-controlled piano is used to recreate the sound of the human speaking voice. The easily grasped premise of this short piece (videos of which are available on YouTube) has helped it spread across blogs and social media.

Ablinger's output revolves around a small number of core interests, such as noise, silence, environmental sound, transcription, and perception. Yet from these simple principles he derives a seemingly limitless and endlessly varied territory of musical investigation. Each element is explored exhaustively, and they are combined and recombined freely, like the colored squares on a Rubik's Cube. In many ways Ablinger is the epitome of the artist in the liquid age: with a conceptual twist or two any one of his works could become any other; his individual classes of material recognize no meaningful boundaries between them. To browse his sprawling website,[45] with its thoroughly hyperlinked interlocking categories, is to get a sense of his fluid and rhizomatic approach. It exemplifies the manner in which material has become separated from meaning. In Ablinger's world, noise, silence, and all points in between are simply relative states, not absolute units.

Silence appears in a variety of ways in Ablinger's work. At one extreme are his *Seeing and Hearing* pieces, or "Music without Sounds." These take several forms— for example, some are series of abstract photographs, displayed in sequence on a gallery wall. In practice, nothing distinguishes these from the truly silent medium of visual art, yet by presenting them as music, Ablinger is suggesting there is something musical (and therefore, on some level, something sonic) about them. Perhaps this is manifest in the rhythm of their arrangement on the wall, or the relationships of colors, or simply in the fact that, as in *Kleines Klavierstück* (2003), they are, although highly abstracted, photographs of a piano (see figure 10).

Another, perhaps richer, seam of Ablinger's work comprises what he calls *Listening Pieces*. These take a number of forms, yet in each it is the body—as a pair of ears, a container for mental processing, and a location in space—that is foregrounded. One subset of these is his *Sitting and Hearing* pieces. These involve arrangements of chairs set out in particular locations. The locations are generally chosen for their particular environmental acoustic, so *Listening Piece in Four Parts* (2001) involved a four-by-five arrangement of chairs set up on a beach, on a suburban baseball field, in a downtown parking lot, and beside a wind farm. As Ablinger describes, the gridded arrangement of chairs not only recalls serial forms of minimalist art but also acts as a "quotation of an audience space that can actually be used to sit down and enjoy the given situation as a concert."[46] Other listening pieces are more prescriptive about what type of action the listener must do, or at least what it is they should be attending to. *Listening Piece in Two Parts* (2005) (which belongs to another subseries of works Ablinger calls *Transition Pieces*) calls

FIGURE 10. Details from Peter Ablinger's *Kleines Klavierstück*, 2003. Courtesy of the composer.

for two adjacent rooms of different sizes and a board placed at either side of the entrance from one room to the other. Board one, in the small room at the entrance to the large room, reads, "Part 1: The change from the large room to the small one." Board two, at the other side of the entrance, reads, "Part 2: The change from the small room to the large one."

These regions of Ablinger's work use listening to indicate the particular interrelation between the body and silence. Yet while his pieces are conceptually rich and his output in this area diverse, each individual work is compositionally—in a more or less old-fashioned sense—quite limited. The work sets up a state of listening or a dynamic listening event, but it doesn't organize that listening other than in a simple on-off sense, supplemented by the suggestions offered by the work's location.

As shown by Cage's experience in the anechoic chamber—when external noise was substituted by the sounds of his own body—silence is a place where the mind-body duality collapses. Even more so than harmony, meter, or noise, silence highlights the subjectivity of the listener. When there is no sound from the stage, listening is the only musical act that remains. Silence, or extreme quiet, may have a more experimental origin than neo-tonality, but its rising status within contemporary music speaks to the same focus on the listener as music's embodied subject.

At its heart remains the figure of the selective, choosing listener/consumer: within a composed silence we are granted permission to listen (or not) to whatever we wish to find.

In his listening pieces, Ablinger sets up relatively straightforward situations and simply invites attention to a place, a moment, or a type of movement. Much greater responsibility (and involvement) is given to the listener in David Dunn's *Purposeful Listening in Complex States of Time* (1997–8), along with a substantial reduction in their freedom to choose how to listen. Again there are no composed sounds, and again the listener/performer is required to direct their attention toward their sounding environment. However, Dunn goes much further than Ablinger in prescribing how the listener/performer's attention is to be directed. There are twenty pages to the score, each representing a separate three-minute composition that is to be realized in a different outdoor environment with a low level of ambient sound. Performances should be documented through sound recordings, photographs, and so on. Within each three-minute piece, successive listening states are notated using a graphical system of noteheads, beams, and staff lines similar to standard musical notation. The duration of each listening state is marked in numbers of seconds. The position of noteheads above, between, or below the two staff lines indicates whether attention is to be at sky level, body level, or ground level. Arrows around the noteheads indicate the direction in which attention should be focused. One, two, or three plus signs indicate proximity to the body (from adjacent to far away). Finally, colors indicate the time state of the sound being listened to: blue for a real-time sound event, gold for a remembered sound event, red for an imagined future sound, and black for "a neutral non-focused time duration."

As a result of such notational detail, Dunn is able to describe ways of moving one's listening perspective through space and time that resemble the gestures and forms of sounding music. A good example of this occurs at the start of the first page. The first three events shorten in length, at three, two, and one seconds, respectively. They also move progressively in space, from behind the listener to the right of them, and from far away at ground level to close by and overhead. All three are marked as imaginary future events, but Dunn draws a curve between them, like a phrase mark in conventional notation, that indicates that all three are to be considered as a single dynamic movement. The effect is of a single upward-spiraling sweep, of some imagined, even fantastical, sound that coils around the listener. This dramatic, six-second movement is followed by its opposite: six seconds of static, unfocused attention. Only after this complimentary pair of ear-opening gestures is the listener asked to focus on a single real-time sound, at body level just behind them to their right. This lasts a full ten seconds, and if the whole sequence is executed faithfully it can prove a revelatory experience.

Dunn's piece requires an extraordinary virtuosity of listening skill—the composer Warren Burt, whose website hosts Dunn's score, admits, "I've made it through a page or two of this score, but never have been able to do more than that."[47] Dunn's ambition, as he explains in an essay that serves as the work's preface, was to go "beyond the event horizon of *4'33"*" and into "a different universe of musical perception where composition might be based upon or at the least inclusive of an awareness of the primacy of mind, where an emphasis is placed upon the processes of perception and not materials."[48]

By composing listening, as a musical activity in its own right, Dunn gives his listener a kind of autonomy usually reserved for the performer. This shift of emphasis, from object to subject, from external artwork to embodied experience, echoes both the shift undertaken in the new musicology, in which what the work is like as an experience for the listener becomes more important than how it relates to an "objective" history, and the "logic of affect" in the commercial market for art music, by which the accessible is deemed good *because* it is pleasurable.

Purposeful Listening takes a more critical stance. Because listener and performer are one and the same person, there is not the same subject/object divide. Moreover, the listener is required to put in the same level of work (including learning and practicing the piece) as a performer might. Dunn's piece builds on the notion of the soundwalk, discussed in chapter 1 in the work of Hildegard Westerkamp. Westerkamp makes explicit the relationship between the embodied listener and ecological responsibility: "As acoustic ecologists we know—in the spirit of genuine ecological consciousness—that we are positioned inside the soundscape: like all human beings we are listeners and sound makers in this world and therefore active participants in the creation of our soundscapes. Soundwalking is a practice that wants to bring our existing position-inside-the-soundscape to full consciousness."[49]

Dunn's motives are also ecological; among his other works is the CD *The Sound of Light in Trees* (2006), a composite "aural portrait"[50] of the inside of a pinyon pine, a type of tree that grows in Mexico and the southwestern United States, and which is under threat from infestations of bark beetles, exacerbated by droughts and warmer winters brought on by climate change. As sound sources, Dunn uses recordings of a range of beetle noises, as well incidental sounds and the sounds of an uninfested tree. The materials of *Purposeful Listening* are not as specifically determined, but the work still encourages "an intensification of awareness towards both the environment and perception."[51]

STYLE AND GENRE

Although the music of the last twenty-five years or so has presented a large number of changes in style and idiom, there have been few genuine innovations in technique, except perhaps in the domain of computer music. In this respect, recent musical history is simply reproducing a widespread trend: the pace of technological innovation, despite how it may feel as we are living through it, has in fact slowed. In terms of its inventions and their impact, the late twentieth century has little that can compete with the television, the jet engine, the Fordist production line, or the Haber process for mass-producing ammonia as a crop fertilizer. Genetic modification in food production, for example, is in many respects just a refinement of a process that has been used by plant breeders for centuries. What *is* new is the way techniques are combined. The largest advances in recent technology are in fact aggregates of already existing concepts. Even the Internet can be interpreted as merely "a super-fast and globally accessible combination of library, post office, and mail-order catalogue."[52]

The units may not be new, but the idea—almost an ethical principle—that things *should* be open to integration like this is characteristic of our times. We have already seen examples of how, in the last twenty years or so, basic musical elements such as harmony, meter, noise, and silence were becoming susceptible to this principle and how they could be used outside the contexts to which they might appear most suited. But toward the end of the century, this principle of integration was expanded beyond the basic building blocks and into characteristics of style and genre, which came to be seen as elements that themselves could be freely chosen and combined.

There are few better examples of this phenomenon than the music John Zorn (b. 1953) made with his band Naked City between 1988 and 1993. Zorn was already an established figure on New York's "downtown" experimental music scene as a composer and free jazz saxophonist. Before Naked City, he was best known for his so-called game pieces, compositions that were written as sets of rules for forms of structured improvisation. *Cobra* (1984), for instance, consists of a set of cue cards that are displayed as desired by the conductor, along with rules governing how the players are to respond to the cards when they are shown or to the actions of other players in the ensemble.

The game pieces drew on the open-form compositions of the 1960s avant garde, but they went further in shifting the compositional emphasis away from prescriptions (of what notes one should play and when) and toward conventions (how one should respond within a given circumstance). This idea extended into the creation of Naked City, which Zorn has described as a "compositional workshop" for exploring the possibilities of the rock band format, itself one of the most conventional of all musical formats. The group lined up as a six piece, with Zorn's sax alongside guitar (Bill Frisell), keyboards (Wayne Horvitz), bass (Fred Frith), drums (Joey Baron), and vocals (Yamatsuka Eye).

The music for Naked City was composed very differently from the game pieces, although a lot of freedom was still given to the players. Each Naked City track was written out in sequence, its order of events marked out precisely for the players to follow. What those events might contain varies greatly—the score for "Snagglepuss", from Naked City's eponymous debut album (1990), includes instructions such as "C Boogie Blues Band," "3 events each," "drum solo," and "drunk falling up stairs." Some events might contain a great deal of freedom in how they could be interpreted; others require a certain amount of preperformance preparation or mutual understanding. In all of them, ensemble unity is essential: every change is as crisply articulated as a CD player skipping tracks. "Krazy Kat" (another piece named for a cartoon character), from the fourth Naked City album, *Radio* (1993), compresses noise bursts, scale practice, cartoon music, references to Stravinsky's *The Rite of Spring* (1913), country and western steel guitar, thrash, and more into less than two minutes. The combinations are even more fluid than on "Snagglepuss"—often one style has dissolved into another before the ear has had a chance to properly grasp what it was.

Zorn's approach, through his game pieces and his later work with Naked City, was initially received as radically new, a rare outpost of the musical avant garde in the 1980s. And it did indeed seem to take some of the implications of the open form ensemble music written by Christian Wolff (b. 1934), Pauline Oliveros (b. 1932), and Cornelius Cardew (1936–81), as well as the polystylism of Alfred Schnittke (1934–98) and Bernd Alois Zimmermann (1918–70), into new territory. Yet the ease with which Zorn's cut-and-paste style has been assimilated into the work of later musicians indicates the degree to which it actually ran with rather than against the grain of wider culture. The aesthetic permissiveness that opened up after postmodernism became an almost moral obligation to cross boundaries of style and genre. Under postmodernism, and in Zorn's music, for example, this was done in a critical fashion, in order to question the existing order of things. As those border crossings stopped being radical and became idiomatic, however, crossover work became a way of appealing to new audience segments and a tool within the marketing of contemporary music.

Crossovers with Electronica

March 8, 2003, saw a remarkable concert at London's Royal Festival Hall. The house was full, and the audience was livelier than usual—young, hip, yet attentive and open-minded. In a major break from protocol, drinks were allowed, albeit in plastic cups. The venue's staff and regulars were outwardly relaxed yet inwardly tense. The United Kingdom's premiere new music ensemble, the London Sinfonietta, was teaming up with the acclaimed electronic dance music label Warp Records to present a concert of twentieth-century avant-garde classics—by Ligeti, Cage, Stockhausen, and Charles Ives—alongside arrangements of Warp Records' artists. Every piece was accompanied by visuals, the ensemble was heavily amplified, videos and dance tracks were played in the interval, and there was a DJ in the lobby afterward. Nothing quite like this had been done before.

The first Warp Works and Twentieth-Century Masters concert may have seemed like a radical new development, but the boundaries between contemporary classical and popular music had been eroding for more than a decade. The earliest crossovers dated back much earlier, to singers like Mario Lanza and even Enrico Caruso. Yet it was reborn as a mass-market phenomenon in the summer of 1990, when Plácido Domingo, José Carreras, and Luciano Pavarotti sang at the Baths of Caracalla in Rome on the eve of the FIFA World Cup final. The Three Tenors, as this operatic supergroup came to be known, proved a huge commercial success. Few subsequent performers came close to receiving the mass adulation that the Three Tenors inspired, but many—including the soprano Charlotte Church, the tenor Andrea Bocelli, and the "operatic pop" vocal quartet Il Divo—have attempted to recapture their crossover appeal.

Ultimately, the Three Tenors and those that followed them were crooners with a patina of respectability, seeking to bring classical music and opera to a mass easy-listening market. Others, however, were attempting to win genuinely new audiences by appealing to youth and channeling a spirit of rebellion. The British violinist Nigel Kennedy attempted to make the genteel music of the baroque—specifically Vivaldi's set of violin concertos known as *The Four Seasons*—hip to an edgy, young audience and along the way achieved sales that most others could only dream of. Kennedy traded on a unique personal blend that was part Yehudi Menuhin and part John Lydon. Other players, including the violinist Vanessa-Mae, used wet T-shirts and other suggestive cover art to help sell their records. *The Four Seasons* itself became a calling card for crossover acts, performed by artists as various as Vanessa-Mae, the Swedish electronic duo There Are No More Four Seasons (2008), and the composer Max Richter (*Recomposed,* 2012).

This spirit of openness went beyond creating new bottles for the old wine of the established repertory; new music ensembles were investigating the possibilities of crossovers. Kronos Quartet is emblematic of this aesthetic sensibility. The group was one of the first to recognize the possibilities of presenting new music in a more youthful way, dressing informally, using lightshows on stage, and collaborating with nonclassical artists (see figure 11). Their repertory is also often chosen for its visceral, almost punk-like, sonic impact, and since 1980 has included an arrangement of Jimi Hendrix's "Purple Haze." The Bang on a Can All-Stars, another group seeking a crossover audience, has released an arrangement of Brian Eno's classic ambient record of 1979, *Music for Airports* (1998). Although not a contemporary music specialist, even Kennedy recorded a version of Hendrix's "Fire" in 1993 and released a full album of Hendrix covers as *The Kennedy Experience* in 1999.

Meanwhile, other dimensions to the classical-electronica crossover were falling into place. Aesthetic overlaps between art music minimalism and popular genres of techno and house were made concrete in 1989 when acid house producer Mark Moore invited Philip Glass to remix the song "Hey Music Lover," by his band S-Express. Glass obliged, providing a seven-minute sequence of looping samples from the original. While it lacks the sophistication of sample-based music made by

FIGURE 11. Kronos Quartet, 1989. Left to right: Joan Jeanrenaud, Hank Dutt, John Sherba, David Harrington. Photo by Guy Le Querrec, courtesy of Magnum Photos.

more experienced technicians, its brutal cut-and-paste style has an energy of sorts. A second, perhaps more auspicious, link was made with British dance music when Glass provided an orchestration of "ICCT Hedral," by the leading techno artist Aphex Twin (Richard James, b. 1971), which appeared as a B-side to Aphex's "Donkey Rhubarb" single in 1995.

In the same year, the writer and former post-punk musician Richard Witts sent recordings by three techno musicians—Aphex Twin, Plastikman (Richie Hawtin, b. 1970), and Scanner (Robin Rimbaud, b. 1964)—to Karlheinz Stockhausen, and interviewed the composer for his responses for a BBC Radio 3 broadcast. In an article for *The Wire*, "Stockhausen vs. the Technocrats," that excerpted part of that conversation, Rob Young reversed the process, asking James, Rimbaud, and Daniel Pemberton (b. 1977) for their views on Stockhausen's pieces *Gesang der Jünglinge* (1955–6), *Hymnen* (1966–7), and *Kontakte* (1958–60), respectively. At this point, in the mid-1990s, there seemed to be little intellectual connection between the two scenes, contemporary composition and electronic dance music. Stockhausen's initial remark was: "I wish those musicians would not allow themselves any repetitions, and would go faster in developing their ideas or language. It is like someone who is stuttering all the time, and can't get words out of his mouth." In their own responses, James, Rimbaud, and Pemberton express limited sympathy with Stockhausen's critique. "Stockhausen should experiment more with standard melodies, try and subvert them," concluded Pemberton. "He should stop being so afraid of the normal: by being so afraid of the normal he's being normal himself by being the complete opposite. He should try to blend the two together: that would be new and interesting."[53]

Yet despite these differences, the crossover impulse continued to grow. In the same year as "Stockhausen vs. the Technocrats" was published, James produced a remix of Gavin Bryars's *Sinking of the Titanic;*[54] two years later he remixed Philip Glass's 1996 *Heroes* symphony (itself based on the 1977 David Bowie album of that name).[55] His absorption in twentieth-century avant-garde composition was confirmed by the inclusion of several pieces for prepared piano on the Aphex Twin album *Drukqs* (2001). At the same time, the Icelandic singer Björk—who, like Richard James, was comfortable introducing materials and procedures borrowed from the avant garde into a pop idiom—began to pursue her own investigations into the pop/art crossover. In 1996 she interviewed Stockhausen for the magazine *Dazed and Confused*, and in 1997 she produced a documentary for the BBC titled *Modern Minimalists*.[56] In 1999, after Björk came for dinner at his house, John Tavener wrote *Prayer of the Heart* for her and the Brodsky Quartet.

So although the ideas behind it had been in the air for some time, the first Warp Works concert in 2003 received a mixed critical reaction. Nevertheless, the idea of exploring the art music and electronica crossover continued to influence both the Sinfonietta's programming and Warp's output for years to come. Aphex Twin's *26 Mixes for Cash* was released in the same month as the concert, and it included his remixes of Glass and Bryars, mentioned above. A second Warp Works concert was devised in 2004. This time arrangements of Squarepusher, Jamie Liddell, and Aphex Twin were performed alongside works by Varèse, Antheil, Cage, and Reich. A double CD of highlights from the two live shows was released on Warp in 2006. Mira Calix (b. Chantal Passamonte, 1970), whose *Nunu* (2003) had been one of the successes of the first Warp Works concert, established herself as an electronic sound artist of some renown. Warp continued to put out her music, and three works by her—extracts from the opera *Elephant and Castle* (2007, composed in collaboration with Tansy Davies), *Memoryofamoment* (2008), and *Dead Wedding* (2007–8)—were released on the label as *The Elephant in the Room* in 2008.

Crossovers with Indie Rock

The London Sinfonietta's interest in the more exploratory areas of popular music didn't end with Warp. Shortly after the first Warp Works concert, the group began an association with Jonny Greenwood, a composer and the lead guitarist of the British rock band Radiohead. In March 2004 the Sinfonietta gave the first performance of Greenwood's *smear,* for ondes Martenot and nine instruments, a piece they released on CD the following year. In 2005 Greenwood also curated a London Sinfonietta concert as part of the Southbank Centre's Ether Festival (within which the Warp Works concerts had previously appeared), featuring *smear* (2004), *Piano for Children* (2005, now withdrawn), and Greenwood's arrangements of two Radiohead songs, "Arpeggi" and "Where Bluebirds Fly."

Greenwood subsequently worked with other leading ensembles. In 2004 he was composer in residence for the BBC Concert Orchestra, for which he wrote *Popcorn Superhet Receiver* (2005), his most acclaimed work to date. In September 2011 he played with Ensemble Modern in Kraków as part of the Sacrum Profanum Festival, and in Wrocław as part of the European Culture Congress. Both concerts were organized by the Polish director Filip Berkowicz, and, completing the circle, both were paired with concerts by Aphex Twin. In Wrocław, Greenwood and James had works of their own performed, alongside pieces by Penderecki that inspired them. Greenwood contributed *Popcorn,* which had been inspired in part by Penderecki's *Threnody,* and *48 Responses to Polymorphia* (2011). James had two works that were effectively live remixes of Penderecki, *Threnody Remix* (2011) and *Polymorphia Reloaded* (2011). In Kraków, Greenwood performed Steve Reich's *Electric Counterpoint,* for electric guitar and tape, at a festival of the composer's music. He and Reich met for the first time, an encounter that brought the London Sinfonietta back into the story with the commissioning of a new work in 2013, *Radio Rewrite,* which was composed using material from two Radiohead songs, "Jigsaw Falling into Place" and "Everything in Its Right Place."[57]

Greenwood's path from rock band to concert hall became somewhat normalized in the first years of the century. Some of this is thanks to the pressures of the box office on ensembles and commissioning bodies—rock star composers are certainly bankable—and Greenwood's own success has surely offered a tempting example. In many ways, however, it is also a logical expansion of the sort of high/low crossover in Turnage's music that began this chapter. It also relates to an older crossover between rock and art music that grew out of New York's No Wave scene in the late 1970s and was pursued in particular by the guitarists Rhys Chatham, whose already mentioned *Guitar Trio* is a seminal contact between punk rock and art music minimalism; and Glenn Branca, who performed *Guitar Trio* with Chatham in 1977 and a few years later became an early mentor to Sonic Youth guitarists Lee Ranaldo and Thurston Moore.

Rock artists who have had fruitful second careers in the concert hall include Tyondai Braxton (b. 1978), Bryce Dessner (b. 1976), and Owen Pallett (b. 1979). This phenomenon isn't confined to a younger generation; older composers who began their musical paths in rock include the American Steven Mackey (b. 1956), the Estonian Erkki-Sven Tüür (b. 1959), and the Russian Vladimir Martynov (b. 1946). This is to say nothing of well-known rock figures such as Paul McCartney (b. 1942) and Karl Jenkins (b. 1944), formerly a multi-instrumentalist with Soft Machine, both of whom have branched out into classical composition. In McCartney's case, this has been somewhat subsidiary to his rock career, although his *Liverpool Oratorio* (1991), for orchestra, chorus, and four soloists, sold well in spite of negative press reviews. Jenkins's move into classical music has been more sustained. An outgrowth of Soft Machine's roots in jazz and progressive rock, Jenkins's interest in the genre developed from his work during the 1980s making music for commercials. Since the crossover success of *Adiemus* (1994), which originated in a theme for a Delta Airlines commercial, Jenkins has focused his attention on a commercially successful brand of classical easy listening/world music crossover. The influence has also worked in reverse. Rock—and particularly the subset that Simon Reynolds and others identify as "post-rock"[58]—has taken on the forms, instrumentation, and techniques of Western art music, exemplified in the music of bands like Godspeed You! Black Emperor, Arcade Fire (whose Richard Reed Parry is also a composer), and Tortoise, as well as Radiohead on occasion.

While Greenwood and Dessner appear comfortable working within the conventional structures of Western art music—writing music for orchestra and large ensembles to play live, unamplified, from scores, and with a conductor—Tyondai Braxton (son of the avant-garde instrumentalist and composer Anthony Braxton) and others are exploring the collision of rock and classical genres more extensively. Tyondai's second solo album, *Central Market* (2009), draws on Zorn's jump-cut aesthetic. Written for chamber orchestra, it features Braxton as a multi-instrumental soloist of sorts, on electric guitar, kazoo, synthesizer, vocals, and more. That this is "art music" is signaled by the frequent cuts in tempo and arrangement, the presence of distinctly "classical" instruments such as xylophone and clarinet, and the use of cyclically recurring motifs between tracks. Yet it is presented as an album (released on Warp, as it happens), divided into seven song-length tracks, with reverberation, amplification, and other studio-bound effects running throughout, all of which clearly place it within the sphere of rock and pop music.

Creating an album, the defining medium of classic rock, rather than a concert work, comes with its own set of possibilities and constraints: it calls for ten or so short tracks that are produced within a studio and can stand alone or work in sequence, and it is usually intended for private listening. New Amsterdam Records, a New York–based label that specializes in releasing such albums, states on its website: "As opposed to the traditional 'live performance' or 'survey' recordings found in the classical music industry, our releases are designed to compete in the mainstream marketplace, with lightly compressed, high-level studio production, handcrafted artwork, and a fluid emotional narrative from start to finish."[59] This is radically different from works that are written for public performance and use a specified set of performers but that may be of any length and in any number of parts.

Until quite recently, such differences went to the heart of what distinguished art music from pop or rock. Yet New Amsterdam, founded in 2007 by composers and Yale School of Music graduates Judd Greenstein (b. 1979), Sarah Kirkland Snider, and William Brittelle (b. 1976), is part of a movement toward music that does not recognize such traditional boundaries. "We're looking for albums that are meant to be artistic products, in and of themselves, and not a reflection of some live ideal," Greenstein has said.[60] Braxton is just one of a number of younger composers for whom the album has become the medium of choice. These composers are too numerous to list here, but Gabriel Kahane (b. 1981), with albums such as *Craigslistlieder* (2006) and *Where Are the Arms* (2011); and Julia Holter (b. 1984), with albums such as *Tragedy* (2011) and *Have You in My Wilderness* (2015), are representative. Again, the formal dimensions of such recordings and their use of studio effects place them firmly within the sphere of "popular" music; but this is tempered by "classical" styles of harmonic and/or melodic development (exemplified on "Last Dance" from Kahane's *Where Are the Arms*). Often the music takes the form of a sort of art-inflected popular songwriting in the line of Noel Coward, George Gershwin, Cole Porter, and Stephen Sondheim, as well as David Bowie, Scott Walker, and others, that draws on influences from both sides. However, this is not always the case, and works closer to a more "conventional" classical mindset also feature in the catalogue, such as *Corps Exquis* (2013), a marriage of soundscapey electronics and live chamber music by Paris-born, New York–based composer Daniel Wohl (b. 1980); and violist Nadia Sirota's recital discs *First Things First* (2009) and *Baroque* (2015), featuring genre-crossing composers such as Marcos Balter (b. 1974), Daníel Bjarnason (b. 1979), Missy Mazzoli (b. 1980), and Nico Muhly. Sufjan Stevens (b. 1975), probably the most popular artist in this in-between area, has turned his work in the opposite direction, writing extended instrumental suites to accompany his own films, such as *The BQE* (2009) and *Round Up* (2014), that may be performed in concert or listened to at home.

The links between these artists and institutions exist within secure and stable national economies and create a mutually beneficial accumulation of cultural capital. For other artists, however, the flexibility to move between types of venue, audience, and genre is a more urgent condition of financial survival. In Berlin in the early 1990s, for example, experimental musicians in what became known as the *echtzeitmusik* scene survived without external support by creating new venues in abandoned buildings, clubs, and bars in the districts of the former East Berlin.[61] In post–civil war Beirut, festivals like Irtijal (an offshoot of the nonprofit association MILL [Musique Improvisée Libre au Liban], founded in 2000 by the trumpet player Mazen Kerbaj and the guitarist Sharif Sehnaoui) act as focal points for a range of experimental and avant-garde forms of improvisation, composition, rock, and electronica. Musicians like Kerbaj (b. 1975), Sehnaoui (b. 1976), Tarek Atoui (b. 1980), and Cynthia Zaven (b. 1970) have to adapt their work for presentation not only in the venues of the music and art worlds but also in the less formal contexts of the commercial music industry, such as clubs, record labels, and radio stations. In such instances, financial and practical constraints lead to the creation of ad hoc institutions and support structures, and thus to particularly flexible exchanges and movements between different musical practices.

WERKTREUE

The final set of borders to succumb to a more permissive, fluid view were those of the work itself. In the nineteenth century and deep in the twentieth, a work of Western art music, as defined in the musical score, was assumed to be a unified, perfectible object. Although interpretations of a single score might differ slightly from performance to performance, it was held that each different interpretation was an attempt to achieve the "correct" or "most faithful" rendering of the composer's intentions. The composer was the supreme authority; the score was a complete and singular set of instructions for realizing his or her vision; and the performer was the medium through which this vision was made audible. A performer's relationship to the score was much like that of a film projector to a canister of 35mm film.

My description is slightly exaggerated. However, a musical work was still considered a self-contained object, something like a painting or a sculpture—except even then it was like a painting or sculpture that you couldn't walk around or place in a different room with differently colored walls, different light, and different objects close by. The advent of recording, and particularly the increasingly powerful role of the studio engineer, started to expose the myth behind this ideology: even a performance that had been committed to tape could be manipulated by a range of studio editing techniques and even be compiled from multiple takes.

The use of open forms and improvisatory or quasi-improvisatory elements by avant-garde composers in the 1950s and '60s challenged the ideology of *Werktreue,* or "faithfulness to the original," still further. When even the composer is admitting flexible elements into their work, such as the order in which events occur, the choice of pitches that can be played, or even whether anything should be played at all, then the idea that the musical score represents anything more than a field of possibilities—rather than a definitive script—is fully established. As with other innovations of the radical avant garde, these ideas and principles continued to be found in music of the 1990s and the twenty-first century, but in a more normalized form. Moreover, the challenges to the *Werktreue* concept came from a range of sources, not just the somewhat self-referential realm of musical notation.

Samplers were an important enabling technology. Developed for commercial use in the late 1970s and popularized in the following decade through hip-hop, techno, and pop, they began to make their way into art music toward the end of the 1980s, with Steve Reich's *Different Trains* being a notable example. In *City Life* Reich went further and brought those keyboards onstage as live instrumental parts. Yet works like these do not challenge *Werktreue.* Reich's samplers bring a new palette of sounds and introduce new ideas about incorporating speech and other concrete sounds into a work of otherwise instrumental music, but *Different Trains* and *City Life* are still unified works in the conventional fashion. The samples they employ are created from concrete sounds and speech recordings sourced specifically and exclusively for these works, as opposed to the hip-hop practice of using samples to situate a track within a network of previous recordings. A greater challenge to the traditional form came from outside the sphere of classical music, as electronica and dance artists began to sample works of contemporary music, thus treating contemporary composition according to the same terms as funk, soul, rock, and other more commonly sampled genres. Reich himself was one of the first to have his music used in this way, when the ambient techno group The Orb (a flexible collective centered around English DJ and producer Alex Paterson) used a sample of *Electric Counterpoint* (1987) for their 1990 single "Little Fluffy Clouds." The Orb's sample capitalized on a synergy that electronica artists were already feeling between their work and Reich's,[62] and Reich samples would continue to be used well into the 2010s, by artists as diverse as Madvillain, Nero, Tortoise, and Susumu Yokota.[63] Reich is perhaps the most commonly sampled contemporary composer, but others have received similar treatment, including Pärt, Górecki, and Feldman. It is significant that minimalist—or minimalist-like—music has proved most open to being sampled, a recognition perhaps of this style's different approach to musical time as a continuous flow rather than as a framed and internally organized singularity, a concept that appeals more to the ideals of flow and fluidity of the DJ set than the work-dominated concert hall.

In 1999 Nonesuch released *Reich: Remixed*, a ten-track album of remixes by British, American, and Japanese producers of Reich's music. Here, definitively, was a new challenge to *Werktreue*: the album introduced the idea that works of contemporary art music could be reworked and reauthored in the same fashion as electronic dance music tracks.[64] *Reich Remixed* was itself preceded in 1997 by *Métamorphose*, an album of remixes of *Messe pour le temps présent* by the French tape-music composers Pierre Henry (b. 1927) and Michel Colombier (1939–2004). This featured mixes by Fatboy Slim, Coldcut (a duo who also appear on *Reich Remixed*), William Orbit, and others. Both albums were issued in conjunction with releases of the original music—in Henry and Colombier's case, Philips rereleased *Messe pour le temps présent*; in Reich's case, the remix album was timed to coincide with the release of Nonesuch's new recording of *Music for 18 Musicians*. Both albums proved successful in their own ways. Nonesuch revisited their Reich concept seven years later with *Reich: Remixed 2006*, a four-track EP including three new remixes and the original mix of *Come Out*. Henry's *Messe* achieved a different kind of success when *Psyché Rock*, one of the movements from the piece to have been remixed several times on the *Métamorphose* album, served as the basis for the theme to the Matt Groening cartoon series *Futurama*.

Since then, works of other composers have had similar treatment. In 2003 the Italian ensemble Alter Ego released an album of music by Frederic Rzewski that featured remixes by Robin Rimbaud (Scanner), Giuseppe Ielasi, and Marco Passarani. In 2007, inspired by *Reich Remixed*, the Grand Valley State University New

Music Ensemble released *In C Remixed*, featuring eighteen remixes of Terry Riley's seminal work of early minimalism. Philip Glass worked with Beck in 2012 on a remix album that also included contributions from Tyondai Braxton, Amon Tobin (b. 1972), and Jóhann Jóhannsson (b. 1969). In 2005 Asphodel Records released an album of remixes of the electroacoustic work *Persépolis* (1971), by Iannis Xenakis (1922–2001). Featuring remixes by artists such as Otomo Yoshihide, Ryoji Ikeda (b. 1966), Zbigniew Karkowski (1958–2013), Merzbow, and Francisco López (b. 1964), this album went into different territory, focusing on textures and soundscapes rather than beats. Xenakis's work wasn't immune to dance-based treatments, however, and in 2012 the French duo ACTUEL REMIX (Xavier Garcia and Guy Villerd) produced a soundtrack for Fritz Lang's *Metropolis*, created first for performance at the Institut Lumière in Lyon and released on CD in 2014, that comprised an extended mashup of samples of Xenakis and tracks by Richie Hawtin (Plastikman).

One of the more sustained efforts in this direction has been the *Recomposed* project, initiated by the German record label Deutsche Grammophon in 2005. The project currently extends to six releases. The most recent of these is *Recomposed*, by Max Richter (b. 1966), mentioned above. For his piece, Richter wrote a new score to be performed by live instrumentalists; earlier releases in the series, however, were based around samples and electronic music production.

DG, one of the world's oldest and most prestigious record labels, is renowned especially for its classical recordings, which have been made by some of the most acclaimed artists in history. The first album in the series turned to the most canonical of those recordings, the discs of nineteenth-century orchestral music made in the 1960s and '70s by DG's signature artist, Herbert von Karajan, conducting the Berlin Philharmonic. Placed in the hands of the German producer Matthias Arfmann, these are transformed into darkly surreal blends of sampled orchestral riffs and dubby drum and bass tracks.

While Arfmann's selections stuck to the central nineteenth-century repertory for which Karajan was known, the second album in the series introduced a more adventurous note. Produced by the eccentric Finnish musician Jimi Tenor (Lassi Lehto, b. 1965), it includes reworkings of *Wing on Wing* (2004), by his fellow Finn Esa-Pekka Salonen (b. 1958), a "sort of a mutant reggae"[65] version of Reich's *Music for Mallet Instruments, Voices and Organ*; three takes on Erik Satie's *Vexations*; and a truly genre-bending version of Boulez's *Messagesquisse* that finds an improbable common ground between such remote points as the hyperactive runs of Boulez's cello part, the burbling electronics of acid house, and bluegrass fiddle music. Matthew Herbert's *Recomposed* reworked Giuseppe Sinopoli's recording of the Adagio movement from Mahler's Symphony No. 10. Herbert is a British electronic musician known for his use of site-specific recordings and concrete sounds; his most well-known records, *Bodily Functions* (2001) and *Plat du jour* (2005), were constructed around (heavily processed) samples of human anatomical sounds and commercial food production, respectively. For his *Recomposed* album, he took a similarly conceptual approach, recording the sounds of Sinopoli's recording played in various environments: in a crematorium, in a coffin, and inside a passing hearse.

The third album brought the series closest to a genuine club aesthetic, with a suite of pieces—including Ravel's *Boléro* and *Rapsodie espagnole* and Mussorgsky's *Pictures at an Exhibition*—reworked by legendary producers Carl Craig and Moritz von Oswald. Remixes like these and many others have no doubt featured in DJ sets since their release; some tracks from the album were themselves further remixed for release as 12" singles. Craig himself has since ventured further into the realm of art music, with collaborations with the orchestra Les Siècles and the pianist Francesco Tristano that combine acoustic instrumental music with live DJ'ing.

As the work concept becomes increasingly destabilized, more and more record labels, particularly those that feature younger composers, have started to include remixes on their releases in order to capitalize on this fluidity. The Nonclassical label releases many remixes of contemporary works, as have other labels, such as Cantaloupe and New Amsterdam. Some DJs have also used unremixed recordings of contemporary compositions, although the rhythmic and textural diversity of much new music militates against this happening more frequently.[66] Nevertheless, it is clear that contemporary composition, often criticized as a final bastion of *Werktreue*, has succumbed in the past two decades to a more fluid idea of what a work is.

Remixing is the most visible manifestation of this, but the challenges have come from other areas too, and not just in conjunction with commercial interests. The creation of the private, mobile listening experience discussed in the previous chapter is another example. Composers too have become more comfortable with the concept of their work existing contextually within the world rather than in isolation from it. The composition of works in series is one case, as they allow a central compositional idea to be returned to over and over, negating the idea of a single ideal expression. Related to this are composite works, such as *Anea Crystal* (2008), by Chaya Czernowin (b. 1957), composed as two string quartet works that can be played separately or combined to form a third work for string octet; *Pedro Páramo* (1992–), by Julio Estrada (b. 1943), which is composed as a series of modules that can be extracted and recombined in various combinations; and *Hommage à Thomas Pynchon* (2001–5), by Claus-Steffen Mahnkopf (b. 1962), a collage of several pieces that take on a different form if played separately.[67] One of the most radical extensions of this principle has been pursued by Robert H. P. Platz (b. 1951). Since the mid-1990s, all Platz's pieces have been conceived as parts of a "continually unfolding overall architecture" in which individual works may cluster together, interlock, or overlap as part of an overall "meta-composition" while standing as individual works in their own right.[68] In highly determined works by Mahnkopf, Brian Ferneyhough, Richard Barrett, and others, the excess of notational detail introduces a different kind of unfaithfulness: multiple, even contradictory layers of information require a constant negotiation between performer and score that does not permit a casual deferral to "the composer's intentions."

In contrast, extremely underdetermined works, such as some Wandelweiser scores, make it impossible to draw a firm line between composers' intentions and sounding results. In very quiet works, the edge between the musical work and the nonmusical world is also impossible to define: the sound of the world is constantly bleeding into the sound of the music (or vice versa). Works of extreme duration, whether very short or (more commonly) very long, face similar issues. Can a very short musical work establish a temporal space all of its own, or is it simply another event within the general soundscape? Conversely, at what point do works of very long duration stop being exceptional events and in fact become part of the soundscape?

The concept of *Werktreue* has faced similar challenges before, and since it is based in any case on mid-nineteenth-century thought, it can only partly represent an ideal for music composed before then. At different times, composers have focused more or less on the physical or cerebral impact of their music: consider, say, the differences between Tchaikovsky and Brahms, or Stravinsky and Schoenberg, to pick just two pairs of contrasting contemporaries. And composers have always had to negotiate their place between popular and "high" culture in order to make a living. However, such matters became more visible and moved closer to the center of concern toward the end of the century as a result of the forces of mediation and the marketplace, and the general breaking down of boundaries and redefinition of the significance of the listener. In the following chapters I will explore these challenges further and also discuss some of the aesthetic modes to which they gave rise.

4

FLUIDITY

Digital Translations, Displacements, and Journeys

COMPOSING IN THE DIGITAL AGE

The birth of the digital age, between Steve Jobs's introduction of the Macintosh computer in 1984 and the creation of the World Wide Web in 1991, brought technical challenges and possibilities to music as much as to any other aspect of life. Consider an MP3 on your computer. MP3 (an abbreviation of MPEG-1 Audio Layer 3) is a coding format for compressing audio data. Put simply, it is a way of making sound files smaller—at CD quality, these can take up more than 10MB of memory per minute of music—without a significant loss in quality. Smaller files are easier to store, and this was an important issue in the early 1990s, when the MP3 was developed and hard drive space was more limited than it is today. As Internet access became more widespread during the 1990s, MP3s also proved relatively easy to transfer over the World Wide Web. Using a 28.8k dial-up modem, of the sort available when the MP3 codec was released in 1995, a one-minute MP3 file, coded at the standard bit rate of 128kbit/s, would take just under four and a half minutes to download. That is desperately slow by today's standards, but it was reasonable when compared to the fifty minutes required for the same amount of music at CD quality. As download speeds increased in the second half the decade, first with 56k dial-up modems and then with ADSL cable connections, MP3s eventually became to all intents and purposes as practical to transfer between computers as text or images. With the advent of peer-to-peer (P2P) file-sharing networks in the late 1990s, those transfers became trivially easy.

The MP3 therefore effectively enabled access to any recorded music from anywhere in the world to anyone with a broadband connection and the right software;

P2P networks—of which Napster was the most well known—became free libraries of the world's music, available to anyone willing to share their own files in return. The impact on the music industry has been profound. Although the Recording Industry Association of America successfully shut down Napster in July 2001, a definitive shift in listening habits, from CDs to online, had begun. Illegal sharing of music online has continued, and to some degree will probably remain, but the attention of record companies and music hardware manufacturers is now firmly on the online market.

As well as increasing music's global transmission, the MP3 has enabled its dematerialization. The story of digitization in the arts runs from the invention of expensive standalone technologies in the 1980s, through their increasing commercialization, miniaturization, speed, and networking capability, to a point where the materiality of cultural objects, of the boundaries between them that define them as themselves—a piece of music, a novel, a photograph—need no longer be a property of these objects themselves. Instead it is the software and hardware that make the pure data "physical." A book is no longer a sheaf of pages bound together; a photograph is no longer an image captured on light-sensitive paper. The MP3 on your computer contains no physical characteristics of its own: it is simply a neutral stream of zeroes and ones. It gains its character entirely from its context: its meta-tagging, the file structure of your hard drive (or that of a remote server on which the MP3 may be stored), and the way in which this context is interpreted by the software on your computer.

Dematerialization does not just have implications for portability, storage, transferal, and scale. It also enables endless possibilities for inter-medial translation and transformation. Because the data file that makes up a particular MP3 relies on peripheral software and hardware, it could be rendered as a visual image or even as a (largely indecipherable) piece of text. The fact that we hear it as music is simply a condition of the software and hardware being used. Inter-medial experiments have been made using sound for almost two centuries—the first sound recording device, the 1859 phonautograph of Édouard-Léon Scott de Martinville, was designed to render sound waves as images on paper. What digitization has done, however, is to take such transfers out of the realm of experiment and into the heart of our daily interactions with our media environment.

The processes of contextualization that give a particular binary string meaning as an MP3 can also decontextualize. This can happen on two levels. On the first, more pragmatic, level, once files can be infinitely duplicated and redistributed, authorship becomes harder to track and assert. Eventually, it can become more or less arbitrary; witness the endless reposting of images or text on Tumblr pages, for example, each post more remote from the original source. Tumblr may track who reposts a particular image, but in many cases the original photographer becomes impossible to trace.

The second level of decontextualization, which has opened up more immediate musical applications, is the way in which a sound, recorded in digital format, can be extracted from its original context and reused in an entirely new musical setting. This is the process more commonly known as sampling. Sampling is related to the much older notion of quotation, but with two important differences. Unlike a musical quotation—such as occurs in a Bach choral prelude, for example, in which an existing melody is copied by the composer as musical notation, to be interpreted by a performer—a sample is a duplication of the original in the same form, a slice of a recording rendered as a new recording. This means that the sample can be a more or less exact copy of the original, capturing not only its rhythms and pitches (as in the Bach example) but also every contour of its timbre and dynamic too. It also means that when we hear a sample (or a sample that we recognize, at least), we are conscious not only of its origin in another piece of music but also of its status as mediated material. We know it is a recording because it comes from a recording that we know.

The second difference from quotation is a matter of scale. A musical quotation needs to be a certain length in order to make sense as such. It is hard to argue that one or two isolated notes are a quotation of something specific, just as it is hard to argue that an individual word can be a quotation from a text.[1] A sample, however, can be of practically any length, down to thousandths of a second.[2] Because a sample captures timbre as well as pitch, its source can be identified in a much shorter timeframe.

The implications of sampling have had substantial and wide-ranging effects on popular music—the standard example being Public Enemy's "Fight the Power," which makes use of the elements of recognizability and scale in the way it constructs an elaborate rhythm track from a canon of black artists excluded from mainstream recognition. Yet sampling does not just enable creations such as this; it also inspires entirely new ways of thinking about music and musical meaning. In chapter 6, for example, I will discuss the development of so-called microsound composition in electroacoustic music, which involves clusters of thousands of tiny sampled sounds to create entirely new sounds; because the resulting macrosounds are determined on such a small level, they can be controlled and transformed with a very high degree of flexibility, giving rise to entirely new kinds of musical development.

As it has in popular music, the power of home computers—and more recently mobile phones and tablets—to act as digital audio workstations has encouraged an explosion of unmappable diversity in electroacoustic composition. The full range of digital routines and processes—including, in addition to those mentioned already, live electronic transformations, limitless soundbanks, the microscopic analysis of sounds, and computerized synchronization between audio and visual media—has dramatically expanded composers' technical range.

Although this chapter focuses on composition, the impact of digitization has not been limited to this. Performance practice has also been affected. Works that even in the late 1980s could only be conceived with the involvement of multiple tape players, bulky mixing desks, and other assorted analog interfaces are now routinely reproduced from a single laptop using free software. The generic designation "tape music" may have persisted in reference works such as *The New Grove Dictionary of Music*, but it became increasingly anachronistic after the 1980s, as first CDs and then lossless digital files became the preferred medium for sound storage and playback. This has given rise to questions similar to those commonly asked in the historically informed performance movement of early music: Should works of the 1950s and '60s that depended on tape remain attached to that medium, or should they be updated to digital? Should those digital files be "cleaned up"? Or does doing so damage the works' authenticity? Some performers, like Langham Research Centre, make "period" versions of John Cage's electronic music using tape players, gramophones, and LPs made in the 1950s, like those Cage would have used himself. Facing in the opposite direction, at the Experimentalstudio des SWR in Freiburg, the designated holders of Luigi Nono's legacy (led since 1989 by the Swiss composer André Richard, b. 1944) are establishing a definitive performance practice through the use of digital technology, to which Nono himself did not have access.

Digital Natives

To one side of the stage a cellist sits with her instrument. Beside her is a large standard lamp. On the other half of the stage is a small string orchestra with chairs, stands, and instruments. The cellist plays a slow, enigmatic solo over a soft electronic bed. Behind her, an old woman is projected on a video screen. She is also standing on a stage, the same one as the cellist, with the same chairs and music stands and the same lamp. But she is alone. As the cellist plays, the elderly woman considers the lamp, oblivious of course to the real-world example just on the other side of the screen. The music is her soundtrack, playing both inside her head and in front of our eyes. The electronics start to crackle and turn metallic in tone. The film cuts to the woman sitting in a forest, still clutching the lamp. As the music begins to fade and fragment, first the lamp and then the film start to flicker on and off, until finally everything—lamps, film, and house lights—fades to black.

Michael van der Aa's *Up-close* (2010), of which this is the final scene, is a hybrid work, part cello concerto, part video opera. Although multimedia works themselves are not new, dating back at least to the first happenings organized by Cage in the 1960s, Van der Aa's use of digital media enables a new kind of storytelling that focuses on contemporary anxieties about identity, the conflict of reality and virtuality, and the psychoses to which these may give rise. The work could hardly have been imagined before the advent of digital technology.

FIGURE 12. Still from a DVD of Michel van der Aa's *Up-close*. Sol Gabetta, cello; Vakil Eelman, actor. Disquiet Media DQM04, 2012.

Digital technology, through sampling and video and the varied ways in which these may be altered to correspond more or less closely to real world and real-time events, enables multiple ways to reflect sound and images. This is Van der Aa's starting point for many pieces, in which live musicians, electronic soundtracks, and, latterly, video combine to create dialogues between the real and the virtual. Live performers are confronted with fractured, extended reflections of themselves and their instruments. Van der Aa's second opera, *After Life* (2005–6), based on the film of that name by the Japanese director Hirokazu Kore-Eda, tells the story of a group of characters who are at the point of death. Each is allowed to choose, and watch on screen, a single moment of their life, which they can then take with them into heaven. *Up-close,* in its duplications of live and recorded action, reality and virtuality, folds that screen over and over on itself until it is no longer clear what is real and what is not (see figure 12). What is the relationship between the cellist and the film? An old woman and her memories? A young woman and her future? Are we witnessing a mental breakdown? Van der Aa's electronic soundtrack, made up of sounds from the worlds of both the film and the concert stage, may bridge the gap, but the two protagonists will always remain divided.

Van der Aa's music exemplifies the way that digital technology can be used to create multimedia spectacles.[3] Works like *Up-close* and *After Life,* as well as the interactive song cycle *The Book of Sand* (2015) and the 3D film-operas *Sunken Garden* (2011–12) and *Blank Out* (2016), use and stretch the most advanced multimedia technology available to create new kinds of musical and theatrical illusion. The inherently spectacular nature of these pieces attracts not only artists but also promoters: no matter the underlying aesthetic justification, a work that uses synchronized video, virtual instruments, and spatialized electronics will always be a sexier sell than one that sets four instrumentalists on an otherwise empty stage. Composers like Van der Aa are not the only ones who benefit from this. Institutions like the Institut de recherche et coordination acoustique/musique (IRCAM) in Paris, the Institute for Music and Acoustics (IMA) in Karlsruhe, the Experimentalstudio des Sudwestrundfunk in Freiburg, and others that seek to fund elaborate in-house technologies for presenting electroacoustic music similarly gain from it.[4]

However, creating an ultra-professional spectacle is not the only reason to go digital. Digitization has sharpened the cutting edge of almost every technological and scientific discipline, but at the other end of the scale it has also created new means of cheap, flexible, and portable sound creation. Matthew Shlomowitz (b. 1975) engages with these aspects in his series *Popular Contexts* (2010–14). To date, there are seven sets of works in the series, for varying ensembles, all of them written using commercial, off-the-shelf software (in particular Garageband, which is routinely packaged with Apple computers) and collaborative sample libraries such as Freesound (www.freesound.org).[5] Shlomowitz is not interested in authentic or ethnographic representation of preexisting sounds, such as soundscape or field-recording work. In contrast to the cutting-edge audio-visual technology used by Van der Aa, Shlomowitz takes an almost self-consciously DIY approach. One important reason he uses preexisting sampled material is purely practical: many of the pieces within *Popular Contexts* are composed around a single topic, such as telephone sounds or transport announcements, and the organization and scale of Freesound makes it quick and easy to gather, compare, and select materials. In most of the pieces, sounds are triggered from a sampler keyboard, which is played alongside an acoustic ensemble. In *Popular Contexts 1*, for piano and MIDI keyboard, the pianist plays both instruments together, creating a clash between the analog and the digital. By relinquishing control of the sound quality of his sources and relying on the recording skills of others, Shlomowitz is able to play with those different levels of fidelity. The resulting sonic naivety is part of the music's charm, but Shlomowitz also plays a more sophisticated game with our perceptions: how exactly do the "concrete" sounds relate to the straightforwardly "musical" sounds of the piano?

A different kind of tension between analog and digital can be heard in *Guide* (2013), by the Canadian composer Cassandra Miller (b. 1976), written for the eight singers of the EXAUDI vocal ensemble. On its surface, the music is distinctly analog in nature: it involves no electronics, multimedia, or even amplification, just eight singers arranged into three groups. What makes it unusual is that a recording is also provided alongside the written score, a 1968 performance of the American country-blues singer Maria Muldaur singing "Guide Me, O Thou Great Jehovah." This is not for use as an electronic soundtrack, but is instead an integral part of how the piece is to be learned.

Miller's piece is a fine example of the collapsing boundaries between musical genres discussed in the previous chapter. Her work is particularly sensitive to how the fundamental characteristics of one genre (in this case country music) might be translated into the framework of another (contemporary art music). The first stage in learning the piece requires the performers to memorize Muldaur's recording until they can reproduce it faithfully, paying particular attention to the singer's idiosyncratic phrasing and articulation. The aim, as described in the performance notes, is "dedication to the humanity of the original recording." At this point, the process resembles an act of oral communication, in which songs are passed from generation to generation by playing and listening, rather than the literate tradition that characterizes Western art music. However, the score then asks for the song to be sung at varying speeds by the eight singers, repeating fragments along the way. These are concepts borrowed from music recording technologies, such as tape loops and variable speed turntables. The result is a dense, undulating mass of song, ringing with the sound of eight voices unshackled from the restrictions of ensemble balance and rippled with details from Muldaur's original.

Oral traditions and media technology are combined in the work's third dimension: its notated score. Here is where the—albeit subtle—digital influence can be found. In her performing materials, Miller provides a detailed transcription—in standard notation—of Muldaur's performance, but this is just to be used as a reference while learning the piece; it isn't what the singers work from in the performance itself. The actual score is written not in standard notation but as glyphs (what the composer calls "neumes," a reference to medieval chant notation) that follow the shape of each phrase of Muldaur's original. These glyphs originate in analyses of Muldaur's recording created in Melodyne, an audio-editing software, which Miller then extracted and saved as digital images in their own right (see figure 13).

When faster or slower (i.e., shorter or longer) iterations of a phrase are required, as happens throughout the piece, the graphical neumes are simply stretched or compressed. Reading from the score, the singers must accordingly adjust all the details of Muldaur's performance, which they have committed to memory, to fit the time that is represented. That is, they must reenact, using the least technological instrument available (the human voice), complex transformations such as time stretching and compressing that are trivially easy within a digital environment.

Fluid Forms

GeneMusiK (2003–), by Nigel Helyer, is not a digital work. Instead, it uses DNA sequencing techniques to compose pieces of music. First, an existing melody is recoded as a DNA strand. This DNA is then created in the lab and allowed to grow within a bacterial culture, which breeds and transforms the original DNA sequence as it does so. After a time, this new DNA is analyzed and resequenced before being coded back as music.

GeneMusiK is an unusual, experimental work, created somewhat outside of the mainstream of Western art music. It is not digital, but it shares with the works

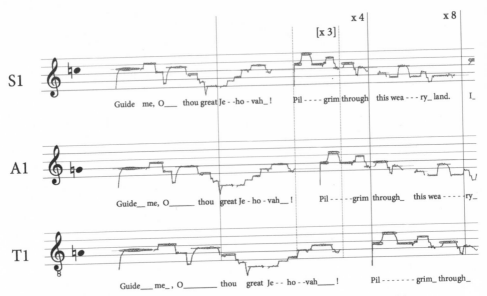

FIGURE 13. Excerpt from the score of Cassandra Miller's *Guide*, 2013. Courtesy of the composer.

already mentioned an instinctive aversion to the concept of formal or generic boundaries. In each piece so far discussed, the identity of the musical material is considered to be completely fluid, endlessly mutable, through whatever process one might imagine. In the case of *GeneMusiK*, these processes are the technologically advanced ones of genetic synthesis; in the case of *Guide*, they are the ancient processes of oral learning and reproduction. In the case of *Up-close*, the fluidity is between the worlds of the stage and those of the film and electronic soundtrack; in the case of *Popular Contexts*, the fluidity is between the sounds of acoustic instruments and decontextualized real world samples.

The idea that contemporary life has become somehow "liquid" has circulated for some time now, influenced in particular by the writings of the sociologist Zygmunt Bauman.[6] Bauman's writings touch on many aspects of contemporary life, but his central thesis is that individuals in late modern society are no longer tied to a single ongoing identity—whether in terms of their jobs or careers, their social position, their nationality, their appearance, or even their gender. Every one of these identities is only temporary, never definitive or absolute. As Bauman puts it, identity is "about the possibility of 'being born again'—of stopping being what one is and turning into someone one is not yet."[7] This fluidity has been enabled (or in some cases, such as those of the refugee or the short-term contract worker, enforced) by a range of technological, political, and economic changes that have taken place since the late twentieth century. So, for example, a person born a man can become a woman, and a salesperson can retrain as a teacher. This gives rise to a form of life that is characterized by movement between identities rather than consolidation and refinement of a particular identity. Bauman calls this "liquid life" or "liquid modernity."

This fluidity is not only enabled but also expected. Consider the way we use social media, for example. As opposed to the static persona presented on a personal webpage (or, before that, via a paper document like a CV), we now construct our identities online as continuous and ever-evolving streams through Facebook, Twitter, and Instagram feeds. Yet continuing the flow is just as important as anything it contains: observe how, when we stop posting regularly, we feel compelled to tell people why—if they haven't asked us already.

Debates about the impact of digital media, the Internet, and this new, "liquid" culture have been ongoing in the visual arts since the early 1990s, and at the center of much of this analysis is the work of the French curator Nicolas Bourriaud. Bourriaud is less concerned with digital arts per se—in fact, many of the artists he writes about work with distinctly low-tech materials—and more with how the psychological, practical, and philosophical implications of the digital era influence how contemporary artists work.

Central to what Bourriaud calls the "radicant aesthetic" is the idea of rootlessness, or of being in motion.[8] That is, the principle that identity is not a constant value but rather one that is in permanent motion. He connects this explicitly to the digital principles of copying, translation, and transcoding—consider the way that a musical sample can be continuously reused and recontextualized—but these processes can be regarded as metaphors for many aspects of liquid life in general. As he puts it, "The computer as object is of very little importance compared to the new forms it generates."[9] What is of interest is the creation of a fluid way of being and the collection of loosely related formal concepts to which it gives rise.

Bourriaud identifies three broad formal concepts—translation, transformation, and wandering—under his heading of radicant aesthetics, and I use these in this chapter to explore three aspects of contemporary composition. Within music, the first of these, translation, encompasses relatively new practices, like transmediation (translating something from one medium into another), as well as those with a long musical history, like transcription (translating something into a different notational form). Musical transformations, Bourriaud's second concept, may be thought of in two types, both of which articulate forms of distancing that echo the essential digital operations of sampling, copying, and morphing. The first works vertically, subjecting the original material to such complex and multiple stages of compositional transformation that the work is heard as simultaneous layers of displacement or disembodiment. The second works horizontally, exposing the material to streams of potentially endless variation that shape the work as a continuous flow rather than a self-contained object (that is, with a beginning, middle, and end). The final section of this chapter takes the third concept—wandering—and explores its appearance in a number of experimental works that are structured around physical topographies and passages through space.

TRANSLATION

Transmediation

The fluid nature of the digital environment, in which material from one medium can be easily translated into another, features prominently in the music of Johannes Kreidler (b. 1980). *Scanner Studies* (2011) uses a program to "scan" computer graphics as though they were musical instructions. So, for example, pixels at the top of the image might equal high notes, and those at the bottom low notes. As the scan moves across the image, it sounds a tone of the appropriate pitch every time it encounters a pixel. A horizontal line produces a sustained pitch, a vertical line yields a sudden cluster of notes, and a diagonal line makes a glissando up or down. The idea is an old one, with an ancestry in Xenakis's UPIC computer system, used turn hand-drawn graphics into sound; and even Arseny Avraamov's and Nikolai Volnov's experiments in the 1930s with hand-drawn film soundtracks. Kreidler uses it to question the nature of musical meaning, transforming semantically loaded images (e.g., the *Mona Lisa* and the word "politics") into meaningless blasts of unpleasant synthesized sound.

Although digital media provide the most obvious channels for experiments like this, transmediation itself is not limited to the digital realm. In fact, Western art music has always entailed moving from one set of codes (notation) to another (its realization as sound). When we listen to a piece of notated music, we are listening to both the composer's written encoding of an idea and the performer's interpretation of it. Our appreciation of the success of a particular performance depends in part on our being aware of this act of transcoding and on how well the performer has achieved it.

This is a distinct difference from the visual arts, where there is not normally a notational or interpretational step between artworks and their audiences. In this respect, Kreidler's work is closer to sound art than it is to the Western classical tradition, although it clearly plays with the values, norms, and assumptions of that tradition, for example in those studies that scan words particularly significant to it—such as Chopin and Beethoven—with predictably bathetic results.

The ease of digital media has brought to the fore the artistic possibilities that working with transmedial situations of all types can create. This is the conceit behind Miller's *Guide*, for example. Moreover, the world that we inhabit is one that is increasingly transmedial anyway; the ubiquity of computers means that we are beginning to stop seeing the borders between text, sound, and image—at least

within the digital environment. Digitization, and other aspects of liquid modernity, are making us care less for the borders between things (or, perhaps, making
us see borders as contingent rather than absolute). As these borders themselves
become trivial, the act of transmediation itself becomes a source for compositional
play; this is the essence of much of Kreidler's work. However, the pieces I have
referred to exist as fixed media (videos and/or sound files) only. If we turn to musical notation, the inherent transmedial nature of notated music can be brought out
to highlight the act of translation that takes place between composer and performer.

One example is *THIS IS WHY PEOPLE O.D. ON PILLS /AND JUMP FROM
THE GOLDEN GATE BRIDGE* (2004), by Jennifer Walshe (b. 1974). The piece is
learned and stored as muscle memory, which the performer realizes in musical
terms in the work's performance. The sequence of recoding from score to physical
action to musical sound is common to all notated music, but Walshe's piece uses
unusual means to bring this process out from behind inherited and historical conventions.

The score is a text. It begins: "Learn to skateboard, however primitively." It is
designed to be printed on a T-shirt together with two or three illustrative photographs, and there is a clear sense that this a piece one should inhabit, like an item of
clothing or a lifestyle, not just read and interpret. What follows expands this opening instruction at some length, using language that is simultaneously bureaucratic
and poetic: "Examine and meditate on optimum skating environments, either real
or imagined, taking in the macro- and micro-structure of these environments. Go
for a walk and imagine being able to skate everything you see—streets, roads, walls,
trees, curbs, planters, slopes, gardens, bins, lamp-posts, footpaths, bushes, cars,
signs, window-sills, ramps, shopping trolleys, pools, slides, bollards, roofs, benches,
cows, hand-rails, fences, edges, lips, steps, drains, ditches, rims, gutters."

For musicians used to the more delicate manual skills of manipulating their
instrument, such instructions can represent quite a challenge. The efforts taken by
two players, percussionist Øyvind Skarbø and clarinetist Rolf Borch, to learn the
piece have been recorded in short documentaries made for the 2010 Borealis Festival.[10] The players can be seen coming to terms with a difficult and unfamiliar
physical task (Borch admits he had never even stood on a board before) and beginning to consider what they are doing as music. "The most obvious is to play
according the physical sounds, to try to recreate the sound of skateboarding," suggests Skarbø at an early stage of his video. "I have some methods and techniques,
which I believe can give the illusion of skating to the listener. Second is to play
according to how I am going to feel, I wonder if I can transfer this feeling to the
music? . . . I also want to try to assign all tricks and movements on the board to
either a sound, a technique or a musical happening on the drums, according to a
rigid system."

Having learned these new skills, the player or players must then recreate a journey by skateboard: "Compose an imaginary path you would like to skate. This path
should push and force you to limits, be rich, beautiful, complicated and stylish,
and incorporate some tricks. The path is limited only by your imagination. Inter-
nalise this path, skate and inhabit it in terms of body, space and time."

This path is then followed in the imagination of the performer as they play the
work. Although the performer may use most of the playing resources at their disposal, the score stipulates that the music be limited to a single pitch. This restriction is severe, but it is designed to eliminate figurative clichés. Quick rising
arpeggios can't be used to represent jumps, for example; the performer must devise
other ways to communicate the feeling of their path. Instead of crude representations, their focus must be on "tiny shifts in muscle, weight, speed, direction." Borch
admitted, "At first I thought this was a terrible limitation to be forced upon me. But
after a while I realised that this is the only way to do it. . . . The skateboard makes
one monotone tone, so it feels natural now. The limitation is now more inspira-
tional, than something that works against me."

THIS IS WHY may be a wholly acoustic work, but the questions it asks pertain
to our newly developing digital consciousness, just as those raised by works such
as Kreidler's *Scanner Studies*. The transfer of information from notation to action
to sound may be familiar to the Western art music tradition, but Walshe turns our
attention to the nature of mediation itself. How exactly is that skateboard route
realized as music, especially as music with such narrowly prescribed means? What
do we as listeners understand by "realization" in this context? What sort of information is or can be transmitted across such a change of medium? The journey
(learning to skateboard) internalized in the work's preparation and outwardly
expressed in its performance is essentially a nonmusical one, but it is the tension
between physical reality and its musical analogy—and the transfer of information
that takes place between one and the other—that is at the heart of the work's
expression.

Transcription

Perhaps the oldest and best-known example of musical transcoding is transcription. In musical terms, this takes two main forms: "notational transcription," the
aim of which is to transfer a musical work from one notational form into another,
such as converting a guitar part from tablature notation to staff notation or con-
densing an orchestral score into music for piano; and "ethnomusicological transcription," in which music (or any other sound) from a live performance or recording is written down in some fashion that can be subsequently read or realized.[11]
Both forms have long been in frequent use—ethnomusicological transcription
since at least the beginning of the twentieth century, and notational transcription
since at least the early seventeenth. In the digital era, transcription has taken on

new possibilities, as computers have made it possible to reduce any sound or sounds to data that can be "transcribed" in any form imaginable—visual or aural.

Few composers have interrogated the nature of transcription in the digital era more rigorously than Peter Ablinger, introduced in the previous chapter. In some works transcription is only loosely involved, but in others the act of transcription—of the ethnomusicological type—is the central theme of the work. *Piano and Record* (2012), for example, stands out for engaging directly with the nature of musical media itself. Its Feldman-esque title would seem to reveal much of what the piece is about—a duet between two more or less archaic technologies—but in fact there is more to the work than meets the eye. The record named in the piece is a blank LP; the sounds it produces are the pop and crackle of dust and static in its otherwise empty grooves. The piano part is a faithful transcription of those sounds (with some qualifications; discussed below), to be played at the same time as the blank disc. Because the piano part is fixed—it is a transcription of a particular playing of a particular blank LP—the LP must be fixed as well, and in performance it is actually played back as a digital recording.

The piano part is composed predominantly of light staccato stabs—transcriptions of the popping static—framed at the beginning and end by a low twelfth drone (an octave plus a perfect fifth) that imitates the AC electrical hum of the record player. When the LP and piano part are played together, the ear endeavors to connect the abstract LP crackles with the seemingly "composed" chords and tones of the piano part; it is clear from their synchronicity that one relates to the other, but precisely how is not always clear. This ontological dissonance is related to the distance between acoustic piano and "real world" samples in Shlomowitz's *Popular Contexts,* but the kinds of links the ear is encouraged to make are different in the two cases. In the Shlomowitz piece, there is no specific link between the two types of sound; they are simply arranged to the same rhythmic grid. In the Ablinger piece, a closer acoustic correspondence is intended between the recorded sound and the keyboard representation of it.

What distinguishes Ablinger's use of transcription from its historical precedent is that the transcribed object it features—a blank recording—is essentially without content. Yet the act of transcription generates a sort of content, a twenty-five-minute piano score full of activity and characterizing features, such as the short stabbing chords already mentioned. Thanks to the regular rotation of the LP, there is also a quasi-minimalistic rhythmic repetition: a repeated crackle of dust is heard in the transcription as a loop. The droning twelfths give the work a sense of departure and return that is almost Beethovenian in its tonal rootedness.

Therefore, in *Piano and Record,* as in several of the works already mentioned, our attention is turned to the act of transcription itself. The blank recording is aestheticized and given compositional form. We are surprised at the amount of "musical" activity to which such a recording can give rise. The simultaneous playing of both source and transcription means that our listening takes place between the two, and we are alerted less to a finished object than to a dynamic compositional act. Ablinger highlights not so much the precision or efficiency of his transcription as the question of how things link up: what survives this radical translation from one form of sonic reproduction to another? To put it in terms of Bauman's liquid life, what of a person remains across multiple changes of identity?

Central to Ablinger's technique across a number of works is the use of grids, or "rasters," to indicate more or less precise divisions of pitch and duration. The title of the *Quadraturen* series (Squarings, 1995–2002) refers exactly to this grid. In these pieces, an "acoustic photograph" (i.e., recording) is made of a particular sound or space (e.g., street noise). The time and frequency of the recording are quantized onto a grid of squares, the dimensions of which may be something like one second (time) against a minor second (interval). That grid is the score, which can be realized by various instrumentations. Ablinger generates his grids from a spectral analysis of the recorded sounds using software specially designed by Thomas Musil, a programmer at the Institute for Electronic Music in Graz, Austria. A simple raster might be measured in the semitones of the piano keyboard on the pitch axis and eighth notes on the horizontal axis. Another might be more precise, but less practical, say cents against milliseconds. The width, and therefore relative precision, of these divisions creates a sort of "pixelated" effect, resulting in a grid of dots in time and pitch space that can be notated as a score. With electronic means, very precise divisions are of course possible; in theory, divisions can be made right down to the level of the digital audio signal of a CD and therefore, for all intents and purposes, the source signal itself. Yet although Ablinger's methods are rigorously executed according to their own terms, his goal is not a precisely audible copy of the original source—a trivial task in the age of digital reproduction—but a sonic recreation that effects a dialogue between the original and the means used to transcribe it. That is, it takes a critical stance toward the (utopian?) possibility of perfect transcription offered by digital technology. The fact that these transcriptions are approximate, often to the point of crudeness, directs our attention to how they were made rather than what they represent.

Where do the boundaries of artistic intervention lie? For his *Voices and Piano* series (1998–), Ablinger also used Musil's spectral analysis software to create transcriptions for piano from recorded source material—this time short extracts of speech by famous figures from history (Arnold Schoenberg, Mother Theresa, Mao Tse-Tung, Billie Holiday, etc.). Ablinger adjusts the parameters of his transcription for each recorded voice, very often in line with certain qualities of that person's speech or character. Mao's transcription is staccato and played predominately in a high treble register; Morton Feldman's is punctuated by long silences, with only a few sounds from the spectral analysis selected for transcription. Listening to more than one piece from the series at a time powerfully highlights the musical diversity that can come from Ablinger's outwardly mechanistic procedures and prompts one to ask further questions about the nature of the transcription that has taken place.

Like Ablinger, Richard Beaudoin (b. 1975) makes transcriptions using advanced sound-analysis technology. Beaudoin uses the Lucerne Audio Recording Analyzer (LARA), designed by the Swiss music performance researcher Lorenz Kilchenmann and operated by the musicologist Oliver Senn.[12] Essentially, LARA is a sonic microscope that can provide exceptionally detailed analyses of a given musical recording, such that individual note lengths can be described down to milliseconds, volume levels precisely quantified, and so on. Beaudoin uses the system to analyze iconic recordings of iconic works, such as Martha Argerich's 1975 recording of Chopin's Prelude in E Minor, op. 28, no. 4 or Maurizio Pollini's 1976 recording of Webern's *Variationen für Klavier*, op. 27, both recorded for the Deutsche Grammophon label.[13] Like a photograph (if stored digitally) can be analyzed to determine the precise position of elements within the frame and the exact color of each pixel, so can a recording be analyzed by Beaudoin's methods to describe precisely the volume and position in time of each note.

This data then becomes raw material for his compositions. In the series *Études d'un prélude* (2009), information about the Argerich recording of Chopin is subjected to a range of compositional procedures, some more free than others. As with Ablinger's transcriptions, the "resolution" of the data is adjusted to bring the detail of the computer analysis within the range of a human interpreter; one millisecond in the original might equal one eighth note in the composition, for example.[14] Beaudoin's *Étude d'un prélude I—Chopin desséché* (2009), for solo piano, remains close to the original. He preserves all of Chopin's original notes, only shifting their rhythms to align precisely with the fluctuations in tempo of Argerich's playing and specifying a dynamic level for every note that matches what Argerich actually played. The big differences are mechanical. First, Beaudoin stretches the piece to five times the length of the original recording (partly to bring those tiny rhythmic fluctuations within the range of what is humanly repeatable). Second, he abbreviates every note to a short, sharp attack—every resonance is removed. By these two simple devices, Chopin played by Argerich is made entirely unfamiliar: by magnifying Argerich's rhythmic fluctuations, Chopin's original meter is almost entirely lost to the ear; by stripping out all of the resonances, the famous composer's signature mellifluous harmonies are completely desiccated— the *desséché* of the title.

Beaudoin often makes comparisons between his work and various visual arts practices. His use of the term "photorealism" recalls the paintings of Chuck Close, and he notes a special affinity for the art of Glenn Brown, who works in a similar fashion, making digital reproductions of older paintings, subjecting them to distortions within a computer, and then painting the resulting images (with further distortions at this level too). Beaudoin's practice also has correspondences with the work of photographer Richard Prince, known for his "rephotography"—taking photographs of photographs—for example, his *Cowboy* series (1980–92), based on images used in advertisements for Marlboro cigarettes.

But while appropriation in art remains controversial—Prince has been sued, although unsuccessfully, for copyright infringement—Beaudoin is tapping into the much older and largely uncontroversial practice of music transcription; all the alterations of tempo, register, figuration, and so on that he applies to his raw data have long historical precedents. Just as Brown's distorted reproductions retain their qualities as paintings, so Beaudoin's work remains obviously "composerly" (where, by comparison, Ablinger's is strictly neutral and nonidiomatic). Unlike Prince, he does not seek to re-present something but rather is engaged in a process of translation, with all the linguistic associations of idiom, tone, and manner that that suggests.

TRANSFORMATIONS

In the 1997 film *Lost Highway*, written by David Lynch and Barry Gifford and directed by Lynch, the saxophonist Fred Madison suffers a drastic crisis of identity, seemingly hastened by menacing videos sent to his home. The last of them shows him standing over the body of his wife, Renee. Fred is arrested for her murder and sent to death row. However, in his cell he undergoes an inexplicable metamorphosis into the car mechanic Pete Dayton. Now an innocent and wrongly imprisoned man, he is set free. Pete begins an affair with the girlfriend (played by the same actress who played Renee) of a local crime boss, Mr. Eddy. As Alice begins to fear that Mr. Eddy has become aware of their affair, she and Pete plot to get away. The night after they leave town, however, Pete turns back into Fred. The film ends with a loop back to its beginning, a mysterious intercom message telling Fred, "Dick Laurent is dead."

Lynch and Gifford's story, a surreal, sometimes gruesome meditation on psychological and physical dislocation, reflections, and the intersection of media and reality, chimes with many of the themes mentioned in this chapter. (One thinks, for example, of Van der Aa's *Up-close*. Yet whereas *Up-close* leaves unexplained much about the relationship of the soloist with what we presume is her reflection on screen, *Lost Highway* makes the transformation explicit: Fred really does change into Pete and, toward the end of the film, back into Fred again.) In 2002–3 that connection was taken even further, as the film was recast as an opera by the Austrian composer Olga Neuwirth (b. 1968).

Neuwirth's *Lost Highway*, with a libretto cowritten by the Nobel Prize–winning novelist and playwright Elfriede Jelinek, stays close to Lynch's film.[15] The plot is the same, and much of the original dialogue is reproduced (only one scene is substantially changed, to allow for a better transfer to stage). Yet the musical setting gives

Neuwirth an additional medium to use to play with the strange metamorphoses of the film's storyline. There are transformations and fluid slides on every level. Voices, in particular, slip between speech, song, and noise, with the help of Neuwirth's live electronics and her sophisticated ear for timbre. The scene of Fred's transformation into Pete is a tour de force, whirling together jittery brass stabs, doom-laden electronic drones, and Fred's own dehumanized vocalizations into a spectral, psychedelic nightmare. On film, this much destabilization would risk incoherence. As music, however, it is almost typical (albeit done to a high artistic standard) of a strand of twenty-first-century late modernism that draws its expression from instability, impermanence, and in-the-moment contingency.

Once stable identity is put into question, once anything—a character, the sound of a blank LP, a familiar historical recording—can be recontextualized in any way, then musical meaning stops deriving from the signifying objects (the original sounds) and starts to transfer to the processes those objects undergo. In Lynch's film, Fred/Pete's transformations are points in the storyline; in Neuwirth's opera, transformation becomes the motivating force for the entire score. Just as *Lost Highway* destabilizes the expected continuities of character, plot, and timeline (and, in the opera, the sounds of voices and instruments), so do contemporary composers upset the stability of their musical materials, either to highlight modern anxieties about identity and responsibility or simply to surf the currents that get stirred up.

Displaced, Disembodied

Several directions in music during the 1960s—such as the rise in electronic music, the increasing complexity of notated acoustic music, and the growth in free improvisation and other open and chance-derived forms of music making—challenged the conventional image of the performer as an interpreting/reproducing machine for the composer's will. In response, works by a number of composers, including Luciano Berio (1925–2003), Giacinto Scelsi (1905–88), Xenakis, Helmut Lachenmann (b. 1935), and Brian Ferneyhough (b. 1943), began to interrogate the relationship between performer and notated score, increasingly emphasizing the actions of performers (in playing their instruments) above the desired-sounding result. These works not only helped further the critique of live, human interpretation that had been initiated in the 1960s but also, paradoxically, in their pure physicality, reasserted the need for live performers.

This compositional path took a new turn in the early 1980s with the work of the German composer Klaus K. Hübler (b. 1956). Around the turn of the decade, Hübler began to develop a new approach to composing musical gestures, based in part on his own extensive studies of Renaissance and Baroque music. His key innovation, which built on ideas already present in works by Xenakis, Lachenmann, and Ferneyhough, was to conceive of the playing of an instrument not as a combination of actions toward a single end (i.e., sounding a particular note) but as a polyphony of differently moving body parts—left hand, right hand, mouth, diaphragm, and so on—that might be "decoupled" from one another and composed separately. In works such as *"Feuerzauber" auch Eigenmusik* (1981), for three flutes, harp (two players), and cello, his first piece to be written in this way; String Quartet No. 3, "Dialektische Fantasie" (1982–4); and *Opus breve* (1987), for cello, Hübler employed a system of "tablature" notation that allowed him to compose individual performer actions on separate lines of music. Tablature, common in music for guitar and other plucked string instruments, is a form of notation that does not map out the pitches that should be played but rather uses a stylized illustration of the instrument (with a horizontal line representing each string, for example) to indicate how the performer should produce a note. It therefore indicates what the performer should physically do (place a finger on the fourth fret of the first string, for example), rather than what will sound. Its usefulness for Hübler was in allowing him to separate individual performing actions from the production of a given sound (Hübler's term for this is "decoupling"), which enabled him to compose those actions more specifically and with greater intricacy.

Hübler's approach was continued by a small number of composers in the 1980s and '90s, notably Richard Barrett (see, for example, *Tract,* 1984–96, for piano) and Franklin Cox (b. 1961; see *Recoil,* 1994, for cello). Independently, and for a little longer, similar ideas were also explored by improvisers such as Malcolm Goldstein (b. 1936), Barry Guy (b. 1947), and Evan Parker (b. 1944).[16] However, it was not until the turn of the century that these concepts were taken up in earnest among a younger generation of composers.

One of these is Aaron Cassidy (b. 1976). The sound of Cassidy's music is of a surface warped, folded, and scored beyond all recognition, like a photograph blistering against a flame. It is like a sonic version of the curved metallic surface of a Frank Gehry building or the smeared paint streaks of a Francis Bacon portrait—both artists Cassidy has invoked in descriptions of his work. The ear struggles to grasp a semantic structure, patterns of repetition or opposition that would suggest an underlying grammar, and instead listens in the moment, hearing the motion of continual uprooting.

Cassidy began investigating the possibilities of decoupling in the late 1990s. In the early bass clarinet solo *metallic dust* (1999), the instrumentalist is given two lines of music: one indicating pitch (or, rather, fingering), and one above indicating dynamics, breath, tonguing, and articulation (or, rather, the actions of the mouth). The two lines are composed in counterpoint to each other, making the sounding results unpredictable. Although the bottom staff appears to notate a straightforward series of pitches and rhythms, how those precisely sound is governed by their interaction with the upper stave of articulations (see figure 14). If these aren't rhythmically synchronized (as is the case for much of the piece), the results will be unpredictable, characterized by the intersection of two simultaneous but independent sets of actions.

Following *metallic dust*, Cassidy began adapting forms of tablature, after Hübler, to emphasize the increasing importance of physical precision over sounding result. His first piece written fully in this fashion was *The Crutch of Memory* (2004). Its instrumental designation—for "indeterminate solo string instrument"—is telling. By making the actual instrument—and therefore its register, tuning, and so on— flexible, Cassidy clearly indicates that the topography of the instrument, rather than its specific sound, is the compositional focus. As his own program note describes, "In this work, I have endeavored to strip away the pretense of pitch in an effort to more directly prioritize the performative actions in the notation."[17]

Figure 15 shows how *The Crutch of Memory* has been conceived across a physical landscape (an instrument's strings and fingerboard) rather than a sounding one (of pitch), as in conventional notation. The top staff, of four lines, corresponds to the four strings of the instrument, with numbers indicating the finger to be used to stop the string. The middle, one-line staff corresponds to finger spacing, on a scale from 1 (as close together as possible) to 5 (the widest possible spacing). The large staff describes seven different hand positions up and down the fingerboard. Speed, pressure, and position of the bow are all indicated above or below the top staff, using a combination of standard abbreviations and shaded blocks (indicating bow pressure). The score thus works as a choreography of the two hands holding the violin and bow, out of which a sound results, rather than as a map of the desired sounds, for which a performer must determine their movements.

In *What then renders these forces visible is a strange smile (or, First Study for Figures at the Base of a Crucifixion)* (2008), for trumpet, Cassidy adapts his notation to include the even more precise details of wind instrument performance, and the score contrasts strikingly with that of *metallic dust*, showing how far his thinking had come. In *What then renders*, the three main bands of information (the description "staff" seems increasingly inappropriate) govern the actions of the embouchure, valves, and slide. Between the bands for embouchure and valves are indications for dynamic—which in the case of the trumpet are broadly identical with the amount of breath pressure.

What then renders belongs to a group of Cassidy's pieces, begun in 2005, that is related to the paintings of Francis Bacon, particularly as described in *The Logic of Sensation* (first published in French in 1981), by Gilles Deleuze. (Several of these pieces are extracted from the composite work *And the scream, Bacon's scream, is the operation through which the entire body escapes through the mouth (or, Three Studies for Figures at the Base of a Crucifixion)*, 2005–9.) Cassidy was attracted to Bacon's work, as was Deleuze, by the sensational physicality of the paintings—paintings of bodies, made by bodies, the smears of paint and twists of form revealing both the fleshy, meaty reality of their subjects and the hand and eye of their painter.

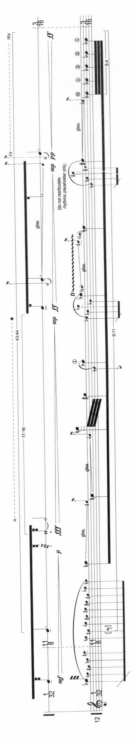

FIGURE 14. Excerpt from the score of Aaron Cassidy's *metallic dust*, 1999. Courtesy of the composer.

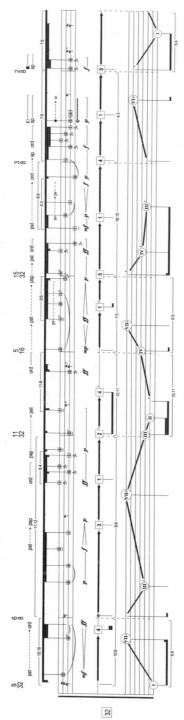

FIGURE 15. Excerpt from the score of Aaron Cassidy's *The Crutch of Memory* (2004). Courtesy of the composer.

Cassidy's *A painter of figures in rooms* (2012) also relates to Bacon, but in this case takes its title from a description by the art critic John Russell. Written for the vocal ensemble EXAUDI (founded in 2002) and commissioned as part of the London 2012 Cultural Olympiad, the piece goes further than any of Cassidy's pieces to date in the precision and multivalency of its instructions. Working for voices alone, Cassidy brings his compositional landscape away from the external world of objects and into the human body—specifically the vocal folds, mouth, glottis, and tongue. The position and tension of all of these, as well as the degree of air pressure, is marked in a form of tablature that forces the performers to rethink entirely how they use their vocal apparatuses, distancing themselves from the most intimate knowledge of their own bodies.

Cassidy's music creates distancing through introducing layers and layers of procedural, interpretive, and translational distortion. The Bacon/Deleuze pieces are musical expressions of deconstructionist readings of portrait paintings whose surfaces are deliberately disturbed beyond recognition. Cassidy's compositional process works similarly, with initially simple blocks of material (set out in the earliest stage on a spreadsheet) pushed through increasingly restrictive and transformative filters and compressions.

Cassidy's methods have connected with a particular stream in new music and have been influential in their own right—he is a popular teacher at the University of Huddersfield in the United Kingdom. Many younger composers have found the logic and practice of decoupling useful not only as a source of new instrumental sound (and, it has to be said, some degree of prestige that comes with the production of ever more novel and complex notational systems) but also as a means of expression that coincides with the deconstructionist philosophies and aesthetics of the time and as a way of capturing and expressing the moment-by-moment contingency of identity that is a reality for millennials. Stefan Prins (b. 1979) has been a leader in this area, using progressive layers of distortion to develop themes of dislocation, alienation, and, in his most recent works, responsibility.

Taking its cue from Samuel Beckett's short 1972 play of the same name, which features a single mouth at the center of a blackened stage, Prins's *Not I* (2007), for electronic guitar and electronics, uses intersecting and conflicting musical planes to explore the idea of disembodiment. The electric guitar is attached to an amplifier, as it normally would be, but between the instrument and the amp is inserted an additional digital sound processor. Controlled by a second musician, this "black box" disrupts the direct amplification of the guitar so that what one hears is frequently not what one sees being played.

Prins developed the idea of technology as a malevolent, alienating mechanism further in *Fremdkörper #1* (2008), *#2* (2010), and *#3* (2010), for differing ensembles. In these three pieces, every instrument within the ensemble is connected to its own amplifier and disruptive black box. *Fremdkörper* is the German term for a

FIGURE 16. Nadar Ensemble performing Stefan Prins's *Generation Kill,* 2012.

foreign or alien body, and Prins's work draws on the word's implications of physical alienation or dislocation. As the live instruments and electronics intersect, it becomes less and less clear which is the original body and which is its alienated extension, setting up a fluid situation in which real and virtual become indistinguishable. The association between Prins's work and Bauman's concept of liquid modernity is made explicit in *Fremdkörper #3 (mit Michael Jackson),* which features an electronics part made up of intros from several Jackson songs that have been highly processed, in most cases beyond recognition. The work's program note draws on Jackson's long history of body modification, citing the singer himself as a "perfect illustration" of a *Fremdkörper,* and connects those physical changes to the electronic transformations of Jackson's music in the piece.

Perhaps Prins's most substantial work so far in this vein is *Generation Kill* (2012). Written for percussion, electric guitar, violin, cello, four musicians with game controllers, live electronics, and video, it plays once more on the ideas of physical dislocation and virtual identity associated with the *Fremdkörper* concept but this time extends them into a critique of modern-day warfare and the nature of responsibility in a virtual combat zone. The four instrumentalists sit behind projection screens. Sometimes they are lit so that we can see them behind the screens; sometimes they are invisible. Most of the time, however, they are in-between, seen through and merging with video projections on the screens. The other four players, with their game controllers, sit facing the screens, their backs to the audience (see figure 16).

In his description of the piece, Prins draws on metaphors of social media (particularly in relation to the revolutions of the Arab Spring of 2011), CCTV surveillance, and drone warfare.[18] The title is taken from the 2004 book and 2008 HBO miniseries of the same name, by the American journalist Evan Wright, an embedded reporter with the US Marine Corps during the 2003 invasion of Iraq, and the piece was inspired by Wright's observation that the Iraq War was fought by soldiers brought up on virtual combat, on warfare as a game on a screen, mediated by graphics, music, and cinematography—"the first PlayStation generation."[19] The work disrupts not only each player's sounds, with electronic distortions, but also their appearance, through the video projections. These projections generally show live footage of the musicians playing that is reversed, sped-up, or otherwise altered. As the piece progresses—noisily, chaotically, a cyborg squelch of flesh and digital bits—the live footage is increasingly intercut with other material: recorded footage (shot from different angles) of the players, live close-up footage of the faces of the musicians with game controllers, and US military footage taken from the onboard cameras of drones and guided missiles.

Prins's music highlights discontinuities and distances between layers of information, constructing a critique—which is vividly explicit in *Generation Kill* but present in all his works—of digitization and its alienating, dehumanizing effects. Yet it highlights the limits of that critique, too. For all its intellectual construction, Prins's music is also thrillingly, even seductively, affective, as it brings to life the disorientation and then somatic disengagement of virtual reality. Prins stages a critique of digitization, but he also invites us to immerse ourselves in it.

Endless Variations

Journeys and representations of fluidity can be enacted within a work itself; they need not depend on precompositional transfers and translations. Enno Poppe's *Thema mit 840 Variationen* (1993, rev. 1997), for piano, is a quintessential expression of Bourriaud's radicant aesthetic. As its title suggests, its seven minutes are made up of 840 variations of a single theme. That theme is simple, minimally constituted, and comprises just two notes. Poppe (b. 1969) applies to this a Lindenmayer system (or L-system), a way of producing strings of symbols that, once converted geometrically, model the branching growth of trees and other plants. Using a small set of rules of transformation (of the kind "A becomes AB," "B becomes A"), which he applies to variables such as interval structure, duration, and direction, Poppe develops a long string of variations on the original two-note "axiom." (The number of variations is not, incidentally, a reference to the 840 repetitions of Erik Satie's *Vexations* (1893), but simply a result of the math used.) The reuse and continual manipulation of very short melodic materials is typical of Poppe's work from this time—see also the cycle of ensemble works *Holz–Knochen–Öl* (1999–2004)—but *Thema mit 840 Variationen* is perhaps the purest expression of his method.

The idea of variations is not new. But by reducing his "theme" to a minimum and greatly amplifying the number of variations he derives from it, Poppe radically alters the balance between theme and form, such that the theme itself disappears into irrelevance, and what is expressed instead is the journey, the work's perpetual rootlessness and reinvention. A classical theme and variations set like Beethoven's *Diabelli Variations* (1819–23) depend on a sense of recognition and arrival with each return of the theme and on an appreciation of how it has been transformed. Poppe's variations, by contrast, are a chaotic stream of change, transformation, and reconstitution. The theme is constant but at the same time eternally ungraspable. (The corollary to this almost cancerous vivacity of musical invention would be a correspondingly rapid discarding of material. The form of Poppe's piece is equally one of hypercreation and hyperrejection. I will return to this theme in the next chapter.)

Another composer to work in a similar way is Carl Stone (b. 1953), although his music often cleaves closer to a minimal aesthetic. Stated in broad terms, Stone's interest is in the electronic manipulation of preexisting music. His work differs, therefore, from Poppe's in that its materials are derived from concrete sources rather than abstract musical formulations. He began composing in a predigital world; as a student at the California Institute of the Arts in 1973–4, he worked in the music library transferring recordings—of the classical repertory, jazz, and world music—onto tape. To speed up the process, the machine he worked with allowed up to three recordings to be made at a time, and Stone soon discovered that it also permitted him to listen to combinations of all three while they were being dubbed: "I could listen to what would happen if you combined Machaut with Ussachevsky, or the music of the Babenzele pygmies with . . . I don't know . . . a Berg chamber piece, up to 3 at a time. And I began to experiment and notice the connections and re-contextualizations that would happen as these things played together."[20]

After his studies, Stone began dividing his time between Japan and the United States, and from this point onward a trans-Pacific fusion of the styles of the American West Coast and Southeast Asia has infected all of his music. This is most simply reflected in his practice of titling all his pieces after his favorite Asian restaurants. More profoundly, his sampled materials are drawn equally from Southeast Asian and Western roots. *Shing Kee,* composed in 1986 and released on the album *Mom's* in 1992, is representative. Kyle Gann has described the process that the first half of this sixteen-minute piece unfolds: "*Shing Kee* was made by sampling a recording of classical pieces by Jap-pop singer Akiko Yano. Stone sampled her singing 'Der Lindenbaum' from Schubert's *Winterreise*—stored several hundred thousand bits of it in digital form—and in *Shing Kee* he plays the samples back, using the computer live to add a few milliseconds at each repetition."[21]

Here, Stone's process is more or less discernible. Its instability derives from its constant evolution. However, the path is still a relatively conventional, additive one: the length of the sample is incrementally increased with each repetition, from the momentary and unrecognizable intake of breath before the voice engages to the recognizable three-second excerpt of Schubert that comes more than eight minutes into the piece. Nominally, the first eight minutes of *Shing Kee* performs a journey from A to B—from the microscopic to the full sample (although the size of this sample is arbitrary, and the process could in theory have been extended to much greater length). What changes is the sampling window: imagined horizontally, it is fixed at its left-hand edge and extends gradually with each reiteration to the right. In theory, it is a process that could be achievable, if prohibitively time-consuming, with tape, and indeed Stone acknowledges that the advent of sampling has not changed his basic aesthetic, only his productivity.

Jitlada, from Stone's 2007 album *Al-Noor,* depends more on digital means of creation, and it takes *Shing Kee*'s transitional form a stage further, putting both edges of the sampling window in motion, moving horizontally through the course of a single long sample.[22] Therefore, while new material is added to the loop at one end, it is also discarded at the other. Although the piece has a generalized consistency of tone—derived from its source material, a cassette of Thai pop—its identity at any given moment is uncertain. We are clearly within a prefabricated musical environment, replete with the rhythms and timbres of commercial pop (even if the specific source is intentionally obscure), but the musical logic has been completely reconfigured. The condition of movement and endless change, without discernible points of departure or arrival, is the music's defining formal characteristic.

Unlike Poppe's mathematical branching systems, Stone's processes are typically gradual, stepwise, and hence traceable. Listeners can directly orientate themselves in relation to where they have just come from and where they are likely to go. Because Poppe's variations do not progress in an audible, stepwise sequence, the sense of formal unrootedness is more pronounced, although the sense of a directed journey is less marked.

The transitional and transformational aesthetic of Poppe and Stone has a precedent in certain works composed in the Soviet Union, such as Sofia Gubaidulina's *Offertorium* (1980) or, earlier still, Arvo Pärt's *Credo* (1967). In both instances, however, although the phase of transition is crucial and constitutes a large part of the works, it is marked by clear points of departure (in both cases, quotations of Bach) and arrival (in Gubaidulina's case, the reduction of Bach's theme from *Der musikalische Opfer* to a single note; in Pärt's case, the gradual distortion of Bach's C Major Prelude from Book 1 of *Das wohltemperierte Klavier* until it becomes saturated noise). In both cases, there is clearly a goal-directed dramaturgy at work, which may also be attached to a wider program about the relationship of the individual to the totalitarian state. If there is a program underlying either Poppe's or Stone's pieces (even if only implicitly) it relates to the identity, freedom, and movement of the unencumbered individual, a story belonging to the decades after the Cold War rather than during it.

There is a further precedent in minimal process music, especially that of Steve Reich (to whom Stone, in particular, owes at least a stylistic debt). However, once again there are distinct structural differences. To take an archetypal example, Reich's *Piano Phase* (1967) is constructed around patterns of tension and release, departure and arrival. Between each sixteenth-note shift in the two-piano pattern is a transition, a passage of musical suspension in which one piano speeds up slightly. This is relieved only when that piano is exactly one sixteenth note ahead of its partner, and the two lock once more into their homorhythmic grind. On the larger scale, the complete phasing process articulates another region of suspension, itself relieved with the final sixteenth-note shift that brings the two pianos once more into unison. Although its processes and the internal relationships to which they give rise are much freer, Terry Riley's *In C* (1964) invites similar moments of centering and decentering, particularly around those cells that contain long sustained notes. It is rare to hear a performance in which these moments don't provide at least a temporary sense of arrival and stasis within an otherwise rhythmically dense piece.

Perhaps surprisingly, given his relatively low credibility today among the "big four" minimalists, it is Glass's early minimal music that most closely anticipates the radicant forms of Poppe and Stone (Glass may have the greater popular profile, but it is Reich, Riley, and La Monte Young that are totemic among experimental and postminimal musicians of all stripes). A piece like Glass's *Music in Fifths* (1969), the aesthetic contribution of which is often discussed in similar terms as *Piano Phase* or *In C*, is radically different in form in that it offers none of the teleological patterning of those works but instead presents itself as a continuous and unrelieved (although not undifferentiated) state of suspension. In other words, it is a pure journey form, in which the piece is suspended between points, in motion but never arriving.

WANDERING

The being in motion of Glass's early music brings us to Bourriaud's final formal concept: wandering, or the journey form. Glass's more recent music may rely on the gestures of functional harmony (and therefore the language of teleological, rather than unrooted, music), but if it is goal-directed, it is often hard to determine what exactly those goals are or what our relation to them might be at any given moment in the piece. The music has the veneer of harmonic function, but it is frequently less grounded and more destabilized than even the early works of Reich or Riley.

Although his style has evolved since the 1960s, Glass has returned to the idea of the journey at different points in his career, most notably in his 1992 opera, *The Voyage*, commissioned by the New York Metropolitan Opera to mark the five-hundredth anniversary of Columbus's landing in America; and *1,000 Airplanes on the Roof* (1988), a music theater work telling the surrealistic story of "M," who recalls (or hallucinates—it is never made clear) a journey through space and his/her encounters with alien beings. Both works deal with the stability and fluidity of identity, particularly in the confrontation with cultural Others. Both also have librettos by the Chinese-American playwright David Henry Hwang, a writer who has made creolization and the destabilization of fixed cultural identities a theme of his work. "In a lot of my plays," Hwang observes, "people become other people. . . . It has a lot to do with the nature vs nurture question. To what degree do you have an inherited identity, and to what degree is your personality shaped by the influences and environment around you?"[23]

Destabilizations such as these are a defining feature of Glass's output. It is well known that his minimalist style derives from his years in Paris, which he spent simultaneously studying formal counterpoint with Nadia Boulanger and Indian music with Ravi Shankar. Yet his music transitions between media just as smoothly as it does between cultural influences—those years in Paris were also spent working on music for film (with Shankar) and for theater (with the Mabou Mines company). That flexibility comes from the essential flatness of his music; as it rolls through its states of harmonic and melodic indifference, it gathers no meaning, which allows scores like the one he wrote for Paul Schrader's film *Mishima* (1984) to pass through the dramatic and psychologically fraught story of an entire character's life (in this case, that of the Japanese author Yukio Mishima, who committed ritual suicide in 1970 after failing to lead a military coup to reinstate the Japanese emperor) with only minimal variations between musical cues.

Certain features of notated music intended for performance militate against the emergence of journey forms. In many of Bourriaud's examples, the journey is undertaken by the artist (with or without a particular object). The journey itself is the artwork, with its concluding documentation providing the only physical manifestation for the purposes of exhibition. In those instances where an object takes part in the journey—such as the Fiat 126 that Simon Starling drove from Turin, Italy, to Cieszyn, Poland, as part of his work *Flaga, 1972–2000* (2002)—the object provides part of that documentation, and its final state gives some expression to the journey. Walshe's *THIS IS WHY* is a musical exception in that the sounding result is similarly an expression of the journey undertaken, but this is only made possible by the piece's unconventional score. Nevertheless, the increasing prominence of sound art, spatialization, and site-specificity, as well as a growing sympathy toward relational and experience-based works of art among commissioning and staging bodies, have supported the idea of purposeful movement through space—the journey—as a way of structuring a musical work.

A classic example, belonging more to the realm of sound art than of composition, is Christian Marclay's *Guitar Drag* (2000). A Fender Stratocaster guitar is tied to the back of a pickup truck, plugged into an amplifier, and dragged at speed along roads and dirt tracks. Bit by bit, it falls apart, sounding its disintegration in a stream of distorted howls. The sound and video filmed from the back of the truck are presented together. It is a complex work. Its imagery (the pickup and the Stratocaster) is high Americana, and on one level there is both humor and melancholy in the way that this symbol of freedom is so ungracefully destroyed. Yet the action also has a much darker side, evoking the lynching of James Byrd Jr., dragged to his death behind a pickup in Texas in 1998, and the dragging of the bodies of US military personnel through the streets of Mogadishu in 1993. The guitar's "journey" is overlaid with meaning; the sound and sight of its disintegration becomes metaphorical.

Koji Asano's *Quoted Landscape* (2001) begins with a similar premise: a microphone being dragged. Like *Guitar Drag*, the music of *Quoted Landscape* derives from the electronic transformation of friction into amplified sound. Yet meaning is stripped out in this instance. There is no video, so the movement of the microphone and the terrain that it passes over can only be imagined. Changes in the ground are articulated through changes in sonic texture, but they never acquire concrete significance. There is also no narrative. Unlike Marclay's guitar, the microphone is not destroyed by this process; it simply tracks what happens to it. A microphone is also a less evocative object than a Fender Stratocaster, with all the layers of meaning that that instrument has acquired through sixty years of rock music. There is therefore less scope for romantic or sentimental interpretation in Asano's piece.

For *The Untuned Piano Concerto* (2006), Cynthia Zaven installed an old, untuned piano on the back of a truck; the truck then drove around New Delhi while Zaven played the piano. Her improvised playing interacted with the sound of the urban environment through which she was passing. Brenda Hutchinson (b. 1954) did something similar for her piece *How do you get to Carnegie Hall?* (1996), spending a month driving a piano from New York to San Francisco and inviting people to play and tell piano-related stories along the way. The resulting recordings were edited down and are used as a backdrop to which live performers respond. As with *Guitar Drag* and *Quoted Landscape*, *The Untuned Piano Concerto* and *How do you get to Carnegie Hall?* both transform movement through or across an environment (space) into music (time). Yet whereas the Marclay and Asano pieces more or less objectively record the sound of a journey according to certain precompositional decisions (the route to be taken, the type of equipment to be used, etc.), those by Zaven and Hutchinson insert more subjectivity into the space/time translation through improvisation and the unpredictable response of the environment or the people encountered on the journey.

Zaven and Hutchinson take conventional (if battered) instruments on a journey. But journeys may take place across the instrument itself. In *expanding space in limited time* (1994), Kunsu Shim marks the passage of a bow across a string. This may be a trivial occurrence in Western art music, but Shim gives it the significance of a journey by isolating the single gesture and expanding it enormously, extending a single bow stroke out across many minutes. *The Harmonics of Real Strings* (2006, rev. 2013), by John Lely (b. 1976), enacts a similar process of slow-motion string playing. In Lely's piece, the focus is on the left hand. While one string is bowed continuously, the left hand moves very slowly along the length of the string, pressing gently so as to sound harmonics at each of the string's nodal points.

Much is left unpredictable in both Shim's and Lely's pieces, but more is predetermined than in the Zaven, Asano, and Marclay works. Ellen Fullman (b. 1957) also works with strings, greatly drawing them out to many meters in length.[24] Her piece *Event Locations No. 2* (2009) is played in a way that enacts a journey in itself, a concept that is an expansion of the single movements in Shim's and Lely's pieces. Fullman's Long String Instrument, as she calls it, consists of metal strings stretched across the performance space, suspended at waist height. When performing, she walks up and down the length of the instrument exciting the strings by rubbing them with her rosined fingertips or specially made wooden blocks. Fullman's work is closer to conventional composition in terms of the relationship between notation and sound specificity. Points in the music are marked spatially on the floor beneath the strings, and her scores are like dance instructions, consisting of instructions for how to walk from one spot to the next (see figure 17).

The conception of notation as a spatial map returns us to the tablature works of Aaron Cassidy and others. The movement of bow and fingers across and along strings articulate tiny journeys through an ever-changing, multidimensional topography. The space of a violin fingerboard may be highly normative and much smaller than the roads and trails of Marclay's *Guitar Drag,* but the principles of transmuting space and movement into sound remain the same; the fact that the two works stem from such different sources and produce such different results only highlights the strength of the journey form as a formal concept.

CRITIQUE

In the world beyond music, the models of fluidity I have described suit modern capitalism well. Flexible workers are more easily exploited. Money that is disconnected from real-world commodities invites risky speculation practices such as short selling. A life lived fluidly requires ever greater levels of consumption so that individuals might "hedge their bets and insure their actions against the mischiefs of fate."[25] Without certainties or stabilities, we are always driven to purchase the next upgrade, the newest model. This isn't just a philosophical point: think of how many items of technology you own that have obsolescence built into them.

The mechanisms of consumption, waste, and obsolescence are brought to the fore in one of the more remarkable examples of a musical journey form, Simon Steen-Andersen's *Run-Time Error* (2009). Steen-Andersen (b. 1976) is a Danish composer who has made much use of digital technologies, music theater, and extended sound sources in his work. His approach to sound resembles Lachenmann's in that he is excited by the peripheral, accidental, counter-traditional, or "undesirable" results of sound production. However, whereas Lachenmann

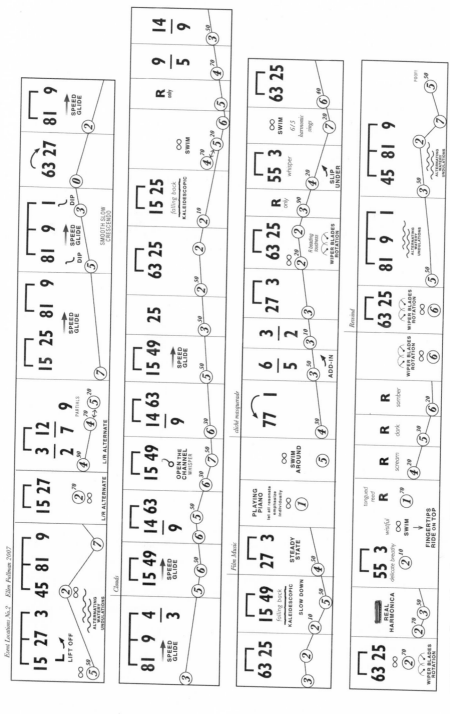

FIGURE 17. Excerpt from the score of Ellen Fullman's *Event Locations No. 2*, 2009, solo composition for the Long String Instrument. Courtesy of the composer.

FIGURE 18. Still from a performance of Simon Steen-Andersen's *Run Time Error,* 2009, at Den Frie Centre of Contemporary Art, Copenhagen, November 14, 2014. Courtesy of Edition·S.

restricts himself to the sounds around conventional playing technique—key slaps, breath tones, and so on—Steen-Andersen's exuberant music revels in pops, squeaks, crackles, and bangs that go beyond the capabilities of traditional instruments. His piece *Black Box Music* (2012), for example, culminates in the amplified sound of balloons, confetti, rubber bands, and more, all whirled chaotically about by a number of electric fans and confined within the space of a small box, the interior of which is projected onto a screen behind the stage.

In *Run-Time Error,* Steen-Andersen takes his fascination with accidental sounds to a new limit. The score contains the instruction that anything within the performing space may only be sounded once. From this unpromising restriction, Steen-Andersen creates a madcap work of sound art that is quite unlike anything else. First, the designation of the performing space is pushed to an extreme and taken to refer to a predetermined path around and through the auditorium where the work is to be presented. Then that path is populated with potential sound objects—pieces of furniture, banisters, light fittings, and so on. These should already be in situ, but they may be prepared beforehand by the composer. After a path and a sequence of sounds has been mapped out, Steen-Andersen runs the route, using drumsticks, an electric drill, and other implements to sound each item in turn. The whole thing is done at high speed and filmed. This recording, made some time before the concert itself, is the basis of the work's presentation, and Steen-Andersen may then apply further manipulations to the video—altering its speed or direction, for example— during the performance, using a joystick controller.

Politically this work is different from the others I have described in this chapter; where works like *Thema mit 840 Variationen, Piano and Record,* or even *THIS IS WHY* conceal the journey dimension of their conception behind the respectability of a formalized musical work (in spite of their substantial differences, all three of these works manifest as concert pieces for one or more instrumentalists playing according to a predetermined musical plan), *Run-Time Error* foregrounds not only the nature of the journey but also its consequences. Perhaps the closest comparison is *Guitar Drag,* but even in that piece the guitar is heroically transformed as a result of what happens to it. The spaces through which Steen-Andersen runs are rarely given a similar chance to express their character; they flash past too quickly. Even then, they are subject to a further layer of seemingly capricious manipulation and distortion through the actions of the joystick.

Two things are striking about the piece. First is its energy: the stipulation that any object may be used only once gives the piece a highly mobile and varied form. Sounds rush past; nothing is static, nothing is repeated. It is an exemplary piece of fluid music in the mode of the Poppe or Stone works mentioned above, but even more so because every moment is aurally unrelated to what comes before it; the only connection is the path itself. Steen-Andersen's anarchic presentation of an ultra-subjective will (see figure 18) is as visceral and thrilling as it is attractive: who watching it would not like to undertake a similar sprint around a building like this?

The second thing is the visible by-product of such a journey: the necessary result of consumption is waste. By sounding everything, Steen-Andersen allows everything to add its voice to the work; but by sounding them each just once, he allows none to develop and live. His path moves forward with the speed and purpose of a wrecking ball, leaving in its wake a trail of waste. Sometimes this is literal as well as figurative: objects are broken, tape is unraveled, papers are strewn. What in *Black Box* is contained within the space of the box, in *Run-Time Error* is spread around the spaces and service corridors of the concert hall, to be somehow collected and disposed of when the performance is complete. Fluidity creates exciting new possibilities for artistic form, but with every new identity, every new skin, an old one must be shed. Poppe composes 840 variations, but each is as easily disposed of as the last. *Run-Time Error* models a hyperconsumption that is both thrilling and magnificent, but which has consequences that are of grave importance for the survival of our species. As with the image of the gradually swamped space of *Black Box Music,* a space that has been silenced by the sheer volume of objects crammed inside it, *Run-Time Error* hints at a very contemporary form of tragedy. Superabundance, as both an artistic mode and a way of being in the twenty-first century, will be the subject of chapter 6, and the condition of loss and ruin that is its flipside will be considered in chapter 7. First, however, the idea of the journey leads us to the influence of globalization and the concept of mobility.

5

MOBILITY

Worldwide Flows, Networks, and Archipelagos

GLOBALIZED NEW MUSIC

Globalization—the increasing interconnectedness of the world through trade, travel, communication, and culture—is not new. Its origins lie in the ancient trade routes between Asia and medieval Europe. Yet the fall of national and regional barriers that followed the collapse of the Berlin Wall, as well as the international spread of neoliberal economic and political policies that came soon after, initiated a more intense phase of globalization that is frequently described in its own right. It was further aided by the development of global communication technologies such as satellite television, the Internet, and the cellphone. These rapidly accelerated the transmission and sharing of information and culture around the world, to the point where today an event can be viewed more or less instantly at any global location. The effects of this compression of time and space—such that both are, at least online, redundant concepts—on our understanding and behavior are certainly great and multiple.

The immediate enabling effects of globalization for a musician are clear. First, the audience for one's work is greatly expanded. Not only because of the (relative) affordability of international travel and the ease of international distribution of recordings and videos—through transnational distribution networks or, more simply, via the Internet—but also because audiences' tastes are becoming increasingly attuned to the full spectrum of what music can and might be around the world. This is not the place for a lengthy discussion of world music, but the success of that genre—an invention of the late 1980s—is one indication of the broadening of tastes.

A second benefit is that these transnational connections and sympathies increase the possibilities for musical exchange and new partnerships, syntheses, and hybridities. A striking example is that of Japanoise, which developed within a cultural feedback loop between Japan and the United States (primarily) thanks to the international movement of artists and to networks of exchange such as Internet newsgroups and, latterly, file-sharing and video websites.[1]

Globalization is not always beneficial, however. The same technologies that create a global market for a musician's work can also distribute it for free and without attribution or compensation. The creations of one region are always open to exploitation by another. The most egregious instances of this are usually when wealthy Western/Northern corporations exploit the creations of Eastern/Southern musicians, but related abuses, such as unlicensed use or adaptations of popular music, also occur in the opposite direction. Globalization is also often seen as a "Westernization" of culture. The endless flow and exchange of culture can lead to a general homogenization and flattening out of difference. When one set of cultural norms is aligned with the dominant economic and political agents of a particular place, they are likely to form a pole toward which homogenization will gravitate. However, this is not a universal view, and consideration must also be given to the agency of subordinate or dominated cultures to appropriate, mimic, subvert, and resist the dominant culture that is imposed on them.[2] Globalization can in many respects be an expression of cultural imperialism; but it can also come from the movements and communications of poorer citizens, such as refugees, economic migrants, or students. Global citizenship is not an exclusive preserve of the wealthy.

There are many ways in which globalization in music might be conceived and its impact analyzed; this chapter does not attempt to explore all of them. Instead it takes one aspect of modern-day globalization—mobility—and uses it as a metaphor for understanding certain features of the contemporary music ecosystem, from the relationships between performers, composers, and institutions, down to individual works themselves. Just as the previous chapter was not only about digitization in new music, so this chapter is not only about globalization. Rather, it uses globalization as a starting point from which to investigate new modes of creation, dissemination, and reception.

Art historians often identify 1989 as the year when globalization entered a new and deeper relationship with artistic production, citing the rise and spread of international art biennials that began at around this time.[3] Biennials are a convenient way to mark the rising influence of globality on contemporary art because they conflate several of its dimensions on a single site: the mixing and curating of international artists; the touristic approach to culture; and the boundaryless flow of international capital. One specific exhibition, *Magiciens de la terre*, held at the Centre Pompidou in Paris in 1989, is often considered as marking a turning point in curatorial focus and style because its self-conscious juxtaposition of Western artists with traditional and contemporary artists from around the world contributed to a radical reassessment of what globalized contemporary art actually was.

Many of the same structural changes that encouraged the rise of the art biennial also apply to music, yet strict comparisons are not easy to make. At first the contemporary music festival—which is itself sometimes associated with a wider arts festival—seems like an obvious analog. Music festivals are typically connected to a single location, recur regularly (annually or biennially), draw a diverse range of artists and productions, serve as meeting places for exchanges between practitioners, attract press attention, and serve the local economy in terms of prestige and tourist revenue.

Yet art and music diverge significantly around a simple difference in form. Art—in general terms at least—is site- and object-specific. It involves the display of an object (such as a painting or sculpture) in a place (usually a gallery, but not always); or, more recently, it may involve an artistic intervention that takes place at a specific site. Music—again, generally speaking—is time- and people-specific. It is less about the production and display of objects in a specific location and more about organizing the activities of people (performers and listeners) within a given timespan (the length of a performance).

This difference becomes important when we consider the role and impact of globalization on the two respective art forms and how they are presented and disseminated. In the era of globalization, art has become more like music; that is, it has become increasingly time-based, as opposed to object-based, and it has more and more come to use people (performers and viewers/participants) as a medium. This shift has been described most succinctly in Nicolas Bourriaud's formulation of "relational aesthetics,"[4] but it may be traced in many forms across arts criticism of the past two decades.

At the same time, music has increasingly begun to make use of specificity and spectacle. Music festivals in particular have responded to the changing expectations of the cultural audience by moving as much of their programming as possible outside the traditional concert hall and into galleries, public spaces, unused industrial buildings, and so on. They have also become more interactive and less formal, pursuing more communal, public, and indeed relational aspects in their programming.

The Bang on a Can Marathon was mentioned in chapter 2. A more recent example is the Borealis Festival, which has been held annually in Bergen, Norway, since 2006. Between 2008 and 2013 it was directed by the British artist, composer, and performer Alwynne Pritchard (b. 1968). One of Pritchard's main ambitions as artistic director was to make audiences more sensitive to the concept of concerts—and by extension individuals' own social, economic, and institutional surroundings—as a construct, having their own weight and history and their own possibility of change. To this end, Borealis included not only relatively conventional concerts in relatively conventional spaces but also events that took place throughout Bergen itself: at the racetrack, the courthouse, private apartments, an IKEA warehouse, and even, in 2013, the city's recycling plant (see figure 19). One of the consequences of this practice was that a wider audience attended these concerts, but more

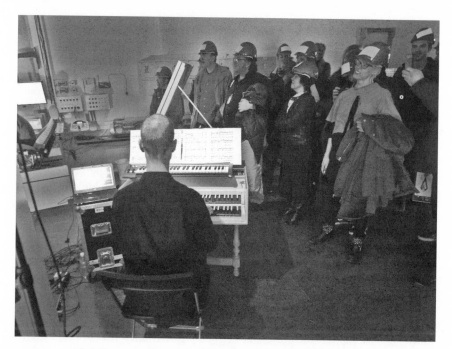

FIGURE 19. Mark Knoop performing at the Borealis Festival, Bergen, Norway, 2013. Photo by Justinas Keršis.

importantly it shifted the boundaries between private listening and public event. In 2010 a performance of *HELIOS NORDWÄRTS* (2010), by Gerhard Stäbler (b. 1949), engaged helicopters and antique fire engines to shift the music's spatial parameters from an indoor performance of string and brass band music to a public spectacle in Bergen's streets and airspace. In concerts like this, additional aspects of the listening experience come into consideration; at the recycling plant, for example, these included temperature and smell, as well as more typical factors such as acoustics and the size of the room.

There are many reasons for these shifts in presentation styles. Art, through the biennial, has become symbolic of the flow of global capital—often concretely, as works are bought and sold—and it relates more broadly to cultural dimensions like fashion, design, and celebrity, all of which are part of the biennial's overall spectacle. Music, as a time-based art originating in experiences rather than objects, cannot attract the same level of investment. Similarly, it does not mesh as well with the visual worlds of fashion and design and therefore has less "stickiness" within the public imagination. By shifting the presentation of some music to the context of something closer to that of the art biennial, festival organizers hope that some of that financial success may rub off. I have already discussed aspects of this convergence in the production of site-specific or multimedia works, which not only counter the usual channels of contemporary arts marketing, but also help establish and define market niches that may themselves be exploited. The transmedial forms and fluidities of genres, styles, and audiences that we have seen in chapters 3 and 4 have also played a part.

If globalization is often described in terms of flow—of capital, ideas, commodities, and people—it may equally be expressed through forms of resistance. Artists may respond to either dimension. As with responses to the marketplace, apparently opposite dimensions may be found in the same work, highlighting the difficulty of passing absolute judgment. What I do in this chapter is point to some of the ways in which these dimensions are articulated—how the mobilizing force of globalization has both enabled and inspired a range of musical responses.

TOWARD A GLOBAL MUSIC: THE SILK ROAD PROJECT

When considering expressions of globalization in music, it may be better to turn to ensembles rather than festivals. For the reasons suggested above, ensembles—around which repertories, instruments, and personnel can be gathered and developed, in which a sense of global mobility can be projected through international tours, and for which financial support and prestige can be built up over time—may be better able to express globalization as a flow of ideas and people through space and time.

The signal example is the Silk Road Ensemble, founded in 2000 by the internationally famous Chinese-American cellist Yo-Yo Ma. With Ma as its chief advocate, the Silk Road Ensemble is capable of attracting substantial levels of capital, interest, and prestige. In large part, this is due to Ma's superstar status, but there is also a correlation with the group's commitment to a globalized, multicultural vision that operates outside of the usual channels of new music. The Silk Road Ensemble's mash-up of global musical styles is an example of the sort of cross-genre permissiveness discussed in chapter 3, and its more instrumental angle attracts investment that more conventional, "abstract" compositional approaches cannot.

The ensemble is part of the larger Silk Road Project, founded in 1998 to "promote innovation and learning through the arts."[5] At the heart of the concept is the network of ancient trading routes from India and China to Europe—one of the earliest instances of globalization—which acts as "a modern metaphor for sharing and learning across cultures, art forms and disciplines."[6] Described as "an imagination platform," the project aims to encourage dialogue between artists, educators, and entrepreneurs. It has been affiliated with several higher education institutes in the United States, including Stanford University, the Rhode Island School of Design, and, since 2005, Harvard University (Ma himself is a Harvard graduate). The project has also organized educational programs in public schools in New York City and Chicago.

FIGURE 20. The Silk Road Ensemble with Yo-Yo Ma, Mondavi Center, University of California, Davis, 2011. Photo by Max Whittaker.

The Silk Road Ensemble is a variable collective of around sixty musicians, artists, and storytellers. They come from more than twenty countries, many of which are along the Silk Road itself. They bring to the ensemble the instruments and traditions of their countries—from the gaita bagpipes of Galicia, played by Cristina Pato, to the Japanese shakuhachi, played by Kojiro Umezaki, to the many other instruments and musical styles of southeastern Europe, Central Asia, North Africa, India, and China.

The composers involved with the group are similarly diverse in origin. The Silk Road Ensemble has commissioned more than eighty original works and arrangements, most of them from composers with backgrounds outside the conventional Western repertory. They include figures like the Azerbaijani Franghiz Ali-Zadeh (b. 1947), the Argentine Osvaldo Golijov (b. 1960), and the American Vijay Iyer (b. 1971), all of whom are well known as Western art music composers. However, many other composers are little known in that music context, like the Lebanese Rabih Abou-Khalil (b. 1957), the Tajik-Uzbek Alisher Latif-Zade (b. 1962), and the Mongolian Byambasuren Sharav (b. 1952).

Silk Road Ensemble concerts blend Western and non-Western, art and vernacular (see figure 20). Some musicians sit while others stand. Some dress relatively formally; others are in shirtsleeves and open collars. Still others (such as some of those playing non-Western instruments) wear traditional national dress.

The instruments themselves are a similar blend, including both Western and non-Western art instruments, such as cello and Iranian kamāncheh, as well as instruments that cross several traditions, such as double bass, violin/fiddle, and a range of percussion. The same variety carries over into the music, which, beyond the sound of the instruments themselves, combines Western elements of harmony and counterpoint with non-Western traditional improvisational styles, melodic ornamentations, rhythms, tunings. Through careful arrangement, in which the characters of individual performers and their instruments each speak as well as blend into the Silk Road Ensemble (which is more like a jazz group than an orchestra in how it operates as a blend of individuals rather than a corporate entity), the effect is an ever-changing melange of voices and perspectives.

The ethos of the Silk Road Project (with the Silk Road Ensemble as its most tangible manifestation) is built on the principles of cultural exchange, learning, and understanding. As Ma explains it, the cultural fragmentation and difference that has been our experience of the world since the 1980s can be resolved through the sharing and passing on of knowledge. Ma argues that by listening and altering our perspectives—on the tuning of a scale or the timing of a rhythm—we can open ourselves to other cultures.[7] Ma's model is transparency, in which progress is achieved through the acquisition of knowledge and understanding within a collaborative creative process. It therefore fits well with the liberal values of a Western university like Harvard.

However, true cultural exchange is extremely rare. More common are forms of "transculturation," which express various symmetrical and asymmetrical power relations. Yet even these are not easy to identify and may be complicated "by the various forms power can take, from economic capital to military might to cultural capital."[8] In the case of the Silk Road Ensemble, one might identify the cultural capital and financial support of Harvard University, the cultural and social capital of Yo Yo Ma, and the hegemonic influence of Western classical music on one side of the equation. However, this must be countered by the influence of the non-Western members of the group—willing participants—who wield power in the form of the diversity, cultural legitimacy, and unique knowledge that they bring to the project. The effect of that power is reflected, for example, in how the Western musicians in the Silk Road Ensemble have had to learn new systems of tuning and rhythm that are outside their training. Then there are the different ways in which members of the group appear on stage and their musical contributions are integrated. Is Ma—a Chinese-American playing a European instrument made in eighteenth-century Italy and wearing generic twenty-first-century clothes—allowed to be less essentialized and more culturally malleable than the Silk Road Ensemble's kamāncheh or pipa players (Kayhan Kalhor and Wu Man, respectively), who appear in traditional costumes that signify particular geographically and historically bounded cultures? Or is it they who exercise a more powerful agency because they, by virtue of their outsiderness, bend the Western musicians' sound toward their own instruments? These are the sorts of questions that watching the Silk Road Ensemble raises. No straightforward answers are given; but that in fact is part of the point.

The music of the Silk Road Ensemble retains many elements of the "classical" Western ethos. Concerts are still given as formal affairs (the Silk Road Ensemble's more informal outreach projects notwithstanding), composers are credited, music is learned from scores, the principles of musical literacy (rather than aural transmission) remain, and so on. Yet in many other respects it isn't "classical" at all. There are many differences in the way that the music is created (with a heavy reliance on arrangements of traditional melodies over original compositions) and performed (with the more vernacular ethos of individual performers working together and expressing themselves as such rather than giving themselves over to the autonomous demands of the composer's intentions). The unique lineup of the Silk Road Ensemble, featuring as it does a range of instruments and vocal styles from non-Western traditions, drives the need for new works and arrangements. It is a very active commissioning body. The fact that the music is composed for and performed exclusively by a closed circle of named musicians rather than, as in the Western classical tradition, composed for generic ensembles or performers is another important distinction. Likewise, very few opportunities exist for the Silk Road Ensemble's commissioned works to be performed by groups other than the Silk Road Ensemble itself. It and its repertory exist in an almost exclusive symbiotic relationship, which raises the question, to what extent are its activities really promulgating a new kind of musical creativity as opposed to assuring the continuation of a particular "brand"?

The Silk Road Project is exceptional, but it is not unique. Similar groups include Amsterdam's Atlas Ensemble (founded in 2002) and the Vancouver Inter-Cultural Orchestra (founded in 2000). Other groups, like the Orquesta Experimental de Instrumentos Nativos (founded in 1980) from Bolivia and the Forbidden City Chamber Orchestra (founded in 2008) from China, use only traditional local instruments to perform compositions such as *Estratos* (1999), by Tato Taborda (b. 1960), and *Whispers of a Gentle Wind* (2011), by Guoping Jia (b. 1963). Earlier examples would include the Ensemble Nipponia (Nippon Ongaku Shūdan), formed in 1964, which performed traditional and contemporary work written for traditional instruments, and World Band, a gathering of Western and non-Western musicians formed at Wesleyan University by Richard Teitelbaum in 1970.

Ensembles like these, and the composers who work with them, challenge the definition of "Western" in Western art music. Yet in many other instances that line remains, and composers from around the world cross it in order to learn, develop, and produce work within unmistakably Western frameworks and idioms. Bright Sheng, discussed in chapter 1, is just one example. Yo-Yo Ma's father, Hiao-Tsiun

Ma, is another: he was a violinist and professor of music in Nanjing, China before moving to Paris, where Yo-Yo Ma was born, and then New York. The border between what we might and might not call Western art music may be more porous and mobile than it once was, but it is nevertheless intact.

There are several reasons for this. Western art forms often attract the highest levels of prestige. This is particularly the case in music, although the precise reasons for this may vary. The first Western musical bodies present in China, Japan, and Korea, for example (starting in the mid-nineteenth century), were military bands. As a result, Western music became associated with values such as strength, discipline, and modernity; this, rather than aesthetics, was what drove early adoptions of Western music.[9] Western art music was seen as an important signifier of modernity, and so "both Western imperialism and the pursuit of Western modernity shaped the development of Western-style music in East Asia."[10] In the early decades of the twentieth century, this led to the establishment of classical music conservatories: Korea's first higher education music department was founded at the Ehwa Women's College (later University) in 1910; China opened its first conservatory in 1927 in Shanghai. In the second half of the century, as state influence on culture diminished in all three countries (after World War II in Japan, after the Korean War in Korea, and after the Cultural Revolution in China), Western music became central to middle-class life.[11] Eventually, beginning around 1959, when the Japanese conductor Seiji Ozawa won the important International Competition of Orchestral Conductors in Besançon, France, the flow of influence between East and West began to move in both directions.[12]

In the Arab Middle East, where the legacy of European colonization remains toxic and violent, Western music does not carry a similar prestige value. (The reverse is the case in Israel, where there is a significant concert music scene on the European model.) However, the music of the Western avant garde is nevertheless admired and its styles and techniques absorbed—to the extent that musicians are criticized by Western commentators for not sounding "Arab enough"—that is, not using Arab instruments, tunings, or other principles. The Lebanese composer and pianist Joelle Khoury (b. 1963) describes the psychological burden of this: "Do we succumb to voyeurism and accept to become a 'vitrine' to the West? Do we play it safe and stagnate into repetitions of the same by sticking to the old? The problem is we need the West since they are the main funders of our works. It is very tricky to remain true to oneself and yet please."[13]

Many Arab musicians have an almost "patriotic" desire to get away from Western stereotypes of Arab music and culture: the clichéd tropes of Orientalism, war, and terrorism. This rejection of traditional music by many Arabic composers is partly due to a frustration with the "endless repetitions, the circling round specific notes," of that music, which some compare to the ineffectuality of Arab politics after the creation of the State of Israel in 1948 and the defeat of Egypt, Jordan, and Syria

FIGURE 21. Tarek Atoui performing in Lebanon, 2010. Photo by Tanya Traboulsi.

in the Arab-Israeli war of 1967.[14] To counter this perceived torpor, many Arab musicians looked to the West in search of a form of modernity. At the same time, the education system in many Arab countries has been based on Western methods (and hence Western values and terms of reference); this remains the case in countries like Saudi Arabia, which seek to modernize their higher educational establishments by importing teaching staff from Europe and North America. The result is a younger generation of musicians who have grown up looking west for a number of complex reasons.

One of these musicians is the Lebanese electroacoustic composer and improviser Tarek Atoui (b. 1980). Born five years into the Lebanese Civil War (1975–90), Atoui left his home country for Paris in 1998. He returned, briefly, to Beirut in 2005, having heard good reports about the quality of the experimental music scene that Mazen Kerbaj, Sharif Sehnaoui, and others were establishing there. He went back again in 2006, this time for a longer period, and was still there when war broke out with Israel that year.

Atoui's own music is deeply embedded in the aesthetics and techniques of the West. His music is sample-based, but he performs it with the physicality of a rock guitarist, using self-built switches and motion detectors to trigger and control the parameters of every sound (see figure 21). As captured in his major work of the late 2000s, *Un-drum* (2009–10), the samples he uses are drawn from a wide range of sources, including field recordings, speech, noise, electronica beats, European art music, and American and British pop and jazz. Yet, like many of his colleagues, for a long time Atoui avoided Arabic influences in his work. Although he began an involvement with the United Arab Emirate's Sharjah Art Foundation in 2008, it was not until 2011, and the collaborative piece *Visiting Tarab*, that Arabic elements began to appear in his work.

Visiting Tarab was a joint commission of the Sharjah Art Foundation and the 2011 Performa biennial in New York. Atoui invited sixteen international musicians, all of them known for working with samples, to investigate with him the collection of historical recordings of Arabic music held by the Lebanese lawyer and musician Kamal Kassar. Kassar's collection, perhaps the largest of its kind, contains many thousands of recordings in all formats, dating back to 1903. After spending time with the collection, each musician took their chosen samples away to work on individual compositions that Atoui then presented and interspersed with his own improvisations. The attraction for Atoui was the opportunity to educate both himself and people from outside Lebanon: "Even though I am from this culture and this region, I knew as little as they did."[15] Atoui revisited this transnational approach, very much in the spirit of the art biennales at which he regularly plays, in *Dahlem Sessions* (2014) for the eighth Berlin Biennale. Again the inspiration was a collection of recordings, in this case the Hornbostel collection of ethnographic wax cylinder recordings held at the Staatliche Museen zu Berlin in Dahlem. The original plan was to use these in a similar way to how he used samples in creating *Visiting Tarab*, but instead Atoui discovered the museum's huge collection of traditional instruments from around the world and decided to use them, attracted by the possibilities they held for interacting with remote cultures: "Playing them today requires reinventing their history, identity, and sound."[16] As with *Visiting Tarab*, he invited a range of collaborators to participate, and he recorded and incorporated their improvisations on these instruments into the final work. In the performances at the biennale itself, Atoui was joined by other live musicians. In these later works, Atoui developed his deployment of samples, staged physically through his interactions with his equipment, into a practice of curating that channels the same energies of borderless exchange explored in his earlier works but now on the level of players and their performances.

There are also practical reasons for the West's influence. One is the flow of money, suggested in the quotation from Joelle Khoury, above. Significant pools of financial support are available to international students to study in Europe and the United States through grants and scholarships provided by bodies such as the Deutscher Akademischer Austauschdienst (DAAD) in Germany or the Fulbright Foreign Student Program in the United States. These can be very generous. Among the schemes funded by the DAAD, for example, is its Berlin Artists-in-Residence program. This awards around twenty scholarships per year to internationally established artists and musicians. The award lasts for a year and includes a monthly stipend for rent, living expenses, travel (including for spouse and children, if required), health insurance, and German language tuition. The International Scholarship Programme at the Akademie Schloss Solitude, another DAAD scheme, is a twelve-month residential grant awarded to up to seventy young musicians or artists (under thirty-five years old). It includes a furnished apartment at Schloss Solitude (an eighteenth-century summer palace near Stuttgart, built by Duke Karl Eugen of Württemberg), €1,000 per month for expenses, a maintenance allowance for two households, project funding, some travel expenses, and a contribution toward health insurance.

Producing new music also frequently requires expensive and rare resources, such as acoustically appropriate performing spaces, electronic music studios, and a corpus of highly skilled vocalists and instrumentalists. This, along with historical reputation, helps account for the continuing gravitational pull of institutions like IRCAM in Paris, Harvard and Stanford University, and the Freiburg Hochschule für Musik: these are places with unique resources in terms of knowledge, skills, and equipment. Examples of their international alumni are numerous, and it is unusual to encounter an early career composer who does not have some connection with at least one of these teaching centers. Nevertheless, the significance of these institutions is gradually being diminished as more centers of excellence appear around the world.

INSTITUTIONS AND THE FLOW OF CULTURE

If the global flow of art is performed by finance and driven by itinerant festivals that serve as marketplaces (often literally so) for the spectatorship, consumption, and purchase of objects, the global flow of music is chiefly performed by individuals (musicians themselves) and driven by the magnetic attraction of the established teaching, research, and performing institutions. Despite the growth in importance of institutions in East Asia and South America, the historical weight of the European and North American institutions still characterizes the predominant types of flow—from non-West to West rather than the other way around—that we see in the globalization of new music.

One of the most successful composers to have followed the flow from East to West is the South Korean–born German resident Unsuk Chin (b. 1961). Before leaving Korea, Chin had some success in her early twenties while at Seoul National University, where she studied with Sukhi Kang (b. 1934). In 1985 her graduation piece, *Spektra* for three cellos, won first prize in the Gaudeamus International Composers Award in Amsterdam, an important international showcase for young composers. In the same year, she moved to Germany, supported by a DAAD scholarship, and took lessons with György Ligeti (1923–2006) at the Hochschule für Musik und

Theater in Hamburg. At that time Ligeti was firmly established as Europe's most visible and respected member of the postwar avant garde. He was a difficult teacher—Chin has said his disciplinarian style effectively silenced her for three years—but he proved to be a lasting influence. Chin's first opera, *Alice in Wonderland* (2007), visits a story Ligeti had long considered for treatment (but never really began); like Ligeti, she composed a series of piano *Etudes* (1995–2003); and her first significant work composed in the West, *Akrostichon-Wortspiel* (1991–3), also draws on Lewis Carroll for its text, as well as on Ligeti's taste for rhythmic patterning and surreal juxtapositions.

A striking feature of Chin's music is how "Western" it sounds. She rarely uses or even evokes East Asian instruments,[17] and her compositional models are largely those of European late modernism, as well as remnants of and occasional allusions to functional major-minor harmony. When a composer is from Korea, the temptation is to overstate the importance of "Koreanness" to their aesthetic, but this is to apply a too black-and-white view of what does and does not constitute a "non-Western" background. Chin herself disavows any stereotypically Asian elements in her work.[18] She describes the conventional orchestra as a European relic of the nineteenth century and uses her non-Western experience to introduce changes of instrumental color, but it is the nineteenth-centuriness of the orchestra, as much as its Europeanness, that is at issue here. In this, her objections are shared by many Western composers. In any case, as the cultural historian Mari Yoshihara points out, it is not possible to make assumptions about what the authentic voice of an East Asian composer might consist of:

> For Asian composers whose cultural and musical identities might be at once deeply Western and Asian, the question of what their authentic voice is and how to represent it with the tools of Western music is highly complicated. Many Asian composers feel that their musical sensibilities are indeed deeply Asian; however, what they mean by the "Asian" musical sensibilities is quite different from recognizably Asian sounds that permeate the popular media.... It is impossible to distinguish which elements of a composition—its Western musical language, Asian sensibility, or multi-genre influences of much of contemporary music—are the most authentic voices of the composer, as it is the very product of those mixtures that becomes his or her individual voice.[19]

In many respects, Chin's upbringing was very European. Her father was a Presbyterian minister, and her dreams of becoming a concert pianist were fostered by her playing hymns at the piano in church, which steeped her in Western triadic harmonies. As a teenager, her musical loves were the symphonies of Tchaikovsky and Beethoven.[20] It was while she was an undergraduate in Seoul that she became aware of the European postwar avant garde and had the idea to study with Ligeti.

Chin's path is not unusual—other Korean composers to have studied and worked in Europe and North America include Isang Yun (1917–95) and Younghi

Pagh-Paan (b. 1945). Yet the experiences of these composers were of a globalization compromised by dictatorship at home. Yun studied in Paris and Berlin, but in 1967 he was kidnapped by the South Korean secret service, charged as a communist, and imprisoned. He was released in 1969 (following an international petition signed by two hundred leading musicians) and returned to live in Berlin. Pagh-Paan traveled to Germany in 1974 on a DAAD scholarship to study at the Hochschule für Musik in Freiburg with Klaus Huber and Brian Ferneyhough. In political exile from the dictatorship of Park Chung Hee, she remained in Germany after completing her studies and went on to teach in Graz, Karlsruhe, and Bremen. Her music has featured a strong political thread, which is related to her personal engagement with a Korean tradition that she could no longer access. Her early works were directly connected to the pro-democracy movement in South Korea: *Sori* (Sound, 1979–80), for orchestra, for example, is dedicated to the memory of demonstrators killed in the Gwangju Uprising of May 1980. After democracy was restored in 1987, her attention turned to a more global perspective on political self-determination while she produced the *Ta-Ryong* series of pieces (1987–99).

Chin's experience was different in that her move to the West was made and sustained without political interference. Chin is a member of the so-called 386 generation: those Koreans who were in their thirties around the time of democratization (the "3" in 368), went to college in the 1980s (the "8"), and were born in the 1960s (the "6"). This is the generation that was most prominent in fighting for and winning democracy in South Korea, and although Chin left the country two years before the first direct presidential elections were held, she benefited from the swift acceptance of Korea into the global political, cultural, and economic system.

Chin's easy transculturalism is perhaps best heard in her 2005 work for two sopranos, countertenor, and ensemble, *Cantatrix sopranica*. Exemplifying the sort of transnational financial cooperation that lies behind many major contemporary works, it was a joint commission by the London Sinfonietta (United Kingdom), the Los Angeles Philharmonic New Music Group (United States), the St. Pölten Festival (Austria), the Ensemble Intercontemporain (France), and Musikfabrik (Germany). Its title comes from a work at the heart of the European literary avant garde, a satiric scientific text by the French author Georges Perec entitled *Experimental Demonstration of the Tomatotopic Organization in the Soprano (Cantatrix sopranica L.)* (1980), which purports to detail the "yelling reaction" produced by throwing large numbers of tomatoes (up to nine per second) at 107 soprano singers under controlled experimental conditions.

Chin's piece sets out from this comic premise to create an "intercultural parody of singing,"[21] a multifaceted exploration of the sound and theater of singing in many different contexts. Its eight movements range from warming up exercises, to pastiches of Baroque opera and Chinese folksong, to mainstream Western contemporary music. Each movement prescribes a different vocal style, such as "childlike" (second movement), "as soft as possible" (fourth movement), and "natural, untrained" (seventh movement). Elements of musical theater are also required, including the use of "theatrical effects or mime gestures" (fifth movement), vocal and facial imitations of Chinese folk singers (sixth movement), and "frozen mime" and "humming with an open mouth as if singing casually for oneself" (seventh movement).

The music suggests an easy postmodern attitude to its sources. Those juxtapositions and contrasts are used to amusing, self-referential effect. The status of the contemporary vocalist is gently mocked, as in Perec's treatise, but Chin appears to be making no deeper point than this. Even the pastiche of a Chinese folksong in the sixth movement, Yuè Guang (Clair de lune)—while set to some of the work's most affecting music—is just another element, on the same plane as the Baroque pastiche in the movement before. The absurdist joke that ends this movement— the two sopranos transforming their "Chinese" intonation into a goat's bleat— indicates the post-racial, post-ideological nature of Chin's borrowings.

For others, the allure of the West is related to the acquisition of cultural and educational capital that cannot be gained at home. Many composers from non-Western countries travel to the West to complete their education, sometimes on the sorts of grants described above, before returning to their home countries. Again, these movements are related to Western-oriented geopolitics. In Syria, for example, the years between the beginning of the Bashar al-Assad era in 2000 and the outbreak of civil war in 2011 saw the emergence of a contemporary Syrian art music. The Higher Institute for Music and Dance was founded in Damascus in 1990 by the conductor, composer, and educator Solhi al-Wadi; a year later, he also founded the Syrian National Symphony Orchestra. The institute became a locus for the study of Western art music for a new generation of Syrian composers— among them Shafi Badreddin (b. 1972), Zaid Jabri (b. 1975), and Hassan Taha (b. 1968)—who would go on to pursue further studies in the West, building up stores of contacts and opportunities as they did so.[22]

The important electroacoustic music scene in South America has been built up through a greater degree of two-way exchange. Some composers—such as the Argentineans Edgardo Cantón (b. 1934), Mario Davidovsky (b. 1934), and Hilda Dianda (b. 1925)—did make early journeys to Europe and the United States. Yet composers in Argentina, Brazil, Chile, and Cuba had in fact begun working with electroacoustic means and devising electronic instruments before such visits. Mauricio Kagel's (1931–2008) first experiments in electroacoustic music date from the early 1950s, before he traveled to Germany in 1957 to work with Stockhausen in Cologne, and the Cuban composer Juan Blanco (1919–2008) registered the design for an electronic organ-type instrument using loops of magnetized wire as early as 1942.[23] Today, the institutional structures around electroacoustic music in Latin America emphasize transnational exchanges of resources, knowledge, and ideas. Argentina's most important studio is the Laboratorio de Investigación y Producción Musical (LIPM) in Buenos Aires. The present-day continuation of the Estudio de Fonología Musical of the University of Buenos Aires (founded in 1958) and the Centro Latinoamericano de Altos Estudios Musicales (founded in 1962 by Alberto Ginastera, 1916–83), LIPM is part-funded by the Rockefeller Foundation and has close ties to the Center for Computer Research in Music and Acoustics at Stanford University and the former Center for Research in Computing and the Arts at the University of California, San Diego. PANorama in São Paolo, Brazil (founded in 1994 by the composer Flo Menezes, b. 1962), has links with several European studios, including IRCAM and the Groupes de Recherches Musicales in France, the former WDR studio in Cologne, and BEAST (Birmingham Electroacoustic Sound Theatre) in the United Kingdom. Since 1996, it has organized the International Biennial for Electroacoustic Music of São Paolo, a globally significant festival of electroacoustic music. Another important festival is Primavera en La Habana, in Cuba, organized by the Laboratorio Nacional de Música Electroacústica in Havana. Both feature a wide range of national and international composers and works.

Transactions and movements like these have helped create what we might call a global new-music hegemony. That is, certain aspects of late modernist style have become vectors of Western high cultural influence, taking the place that tonality had in the nineteenth and early twentieth centuries. However, the story is somewhat different from that of the spread of tonality. For one thing, these aspects do not penetrate into the sphere of popular culture in the same way that tonality, equal temperament, or instruments like the piano or guitar have. In that sense, then, whatever force they might have as carriers of Western influence or soft power remains circumscribed within that instinctively self-critical and self-aware high cultural sphere. However, many of the techniques, materials, and precepts of the late twentieth-century Western avant garde are flexible and nonsituated enough to transcend cultural signification. Noise is noise. Silence is silence. A digital workstation is culturally neutral, whereas an orchestra is not. The flexible, fluid, non-ideological, pragmatic, postmodern techniques of the late twentieth century can serve as corridors for contact and collaboration rather than instruments of domination and suppression.

EMBODIMENT

As publication, performance, and recording rights have dwindled as stable sources of income, short-term grants, residencies, and scholarships have grown in importance within the economy of new music. As in the visual arts, this has encouraged a form of nomadism, in which composers—particularly those unwilling or unable to take up a full-time academic position—live from commission to commission. Whereas artists in this situation find themselves composing for particular sites,[24] composers will find themselves composing for particular players or groups of players.

The rise of the performer as a "site" is a product of several late-century forces: the increasing autonomy of new music ensembles and their need to establish unique "brands" for themselves constructed from the repertoire that they curate; the mobility of the artist as freelancer; the legitimacy that performer collaboration suggests (a seductive riposte to the stereotype of the modernist in the ivory tower); and a more general turn across the arts toward an interest in site, collaboration, and process as practice.

In this way, the global flow of music and culture may be expressed through the bodies of musicians and artists. As the performance of new music has become an increasingly specialized skill—in some instances requiring a dedication to practice and the acquisition of novel techniques to the exclusion of almost all else—those performers who have taken the time to master this skill have become vectors in the global transmission of that music.[25] The Silk Road Ensemble is a good example. Its performers are not only drawn from all parts of the world, in support of the its multicultural aesthetic, but they are also masters of their instruments, with highly specialized skills: ways of moving, touching, and holding. In this manner, their national culture is embodied within them. Furthermore, each brings to the Silk Road Ensemble their own personal histories of interactions with other members of the group, creating a unique repository of understanding. Rather like Miles Davis bringing together different groups at various stages of his career, the Silk Road Ensemble is defined not so much by its instrumentarium but by the specific individuals playing within it.

This model has increasingly shaped the creation of contemporary music ensembles. Consider John Zorn's Naked City group, introduced in chapter 3. Naked City depended on the combined skills of its members to play Zorn's radically disjunctive scores—this was not music that others could easily take up. Zorn's role as composer therefore extended not only to the production of scores but also to the curation of the group. In improvisational contexts like Naked City, the embodied relationship between music and performer is especially important, as performers bring sets of skills and techniques that they have developed in a highly personalized fashion and that function as part of their personal "brand." For vocal performers, these techniques are even more personal, coming as they do directly from the performers' physiology. Musical collaboration involves combining these competing embodiments, using strategies of synthesis or juxtaposition that are more or less fluid or rigid.

The Composer-Performer

The composer, performer, and electronic musician Pamela Z (b. 1956) is in many ways a quintessentially twenty-first-century musical artist. A direct artistic

FIGURE 22. Pamela Z performing at Ars Electronica 2008, Linz, Austria. Photo by rubra, courtesy of Ars Electronica.

descendent of other female composer/performance artists, like Laurie Anderson (b. 1947) and Meredith Monk (b. 1942), Z works within a form of music making and structure of artistic creation and ownership that didn't exist (within Western art music anyway) before the late 1970s.

Technology, particularly digital technology, is central to her work. In the early 1980s, she began using digital delays after hearing pieces by the bassist Jaco Pastorius, and, in conjunction with her voice, they have since become her signature instrument. While digital delay and live looping have since become commonplace, Z was a pioneer of the techniques. Her musical language is built on the rhythms and melodies of speech, on looping and layering effects, on repetition, and on the tension between recorded sound and live sound. A synthesis of African American vernacular forms and white classical styles, it is also indebted to musical innovations of the 1960s and '70s by Terry Riley, Steve Reich, Alvin Lucier, and others.

In the mid-1990s, Z added to her setup the BodySynth, a musical control system developed in 1994 by Chris Van Raalte and Ed Severinghaus (see figure 22). A system of electrodes attached to the body, rather like an electrocardiograph, it detects muscle movements and translates them, via computer, into musical parameters. This means that Z can perform without having to sit behind a laptop or keyboard, allowing her to make movement and gesture as much a part of her work as sound. Combined with the duplicating selves of her digital loops, it serves as a prosthetic extension by which the movements of her body and the sounds of her voice are reshaped and reformed across several musical dimensions.

The subject of mobility is often explicit in the titles of Z's works. *Parts of Speech* (1995), *Voci* (2003), *Baggage Allowance* (2010), and, in particular, *Gaijin* (2001) all point toward topics of travel, language, foreignness, and negotiation with a foreign culture. *Gaijin* is Japanese slang for foreigner, applicable to anyone who doesn't look Japanese. Regardless of how assimilated one might be into Japanese culture—learning the language and customs, making a home, even starting a family in Japan—a non-Japanese person will always be *gaijin,* on the basis of appearance alone. The African-American Z felt this foreignness acutely while on a residency in Tokyo in 1999, and she explores this experience in the series of short pieces that make up *Gaijin.* One of them, "Nihongo de Hana soo" (Let's speak Japanese), which takes its title from a language textbook, illustrates the borders created by language. Against a dense, disorienting, and insistently repetitive background of Japanese phonemes and nonverbal vocal loops, Z reads from a textbook some of the things that are difficult to do in a language not your own: apologizing for being late, asking for directions, giving and receiving gifts, and so on. Other movements feature an application for a green card and texts in multiple languages about identity and alienation. Throughout the piece, the key is the *gaijin*'s awareness of her fundamental outsiderness and her attempts to mitigate this.

The mobility—reflected in an itinerary of performances, festivals, and educational institutions—that Z and other nomadic artists, such as Tarek Atoui, are able to exercise is a marker of privilege and an important source of cultural capital. It provides the opportunity to present one's work to a greater international audience, and it enables interactions with musical and artistic traditions outside one's own. However, the ability to access and participate in this flow is unequally distributed, as the ethnomusicologist Thomas Burkhalter points out: "Sounds and sound formations may travel worldwide, but for the musicians, national and political borders are still binding."[26] It has become increasingly difficult for Arab musicians like Atoui to obtain visas to perform in Europe and the United States, for example.

Mobility also affects financial capital.[27] Western art music, exemplified by the notated, copyrighted score and realized in music of formal complexity and specificity, is traditionally an economy based on property rights and commodifiable works. It is opposed, however, by an economy of music based on performance, presence, and experience, exemplified by the mobile composer-performer. Moreover, the focus of Z's music on patterns of rhythm, cuts, and repetitions connects it to a wider Afro-diasporic music that encompasses jazz, dub, and hip-hop.[28] Through the digital delays that loop and layer her own voice and her virtuoso changes between vocal styles (a particular feature of *Voci*), she presents identity as a matter of polyphony, sometimes between irreconcilable parts. The emphasis on storytelling over object creation—*how* the story is told, through style, flow, and characterization, rather than *what* the story is—in Z's music and in the recent curated works by Atoui connects these two artists with this alternative economy.[29]

The Specialist Performer

Despite these examples, music can also be embodied by a performer working wholly from a score composed by someone else. However, although notation has a semblance of universality, notated works are not in fact equally transferrable between players. Some scores, particularly those of an especially complex nature, require an investment of time to learn that few players are able or willing to make. In cases like these, knowledge of the work, acquired through hours of patient rehearsal and study, become embodied in the muscle memory of a small and self-selecting group of practitioners, like the patterns and forms of kung fu or tai chi.

From its formation in 1986, by guitarist Daryl Buckley and other students and former students of the Victoria College of Arts in Melbourne, the ELISION Ensemble, introduced in chapter 2, set out to perform radical and innovative Australian composition and to introduce works of the European avant garde to Australian audiences. At that time, in the late 1980s, it was something of an anomaly; there were practically no other Australian musicians performing such a repertory. A postcolonial inferiority complex in official Australian arts culture fostered a widely held belief that Australian new music was not up to much and that those with any talent would leave for Europe as soon as possible. Nevertheless, ELISION fit well with Australia's underground and experimental culture, which is marked by resistance to the official view and a desire to take personal ownership of the arts. The group was formed to challenge official negativity and foster an Australian new music scene of an international standard. By the early 1990s, it was already beginning to meet this goal, establishing a unique profile for itself not only in Australia but also internationally. This profile might be described across four dimensions: an openness to innovative forms of music making and presentation, including site-specific work, group improvisation, and collaborations with installation artists (as already seen in chapter 2); a unique and flexible instrumentarium that includes both Western and non-Western instruments; a commitment to artistic realization of the most technically uncompromising repertory; and close and extended collaboration with composers.

Any of these dimensions may be replicated by other ensembles, of course, and none of them is unique to ELISION. Ensemble Musikfabrik (founded in 1990), for example, has forged extended working relationships with composers such as Rebecca Saunders (b. 1967). It has also worked with installation artists and employed improvisation in some of its work. Ensemble SurPlus (founded in 1992) and Ensemble Exposé (founded in 1984), meanwhile, have also devoted themselves to the virtuoso end of the new music spectrum. Yet the four dimensions together define ELISION's operational territory and its particular, unrepeatable qualities.

The question of instrumentation is the most obvious. ELISION's regular lineup includes not only the usual strings, wind, brass, and percussion but also an electric guitar (played by Buckley), koto, vocalists, recorder, harp, and saxophone. This automatically encourages the creation of an almost unique repertory, since most other ensembles will find it hard to gather the same spread of musicians. An extreme example of works like this that have been written for the group is Richard Barrett's *world-line* (2012–14), written for a quartet of trumpet/quartertone flugelhorn, percussion, electronics, and an electric lap steel guitar custom-made by the lap steel guitar maker David Porthouse. In this case, particulars of the instrument and the evolution of its design—the tuning of its strings, the pitch benders on three of its strings, and the overall ergonomics of the new instrument—became part of the compositional process.

Related to instrumentation are personnel. Many of ELISION's past and present members, including cellist Séverine Ballon, percussionist Peter Neville, saxophonist Timothy O'Dwyer, and soprano Deborah Kayser, are more than just virtuosos on their instruments; they are possessed of unique and distinctive skill sets and musical personalities. Each player feeds directly into the music that the group creates. This enables fluid shifts between notated and semi-notated or fully improvised music and also helps foster a collective commitment to an extremely difficult repertory—another dimension of ELISION's profile.

The final dimension is ELISION's habit of working closely with composers over extended periods, often developing not just one work in collaboration but a series of works. The group's association with Barrett began in 1988. Buckley was given a tape by a friend of a performance of Barrett's *Coïgitum* (1983–5), for mezzo-soprano and four instruments, which had been performed at the Darmstadt Summer School for New Music that year. It came with a warning: "Heavy dots. No one will ever play this in Australia." On the lookout for distinctive repertory that would establish ELISION's creative focus, Buckley saw a challenge, and in early 1989 he contacted the composer. Within a year, ELISION commissioned and performed *Another heavenly day* (1990), for electric guitar, E♭ clarinet, and double bass, the first of what would become a long line of collaborative works and the beginning of a three-decade creative partnership.

The piece *world-line* celebrates the team of players that Buckley has put together over the years; it is a gift exchanged between two long-standing friends and colleagues, from composer to performer. In performance, Buckley's guitar holds center stage and is the only instrument to play in every section of the work (with the exception of a short electronics solo in the middle). Barrett, by contrast, is offstage, playing the electronics. Buckley gets a moment with every pairing of instruments, but especially touching are the two duo sections with Neville.

Buckley and Neville are two of the founding members of ELISION, and they have played together all of their professional lives. It is fitting, therefore, that at these two points Barrett steps away from giving instructions as a composer and lets the players engage in a few moments of free improvisation with each other.

Although Barrett's works for ELISION are tailored specifically to the abilities and resources of the ensemble, many do find a wider performance context. In particular, several solo works have been taken up by other musicians. Nevertheless, Barrett sets high barriers for performance, and not only in terms of technical difficulty. Frequently, the works have other dimensions—usually to do with instrumentation or a particular combination of musical skills—that seem designed to restrict their performance to the players for whom they were written. *Interference* (1996–2000) is an obvious example. Composed for solo contrabass clarinet (doubling on a pedal bass drum), its instrumental writing is already difficult on a level that makes it accessible to only a small number of players. But Barrett goes further, requiring the clarinetist to sing, across a four-and-a-half-octave range, no less. That combination of skills reduces the pool of possible performers even more, although it is a good fit for its dedicatee, the Australian clarinetist and vocalist Carl Rosman.[30]

The sheer technical difficulty of these works means that a substantial commitment is necessary just to learn the requisite physical movements. But the nature of embodiment in these pieces goes further than committing notes to muscle memory. An internalization of the work's nascent performing practice is also demanded. That is to say, such a work requires the development of techniques and ways of prioritizing and negotiating layers of musical information that are unique to that piece. In playing one of these works for the first time (and often being the only players who will play it for some time to come), ELISION's musicians are charged with developing a particular performance practice for each new work. The players are therefore mobile—as highly specialized virtuosi, they are in global demand and exemplify the nomadic artist—but the works, paradoxically, are to a large extent site-specific in that they are tied to those bodies.

Works in ELISION's repertoire frequently require players to rethink their relationship to their instrument and even to unlearn much of what they already know about it. The tablature scores of Aaron Cassidy, for example, ask their performers to reconsider their instruments not in terms of what they need to do in order to sound a given pitch or timbre at a given volume but in terms of how they move their fingers and hands, shape their lips, and position their tongue. For a guitarist, notation of this sort is familiar; for an oboist, it is alien territory. The pianist Philip Thomas (not a member of ELISION) notes how he has to rebuild his approach from scratch every time he performs *être-temps* (2002), by Bryn Harrison (b. 1969), a composer who has written for ELISION. This is not because he is not able to get the whole piece "under his fingers," as it were, but precisely because, after many hours of practice, he *is*. The poetics of the work, however, demand a sense that the piece's difficulties are being addressed as though for the first time.[31]

Barrett's music is sometimes described as "ergonomic" because of its detailed, precompositional scrutinization of *how* instruments are played and the way it and the performer's body interact. In contrast to Cassidy, who dissects performance actions to compose with them independently, Barrett considers the overall relationship of the performer's body to their instrument, drawing out its characteristic features. The early cello solo *ne songe plus à fuir* (1985–6) can stand in for Barrett's later practice. Before composing the piece, Barrett reconsidered the cello as "more or less just a resonant box with four strings on it; then, the player has two hands, one of which holds the bow, both of which are able to move in three dimensions."[32] Barrett's practice strips the cello of its associations with the Western musical tradition and, to an extent, delocalizes it, removes it from its geographical specificity, and restores it as a musical object that is as mobile and unencumbered as its performer. This link between performance parameters and identification with tradition is realized more completely in *EARTH* (1987–8), for the unusual duo of trombone and percussion, which attempts "to get towards a kind of folk music, though not one tied down to any particular place in the world."[33]

Both these pieces were composed before Barrett began working with ELISION. Yet that partnership—which enabled him to collaborate closely with players who were all keen to rethink and reinvent the received wisdom about their instruments and what they could (or should) be capable of—has allowed his early investigations to flourish. *CONSTRUCTION* (2003–11) may be the definitive statement on that partnership. Involving sixteen instrumentalists, three singers, electronics, and an eight-channel sound diffusion system, it is made up of twenty sections, comprising a total of two hours of continuous music, and is another example of the concert-length works in which ELISION specializes. For reasons of money alone it seems unlikely to be performed more than a handful of times by ELISION or anyone else.[34] As is the case with Barrett's other work-cycles—*Negatives* (1988–93), *Opening of the Mouth*, and *DARK MATTER*—each section can be performed as separate work in its own right. Five make up a miniature violin concerto (with the title *wound*); five others make up a song cycle that sets (in highly abridged form) Euripedes's *The Trojan Women*. The fifteen-minute *heliocentric* (the sixth section of *CONSTRUCTION*) itself incorporates three duos that can all be performed separately: *Adocentyn* (2005–11), for bass flute and bass recorder; *Hypnerotomachia* (2005–9), for two clarinets in A; and *Aurora* (2005–10), for quartertone flugelhorn and alto trombone.

Appropriately, the theme of *CONSTRUCTION* is utopias; its central inspiration is Vladimir Tatlin's never-built Monument to the Third International, which Barrett describes as "a kind of non-existent monument to all unrealised and unrealisable utopian visions."[35] The overall form of the work is too rich to go into here; I will just focus on the final and longest section, *ON*. Lasting around twenty minutes (although in theory indefinite in length), this is a collective improvisation involving the entire ensemble for the first time during the work. Barrett says of the section: "The way out of all the confrontations which have articulated the previous 100 minutes is to be found by the entire performing ensemble as a collective, and found anew in each performance, each time evolving in a different way from the previous music and—I dare to hope—discovering a new music which couldn't have been brought into being any other way."[36]

This ambitious goal is to be achieved through the collective muscle memory of the performers themselves. Having learned and internalized the music of the preceding nineteen sections, they base their improvisation on those materials, following a timeplan that replicates the proportions of the whole work at a smaller scale, with ten seconds of ON corresponding to one minute of the original. ON may be performed as a separate work—versions of it have been—and it need not involve players who are intimately familiar with the rest of CONSTRUCTION. However, it is also an expression of an extensive working relationship with specific players (some of whom have known Barrett's music for more than twenty years), and it would have been hard to conceive without that already in place.

NETWORKS

Globalization today is almost synonymous with the Internet. The Net has not only enabled globalization's modern-day form but also, in its early days at least, served as its ideological model: it was believed that, thanks to the network, the world would become one of universal access to culture and resources, flat hierarchies, and the smooth flow of information, unimpeded by physical and political boundaries. With the birth of the Internet, networks, personal mobility, and globalization would come together as complimentary forces, and musical works would be able to participate in the global flow as performers.

In fact, concepts of global music predated the net. Sound artists in the 1960s and '70s were already using telephone and radio networks to coordinate and mix musical performances between remote locations. Initially these links were relatively local. *Public Supply I* (1966), by Max Neuhaus (1939–2009), used input from ten telephone lines within the broadcast area of a New York City radio station. The first of the *City-Links* series (1967–81), by Maryanne Amacher (1938–2009), collected the sound environments of eight locations in the Buffalo area, transmitted them by telephone line to a central studio, and then mixed and rebroadcast them as a twenty-eight-hour performance. Later works in the series all utilized telephone or radio connections to transplant the sound of one acoustic space into that of another; in many cases, these remained local spaces.

Ambitions for such works grew, however. In *Radio Net* (1977), Neuhaus expanded the compositional principle of *Public Supply I* to utilize the whole of the

National Public Radio (NPR) network. Input could be phoned in by NPR listeners in five cities (Atlanta, Dallas, Los Angeles, Minneapolis, and New York). Taking advantage of the system of telephone lines used by NPR to connect its two hundred stations across the United States, Neuhaus created five sound-processing loops, one for each of the call-in cities, that stretched across the country, circulating the sounds and then broadcasting them back onto the network. *Nineteen Eighty-Five: A Piece for Peace* (1984), by Alvin Curran (b. 1938), was produced and simultaneously broadcast across Europe on January 1, 1985. It involved three hundred musicians who were divided between three venues in Amsterdam, Frankfurt, and Venice. The three groups' performances were recorded and sent to a central studio in Frankfurt, where they were mixed by Curran. The combined mix was then broadcast back to the participating countries. The three groups could not hear one another while they were playing, but they were directed centrally from Frankfurt. Because of the time delays involved, they were never expected to coordinate rhythmically, but there were points in the work in which "slow moving melodies and tonal chorals . . . like clouds, move through one another."[37] The larger scale conception that technological developments had made possible attracted Curran to a utopian program that is only implicit in the earlier pieces by Amacher and Neuhaus:

> The medium of RADIO offers vast possibilities to a composer: to create and combine sounds in places far beyond the confines of a single concert-hall. One can literally compose with the land, air and sea—uniting sounds from great distances and from totally diverse geographies. My task here is to compose a vast soundscape using all of these elements "al fresco" (live) via satellite radio broadcast, where the medium is not only the message, but a metaphor for human peace.[38]

Despite the technical limitations of these works (*Public Supply I* involved nothing more sophisticated than ten telephone handsets in the radio studio, jerry-rigged with microphones over their earpieces so that the sounds of callers could be picked up by the studio recording equipment), they were ideologically inspired by the concept of perfect communication between people or spaces that were remote from one another. When the Internet seemed to bring those possibilities even closer, that ideology followed into the first experiments in Net art and Net music in the early 1990s.

As musicians began to experiment with the Net itself, however, it became apparent that these hopes were still far from realized. In some cases, it emerged that they were actually unattainable. Much of the development of networked music in the Internet era has concerned ways of addressing those early ideals and working around or coming to terms with their shortcomings. As networked music came up against reality, it became less about exploiting the possibilities of unimpeded flow and more about thematizing the tension between potential (a fully networked utopia) and reality (the limitations of the technology). In other words, as this tension began to manifest in the mid-1990s, the Net changed in status from solely serving as an enabling force to also functioning as an inspiring one.

It didn't take long for the ideal of unimpeded global communication to run up against the realities of bandwidth, buffering speeds, and browser capabilities. Even if we set aside these current limitations, we can't get around physics. If data were to travel at its maximum speed (that is, the speed of light) across a perfect network with unlimited bandwidth, the delay between two opposite points on the globe would still be at least sixty-five milliseconds—more than three times longer than what the human ear perceives as simultaneous.[39] This has a direct impact on music: acceptable synchronization, such as an ensemble might easily achieve on stage, would not be possible between performers so geographically remote. Because such synchronicity is a founding value of most "good" musical performances, it was soon clear that Net music would have to build itself on new foundations. One of the first major compositions for the Net, *Cathedral* (launched in 1997), by William Duckworth (1943–2012) and the media artist Nora Farrell, sidestepped this issue by existing as a multiform work involving an interactive website for single users; a virtual instrument, the PitchWeb; and an offline band of improvisers, the Cathedral Band. This meant that it existed in real/temporal and virtual/nontemporal spaces that only needed to be coordinated on occasions when online Pitch-Web players joined the Cathedral Band in live performances. Even then, the broadly improvisatory context of the Cathedral Band's performances meant that issues of delay and system limitations could be readily absorbed.

Latency—the unavoidable delay of a networked system—is now accepted by Net musicians, who either work around it or incorporate it as a feature of their art. Atau Tanaka is among those who have given most thought to this. Works like *NetOsc* (1999), written for the Sensorband trio of himself, Edwin van der Heide, and Zbigniew Karkowski, play with latency as the Net's "acoustic resonance." John Roach and Willy Whip's *Simultaneous Translator* (2007) uses live data about the lag of router-to-router transactions across the Net to shape certain musical parameters. Of course, by the 1990s, musical innovations in open form, free improvisation acousmatic music, and aleatory, parametrical composition were well enough established for there to be no need for dramatic innovations in musical form or technique. At least the battles that made networked music aesthetically possible had all been fought.

When it comes to considering the web as a flat, nonhierarchical landscape, an important early work is Randall Packer's (b. 1953) *Telemusic #1* (2000), a collaboration with Steve Bradley, Gregory Kuhn, and John Young. One of the principal concerns of the piece was "dissolving the spatial and temporal constraints of the performance environment and transforming the World Wide Web into an unseen ensemble of audience participants."[40] It was performed in two spaces simultaneously: one physical and one in cyberspace. Online, participant-listeners could navigate a 3D Flash environment populated by bits of text. Clicking on a text would trigger an audio sample of those words, which would be processed live and projected or streamed back into the physical and virtual spaces. In the physical space, these texts were spoken aloud. Participant-listeners would then hear a composite of the activities of themselves and everyone else participating in the work. The idea was developed further in *Telemusic #2* (2001), in which each participant-listener's IP address was used to create a unique sonic identifier, making it possible to hear the virtual space as a plurality of individuals rather than an undefined homogeneity.

In Net works like these, art becomes about constructing an environment that the user enters rather than delivering a precisely conceived message.[41] This is analogous to the shift that took place in site-specific art over the same period, from the 1970s to the 2000s, although in music's case it was driven as much by technological expediency as political critique. Packer even predicted "a form of music vision that is no longer dependent on the location of the audience member, or even the location of the performance space."[42] The image is seductive, but given the speed at which technological developments are taking place in other areas, it is notable that it has not yet come to pass. Once more, the potential of Net music is in tension with the reality of it.

Packer's vision rests on the principle of technological sophistication, and therefore privilege. The fact is that engaging in Net art—whether as a participant or as a creator—requires certain advantages that remain far from universal: a good quality computer and high-speed Internet connection (or access to a relatively well-appointed gallery where such a work may be installed), sufficient leisure time, and appropriate physical and intellectual abilities to work whatever interface there may be (interfaces may not be easily accessible by those with certain learning difficulties or restricted mobility, for example). These privileges are related to those surrounding conventional acoustic music composition, discussed above. Some of the barriers to access are lower (a laptop is generally cheaper and more practical than a piano, for example), while others are higher (high-speed Internet connections require infrastructural investment at the national level, whereas acoustic music just needs local players and instruments). As with acoustic music, we are back to a pattern of nodes, and hence dominant languages, aesthetics, and styles, rather than true global heterophony.

OBJECTIONS

Just as networked music has revealed the limits of the global ideal of the Internet, so have other works confronted globalization or cultural interrelations in terms other than synthesis or accommodation. One notorious provocation is *Fremdarbeit*

(Outsourcing, 2009), by Johannes Kreidler. Commissioned by the Klangwerkstatt Berlin contemporary music festival, *Fremdarbeit* performs and makes explicit the financial inequalities and systems of exploitation that still underpin globalization.

To create the work, Kreidler hired a Chinese composer, Xia Non Xiang, and an Indian audio programmer, Ramesh Murraybay. Each was commissioned to create a new piece in Kreidler's style for the ensemble he had been assigned by the festival. The first movement is by Xiang, the second by Murraybay. Xiang agreed to complete his movement for $30, Murraybay for $15; both composers were then asked to collaborate on a third movement for $45. (By way of comparison, Kreidler's fee from the Klangwerkstatt Berlin was €1,500.) Both men were given copies of recent pieces by Kreidler as source materials. According to their instructions, Xiang made a stylistic copy of Kreidler's music, and Murraybay programmed an algorithm that could generate something like the piece of Kreidler's that he received, based on calculations of timbre profile, amount and type of sampled material, volume levels, and so on. Like Kreidler's works discussed in chapter 4, *Fremdarbeit* relies on transcription and translation, although here the "automated" processes are undertaken by hired laborers rather than technology.

In a performance of *Fremdarbeit,* the three movements are framed by a spoken introduction in which Kreidler lays out the precise manner (including the financial exchanges) in which the piece has been created. In a sense, the sound of the work—except the extent to which it may or may not resemble music written by Kreidler himself—is beside the point. The gesture is about the relativity of ownership, creativity, and legitimacy within the global marketplace. When a heckler at the work's first performance complained that "What we're hearing is not your music!" Kreidler responded, deadpan: "Of course it is my music. I bought it. Legally, it is my music—I own the patents."[43]

As a well-funded, white, middle-class German, Kreidler is, of course, acting from a place of considerable privilege himself. For better or for worse, the critique that *Fremdarbeit* proposes should at least be seen from that vantage point. Yet there is more to *Fremdarbeit* than even this. As Martin Iddon observed, no trace of either "Xia Non Xiang" or "Ramesh Murraybay" can be found online; furthermore, neither name is believable in their respective languages.[44] The photographs Kreidler supplies of his supposed collaborators appear to belong to two other people entirely: a physics professor at Stanford University and an engineer based in the Minneapolis–St. Paul area. It may be said, therefore, that the concept of *Fremdarbeit* is not that its music is not what it seems but that the whole production of the piece, including its supporting backstory, is a fiction. "What *Fremdarbeit* makes *visible* is surely not outsourcing and its iniquities," writes Iddon. "These are familiar to any Western audience. What it *does* make visible is the degree to which any musical endeavour is almost unavoidably complicit in some sort of history of exploitation, if not in actual exploitation in the moment of its instantiation."[45] In so doing, however, it is compelled to repeat a colonial discourse through its use of recognizable stereotypes: the plagiarizing Chinese and the computer-coding Indian.

Other composers have approached the premises of Western art music from the outside, as it were. One of these is the Philippine composer Alan Hilario (b. 1967). Like others discussed in this chapter, he benefited from a DAAD scholarship; he used it to study in Freiburg in 1992 with Mathias Spahlinger (b. 1944) and Mesías Maiguashca (b. 1938), an Ecuadorian who settled in Germany after studying with Stockhausen in the late 1960s and becoming part of his circle. Since completing his studies, Hilario has continued to work as a freelance composer, remaining in Germany in order to do so—it being one of the few countries where such a career within a style as rarefied as his is possible. In this respect, he is an excellent example of the globalized composer, whose education, travel, stylistic development, and career have been nurtured by the attractive power of Western money. What makes Hilario stand out is the extent to which he is conscious of his fortune and how he incorporates his non-Western—indeed Third World—experience into his work.

A straightforward example is *katalogos* (1998, rev. 2008), which features an array of percussion instruments drawn from around the world. When those instruments are all seen under the stage lights, as part of an ensemble that also includes English horn, bassoon, French horn, viola, and cello, the question raised is clear: Western music has been considerably enriched by plundering the sounds of the world's musics, but have those benefits been reciprocated? The piece *kibo* (1997), for solo violin or viola, directly stages the concerns of Third World musicians. The instrument in *kibo* has been radically distanced from its Western norm. The first and third strings have been removed entirely; the other two have been tuned down at least two octaves, reducing tension to an extent that they are almost unmanageable. Hilario's inspiration was the street musicians of Manila, who often play with broken strings. Too poor to afford replacement strings, they detune the others to reduce the chance of them breaking too. The piece dramatically presents the relationship between music and money: the poverty of the Manila street musician is reflected in the poverty of sound that *kibo*'s violinist or violist can produce; the music is a catalogue of unpredictable, nonresonating scratches and plucks. The title is a Tagalog word meaning "movement after silence," and the piece ends with the player removing the instrument's bridge entirely, reducing the two remaining strings to almost complete soundlessness, while continuing to saw hopelessly at them with the bow.

Hilario explores the confrontation between traditional cultures and the West further in *phonautograph* (2002), for countertenor, four female voices, trombone, four turntables, and live electronics. The phonautograph, invented by Édouard-Léon Scott de Martinville in 1857, was one of the earliest sound recording devices. Not designed for sound playback, it recorded sound waves as visible tracings on smoke-blackened paper. Hilario extends the idea of visually manifest sound by using vinyl records with cuts made across their grooves. When played, these produce regular or irregular rhythms of pops, depending on whether the cut has been made perpendicular to the record's edge or at an angle. The records used are chosen from flea markets and represent musical styles that have already had considerable influence on other cultures—that is, styles of "traditional" Western music that make use of equal temperament, major-minor harmonies, and so on. In the live recording of the premiere at the Donaueschingen Musiktage in 2002, the records used appear to be of old marching band music. Just because records like these are now extremely cheap to buy, notes Hilario, does not mean that their music no longer has any listeners: "On the contrary: it is only the music storage technology that has been displaced. This kind of music . . . has spread its influence and authority faster than ever, aided by the rapid development of advanced communication technology."[46] As with *kibo*'s slackened strings, Hilario's physical intervention in his performing materials (scratching the records) emphasizes his critical approach. Echoes of the cultural—colonial—markers he describes are evident, but they are radically disturbed by the pop, crackle, and skips of the records themselves. In turn, those sounds create a new music of loops and pulses, which Hilario augments and further distorts through his music for the voices, percussion, and trombone.

Still other composers have refused to engage with orientalist expectations of what a "non-Western" composer should sound like; among those already mentioned are Tarek Atoui and Unsuk Chin. Nevertheless, by virtue of being non-Western, musicians like Atoui or Chin are able to access certain venues, festivals, and record labels. This is partly a trade on hip exoticism, but it also has to do with the challenge—or lack thereof—these artists present to normative Western ideals. The channels open to Atoui, through the relatively culturally neutral context of electroacoustic improvisation, are different to those open to Chin, a concert hall composer, yet both composers benefit to some extent from their status as cultural outsiders. These channels thus point once more to the ways in which the boundaries of what might be considered Western art music are enforced institutionally as well as stylistically.

The composer and oud player Mahmoud Turkmani (b. 1964), another Lebanese musician, turns toward insider expectations of what he should do. Like many other Arab musicians, he criticizes the Europeanization of Arab music, particularly the softening and sweetening of traditional music that has taken place in recent decades. Unlike some of his peers, however, he continues to draw on Arab influences in his work, especially the fundamental musical tradition of maqam. Yet his maqam compositions and performances take deliberately surprising and nonidiomatic paths, introducing a dimension of inauthenticity that may be perceptible only to Arab listeners familiar with traditional maqam performance. Turkmani argues that this gesture is a more radical postcolonial response than the simple Arabization of

European classical music through approximations of traditional scales and ornamental figures.[47]

Archipelagos

Drawing on the legacy of slavery, the experience of colonialism, and the geography of the Caribbean, the Martiniquan theorist Édouard Glissant (1928–2011) developed an alternative theory of globality that not only celebrated diversity but also emphasized the inevitable and desirable opacity of human and community interactions—a concept that he termed "Relation." Globality, in Glissant's terms, was the contemporary experience of the world as "both multiple and single," distinct from globalization, which he described as "uniformity from below" driven by "multinationals, standardization, [and] the unchecked ultra-liberalism of world markets."[48] Glissant's world prefers unpredictable heterogeneity to homogenizing synthesis

To provide a model for understanding this new global reality, Glissant refers to the Caribbean archipelago, a collection of local cultures within a wider shared identity—a simultaneous combination of coherence and difference. The concept has subsequently been taken up by art critics to describe the phenomenon of works or exhibitions that exceed the bounds of a singular presentation. These have become a recurring feature of work presented at biennials (as described at the start of this chapter) and so express, model, and legitimate the idea of global flow. One such example is *Utopia Station* (2003), by the artists Molly Nesbit, Hans-Ulrich Obrist, and Rirkrit Tiravanija.[49] Although it originated at the Venice Biennale, where it was first shown, *Utopia Station* also consisted of interlinked yet isolated presentations that took place around the world in 2003 and subsequent years. Made up of such numerous iterations, each of them only partial, it was unlikely that any individual (other than the artists themselves) would ever experience the complete project, giving the whole a structure of isolated fragments that are not designed to form a complete whole. If contemporary art expresses globalization through the activities of the biennial, *Utopia Station* presents it not as a unifying force but as a vector for plurality and difference.

The idea of the archipelago suits the itinerant nature of the exhibition, but it need not apply exclusively to the visual arts. Musical analogs have proliferated in the late twentieth and early twenty-first centuries. One of these can be found in the music of Manfred Werder. Werder, a cofounder of the Wandelweiser group, is deeply attached to environmental sounds and to a severe reduction in the number of activities or noises his music introduces into a space. More than that of many of his colleagues, his work appears to be about devising ways of articulating, framing, and coloring periods of nonactivity. His approach is distinctly low-tech. In line with the presentational style of Wandelweiser CDs (discussed in chapter 2), his scores are designed for reproduction and distribution on paper, with considerable attention given to matters such as font and page layout. Yet his music also speaks of digital-age conditions of liquidity, transience, and obsolescence. An exemplary early work is *stück 1998* (1997–2001). This is printed on a total of four thousand pages, and the "pageness" of each of these is an important constituent of the work's form. Each contains forty "sound units" (six seconds of a notated single pitch, followed by six seconds of silence), arranged on the page according to an identical grid layout. Each page takes eight minutes to perform. A complete performance would therefore take 533 hours and 20 minutes.

It belongs to a group of extreme-duration works and sound installations that includes Cage's *ASLSP* ("As Slow as Possible," 1985–7), which since 2001 has been performed in a 640-year-long realization at the church of St. Burchardi in Halberstadt, Germany; and Jem Finer's *Longplayer* (2000–) installation at the Trinity Buoy lighthouse in East London. From a somewhat different aesthetic position is Frederic Rzewski's (b. 1938) approximately ten-hour *The Road* (1995–2003), for solo piano, of which the composer has said, "I wanted to write a piece that was so long that people would be unlikely to hear it all in one sitting. In that sense it reflects the fact that in real life you don't really get the whole thing all at once."[50] Yet all of these works have been conceived with the expectation of a single continuous realization (even if audience members are expected to come and go). Werder's *stück 1998* is different, as it makes use of a kind of rolling performance practice. Pages are to be performed in succession, either one at a time or in groups, and each performance must end at the bottom of a page. The next performance, whether or not by the same performers, continues at the top of the next page. Once a page has been played, it is not repeated.[51]

In this way, *stück 1998* exists as a fragmentary, archipelago-like series of partial realizations, in many ways similar to the unfolding nature of *Utopia Station*. Werder maintains a list of performances.[52] This is primarily a way to keep track of where the piece currently is in its realization, but it also highlights the work's dispersal across a wide geographical and temporal frame: pages have been performed not only in cities across Europe and in North America but also in Buenos Aires, Santiago, Mexico City, and Seoul. As with *Utopia Station*, it is doubtful that anyone—even the composer—has heard all pages of *stück 1998* so far performed. Yet the neutrality and simplicity of each page, all of them formally much the same, makes it possible to a degree to imagine, on looking through the list of previous performances (and their instrumentation), what those performances may have been like. So, while the work excludes any listener from the possibility of hearing it in its entirety, it nevertheless permits an imaginative completion for anyone who has heard it in part.

James Saunders's *#[unassigned]* (2000–2009) takes a different kind of archipelago form. In this case, there is not one single work whose boundaries make it impossible to hear in full. The piece is in fact a series of works, each complete in itself. Each work is unique and intended to be performed only once. When Saunders composed a work, he gave it a title that incorporated the date of its first (and only) performance; for example, *#051000* was the name given to a work performed on October 5, 2000. On the handful of occasions that a work in the series was prepared for recording, "*-[R]*" was added to its title.

The archipelago nature of *[unassigned]* comes from its modular construction. Each piece in the series draws on a pool of musical materials selected and combined for that particular iteration. New modules could be added to the pool at any time, and existing modules could be accepted or rejected as desired. Some modules appear in many works; others only appear once or twice. In no work is the complete pool heard, however, and although Saunders is happy to disclose the modular principles behind his work, the actual connections between pieces remain obscure. This is particularly because, apart from the few recorded examples, most of the works have been heard in public only once.[53] Now that *#[unassigned]* is finished, the pool projects across a defined temporal and geographical space that is the compositional history of the series and acts as a partial repository for what it gave rise to.

Some works come closer to the nomadic, itinerant form of the traveling exhibition, and in many respects nomadic and archipelagic works are different sides of the same issues of scale and mobility. Craig Shepard's *On Foot* (2005) involved a 250-mile walk over thirty-one days across Switzerland. Each day, Shepard wrote a new piece for pocket trumpet, which he then performed at 6pm wherever he happened to be at that time—whether on a mountaintop or in a town square. Seth Kim-Cohen's (b. 1964) *Brevity is a Sol LeWitt* (2007) requires the creation of a ninety-nine-note piece, built up one note at a time at successive concerts by a single ensemble. Using a relay system described in the work's score, one player plays a note, which is then transcribed by a second player according to parameters set out in a "tableau de notation" (see figure 23). This completes the first concert. At the next concert, a third player plays a second note, which is again transcribed. This process continues in the following concerts. After each new note is added, a card is sent to the composer describing the setting—weather, audience, type of room, and so on—in which that note was performed, "a postcard update from the midst of your journey."[54] The work ends at the one hundredth concert, when the ninety-nine transcriptions are distributed randomly among the players, who then perform them.

Opacity: Liza Lim

Questions of knowledge, and the ways in which it might be shared or hidden, are a feature of the music of Liza Lim (introduced in chapter 2). Like Richard Barrett, Lim has a longstanding relationship with ELISION, which has produced a number of her ensemble and solo works, as well as *Bardo'i-thos-grol* and her first three operas.[55] She has also developed a more recent but similarly productive relationship with Musikfabrik. In reference to her bassoon solo *Axis Mundi* (2012–14), composed for Musikfabrik's Alban Wesly, Lim has written, "The creative 'DNA' of

Tableau de Notation

Date of Performance:

Location:

Performer of Note:

Notator:

A. Pitch (circle one):

fruit bat ultra high	sparrow high	ambulance medium high	human medium	Andre the Giant medium low	fog horn low	seismic event ultra low

B. Duration (circle one):

pre-cognitive	augenblick (the blink of an eye)	shooting star across the night sky	completely opening and then closing a door	walking, not running, up a flight of office building stairs	respectfully reading a short poem such as this one: This Is Just To Say I have eaten the plums that were in the icebox and which you were probably saving for breakfast Forgive me they were delicious so sweet and so cold (William Carlos Williams)

C. Personality of Note
(circle all that apply):

sweet	stinky
refined	coarse
stubborn	relaxed
mathematical	poetic
unassuming	pretentious
laden	light-hearted
opaque	translucent
generous	stingy

D. Physicality:

D1.) Performer's Degree of Theatricality (circle one number on scale):

Inanimate Object ----------------------➤ Al Pacino

1   2   3   4   5

D2.) Performer's Head Position (circle one):

D3.) Performer's Body Posture & Location (circle all that apply):

sitting	standing	reclining	prostrate	rectilinear
on stage	in/among audience	walking	running	jumping

Brevity Is A Sol LeWitt
Seth Kim-Cohen
Page 4 of 4

FIGURE 23. *Tableau de notation* for Seth Kim-Cohen's *Brevity is a Sol LeWitt*, 2007. Courtesy of the composer.

the performer is an intimate part of the compositional work, just as the compositional work becomes part of the life-history of the performer's technical apparatus and musical functioning."⁵⁶ This model is explored deliberately in the piece through the use of unstable and imprecise multiphonics to create what the composer calls "a contoured landscape of continually morphing shapes through which the performer travels anew in each iteration."

Invisibility (2009), for solo cello, was written for ELISION's cellist, Séverine Ballon. As an improviser, Ballon has developed a large and personal repertory of playing techniques, including various types of bowing and varieties of harmonics. In the precompositional phase of *Invisibility*, Lim spent time discussing these techniques with Ballon, seeking ways in which to incorporate them into the piece. In addition, Lim considered Ballon's own qualities as a performer and as an individual.

The piece belongs to a group of works Lim composed in the 2000s that was inspired by the Yolngu culture of Arnhem Land, in northeastern Australia. The Yolngu are among the better-known Aboriginal groups in Australia, and they are celebrated for their artworks, particularly bark paintings, which are some of the best-preserved artifacts of any Aboriginal art. As part of the research for her pieces, Lim spent time with the Yolngu, as a conscientious observer rather than a cultural tourist. The imagery used in Yolngu art, which combines realistic figures with highly stylized geometric patterns, admits many possible interpretations that are linked to socially organized structures of knowledge and secrecy.⁵⁷ Certain meanings may be accessible to anyone—including outsiders—but deeper levels are increasingly hidden and only available to the initiated or privileged. The interpretation of a single painting can thus appear to vary radically between individuals; however, each interpretation is a single perspective on a wider truth.

Another characteristic aspect of Yolngu art is what is known as *bir'yun,* or "shimmer." This is a visual effect created by fine crosshatching drawn in highly contrasting colors over the surface of a painting. It projects a shimmering brightness that is seen by the Yolngu as emanating from the ancestral creators of their mythology, and it thus endows the paintings themselves with ancestral power. A painting's shimmer is not only read as a representation of that power but is also felt as a direct manifestation of it. That power is a dangerous and highly restricted form of knowledge: when a person whose body has been ritually painted with *bir'yun* patterns returns to the main camp, the crosshatching is smeared to erase its brilliance and thus its ancestral power.⁵⁸

While no secret meanings are revealed in *Invisibility* or in Lim's other Yolngu-inspired works (to do so would be a gross betrayal of the trust she had won from the community), the process of knowledge transfer and sharing, particularly of an intercultural sort, and the aspects of opacity that are bound up with that are intrinsic to the work. Many of Lim's works address aspects of non-Western culture, from the Yolngu pieces to Chinese street theater in *Yuè Lìng Jié* (1999) to Persian poetry in *Tongue of the Invisible* (2010–11). In all of these, Lim considers her use of another cultural complex as more than a metaphorical translation from one medium to another: "I'm thinking in a more abstract way. So, regarding Japanese music I'm interested in proportions of asymmetry and asymmetrical temporal models rather than how it sounds Japanese."[59]

Although Lim's method is largely intuitive, she refers to the theory of pattern languages developed by the architect Christopher Alexander.[60] Alexander defines a "pattern" as an abstracted, highly generalized solution to a design problem—creating a place for waiting, for example—that is made up of a balanced collection of forces and desires. So, for example, a waiting place requires an entrance, room for those waiting to congregate, some form of comfort, and so on. The pattern may be applicable to several situations—in this case, a bus stop, for example—but its form is fixed. A "pattern language" is the collection of interlinked patterns that make up a more complex structure, such as a doctor's office or a city transit system. The key is that functions and forces are what make up the pattern, whereas concrete objects are possible design solutions. Thus, the pattern of another cultural object, such as Yolngu painting, may be approached and understood through its underlying pattern, which can then be resolved and given new expression within the vocabulary of the Western concert hall without resorting to a colonialist appropriation of mere surface features. Or, as the composer puts it, "It is a way of approaching a knowledge system which utterly fascinates me but of which I am clearly not a part."[61]

In *Invisibility*, the knowledge system of Yolngu art is composed through the ergonomics of the piece as much as its sound. This is manifest through two performance instructions that render the score a distant relative of the sounding result. The first is the use of two bows. One is standard, but the other is a so-called guiro bow, an invention of John Rodgers, in which the bow hair is coiled around the wood, like a damper spring. When drawn across the string, it creates an unevenly serrated, stop-start sound. Lim's program note makes the connection explicit: "Like the cross-hatched designs or dotting effects of Aboriginal art, the bow creates a highly mobile sonic surface through which one can hear the outlines of other kinds of movements and shapes." The sonic surface—fractured, brittle and endlessly detailed—is emphasized as the work's core "theme." When the piece is seen live, this is emphasized still further: crosshatching is suggested not only by the bow's sound but also by its appearance. Furthermore, the unpredictability of the abrasive playing surface creates a clearly visible dislocation between the actions of the performer and the precise sounds being created.

Already, this suggests a level of secret knowledge within the piece, since only the performer can know exactly the relationship between her bow movements and the sounds being produced. Lim has built on this possibility in the second crucial performance instruction: a radical scordatura. The score asks that the bottom string (C) be lowered by a semitone to B, the next string (G) be taken down by a tone to F, the third string be left untouched at D, and the highest string (A) be drastically flattened by a tritone to D♯. No doubt harmonic considerations played a part in the selection of these pitches (the work's final section is played almost entirely on open strings), but Lim's primary goal is to destabilize the relatively even spread of string tension in the standard C–G–D–A tuning. The A string in particular will feel dramatically different under the cellist's fingers.

Lim's preface to the score highlights how physical performance parameters become part of the material of the piece: "The work is a study in flickering modulations between states of relative opacity/dullness and transparency/brightness, between resistance (noise, multiphonics and other distorted sounds) and ease of flow (harmonics, clear sonorities). Striated, shimmer effects are created in the interaction between the competing planes of tension held in the retuned strings as they are affected by fingers and the varied playing surfaces of the two bows travelling at changing speeds, pressure and position."[62]

Thus Lim's notation contains something that can only be accessed through *doing*. To a degree, this is the case in all music written to be performed by others, but in setting up the cello's strings and bow in such an unusual way, Lim has made the relationship between action and meaning central to her piece. The score may only be a distant relative of the sound, but it is not arbitrary: its details and specifications are as much part of the piece as anything else and are crucial to the ritual process that is consummated in performance but that also includes composition, collaboration, practice, contemplation, and improvement. That background—that the work has been "lived" for a time before its public emergence—is an extension of the idea of public and private spheres of knowledge and experience, and it is critical to the work's identity as a shared ritual object in which composer, performer, and listener all have a stake.

Relatedness: Michael Finnissy

The oeuvre of the English composer Michael Finnissy (b. 1946) is as diverse as it is large. In 2015 his website listed more than three hundred works (although this list only went up to 2009).[63] They range from works of music theater, to chamber works involving every conceivable combination of instruments, to works for solo instruments. Yet certain aspects tie the varied collection together. It is often observed, for example, that Finnissy's musical technique is dominated by a combination of transcription and juxtaposition.[64] In some ways, these are opposing dynamics: one is tied to a logic of continuity and preservation across differences in media and the other to discontinuity and disruption within a single medium. Finnissy is not the only musician to work with this combination; as mentioned earlier, the practices of cutting, mixing, and versioning are also the basis of most Afro-diasporic music. Yet Finnissy's application of these two techniques speaks to a particular expressive mode of collage, identity recreation, and formal transformation.

Although he has worked almost exclusively with acoustic instruments (only *Nowhere else to go* [1989, rev. 2003] features electronics; a handful of others use prerecorded sounds), his sensibility is increasingly in tune with the fluid circumstances of the digital era (described in the previous chapter), in which materials and identities can be transformed and juxtaposed endlessly.

Finnissy's use of transcription is particularly apparent in his music for piano, his own instrument. His prodigious output for piano is dominated by five substantial works or work cycles. Beginning with *English Country-Tunes* (1977–85) and moving through the *Verdi Transcriptions* (1972–2005) and *Gershwin Arrangements* (1975–88) to *Folklore* (1993–4) and *The History of Photography in Sound* (1995–2001), this sequence traces Finnissy's increasingly sophisticated and complex use of transcribed and borrowed materials.

Despite its title (which can also be read as an X-rated pun), *English Country-Tunes* contains just one borrowed melody.[65] It is with the *Verdi Transcriptions* that Finnissy's rewriting of music that is not his own begins in earnest. Like those of Liszt or Busoni, but much more so, Finnissy's "transcriptions" are as much acts of creation as they are acts of mechanical procedure. In the strictest sense, a musical transcription should be a matter of just renotating an existing work for new forces, preserving as much of the original as possible—a piano reduction of the orchestral parts of an opera, for example. Yet Finnissy understands transcription as a negotiation not only with the notation of the original but also with its reception history. He situates his transcriptions within a potentially inexhaustible chain of transformation and identity (re)creation, illustrated by his comment on one of his Verdi transcriptions: "I worked from an earlier transcription by Alexander Abercrombie, generally increasing the harmonic ambiguity, eliding the original phrases, re-voicing Verdi's (orchestral) texture, creating a kind of production of the scene in my imagination."[66]

The sources for Finnissy's transcriptions are all musical, taken either from the Western classical tradition or from traditional music. Unlike Ablinger, he is not interested in transcribing nonmusical sounds; nor is he interested in recorded artifacts, as Beaudoin and Miller are. It is the linguistic and cultural content of his chosen materials, as written, that interests him. Over the years, Finnissy has shown a preference for certain repertories—Balkan and East European folk music, for example, as well as the music of nineteenth-century pianist-composers—but his tastes are wide-ranging. Apart from early and mid-twentieth-century jazz, however, he shows little interest in Western popular music.

As suggested above, Finnissy's transcribing practice stretches the limits of the term.[67] Some of his pieces remain relatively close to their sources.[68] These include his transcription of the Romanza ("O cieli azzuri") from *Aida*, a part of his *Verdi Transcriptions*, in which the original melody can be clearly heard, although within a new harmonic and contrapuntal context. Most of his works go much further, however. *Wenn wir in höchsten Nöten sein* (1992), for example, is an elaborate reimagining of Bach's so-called deathbed chorale, supposedly the last piece the German composer wrote. While the basic contour of Bach's original is maintained throughout, it is almost completely submerged beneath frequent alterations of meter, register, harmonization, and texture.[69] Other works use cut-ups and serial operations that disrupt even the line of the original. Yet when one transformational procedure is applied, often another is held back so that some essence of the original can still be discerned. Ian Pace writes that, even in Finnissy's most radical transformations, "a kernel of a source's intrinsic characteristics, however small, will continue to be present in the work which has been created from that source."[70]

Finnissy's most characteristic move, however, is to incorporate into a piece material from secondary sources, either by the same composer or, more commonly, by someone else altogether. This is the essence of the second part of his compositional voice: juxtaposition. Finnissy chooses his combinations for a range of reasons, including caprice, musical correspondence, and historical connection. The *Verdi Transcriptions,* the title alluding to the origin of the series in Liszt and the late nineteenth-century virtuoso piano repertory, include a number of homages to Romantic pianist composers, including Alkan, Busoni, Schumann, and Liszt himself. *Wenn wir in höchsten Nöten sein* includes melodies from Alban Berg's Violin Concerto of 1935, which itself quotes Bach, and so folds into its transcription some of the history of Bach's own music.

There is a connection here with the fluid and unrooted forms discussed in the previous chapter: from *Verdi Transcriptions* on, Finnissy's music increasingly expresses not just the original materials that he has collected and transcribed but also their status *as transformed material.* Materials are always presented in a state of change rather than reification—even across the five hours of *Photography,* the music rarely stays in one place for more than a few bars without throwing itself into question again. That undoing is achieved in many ways, including harmonic and rhythmic instability, processes of radical ornamentation and reduction, layering and juxtaposition, and sudden changes in texture and mood.

Photography may be the longest and, in many respects, most complex and sophisticated expression of Finnissy's transcriptional method to date, but the earlier *Folklore* presents a more interesting study in how he uses borrowed materials within a critique of regional, national, and global identities. Finnissy's interest in folk music is multifaceted. It began at a young age, sparked by family friends from Poland and Hungary, and one of his earliest acknowledged works is a set of *Polskie Tance* (Polish Dances), written when he was nine. Later his interest acquired a political dimension that is connected to the relationship between private and public space, art and commerce, and the individual and society. As a gay man in postwar England—and therefore regarded as just as much an outsider as any foreigner—he soon discovered that his native folk music felt just as alien to him as that of other countries.

In the early 1980s he began writing works that explicitly engaged with national folk musics—often of unusual origins (not the usual Western European sources but Albanian, Korean, Australian Aboriginal, and so on)—many of them for solo instruments. Yet he was also acutely aware of the potential pitfalls of a Western composer appropriating the music of other cultures. As a result, he has sought to avoid fetishizing or sentimentalizing his materials and has attempted not to give in to a cheap and easy multicultural eclecticism. His works are thus multilayered, non-nostalgic, and designedly difficult, for both listener and performer. His is a vision of folk music that is powerful, strong, noble, challenging.

The music of *Folklore* is primarily derived from folk musics from around the world, which Finnissy has transcribed, ornamented, supplemented, and generally stretched and distorted in his typical fashion. It is divided into four large sections, each of which focuses on a different region or regions of the world: Scandinavia; Scotland, Romania, England, China, and African America; Sweden, Romania, France, Serbia; and India, Korea, China, and North America.

The opening of Section II provides a good example of how Finnissy deploys his materials. It begins as a monody, a single melody, played in a high register. It is heavily decorated with ornaments that Finnissy has drawn from Scottish highland bagpiping, in particular a type of ornament known as a Hinbare (other ornament types feature elsewhere). These ornaments are effective musically because, in combination with the piano's sustain pedal, they provide a way of inserting harmony into a line of monody. Other elements are added soon after: allusions to Romanian folk tunes, a short homage to the American composer Christian Wolff, and hints of the African American spiritual "Deep River" (which is the only source to appear twice, returning in Section IV).

Throughout *Folklore*, Finnissy is sensitive that what he is presenting can only be a simulacrum, an impression, of traditional musics. The fact that everything is written for a piano—equally tempered, acoustically "clean," the icon of Western art music[71]—makes this clear from the outset. For this reason, many of Finnissy's folk references are deliberately made via transcriptions and/or arrangements of others. The Scandinavian material in Section I, for example, is derived from the work of Edvard Grieg and the folksong collector Ludvig Mathias Lindeman. The brief insert of Chinese folksong in *Folklore II* is presented in the arrangement made by Cornelius Cardew, with the addition of random grace-notes laid over the top, a reference to a technique developed by Cardew himself in his earlier experimental years. Most significantly, both references to "Deep River" in *Folklore* are filtered via Michael Tippett—another homosexual, politicized English composer—who featured an arrangement of the spiritual in his antioppression oratorio *A Child of Our Time* (1939–41). Tippett is the dedicatee of *Folklore II*.

While some elements in Finnissy's works are recognizable (such as "Deep River") and others may be guessed at in origin by listening (the bagpipe ornaments, for example), it is not important that everything be heard for what it is. More important are Finnissy's formal techniques, borrowed from the language of film and film editing, in which disparate elements are combined, juxtaposed, altered, and sequenced.

Many of his sources symbolize the outsider: Tippett and Cardew are two examples, and another English outsider, Kaikhosru Sorabji, features elsewhere in the piece. The presence of an African American spiritual is an obvious reference to outsiderness, and the general use of folk music—music produced by peasant cultures marginalized by mainstream bourgeois society—is of course the largest reference. In deference to his own outsiderness, Finnissy makes use of an English folk tune just once, the song "Let Him Answer Yes or No" from his home county of Sussex. Along with the references to Tippett's arrangement of a Negro spiritual and Cardew's arrangement of a Chinese folk song, this makes up the work's sole English portion.

Nearly all of the references within *Folklore* are therefore "remote" to Finnissy. It is not music in which he can participate. But in a globally interconnected, multicultural world, it is also not music he can ignore. We no longer live in a world in which closed, collective ethnic groups exist; we all rub alongside one another and mix together, much like the different musical elements in *Folklore*. We might be born into an indigenous culture of one sort or another, but we may nonetheless be more profoundly influenced by something from outside our culture—as Finnissy was by his early introduction to Eastern European folk music.

Finnissy's approach is also a radically personal one. Romanian music means something different to a Romanian who has grown up with it than it does to a casual listener from outside that culture. But Romanian music can be more significant to a British composer than the folk music of his own country. It is questions like these, of identity and of the relationship between us as individuals and the society to which we belong, that Finnissy is attempting to ask.

Finnissy's borrowed elements almost never appear in isolation; they are usually combined with something else, whether in simultaneous layers or linear juxtapositions or synthetically merged together. Maarten Beirens has observed that, "in that respect, the recognizability of the sources of the material is of little importance; what is essential is the way the material is combined, interspersed, alternated, modified, followed with or by other material."[72] Finnissy therefore articulates not only the fundamental fluidity of his transcribed or uprooted materials but also relative degrees of viscosity between objects, cultural artifacts, individuals, and societies. That is, in sympathy with Glissant's concept of Relation, he frames, highlights, and celebrates degrees of difference and incompatibility between cultures rather than make claims for a homogenous "global village." Finnissy's music takes the ideas of cultural confrontation and relatedness addressed by other composers mentioned in this chapter to their logical conclusion—or, rather, it points toward that conclusion (in its absurd excess), stopping just short of realizing it.

The sheer scale and density of Finnissy's later piano cycles, as well as their pro-liferation of external references, points to a latent condition of excess that lies within any attempt to capture the global. Any such project will be marked by an acceptance of incompletion and/or overdetermination. This has been theorized perhaps most succinctly by the Dutch architect Rem Koolhaas with the term "big-ness."[73] Above a certain size, Koolhaas explains, "a building becomes a BIG build-ing." This is not just a matter of dimension, but a shift in the ontological state of the building itself.[74] "Such a mass can no longer be controlled by a singular architec-tural gesture, or even by any combination of architectural gestures," he continues. "The impossibility triggers the autonomy of its parts, which is different from frag-mentation: the parts remain committed to the whole."[75] In Finnissy's piano cycles we see perhaps the threshold of where a musical work becomes a "BIG" musical work—a threshold that Finnissy determinedly pushes back with each new cycle. In the following chapter, the notion of excess, as an aesthetic pursuit in its own right, is considered at greater length.

6

SUPERABUNDANCE

Spectacle, Scale, and Excess

LICHT

When four Alouette III helicopters of the Royal Dutch Air Force's Grasshoppers display team took off from Deelen Air Base, north of Arnhem, on June 26, 1995, each with a member of the Arditti String Quartet inside, a new line was crossed in musical extravagance. Grand gestures are not new to Western art music, from Pérotin to Mahler, through Tallis's *Spem in alium* (circa 1570), Monteverdi's *Vespers* (1610), and Wagner's *Der Ring des Nibelungen* (1848–74). Yet even in this company, Stockhausen's *Helikopter-Streichquartett* (1992–3) is something else. Lasting thirty minutes, it requires a string quartet to be flown in helicopters over the auditorium, its music counterpointing the *chop-chop-chop* of the helicopter blades and the rise and fall in pitch of the engines. The helicopters' movements are choreographed, and the sound and video, starting with the players approaching and climbing into the helicopters, continuing through their performance, and ending with their return to earth and the auditorium—where they then participate in an informal Q and A about their experience—is all fed back to the audience via four screens and surround sound speakers.

Helikopter-Streichquartett requires a suspension of credulity to not be seen as a monstrous indulgence. Even with the greatest sympathies toward Stockhausen's musical vision, it is hard to ignore that it stretches to the limit the ratio of financial cost to artistic value. The environmental cost, not usually a consideration in productions of contemporary music, is also unignorable. Indeed, protests from the Austrian Green Party contributed to the cancelation of the planned first performance in 1994. Stockhausen (1928–2007) was no stranger to such extravagances. His works had already called for concert halls to be redesigned to accommodate multiple antiphonal orchestras (*Gruppen*, 1955–7), for outdoor performances by multiple ensembles over a large space (*Sternklang*, 1971), and for sound projection across a spherical auditorium enclosing fifty groups of loudspeakers (various works, World Expo 1970, Osaka, Japan).

And in fact, the *Helikopter-Streichquartett* is only the most logistically complex section (Act 3) of the most logistically complex part (*Mittwoch*) of probably the most logistically complex musical work ever conceived (the operatic heptalogy *LICHT*, 1977–2003). *LICHT* demands an investment of resources that may be unmatched by any other work in any other live medium.[1] It has always operated at the limits of the possible, but over the decades Stockhausen worked on the cycle, the parts the staging and technical production became increasingly complex, paralleling the composer's growing ambitions. *Donnerstag* (1978–81) requires a solo trumpeter to play inside a giant rotating globe; *Samstag* (1981–3) calls for "an orchestra in the shape of a face"; and the final part, *Sonntag* (1999–2003), ends with two versions of the music (for orchestra and for chorus) played simultaneously in (and broadcast back and forth between) separate concert halls. This was all in spite of the fact that commissioning pressures forced the composer to use fewer instrumental resources in later parts and to rely to a greater extent on electronic sounds. "One can only speculate," wrote the Stockhausen scholar Robin Maconie, "about what might have been had the composer's vision taken hold of a wider musical constituency, and attracted more generous funding and support."[2] The only musical comparisons in terms of duration and conceptual extension are Robert Ashley's (1930–2014) trilogy of opera cycles,[3] which encompasses the heptalogy *Perfect Lives* (1978–80), the trilogy *Atalanta* (1982–7), and the tetralogy *Now Eleanor's Idea* (1993); and R. Murray Schafer's (b. 1933) twelve-work *Patria* cycle, which has been ongoing since 1966. However, Ashley's fourteen operas are individually much smaller in scale than Stockhausen's seven, with many lasting only half an hour or so and involving a handful of musicians. None requires staging anything nearly as ambitious as Stockhausen's. The internal connections in Ashley's works are looser too; there are shared characters and a common tempo, but little else. *Patria* is a more unified conception, and although it outdoes *LICHT* in terms of duration (the final *Epilogue*, for example, requires two groups of participants to learn their own clan rituals over the course of a week), its demands are in terms of location—much of the work is staged in wild outdoor environments—and audience participation rather than theatrical staging.

In the 1950s, Stockhausen was a leading exponent of serial composition. Put very simply, this was an extension of Arnold Schoenberg's idea (developed in the early 1920s) of arranging the twelve notes of the chromatic scale into a particular sequence (or series) and using this—rather than a melody, harmonic sequence, or rhythmic pattern—as the starting point for a musical composition (although serialism did not preclude any of these featuring in the finished work, of course). Stockhausen, along with other young composers who had come of age during World War II, such as Boulez, Karel Goeyvaerts (1923–93), Gottfried Michael Koenig (b. 1926), Nono, and Henri Pousseur (1929–2009), saw in Schoenberg's principle, and its extension in the music of his pupil Anton Webern, a way of radically reconceiving of musical space in all dimensions—not just the horizontal line of melody or harmonic progression—by applying the serial principle not only to pitch but also to other aspects of music, such as duration, volume, and timbre. The trend of strict serialism may have been short-lived (composers quickly became interested in ways of turning those points into masses and lines), but the way of thinking to which it gave rise—that a work could be determined by a single germinating idea, whose dimensions were explored in every direction—had an enduring effect.

Stockhausen's musical style and techniques developed greatly throughout his career, but this basic principle remained, and in *LICHT* it is carried to its limit. All seven operas (twenty-nine hours of music) are based on a single "superformula," a musical idea written in three parts of just nineteen measures. It is never played as such, but if it were it would last barely a minute. The three parts represent the three main characters of the cycle—Michael, Eve, and Lucifer—and each opera takes a two-, three-, or four-measure segment of the superformula as its basis. *Mittwoch*, for example, is based on measures six and seven. By zooming in on each group of measures, Stockhausen is able to extract and extrapolate the music for the entire opera. An early part of this process would be expanding the superformula durations enormously to create a basic structural outline for the work. Later stages involve constructing a new superformula for the opera itself and then creating actual materials—leitmotifs, pitch series, gestural types, and so on—from this.

LICHT exhibits an aesthetic of superabundance in two ways. The first is represented by the work's consumption of resources, exemplified by *Mittwoch*'s helicopters. The second is that it exceeds its formal propositions, stretching the internal unity and integrity of the superformula idea to its limits. The principle of musical unity that underlies the superformula extends into Stockhausen's staging instructions. Each opera is prefaced by a list of twenty-four "features of the scenic aspect," with each feature having seven different possibilities, so that the seven operas spell out not only the seven days of the week but also seven scents, seven elements, seven bodily organs, seven colors, and even seven "divine principles" (in the case of *Mittwoch*, for example, these are "intuition and harmony"). There are also seven precious stones, seven shrubs, seven animals, seven planets, and more. The helicopters' flight into the sky beyond the opera house, their performance experienced only via a series of proxies (video feeds, reports from the players, possibly a spiritual intuition), symbolizes this extension of the earthbound pragmatism of compositional technique into genuine flight and outlandish fantasy.

REVELING IN THE RESOURCES

For all the hyperbole, *LICHT* reflects a wider trend around the turn of the twenty-first century toward the spectacular. The reasons for this are many. Some have already been touched on in previous chapters, and others will be set out here. Once again, technology and globalization are key drivers. Both together mean that we inhabit a world that is more complex, dense, multivalent, and multilingual than ever before. Global information technologies may have connected us to the world with a previously unimagined vividness, but the deluge of information that has come back has obscured that world more than it has made it clear.

Technology and the expansion of our activities onto the global scale have also given us new concepts of scale. Thanks to developments in particle physics, astronomy, and genetics, as well as international travel, finance, and communication, our lives have become more acquainted with the immensely large and the subatomically small. The 1990s began with the famous photograph of Earth as a "pale blue dot," taken at the request of astronomer Carl Sagan from the *Voyager 1* spacecraft as it left the solar system. This radical new image of Earth was the starkest possible expression of the vastness of the universe and the ephemerality of human existence that comes with the awareness of that. Our common cultural horizon today easily accommodates both trillion-dollar deficits and the Higgs boson.

As concepts of the very big and the very small have grown, so our concept of what is normal and ordered has dissolved and disintegrated. This has been reflected in the changes in marketing and reception structures for music and art described in chapter 2, which have turned away from the formal and contemplative to prioritize the informal and experiential. The collapse of musical ideologies like *Werktreue*, under pressure from postmodern aesthetics and new marketing strategies that sought crossover audiences and distribution paradigms outside the circumscribed realm of Western art music, has opened up new possibilities for excessive and destabilized forms. Finally, the fluid and journey forms of music described in chapter 4, which are predicated on processes of consumption and waste, further articulate aesthetics of superabundance and excess.

Circuses and Spectacles

Although Stockhausen could not have anticipated such economic shifts when he began *LICHT,* the work's style of immersive spectacle, and that of other works he composed in the 1970s, such as *Sternklang,* has come to seem increasingly in step with its time. Performances of individual operas from the work are sufficiently exotic to attract global audiences; Birmingham Opera's performance of *Mittwoch,* for example, drew listeners to the United Kingdom from as far away as New Zealand. Some people even bought tickets for the complete four-night run, presumably surmising that they would not have the chance to hear the opera in concert again. Each night was sold out. *Mittwoch* also proved surprisingly attuned to postindustrial narratives of cultural regeneration. Birmingham Opera's production of it was a centerpiece of the 2012 Cultural Olympiad, which was attached to the 2012 London Olympics—indeed, it is hard to imagine that the performance would have been able to get enough funding without such backing. It was staged in a former chemical plant close to the center of Birmingham, a British city that has received large investments in the retail dimensions of urban regeneration. The space itself was not only flexible enough to meet the opera's many theatrical demands but also offered a trendy air of industrial decay and urban renewal and symbolized the late capitalist shift from manufacturing to services. As the structures of commissioning, promotion, and presentation of art music after 1989 came to place a greater emphasis on the spectacular and the singular, it is not surprising that there has been a growth in the number of works that, like *LICHT,* employ a large-scale, spectacular, and/or carnival aesthetic.

Despite the more socially conscious status of such works today, however, they find an important inspiration in the radical avant garde of the 1960s and '70s. Many find their chief precedent in the work of John Cage, in particular his idea of the "musicircus." This was a concept drawn up by Cage in 1967 for a multimedia happening at the University of Illinois, but the composer revisited it increasingly in his later works, including__, __ __ *circus on* __ (realized in 1979 as *Roaratorio, an Irish Circus on Finnegans Wake*) and his five *Europera*s (1987–91). The idea is simple but extremely flexible: a musicircus is essentially a (chance-derived) system for organizing the simultaneous performance of many musicians and performers. It has proved an especially durable idea for the changed status, function, and audience of the municipal arts center at the turn of the millennium, presenting a playful, polyglot, fluid environment that is as attractive to children and casual visitors as it is to the connoisseur.

Works in which an overfilling, multisensory experience of sound, space, and visuals is substituted for precisely delineated meaning are not confined to music. Among other examples we might include the "relational aesthetics" of artists such as Rirkrit Tiravanija and Philippe Parreno,[4] the "immersive theater" of Punchdrunk and Théâtre de Complicité, and the "humanist memory theater"[5] of Daniel Libeskind's architecture. As we have seen, this turn toward experience can be understood as an articulation of both globalization and changing funding structures.

Among the most productive inheritors of the musicircus idea is Alvin Curran. The use in *A Piece for Peace* (described in chapter 5) of uncoordinated and spatially distinct ensembles (in separate countries in this case) owed much to the musicircus idea, which was already central to Curran's thinking by this time, particularly evident in the series of works known as *Maritime Rites* (1979–). The first of these was composed for students of Curran's in Rome and was performed by them on rowing boats on the lake of the Villa Borghese. Groups of performers on each boat sang sustained chords, which were spatialized and set in motion according to the unpredictable drifting of the boats. Subsequent versions (of which there have been around twenty to date) expand on this core image; Curran has placed few restrictions on the work's possibilities beyond the common threads of water, spatialization, and boats. However, these already suggest certain musical ideas: horns, for example, both onshore and onboard the ships, feature in most versions. Most versions are composed with the specifics of the location in mind. The 1991 version for Sydney Harbor featured aboriginal musicians; the 2007 version for Kinsale, Ireland, featured a local rock band. Not all versions are on a large scale: the one Curran created for New York in 2012 was devised for small groups of brass and wind instruments on the Central Park boating lake, a transplantation of the structures and sounds of international shipping into the refined and cultivated space of a pleasure garden. Nevertheless, *Maritime Rites* has presented opportunities for cities and arts festivals to project their own grandeur, history, and location. The flexibility of the work's core concept and the relative homogeneity of shipping activities makes this possible, allowing for local specificities to be incorporated (a particular foghorn, say, or the acoustics and scale of a harbor) without difficulty.

One of the largest iterations of the work to date was *Maritime Rites Tate,* which took place on the River Thames in London in 2007. The potential of *Maritime Rites* to capture moments of local commemoration or celebration had by that time become part of the process of the pieces. *Maritime Rites Kinsale,* for example, both provided the local arts festival with a "large-scale, site-specific musical spectacle"[6] and served to commemorate the lives of local fishermen who had died in trawler accidents that winter.[7]

Maritime Rites Tate proved to be an even more spectacular example of the intersection of commerce, public relations, public art, and entertainment, particularly such as was possible before the 2008 financial crisis. Commissioned by the Tate Modern gallery as part of its UBS Opening: Live series of performance works,[8] it also served as the opening event of that year's Thames Festival, an event that since its beginnings in 1997 "has played a significant role in the cultural and economic regeneration of London's South Bank, helping to transform it into one of the most-visited, international cultural destinations."[9] It took place, therefore, at a symbolic intersection of an international fine art franchise (the Tate), a Swiss bank (UBS), and the public image interests of London itself. Taking place on the river and riverbank outside the Tate Modern and on the Millennium Footbridge, which links the Tate with St. Paul's Cathedral and the City of London, the location perfectly encapsulated that intersection.

Curran's music made use of these collisions of history and place: mixed with the maritime sounds of boat horns and whistles, and the bells of St. Paul's, was an orchestra made up of UBS staff, the London Symphony Orchestra, and an improvising quartet of Evan Parker (saxophone), Anton Lukoszevieze (cello), Melvyn

Poore (tuba), and Curran himself (keyboards) that was placed on a floating stage in the middle of the river. The spectacle consciously recalled the Thames pageants of George I, a fact acknowledged by the use of some of Handel's Water Music. The space defined by the two riverbanks, and connected by the Millennium Footbridge, became a reverberant auditorium. Echoes from the buildings on each side seemed to collide overhead.

Curran's eclectic, multilayered style allows him to make connections between disparate elements like these, but it is not the only way in which such a piece may be arranged. Lisa Bielawa's (b. 1968) two *Airfield Broadcasts* (2013), written for two disused airfields that are now public parks, Tempelhof in Berlin and Crissy airfield in San Francisco, present a contrasting example. I will focus on the first, *Tempelhof Broadcast*, but the musical design was similar for both. Tempelhof is a historically significant space for Berlin. Built in 1927, the airport was substantially reconstructed by the Nazis, who installed its vast, iconic curving terminal building. It served as the point of arrival for the Berlin airlift of 1948–9, and throughout the Cold War it was an American air force base. As reunified Berlin's air traffic shifted to Berlin-Schönefeld International, plans were made to close Tempelhof. In 2009 it reopened as a public park, run and maintained by Grün Berlin, a state-owned company dedicated to managing Berlin's outdoor spaces. Like the Tate Modern, a modern art gallery housed in a former power station, Tempelhofer Park is a prime example of the urban reclamation of former industrial spaces as sites of entertainment, leisure, and education. Also like the Tate, it has been successful and largely welcomed. However, it has not been without controversy, and at the park's opening, concerns were raised about whether the boundary fences (and nighttime closures) made it a truly public park; likewise, objections were voiced about the effect this regeneration would have on the housing costs of those who lived close to the field.

Airfield Broadcasts used audibility, spatial distance, and ensemble coordination as compositional parameters. Bielawa had explored these elements before in smaller works such as *The Right Weather* (2003–4), for members of the American Composers Orchestra distributed around Zankel Hall, New York, and *Chance Encounter* (2007), for twelve musicians in "a transient public space." In the video documentation for preparing *Tempelhof Broadcast*, she explains the protocol used to devise one section of the work (see figure 24).[10] Two groups of ensembles are arranged such that the ensembles within each group are close enough to hear each other but far enough apart that they can't hear any ensembles from the other group. From onsite experiments, Bielawa calculated this distance to be about 250 meters, although this varied depending on the prevailing wind direction and whether the instrumental sounds were high or low, and both of these parameters extended into her compositional design. Each ensemble group had a lead ensemble, which gave audible cues for when the other ensembles should enter with their material (assigned from a list of possibilities that accorded to the players' profi-

FIGURE 24. Distribution of performing ensembles (shown as black dots) for Lisa Bielawa's *Tempelhof Broadcast*, 2013.

ciency). Although the two ensemble groups could not hear each other, anyone between them could listen to their uncoordinated antiphony. Midway between the two groups stood a final ensemble, a group of trumpets, which gave a signal to both group leaders to end this section of the piece.

Between sections, the hundreds of musicians brought together to perform *Tempelhof Broadcast* walked in groups to points in the park according to a carefully preplanned choreography, gradually spreading farther apart and finally leaving Tempelhof and continuing to play in the surrounding streets. As they did so, and as it gradually became impossible to hear everything that was happening at once, the aural and spatial unity of the work gradually dissolved. The composer suggested that one way to listen would be to get on a bike and cycle around the park, like the many day-to-day users of Tempelhof park did, either following a single ensemble or sampling several in sequence.

Events like *Maritime Rites* and *Airfield Broadcasts* may draw their language and formal processes from the countercultural forms of Fluxus and the Cageian happening, but their commissioning and performance now (however unintentionally) lend support to the modes of spectacular capitalism. This is clear as much from their aesthetic effect as it is from the specific circumstances of their creation. Their sheer scale renders them "experiences," in the vernacular of early twenty-first-century arts marketing.[11] In both cases, although the works present some challenging ideas in themselves, these are pieces of public art that do not set out to critique but rather to engage and enthrall a large audience. Bielawa's language is more consonant, rhythmically and tonally, than Curran's and not as stylistically eclectic; it might therefore be described as more approachable, although that must be counterbalanced by its formal "correctness" as compared to the freeform exuberance that Curran's style permits.

The experience of *Airfield Broadcasts* wasn't even limited to attendance at either site. Both performances were broadcast online, and Internet users could click on an interactive map of each site to listen to the sounds taking place at that point in space. In this respect, the *Airfield Broadcasts* extended the archipelago idea to the virtual space of the Internet. The Web provides an ideal space for wider audience engagement and participation that can extend beyond ways to listen to or see the work itself—as was the case with *Airfield Broadcasts*—and into modes of public reception such as sharing photographs, sounds, and verbal responses across social media. In this context, the excess of *Maritime Rites Tate* is of a more historical type; it is a Dionysian display of resources and sounds, but one that is still contained within a single place and time. *Airfield Broadcasts* represent a more radical, more contemporary proposition, in which the work—using an engaging, consonant style that draws the listener in—quite simply exceeds the spatiotemporal boundaries of the site and event.

FROM ORNAMENT TO EXCESS

The music of the past century was characterized by its desire to express completeness in its use of the resources available to it. As the musicologist Herman Sabbe observes, these traits may be seen across several strands of musical invention: "the permanent integration of all elements and their total determination in the case of multiple serialism; total indeterminacy in the case of chance music; and the availability of all musics in 'quotation' techniques."[12] *LICHT* itself is one consequence of this kind of conceptual saturation. By the end of the century, however, the desire for inclusiveness had morphed into something new: beyond describing, exploring, and expressing complete worlds, composers began to seek conditions of excess and surplus, extremities of scale in which material overflowed form or form overstretched material. As the works by Curran and Bielawa show, this sometimes took place in alliance with contemporary structures for the commissioning and presentation of major new work—and its expected relationship to the audience "experience"—but it also took place on a more technical level as the implications of the serial avant garde were explored in new directions against the late twentieth-century context.

Boulez: Ornamentation

Where Stockhausen's serial practice led him to ever more complex elaborations of a global unity, his brother-in-arms of the serial 1950s, Pierre Boulez (1925–2016), pursued an aesthetic driven by outward transformation and ornamentation. Stockhausen's ideas start from a universe and work inward to fill in the gaps; Boulez's start small and work outward, dividing, evolving, and proliferating, like tree branches or bacteria. This is apparent not only in the titles of individual works—*Répons* (Response), *Pli selon pli* (Fold within fold), *Constellation-Miroir* (Constellation-Mirror)—which emphasize forms of duplication and echo, but also in his general working practice, which, since the 1960s, has been characterized by patterns of revision and recycling. Already present in Boulez's practice, these patterns came to dominate his music after the completion of *Répons* in 1980, and almost all of his compositional work since then was predicated in some way on earlier pieces. From 1978, for example, he was involved in a project to orchestrate the twelve *Notations* for solo piano, which he had originally composed in 1945. Another group of pieces—including *Mémoriale* (for flute and ensemble, 1985, rev. 1991–3) and *Anthèmes* (for violin, 1991; supplemented with electronics as *Anthèmes II*, 1997)—is related to the ensemble work . . . *explosante-fixe* . . . , which was planned in 1971 and itself realized in multiple different versions between 1972 and 1993.

Of the very small number of apparently sui generis new works Boulez composed after 1980, among the most notable is the short piano solo *Incises* (1994–2001). It is not so much on its own; in its first version (it has itself been revised and enlarged twice) it lasts just three and half minutes. Its significance lies in the fact that it also serves as the source material for the much longer ensemble work *sur Incises* (1995–8), Boulez's most important work of the 1990s and a brilliant example of his practice of extending through methods of ornamentation and reworking. Written for three pianos, three harps, and three percussionists (one playing vibraphone, steel drums, and crotales; one playing vibraphone, glockenspiel, and timbales; and one playing marimba, tubular bells, and crotales), *sur Incises* expands the miniature *Incises* into more than half an hour.

Over the course of *sur Incises,* the material of *Incises* is stretched across a territory that was previously only latent. A feature of its expressive language is the distance that can be constructed between the two pieces. The sort of procedures Boulez uses can be heard from the start. *Incises* begins with a single held note, anticipated by a quick dissonant chord and followed by a quick downward flurry. In its original form, this lasts just a second or two, and the music quickly moves on. In *sur Incises,* Boulez turns these two small gestures into more than thirty seconds of moody atmosphere, zooming in and distributing the sounds among the ensemble in a series of echoes and elaborations in which the held note becomes an everpresent drone punctuated by sudden attacks as it is passed among the ensemble and the downward flurry becomes a long marimba melody that threads sexily around the central pitch. The music recognizably references the *Incises* original, even though six measures go by before anything is heard that hasn't been varied in some way. "Frequently a gesture from *Incises,* rather than being stated then developed, will seem to gradually emerge as a *consequence* of the music," writes the composer Tom Coult in an analysis of the piece.[13]

The ways in which the musical material is expanded are reflected in the ensemble, which is devised to augment and expand the sound of the original solo piano. The instruments chosen all share a similar sonic envelope with the piano: sharp attack, followed by a slow decay. (Conceiving of a sound in such terms itself derives from the parametrical thinking of early serialism, as well as advances made in the 1970s and '80s in the computer analysis of sound.) Across the ensemble, however, the precise morphologies differ. For the glockenspiel and vibraphone, the decay is longer and fuller; for the harp and marimba, it is shorter. The attacks of the steel drums are softer, while those of the crotales are harder. The instrumentation further reflects the structure of the piano itself, with the strings represented by the harps, and the soundboard by the bells and keyed percussion.[14] However, this analogy oversimplifies the network of sonic relationships between the instruments. Indeed, rather than thinking of the ensemble as a single spectrum of timbre, it may be more useful to consider it in terms of a terrain of interrelated timbres. Boulez himself noted, "What I wanted here was the idea of a mirror of the piano sound modified by the percussion and harp, also the idea of echoes mirroring the same type of sonority."[15] This terrain might be described across three axes—relating to pitch/noise, attack, and resonance—and we might be able to describe it in general terms: the piano is less noisy than timbales; crotales are more resonant than marimba; the harp is sharper in attack than steel drums. But the specific placement of sounds on this terrain in fact depends on more mutable factors than instrument type: stick type (for percussion), dynamic level, and register can all dramatically change the timbre and acoustic profile of a note. To a certain extent, any instrument might appear almost anywhere on the terrain, and the timbral design of *sur Incises*, just like its musical elaboration, is more complex and interrelated than a simple outward expansion. Rather than a model of inclusiveness, of the sort to be found in much music of the earlier twentieth century, this is something else: a glittering overflow of energy that reflects and renews itself at every turn.

Kurtág: Saturation

Boulez was not the only composer at the end of the century who liked to revisit earlier works. So too did György Kurtág (b. 1926). Since the 1980s, Kurtág's output has become more intertwined and self-referential than even Boulez's. Just the titles of Kurtág's works signal their density and polyphony of external reference: *Merran's dream (Caliban detecting-rebuilding Mirranda's dream)*, the title of a 1998 piece for piano, is typical. In profound tension with this is the slightness of the music itself, both in duration and apparent complexity. *Merran's dream* lasts just a minute and a half and is mostly made up of narrow, mid-register chords, like a strange chorale. Further, everything within Kurtág's output is a potential component for a new work, a node within a complex network of revisions and recyclings. Again, *Merran's dream* serves as an example: originally written for piano, it has subsequently appeared in a version for string orchestra, as part of *New Messages* (1998–2008), for orchestra. Kurtág's means, and much of his aesthetic, may be rooted in the classical tradition, but it is impossible to miss the relevance of his work to the age of hypertext, subatomic physics, and quantum theory.

After a difficult early career marked by faltering productivity, Kurtág came into his mature compositional style almost by accident, through a request in 1973 from the Budapest piano teacher Marianne Teöke for a set of short pedagogical pieces for young children. These became *Játékok* (Games, or Playthings), an open-ended series of piano miniatures not dissimilar from Bartók's *Mikrokosmos* (1926–39) in the way they set out a complete piano tutor from beginner to advanced student; *Merran's dream* belongs to Book VII of the series. Having previously been a slow composer, Kurtág expanded *Játékok* relatively quickly, publishing four volumes in 1979. These were swiftly followed by two more, and he finished a further two in 1998. In all, the series' eight volumes bring together a total of more than four hundred pieces, ranging in length from a few seconds to five or six minutes, and written for two, three, or four hands. Once he had begun *Játékok* in earnest, Kurtág became more productive in terms of both the number and scale of his pieces. By the end of the 1980s he was working on larger ensemble works, culminating in *Stele* (1994), for Claudio Abbado and the Berlin Philharmonic.

What Kurtág discovered in writing *Játékok* was a musical language that was serious and yet playful. It could sit in the same tradition as Bach, Beethoven, and Bartók, yet it did so through almost capriciously nondescript materials, such as the thumping of fists on the keyboard in *Hommage à Tchaikovsky* or the outwardly fanning glissando in *Perpetuum mobile* (both from Book I). Materials like these are almost banal in their simplicity, and Kurtág has used the term "objet trouvé" as a description, less to indicate a Dadaist appropriation of the industrially fabricated "readymade" than to describe the highly personal process of improvised discovery. However, such materials are rarely as simple as they seem. Kurtág's materials—his individual notes even—are loaded with associations and references that are both private and public. Two pieces dedicated to other Hungarian composers—*Hommage à Jeney* (1979) and *Hommage à Vidovszky* (1979)—carry the subtitle, "Phone numbers of our loved ones." The title of another, *Les adieux* (1979), refers explicitly to Beethoven's Piano Sonata No. 26, transmuting that piece's famous opening three chords into just two of its own, quite different but somehow evocative. Any individual piece might combine allusions to the avant garde, the historical tonal tradition, and childlike experimentation and play, as well as references more or less overt to works in Kurtág's own output or those of other composers. Kurtág's methods share something with the densely interwoven allusions and references of Michael Finnissy's piano works and the work cycles of Richard Barrett. All three composers, in the discourse around their pieces expressed through program notes, dedications, and titles, imbue their notes with a seemingly impossible quantity of external references. In the cases of Barrett and Finnissy, this leads to music that exceeds its capacity for meaning management through its density and multivalency. In Kurtág's case, however, the reverse is true: the process of pruning the music's density back (in terms of number of notes per page) increases the burden of signification for each single note, so that a lifelong friendship can be compressed into just a few measures and a masterpiece of the piano repertory into just two chords.

A key work is *Grabstein für Stephan*. Although composed in 1989, it was based on an earlier set of sketches for guitar made in 1978–9. This wasn't the first time Kurtág had drawn on an earlier piece in this way—his previous ensemble work . . . *quasi una fantasia* . . . (1987–8) borrowed a movement from the *Hommage à Mihály András* of a decade earlier—but after *Grabstein*, it became an increasingly frequent practice for Kurtág, and *Játékok* proved a valuable resource. As with many of Kurtág's larger instrumental works, the forces are distributed spatially. A guitarist sits at the center of the stage, which is shared with an ensemble of "harmony instruments"—piano, harmonium, harp, celesta, cimbalom, and tuned percussion. Four smaller groups—of wind, brass (two groups), and strings—are spread antiphonally around the auditorium. Among them is also a sextet of referees' whistles and air horns, which, along with the brass, interject at full volume and with shattering force at three points in the piece.

The piece begins with a slow strum across the guitar's six open strings, a quintessential Kurtágian objet trouvé. This is repeated with slight variations throughout *Grabstein's* ten-minute duration. Each iteration is doubled in various ways by the "harmony" ensemble; sometimes they are interspersed with short, aphoristic comments from the other ensembles. There is always a strong sense, however, that the guitar is the music's core. Even the interruption of horns and whistles can be heard as an immense and perverse magnification of the discordant reverberation of its strings.

In *Grabstein*, Kurtág performed an act of radical expansion not unlike that of *sur Incises*, inflating his material (the open-string guitar strum) far beyond its original size and meaning. Yet Kurtág's methods, unlike those of Boulez, are not developmental or permutational. He does not expand his material linearly according to its harmonic, rhythmic, or melodic properties. Instead, he shows it spilling outward along other, less easily quantifiable paths, such as timbre, space, and association. *Grabstein für Stephan* reaches out through echoes, shadows, and reflections; these are the more mysterious structures of memory rather than the living forms of the organic.

After *Grabstein*, the principle of decenteredness increasingly became a feature of Kurtág's output, and in the 1990s extended into the form of his pieces themselves. Kurtág had always composed in small fragments, either keeping his music short or extending it—as in *Kafka-Fragmente* (1985–7)—in chains of short movements. However, these chains were usually determined by the composer. In *Signs, Games, and Messages* (1989–), a collection of short pieces for one, two, three, or four string players, the order and number of movements to be played is left up to the performer(s). Kurtág had been performing *Játékok* in this way himself for many years, giving recitals with his wife Márta of selections from all eight volumes, interspersed with his own arrangements of early music and occasionally with music by entirely different composers altogether. However, with *Signs, Games, and Messages* and other work-collections such as *Messages* (1991–6) and *New Messages* (1998–), for orchestra, this open-ended approach is made official. The endless networks of possible connections and associations contained within those work-collections have become "almost completely saturated with possible meaning."[16]

It is also possible to see Kurtág's later open form works against the contexts described in previous chapters. The extreme multivalency of his work, in which single notes might point toward several sets of meanings at once, has echoes in the translational techniques discussed in chapter 4. There is something of the archipelago too, in the way in which individual performances offer only partial views of an open-ended whole. Yet what makes Kurtág's music exceptional is its relationship to the personal. The archipelago Kurtág constructs is an archipelago of the self—exemplified in *Játékok* but extending across all his work. The polyphony of images and associations manifest in a performance of *Signs, Games, and Messages* speaks of fluidity and contingency; the excesses of past and future that contemporary life opens to us and forces us to leave behind; and the infinite and incompletable project of identity.

Ferneyhough: "Complexity"

Over the last two or three decades, the music of Brian Ferneyhough (b. 1943) has taken on an almost talismanic quality. Not one of the world's most regularly performed living composers (although the obscurity of his music can be overstated), he is nonetheless one of its most frequently referenced, whether as the originator of a style and aesthetic that has excited many younger composers or as an anachronistic adherent of old-school modernism. Much has to do with his reputation as a teacher. At the Staatliche Hochschule für Musik in Freiburg (1973–86); University of California, San Diego (1987–99); and Stanford University (2000–), he has taught at least two generations of composers in a fashion that is widely admired.[17]

Ferneyhough's status also comes in large part because his style—like that of other icons before him, such as Cage, Ligeti, or Reich—can be condensed to a single, usually unhelpful, word. Cage's is "chance," or perhaps "silence." For Ligeti, it is "atmospheres." For Reich, it is "minimalism." Without question, Ferneyhough's word is "complexity."

Although Ferneyhough had been composing works that might be described in this way for two decades, the term firmly attached itself to his music in 1988 with the publication of the article "Four Facets of the New Complexity," by the Australian musicologist Richard Toop.[18] Toop's focus was the (mostly) younger quartet of Finnissy, Barrett, Chris Dench, and James Dillon, but Ferneyhough's influence on all four hangs over his analysis. Since then, "complexity" as a musical description has become so tainted with stereotype and misinformation that it is almost impossible to reclaim in a neutral sense. Like Milton Babbitt's 1958 article "Who Cares If You Listen," Toop's piece—through no fault of his own—has become notorious much more for its title than for anything contained within it. The term wasn't even his but had been circulating for several years, possibly coined by the Belgian musicologist Harry Halbreich. Nevertheless, "complex" remains a good description of Ferneyhough's music and is hence difficult to avoid.

Complexity should not be reduced, however, to "difficulty." Alkan is difficult, as are Liszt and Paganini. Ferneyhough's music is, without doubt, difficult to play. Yet complexity in this context refers more usefully to the music's construction through multiple, and sometimes conflicting, layers of information, its polyvalency, and its structured chaos. This is not a question simply of density of information, although that is also a feature of the music, but of the multiple lines of force that must be negotiated and balanced at any given moment. Paganini's music is difficult because it adds dense figuration and ornamentation to a single musical trajectory (a melody or a harmonic progression), using many notes to the bar. Ferneyhough's is complex because it describes multiple intersecting and conflicting frameworks at once.

Ferneyhough's music begins from the premise that a given chunk of material— a musical building block—carries within it a set of implications. It suggests certain ways in which it would like to unfold—for example, certain narrative arcs. It also contains a certain density of information, which further suggests an ideal time-frame in which it can present itself and be understood by a listener. Accepting this to be the case, for now, Ferneyhough's aesthetic derives from thwarting or challenging these implications, setting up situations in which the material is forced to exceed its implied limits. In his quasi-violin concerto *Terrain* (1992), for example, the soloist's opening passage is split over two staves that continually "interrupt" each other, as notes on one line are timed to begin before notes on the other line should have ended. Divided between two instruments, these could create a continuous polyphonic exchange, but compressed as they are into the single line of one violin, we hear how neither part quite has enough time to speak. Similarly, the orchestral *Plötzlichkeit* (2006) squeezes 111 densely packed sections into its twenty-three minutes to achieve the "abruptness" or "suddenness" of its title.

In the 1970s, Ferneyhough's complexity was in fact closely aligned with virtuosity. In the series of solo works that made his reputation—*Cassandra's Dream Song* (1970) and *Unity Capsule* (1975–6), both for flute; *Time and Motion Study I* (1971–7), for bass clarinet; and *Time and Motion Study II* (1973–6), for cello and electronics— the performer's ability simply to get through everything in the score becomes a compositional parameter in its own right. However, as performers have caught up with the demands of his music—and a growing number of ensembles like ELI-SION, Ensemble SurPlus, and Ensemble Exposé have made playing this repertory a specialty and a matter of brand identity—Ferneyhough has shifted his attention away from the relationship between the score and the performer to that between the sound and the listener. The imperfect capacity of memory is now the forum for his experiments. How we understand a piece of music—what a given melody or sound means, how we perceive the work's structure, how we sense how far into a piece or how near the end we are at a given point—is determined by our short-term listening memory. In a song, for example, we recognize a chorus for the first time by how it relates to the verse that we have just heard and for the second time by the fact that it has come around again. Both thoughts depend on our memory's ability to hold chunks of music in mind and make quick comparisons between them.

Ferneyhough's more recent music disrupts these pathways of memory, over-loading, thwarting, or redirecting them. *Incipits* (1996), for viola and small ensem-ble, for example, is composed of seven separate "beginnings,"[19] which draw the listener into a set of expectations that they must keep having to drop and reboot (a musical parallel to Italo Calvino's novel *If on a winter's night a traveler*). Memory here is activated, only to be forcibly wiped clean. This principle is taken a stage further in *Plötzlichkeit* and the mini-concerto for guitar and ensemble *Les froisse-ments d'ailes de Gabriel* (2003) ("245 bars of total non-sequiturs"[20]), extracted from Ferneyhough's opera *Shadowtime* (1999–2004), about the life and thought of Wal-ter Benjamin. On a superficial level, *Les froissements* is an evocation of the rustling wings of the Angel Gabriel, sounded through the music's compressed, fluttering textures. More profoundly, however, it is a Benjaminian meditation on the nature of time. Angels, it is supposed, are unable to perceive time in any human sense, and the way Ferneyhough deliberately overpacks his music with information, starting and restarting it every few seconds to create a perceptual overload, thwarts the memory's ability to create a meaningful structure. Each event is too dense to be fully absorbed in the given time, so when the next one comes along we are already running just to keep up. (In this way Ferneyhough's Angel Gabriel recalls Benjamin's Angel of History, whose wings are continually buffeted by the debris of history piling up before it.) Time after time, what we have just heard is pushed into the background by what follows next, until all we can be sure of is the immediate present, completely out of time.

This brings us to the third reason for Ferneyhough's talismanic character. Proc-esses like the ones described above, as well as the use of nonmetrical rhythms and fleeting pitch relationships, are designed to violate and disturb conventional lis-tening patterns and expectations and thus inevitably attract a lot of resistance from audiences and critics. "Complexity" itself has become a derogatory term. Yet what Ferneyhough is modeling is not confined to the realms of abstract philosophy. In fact, the disorienting, destabilizing, and deferring processes of his music share much with the day-to-day aspects of our twenty-first-century lives. The successive layers of interpretive difficulty displace the musical content in successive steps away from the concrete and the real and toward a virtual, or unreal, musical space. By applying these distorting layers progressively, each one destabilizing the last, Ferneyhough's music crosses a threshold into a more metaphysical realm. Consider his use of nested rhythmic subdivisions. Even a simple triplet rhythm (three in the time of two) creates a temporary "virtual" rhythmic space of three beats within the "real" space of two. Yet it also maintains a tension, as both the articulated three and underlying two can be held simultaneously in the mind. However, when further rhythmic distortions of this type are piled on, as Ferneyhough's rhythmic calculations frequently require, the anchor of the underlying beat is very quickly lost. The original tension goes, and the music gives itself up to the virtual rhythmic space that skips and skims over the top.

Just as the sonata form says something about the metaphysics of the eighteenth century, so Ferneyhough's complexity relates to the metaphysics of the twenty-first. His method of progressively shifting away from the real may take place in an exclusively musical space, but it is formally similar to modern-day financial models, public transport payment systems, and media storage structures, in which everyday transactions no longer take place between people and objects but in a remote—and fragile—digital space of databases and cloud computing. This sympathy with the times (if not necessarily with the immediate desires of its potential audiences) has helped make it a popular point of departure for many younger composers.

Mahnkopf: Excess

By constructing a sort of music-plus that stretches and exceeds the formal boundaries of its original material as an aesthetic principle, Ferneyhough's music shares something with the works by Boulez and Kurtág described above. Yet of the work of these three composers, it is Ferneyhough's construction of virtual musical spaces that has been explored the furthest by younger generations. In *Generation Kill* (2012), Stefan Prins articulates layers of distortion more aggressively than Ferneyhough had by using visual projections of the musicians (both live and on video), which are themselves distorted and warped. These make explicit the critique suggested by Ferneyhough's operations, through the theme of military game playing. In pieces by Evan Johnson (b. 1980), a more subtle critique is described. In *vo mesurando* (2012), for four high voices, for example, the music reaches a point of almost total erasure, in spite of its forbiddingly prescriptive notation. The multiple planes of activity, which in Ferneyhough interrupt the passage of time, simply start to cancel one another out, permitting only the slightest glimpses of actual music to slip through the gaps. As the composer writes, "The material and energies of the work are private, quite often simply inaudible . . . . These are all madrigalian figures that you are overhearing, but they are not for you."[21] The distance between

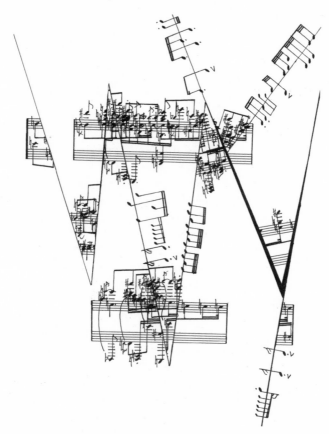

FIGURE 25. Excerpt from the graphic score for Will Redman's *Book*, 2006. Unsystematic Music ASCAP.

figure and ground, concrete and virtual, becomes so great that the whole system seems to rest on the knife edge between total collapse and genuine magic. In Will Redman's (b. 1975) *Book* (2006), that implicit catastrophe is realized in surreal graphic scores that set up Ferneyhough-like expectations of musical detail only to explode them in flamboyant sprays of notes (see figure 25).

In terms of notational complexity, at least, Claus-Steffen Mahnkopf (b. 1962) is chief among Ferneyhough's successors. It is unwise to make predictions based on present conditions, but Mahnkopf's *Hommage à Thomas Pynchon* (2001–5) surely represents something close to the horizon of musical expression of formal and material superabundance. Composed for Ensemble SurPlus, and given its first performance at the MaerzMusik festival in Berlin in 2005, it is a cycle of three works—*The Tristero System* (2002), for ensemble; *The Courier's Tragedy* (2001), for solo cello; and *D.E.A.T.H.* (2001–2), for eight-track electronics—that are performable separately or in an integrated sequence as the *Hommage*. A fourth piece, *W.A.S.T.E.* (2001–2), for oboe and electronics, belongs to the same cycle of separate pieces. It is not heard as part of the *Hommage* polywork, however, although its sound materials contribute a substrate to *Hommage*'s electronic components.

Hommage à Thomas Pynchon is a work of unidentifiable genre. It is part ensemble piece, part concerto, part music theater, and part sound installation. It begins with *The Tristero System*, for an ensemble of thirteen instruments (two pianos, two percussion, two bass clarinets, three trombones, and four piccolos), offering, as Mahnkopf describes, "sufficiently repellent post-urban sonic material."[22] The work lasts eighteen minutes. At the same time, a software program that Mahnkopf calls the Pynchon Architecture is launched. Using the sounds being performed on stage, and working in real time, the program creates a new layer of electronically transformed music, which is freely faded in and out of the hall's loudspeakers by the sound engineer. The musicians leave the stage when *The Tristero System* is finished, but the Pynchon Architecture continues. After around ten minutes, and without a break in the music, a solo cellist (whose part is notated across an unprecedented ten staves at once) appears and performs *The Courier's Tragedy*, a musicotheatrical attempt to "defeat" the electronics. This attempt fails, and after twenty minutes, the cellist also leaves the stage. The Pynchon Architecture carries on, however, and around an hour after the start of the work, the hall doors are opened to reveal that the electronic music is proceeding in four additional spaces, in a different configuration in each room. At this point, the music in the main hall is replaced with the tape piece *D.E.A.T.H.*, played on an indefinite loop. Mahnkopf's preferred form is of "a music without any temporal end, one that made the greatest possible provocation of the art world, a permanent threat: an untreatable paranoia, as it were."[23] However, he concedes that "one must, in the end, organize a 'concert', an event with a fixed time and a predefined location."[24]

The theme of excess was thus coded into the work from the very start: the cycle's planned duration and content were guaranteed to exceed the practical requirements of performance. This applies not only in the simple terms of duration but also in the fact that an entire eighteen-minute component of the Pynchon cycle, *W.A.S.T.E.*, was composed in the express knowledge that it would barely feature as an audible part of the *Hommage*. Mahnkopf has written that the attraction of Pynchon's work (specifically the novel *The Crying of Lot 49*) lies in a similarly polyphonically and illegibly layered reality: "The listener hears that he cannot hear everything, just as the reader of Pynchon is constantly led to suppose that, as well as the story that has been told, there are also other, presumably equally valid descriptions of reality."[25]

Hommage à Thomas Pynchon would be unremarkable if its complexity ended there, however. As we have seen in chapter 3, Mahnkopf is not alone in composing polyworks, in which multiple complete pieces serve as polyphonic layers to one another. What makes his work extraordinary is the extent of his compositional operations on his material—grotesque and even alarming extensions of the kinds of displacement and distancing I described in chapter 4. The work is too substantial to consider in detail here, but a brief walk through the electronics used to create the Pynchon Architecture will give a sense of the complexity of operations at work.[26]

Two main components underpin the Pynchon Architecture: sound files of *The Tristero System*, recorded live as the music is being performed, and a long number sequence that Mahnkopf calls the Pynchon Sequence. The sequence is derived from a list of every letter (upper and lowercase) used in the book, ordered according to frequency and assigned a number (from one to fifty-one). Substituting these numbers for the letters used in the text produces a sequence more than two hundred thousand digits long.

Mahnkopf's program subjects the recorded *Tristero* material it to a series of five operations, each of which uses aspects of the number sequence. Nodding ironically toward Pynchon's American nationality, Mahnkopf calls these Aggressor, CIA, Pentagon, White House, and NASA. (A sixth operation, named Cox Machine, after the cellist Franklin Cox, draws not on the *Tristero* material, but that of *The Courier's Tragedy*.) Each of the five units applies its own set of actions before passing the results on to the next unit.

The Aggressor receives the raw sound files and arranges them according to instrumental group before applying various transpositions, inversions, and reversals. These actions are related to the original methods of Schoenberg's serial technique, but because they happen within the computer, various further distortions also apply (units that are transposed up or down also sound faster or slower, for example). The Aggressor also performs a number of switching operations, governed by the Pynchon Sequence, between "normal" and "interference" types of material. The CIA unit then applies a secondary switching system between the various layers of processed instrumental material generated by the Aggressor. This is also guided by the Pynchon Sequence, but it is applied at a slightly larger scale so as to avoid any synchronization. The four-channel sound output is then fed into the Pentagon unit, which determines the distribution of the sound among the four acoustic spaces that open up outside the main hall in the final section of the piece. Again, the Pynchon Sequence determines the rhythm by which the distribution pattern between the four spaces switches. Once more, the sequence is applied at a further slightly larger scale, so as to avoid synchronization with the preceding switching processes.

By this stage, the pieces of original recorded material (transposed, inverted, reversed, or left alone as according to the Aggressor) are arranged in a sequence that switches between normal and distorted forms. This sequence is further distorted by switches between different layers of similarly processed material and distorted once again through constantly shifting spatial distribution. Yet the most dramatic transformations are yet to come, with the White House unit. In this unit, the sounds are electronically processed according to eighteen types of procedures, ranging from alterations in dynamic to the addition of various types of reverberation to granulation and filtering effects. These procedures last between two and eighteen minutes and in themselves often rely on internally complex manipulations. Mahnkopf applies them, in an order determined (once again) by the Pynchon Sequence, to each of the four channels of music in turn so that the series of operations is different (and hence unsynchronized) for each channel. By allowing this order to be looped, Mahnkopf creates a self-generative work that can be extended indefinitely, although in practice a finite time is defined; for the work's premiere, this was set at seven hours. Finally, the NASA unit determines the spatial movement of the sounds across a six-channel speaker system for each of the four acoustic spaces. Yet even this final presentation is not left undistorted, as additional speakers in each of the rooms play further electronically derived material, via the Cox Machine unit, and a recording of percussion sounds composed according to the occurrence of punctuation marks in Pynchon's novel.

At the end of this collection of processes, Mahnkopf has created an electronic music whose relationship to its original material (the ensemble music of *The Tristero System*) is tenuous at best. Yet some sort of continuity is nevertheless expected; as with Michael Finnissy's transcription procedures described in the previous chapter, some memory of the source must remain regardless of what transformations are applied. When such connections are stretched to their absolute limits, as they are in *Hommage à Pynchon,* the nature or fact of their existence becomes an almost mystical article of faith, akin to Mahnkopf's own recoding of *The Crying of Lot 49* into a number sequence based on the book's typographical characters. At this level, excess becomes an expression of the infinite connectivity of things—across all boundaries, across all media, across all modes of transformation and translation—a compelling, if disconcerting, vision of technologically managed supermodernity.

EXTRAHUMANITY: TECHNOLOGY AND EXCESS

Excess, in its historical sense, has always been concerned with pleasures of the flesh. Dionysus and de Sade saw the body as a vehicle for transgressing social norms and regulations. Now we can exceed even our bodies through prosthetic, virtual, and genetic technologies. Of course, technology has always been about augmenting our human capabilities. But recent developments in synthetic limbs and organs, genetic modification, virtual reality, and so on put into question what it is to be human, to inhabit this fleshly body. Present-day technology gives us access to hitherto unimagined scales, from the interplanetary to the subatomic. Technologies of data storage and the attendant industries of restoration and preservation have made trivial the creation of impossibly huge, Borgesian libraries. Processor speeds have reached a point where it is possible for us to interact with computers more or less in real time, playing music alongside them or using them as extensions of our own instruments.

Prosthetics and Augmentation: The Studio

It is an intriguing coincidence that two of the leaders of Europe's postwar modernist revival should turn at the same time to the realization of massive, even utopian, projects in the mid-1970s. In the same year that Stockhausen began work on *LICHT,* Boulez became director and de facto artistic figurehead of the Institut de Recherche et Coordination Acoustique/Musique (better known as IRCAM), the French state-funded research institute of acoustics and music technology.

In its scale and influence, IRCAM represents the quintessential example of the channeling of financial, computational, and intellectual resources into creating new music. Although it was initially a site of considerable innovation, in the 1980s it drifted into a cycle of self-justificatory research design, common to many academic institutions, in its continuing pursuit of funding. The compositional work that took place was affected and could even be accused of a certain degree of bloat. Works were composed to showcase new technologies; new technologies were designed (more or less bespoke) to accommodate the wishes of composers.[27] Lurking underground, beneath the Place Stravinsky in Paris, IRCAM was a symbol of modernist excess and isolationism.

This began to change in the 1990s. Boulez retired as director and in 1991 was succeeded by Laurent Bayle. The institute started to become more accountable. It opened itself up. New building work took place, and much of the facility was both literally and symbolically moved above ground. IRCAM opened an extensive multimedia library in 1996 and launched a large and user-friendly website, today one of the Web's most authoritative sites on contemporary music. Cross-media collaborations were instigated, and in 1999 a choreography department was opened. In line with the trend toward instrumentalization, both education and marketing departments were created. The former offers a range of opportunities, including children's workshops, software training, a summer school, and graduate composition courses that have become a rite of passage for ambitious composers in their twenties and thirties. The marketing department opens IRCAM to the public in other ways, most importantly by selling and distributing its software through channels such as the subscription-based IRCAM Forum.[28]

The result is that IRCAM's place within the contemporary music world has become even more important than it was during Boulez's tenure, even though it is not as loudly heralded. The number of composers under, say, fifty who have at least some experience at the institute is remarkable. Its software developments have been even more significant. Two of the most successful are the visual programming languages Max and OpenMusic. Max was written at IRCAM around 1986, by the composer and programmer Miller Puckette (b. 1959), and was first used to realize Philippe Manoury's (b. 1952) *Pluton* (1988), in which a computer creates a live electronic accompaniment synchronized with a solo piano. Max was licensed by IRCAM first to Opcode Systems (in 1990) and then to Cycling '74 (in 1999), who are its current developers, and it has since been renamed Max/MSP. An on-screen interface for creating and processing electronic sound in real time, Max is essentially a virtual equivalent to the table of effects pedals used by noise artists, although it is of considerably greater potential and finesse. Individual sound processing modules (called patches) can be designed and then linked together in any possible combination before being outputted to a speaker system. Because of its fundamental flexibility (it is unattached to any particular aesthetic) and its intuitive interface, Max/MSP has been used widely by musicians not only within the art music and experimental sphere but also in the pop and rock scenes.[29] OpenMusic is a more specialized compositional application. Similar to Max, it uses modular patches that can be designed by the user and arranged in any combination. However, whereas Max is a means of processing sound signals, OpenMusic is a means of processing pitch and/or rhythmic data, which is then output as conventional notation. It is therefore a tool not for live sound synthesis but for precompositional planning and calculation. OpenMusic has been widely used by composers interested in harmonic spectra, such as Michael Jarrell (b. 1958), Tristan Murail (b. 1947), and Kaija Saariaho (b. 1952), as a means of generating and transforming chord sequences based on individual sound spectra; it has also been used extensively, by Ferneyhough, for example, as a means of calculating rhythms.

IRCAM may be large, but it is not unique. Similar stories may be told, at varying scales, of other institutions around the world, including the Experimentalstudio des Sudwestrundfunk in Freiburg and Stanford's Center for Computer Research in Music and Acoustics. At much the same time as IRCAM was undergoing its changes under Bayle, a new studio, the Institute for Music and Acoustics (IMA), was opening at the Zentrum für Kunst und Medientechnologie (ZKM) in Karlsruhe, Germany.

By sheer coincidence, the IMA was founded in the same year as the Berlin Wall came down, and its early history is shaped by the wider situation in Germany. By the late 1980s, the famous WDR studio in Cologne, where Stockhausen first worked, was almost defunct; the Feedback Studio, also in Cologne, home to a number of former members of Stockhausen's performing ensemble—including Clarence (Klarenz) Barlow (b. 1945), Peter Eötvös (b. 1944), and Mesías Maiguashca (b. 1938)—was still operational but very limited in equipment. There was a studio in the former East Germany at the Akademie der Künste in East Berlin, but this quickly disappeared after reunification. The IMA therefore entered something of a vacuum. Its importance within German electroacoustic music since 1989 is high-

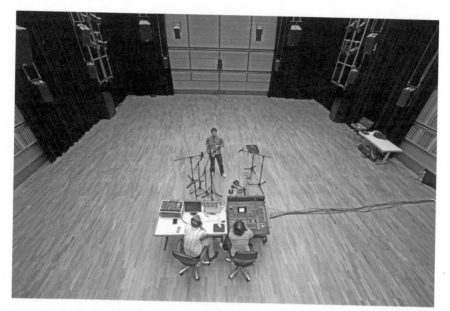

FIGURE 26. The Klangdom at ZKM_Cube. Photo by ONUK, courtesy of ZKM | Karlsruhe.

lighted by the fact that, in 2004, Stockhausen himself produced *LICHT-BILDER*, the final section of *LICHT,* at the IMA, a symbolic passing of the baton from Cologne to Karlsruhe.

Like IRCAM, ZKM (and by extension the IMA) oriented itself between the needs of the arts, research, and industry. Its first director, the art historian Heinrich Klotz, proved adept at arguing for the economic and technological benefits of supporting cutting-edge media art, garnering the political and financial support crucial to ZKM's early survival (although as the IMA's first director, Johannes Goebel, observed, these arguments were "happily never questioned"[30]). Its signature technology is a forty-seven-speaker, 3D surround-sound system known as the Klangdom (see figure 26). As its name suggests, the Klangdom is a dome of speakers, arranged above and around the audience. This is linked to custom software, Zirkonium, which allows for highly sophisticated multichannel spatialization of sound. Sounds can be programmed not only to be produced from any point within the dome but also to move in any shape—left/right, up/down, in spirals, in circles, and so on—across and around the space.

As technologies like this show, today's electronic studios express abundance and excess not only through their consumption and justification of financial resources but also through the creation of electronic augmentations that take the human performer into superhuman and even virtual realms. In the Klangdom, for example, performers can create live spatializations of their music using motion sensors so that the sound moves according to their own gestures. At the Massachusetts Institute of Technology Media Lab, a whole series of electronically augmented instruments—hyperinstruments—have been developed that use detailed analyses of performance gesture and sound production to radically alter the music that is heard.

The hyperinstrument project—known as the Opera of the Future research group—was begun by composer Tod Machover (b. 1953) in 1986. Before coming to MIT, Machover had worked at IRCAM, where he composed works that combined live performers and computer-generated sounds. Hyperinstruments extend this idea but with a view to creating technology that is responsive enough to be used not only by leading professionals but also by amateur and young musicians. The project's first significant creations were string instruments: hypercello, hyperviola, and hyperviolin. These used various forms of gesture and sound recognition technology that converted a player's technique and phrasing into hard data, which could then be used to trigger electronic transformations of the sound itself. The new instruments were given their first repertory in a trilogy of works composed by Machover: *Begin Again Again* (1991), for hypercello, written for Yo-Yo Ma; *Song of Penance* (1992), for hyperviola and chamber orchestra, written for Kim Kashkashian; and *Forever and Ever* (1993), for hyperviolin and chamber orchestra, written for Ani Kavafian. Later, a second generation of hyperstring instruments was produced, along with a hyperbow. The bow collects data about bowing parameters—speed, force, position—and uses these as the basis of sound transformations; so a greater bow speed might trigger one set of transformations, while a decrease in pressure might trigger a different collection. In this way, the electronic sounds derive directly from the performer's playing and can be as closely controlled by them as their regular sound production. (Unlike Stefan Prins's interfering "black boxes," the computer of a hyperinstrument is a faithful extension of the performer's movements.)

Although the original hyperstring instruments were given to leading professionals like Ma and Kashkashian—no doubt to help cement the legitimacy of the new inventions—MIT's work has also been directed toward popular and amateur usages. Hyperinstrument technology may have its origins in high modernist institutions like IRCAM, but it has had greatest impact in the production of interactive toys and media. The toys produced by Opera of the Future include Beatbugs, Fireflies, and Music Shapers, which all use simple, tactile interfaces to control musical parameters such as rhythm and timbre, allowing even very young users to create satisfying musical effects. Some of these instruments can be wirelessly linked together and therefore interact, sharing and mutually transforming each others' sounds in virtual, data-designed ensembles. Machover's *Brain Opera* (1996), a major work now permanently installed at the Haus der Musik in Vienna, fills a room with interactive electronic sound sculptures that are collectively dubbed the Brain Forest. They are designed to be organic, playful, and intuitive, and their different interfaces use hyperinstrument principles to engage the public in sophisticated live electroacoustic improvisations created from relatively simple inputs. In the work's original version, these inputs were combined with others from online participants (an example of the networked music discussed in chapter 5) and a live performance by Machover and two others.

The economics of managing a studio mean that technologies are often developed in line with research and/or market applications, as has become the case with IRCAM's software and MIT's musical toys. One of the most successful such outcomes is the game *Guitar Hero*, developed from hyperinstrument technology by two of Machover's students, Alex Rigopulos and Eran Egozy. However, a more DIY approach to running a studio is also possible, exemplified by the Studio for Electro-Instrumental Music (STEIM) in Amsterdam.

Rather than being a studio directed toward the creation of certain technologies and driven by an overriding academic, creative, or industrial agenda, STEIM is more of an enabling facility for composers, performers, and instrument builders. Presently supported by the Dutch Ministry of Culture, it was founded in 1969 by composers Louis Andriessen, Konrad Boehmer, Reinbert de Leeuw, Misha Mengelberg, Dick Raaijmakers, Peter Schat, and Jan van Vlijmen to house the built-from-scratch electronics used in their collaborative opera *Reconstructie* (1969). Since then, and in line with the antiauthoritarian instincts of its founders, its focus has been on the creation of new instruments and instrumental interfaces with a practical, work-specific application—allowing artists to realize their ideas—rather than on more abstract concepts beholden to institutional justifications.

STEIM's focus, particularly under the long directorship of Michael Waisvisz (from 1981 until his death, in 2008) has been on developing physical interfaces for live electronic music, such as the motion sensors used by Tarek Atoui. Frequently, these take on a prosthetic dimension, a good example being the Lady's Glove of Laetitia Sonami (b. 1957). First designed in 1991, the Lady's Glove went through several iterations, each incorporating more and more sophisticated technology. (Sonami stopped using it in 2014.) The version designed in 2003, with assistance from STEIM, contained an array of pressure pads, motion detectors, light sensors, and more, all designed to be worn like an evening glove. The glove's outputs are sent to a computer running Sensorlab, one of STEIM's own software programs, as well as Max/MSP, and by wearing it, Sonami was able to create music from the movements of her hand. In an interesting commentary on the tendency of technology to overtake our intentions—even in a low-key scenario such as STEIM encourages—Sonami has noted that, over time, the glove stopped being a controller and became more of an instrument, even an extension of her own body.[31] But at the same time, the beauty of work with prosthetic controllers or instruments lies not in giving up wholly to the machine but in working with the space that remains between the body's limits and their mechanical extension.

Massification

As well as the sort of ornamental, supplemental, prosthetic extensions described above, computer technology has also encouraged phenomena of massification and multiplication. These concepts have been around for much longer than twenty-first-century technological advances, at least since the advent of tape. They may be found in classic works that use multiplying tape recordings to overwhelm the speaking voice, such as Steve Reich's *Come Out* (1966) or Alvin Lucier's *"I am sitting in a room"* (1969), both of which predate IRCAM. However, practices of massification and multiplication were greatly accelerated, and the possibilities of overstretching the medium more thoroughly explored, with the greater processing speeds, dimensions, and storage capacities enabled by digitization. Techniques such as digital delays, live looping, granular synthesis, and more simply weren't possible before the 1980s, and they gave rise to new styles and aesthetics. These changes became allied, once again, to the commercial factors around commissioning and performing, leading to a kind of work that was very different from the experiments of the 1960s and '70s.

The developments described in the previous chapters have also given composers an unprecedented range of choice and possibility. Social and cultural liberalism has seen previously established barriers between styles, genres, and audiences thoroughly challenged. Technology has done the same for national, temporal, and medial differences. Alongside and partly integrated with these advances are late capitalism's ever-increasing demands for commodity consumption. Yet, as we have seen with Simon Steen-Andersen's *Run Time Error,* models of joyful proliferation, augmentation, and embellishment are inevitably accompanied by casual wastage and anxiety. Every update or upgrade is a step further into a limitless universe, but it leaves behind something outmoded and unusable. "Consumer society," notes Zygmunt Bauman, "cannot but be a society of excess and profligacy—and so of redundancy and prodigal waste."[32]

The sound artist JLIAT (James Whitehead, b. 1951) considers the relationship of scale to superabundance in the digital era: "Today I can hold in the palm of my hand sufficient storage capacity for more than seven years of music. Ten of these devices would store an un-listenable quantity—yet one that is by all means an objective reality—and the data that exists in data farms far exceeds any single human experience."[33] This image recalls the stories of Jorge Luis Borges—"The Library of Babel," "The Aleph," and "On Exactitude in Science"—but transferred from the world of books and maps to the digital age. JLIAT's "thought experiment" *All Possible CDs* (n.d.) is a proposal for the creation of every permutation of bits that can be stored on a seventy-four-minute CD; that is, $2^{6,265,728,000}$ possible CDs, or many, many times more CDs than there are particles in the universe.[34] At the opposite end of things, the speculative text *The shortest piece of music* (2014) discusses the different ways in which the shortest possible sound might be conceived: as a single sample on a CD, a work lasting the duration of the Planck time,[35] or the shortest imaginable length, unrelated to physics or methods of CD manufacture.[36]

1TB (2011–12) represents an unusual case in that it is a realized object. It comprises 233 DVDs, packaged in a single DJ box. Yet it remains as much a conceptual work as it is a physical object. Each disc contains just over seventy-three and a half hours of music, compiled from randomized selections from a database of heavily processed harsh noise samples. The whole set amounts to 1TB (one terabyte, or one trillion bytes) of data, equivalent to around five hundred million pages of text. Listening to it all would take just under two years.

One might be tempted to draw a comparison with Werder's *stück 1998*, another piece whose duration renders it impossible to be heard in full. Both articulate a notion of superhuman scale enabled by changes in the musical language of the past twenty years. However, since Werder's work exists as a score, there is the expectation that it will be realized, in increments, and eventually concluded (although at the current pace of the piece, this will not happen until 2086). It will also be listened to and framed within (relatively) conventional concert spaces. The duration of *stück 1998* is therefore active and actual. That of *1TB*, however, is potential; it will almost certainly not be played or heard as a single duration, even one broken into segments. Where *stück 1998* expresses a fragmented continuum or archipelago, *1TB* expresses a single, unapproachably large mass. JLIAT notes that other long duration works, like Cage's *ASLSP*, "rely on future machines/cultures to fulfil their speculations."[37] By contrast, *1TB* is physical, real, encoded onto twelve-centimeter discs, and a "completed" work. It simply awaits a listener, albeit one with an improbable amount of time and patience.

Both *1TB* and *stück 1998* deal with excess on a horizontal plane; they exceed their formal propositions along the dimension of time. Carsten Nicolai's *Realistic* (1999), however, uses technology to address the idea of vertical excess, in which it is the density of the work that destabilizes its unity and comprehensibility. A tape recorder and a microphone are placed on a table in the center of a room. The recorder is running, and the sounds of the room are being recorded. However, the tape has been cut into a short loop, and the recorder's erase head has been disabled. This means that as the machine runs, it continually layers the room's sound onto the tape; each circuit of the tape loop adds another layer of sound. Every environmental sound—made by visitors, the building, or even the machinery itself—is recorded. The recording is made in high fidelity, but it is almost immediately rendered useless as a meaningful record through the process of looping and layering. The value in our limitless capacity to record and preserve is nullified by the senselessness of data massification.[38] It is a more direct form of the sort of limitless mutation that erodes identity that is found in *Hommage à Thomas Pynchon.*

Realistic and *1TB* highlight how scale, the relationship of the work to the archive, the temporal limits of a musical work, and other elements have become aesthetic categories. Both pieces confront the fact that the seemingly impossible has become today's reality: JLIAT's impossibly immense work is contained in a single portable carry case; Nicolai's tape loops are displayed on the wall of the installation, which is, after all, titled *Realistic*. Both represent extreme states of massification, possible only because they step beyond the bounds of score- and time-based composition and into the more conceptual realm of sound art. Nevertheless, they are part of the same continuum of thought and products of similar forces of enablement and inspiration as many more "conventionally" composed works.

Microsounds

Advances in computer speeds and memory capacity in the 1980s allowed not only greater complexity of live electronics and the prosthetic expansion and multiplication of the performer through instrument-computer interfaces, such as described above, but also conceptions of compositional methods on hitherto unimagined small scales. One of the most important developments was that of "granular synthesis," the idea of composing with minute particles of sound as short as one millisecond in length. This concept originated in the work of the physicist Dennis Gabor, which proposed that sound, like light, may be thought of as a stream of elementary sound particles rather than as a waveform, as had previously been believed.

Inspired by Gabor, Iannis Xenakis began investigating the possibilities of granular synthesis for composition. The principle of combining small musical units to create masses, swarms, flocks, and other large-scale, dynamic structures had been present in Xenakis's music since his orchestral works of the 1950s (e.g., *Metastaseis*, 1954, and *Pithoprakta*, 1955–6), composed not long after Gabor began presenting his research. Xenakis developed these ideas further in the tape pieces *Concret PH* (1958), composed of one-second fragments of the sounds of burning wood, and *Analogique B* (1958–9).

Xenakis's work was severely constrained by the technology available to him at the time, and in the end he did not pursue his ideas much further in the digital domain. The next stage was carried out by his student, Curtis Roads (b. 1951). Roads produced his first studies in digital sound particle synthesis in 1974, working painstakingly and slowly between several facilities at University of California, San Diego (including the Scripps Institute of Oceanography, where he was able to transfer data on tape onto a disk cartridge). However, it was not until 1986 that granular synthesis was first implemented in real time, in Barry Truax's *Riverrun*. Truax (b. 1947) remained an important innovator in the following years. In works such as *Beauty and the Beast* (1989) and *Pacific* (1990), he used granular synthesis to time-stretch his source sounds without altering their pitch, a technique that is now commonplace in electronic music of all types. By the end of the decade, developments in software and hardware had made it possible to experiment with granular synthesis on desktop computers and to edit sound graphically, even at the level of the sound grain.[39]

Roads coined the term "microsound" to describe electroacoustic composition that began on this granular level.[40] Key to this technique is the "plasticity" of the sound, a result of its manipulation at the particle level. This, he writes, "allows mutation to play an important compositional role, since every sound object is a potential transformation"[41]—an aesthetic principle that has clear links with some of the models of fluidity described in chapter 4.

The combined aesthetics of massification and plastic transformation are exemplified in Horacio Vaggione's *Schall* (1994), a key early work of its type. Vaggione (b. 1943) was a pioneer in the 1960s in the interaction of computers and live instruments. Beginning in the 1990s, his works have increasingly used techniques of digital sound manipulation, such as granular synthesis. Like many of his works, *Schall* is composed of tens of thousands of sound particles, in this instance all derived from sampled piano notes. Although granular synthesis composition typically uses automated procedures, Vaggione works directly, point by point, painstakingly selecting tiny samples of sound from a large dataset and organizing them on screen in a process that Roads calls "micromontage."[42]

The use of granular synthesis provides a link between music and so-called "big data"—the widespread use of very large datasets to construct and predict trends and patterns, whether in genetics, meteorology, or the stock market. Although microsound composers use digital grains to synthesize more complex sounds—in Vaggione's case almost working by hand—other composers have translated data more directly into sound and visuals. The most notable of these is the sound and visual artist Ryoji Ikeda (b. 1966), who exploits the spectacular possibilities of massed data. Often, as in installation works such as *The Transfinite* (2011) and *data. path* (2013), the scale and density of the data presented, transformed into electronic sound and highly abstract black and white projections, takes on a sublime quality, becoming a meditation on the structures behind contemporary life (see figure 27).

Multiples

A singer is alone on stage, accompanied only by a microphone and an electronic box at her feet. As she sings into the mic, she uses a pedal switch on the box to capture short melodic loops. While the loops continue, she sings a new melody over the top; with a couple more taps of the foot this is added as a second looping layer, and her voice moves on again. She continues in this way.

The box is a digital delay system, a simple means of recording a sounding input and then playing it back as an indefinitely repeating loop. With skill, a single

FIGURE 27. Ryoji Ikeda's *data.path,* 2013. Photo by r2hox, www.flickr.com/photos/
rh2ox/9989876925/, licensed under CC Attribution-ShareAlike 2.0.

performer can quickly build up an elaborate accompaniment made up entirely of
recordings of herself. Although the technology is a little older, commercial digital
delay unit effects boxes (such as the popular Lexicon PCM42) were developed in
the early 1980s, making delay effects, live sampling, and looping affordable to
many musicians. These made it possible for one player to generate a whole ensemble. At first they found a place in popular music and jazz, but they quickly drew the
attention of experimental musicians too, including Diamanda Galás, Pauline
Oliveros, and Pamela Z, who were among the pioneers of this new technology.

In some respects, digital delays did not add anything new to the musical vocabulary available to composers in the 1980s. Loops and layers were invented as formal devices soon after the invention of magnetic tape, and the idea of composing
works of music wholly or substantially out of such materials was at least as old as
Terry Riley's experiments of the early 1960s. Steve Reich's refinement of such processes, through his own tape works of the mid-1960s and the instrumental works
that followed, helped create a set of formal and aesthetic norms for such music,
which soon came to be known as minimalism. One, albeit limited, way of viewing
the digital delay is as an after-the-event tool devised to assist in the rapid creation
of the close canons that characterize such works, particularly in a live setting. At
the very least, minimalism created a vocabulary and a set of stylistic tropes that
suggested one set of ways in which delays could be used.

There is a clear difference between the lengthy precompositional work undertaken by Reich in perfecting his loops for *Piano Phase* and *Violin Phase* and the more improvisational processes that digital delays admit. How do we compare and evaluate the results of two distinct compositional processes that have arrived at superficially similar ends?

One of the key differences between Reichian notated loops and the (no less composed) live loops of a performer like Z or Oliveros is the most obvious: the presence of a live performer at the heart of the process. When live looping, everything fed into the delay system emanates from a single performer; likewise, a single performer must form and sustain her presence within an automated environment that is singing back to her. The stage performance and composition involve self-augmentation and self-multiplication; their meaning extends to questions of embodiment and identity, and not just the abstract level of interactions of material.

The philosophical, aesthetic, and even political challenges live loops present are perhaps most fully explored in Ferneyhough's *Time and Motion Study II*, in which the solo cellist must grapple not only with ferociously challenging writing for her two hands but also with a tape-delay system operated by two foot pedals (a precursor of the more flexible digital units), vocalizations, and the very real bonds of a system of contact microphones on her throat and instrument. Not for nothing is the work sometimes referred to as "electric chair music."[43] However, in more recent works involving multiplying voices, the performer is less physically unrestrained. Another cello piece, David Lang's *world to come* (2003), offers a good comparison. Whereas Ferneyhough's tape-delayed cellists bounce back on the live performer, regulating and confining her musical identity, Lang's multiple parts (which are prerecorded tracks rather than live delays) ripple outward, splitting her personality. The principle is similar to how Galás multitracks her vocals, although Lang's postminimalist aesthetic is more immediately approachable. The work has an association with 9/11 (Lang has noted that the initials WTC can stand for both World Trade Center and world to come), and the piece was inspired by the idea of a "cellist and her voice [becoming] separated from each other" and struggling "to reunite in a post-apocalyptic environment."[44] The performer isn't just made plural; her expression is made to exceed her bodily limit. In this respect, the precursor is *"I am sitting in a room"*, in which the process of using a pair of tape recorders to loop and rerecord the sound of the performer's speech within the space audibly dissolves the vocal identity of the performer into the abstract, architectural properties of the room itself. Yet where Lucier's piece enacts a mono-directional process, ungovernable once set in motion, Lang's is freer, compositionally speaking, and can build cuts or layers into the music, changing and shaping it so that it is no longer about only the process but can accommodate narratives outside of itself as well.

Masses

Related to the technique of multiplication is that of composing for large numbers of instruments of the same type. Works like this have become increasingly popular. One of the first well-known examples is Rhys Chatham's *An Angel Moves Too Fast to See* (1989), which calls for 100 electric guitars. So too does Glenn Branca's Symphony No. 13 *Hallucination City* (2001, rev. 2006). Chatham, however, surpassed both in 2005 with *A Crimson Grail* for 400 guitars. Wendy Mae Chambers (b. 1953) has also composed for large numbers of identical instruments, including a Mass (1993), for 77 trombones, and *Kun* (2009), for 64 toy pianos. Salvatore Sciarrino's *La bocca, i piedi, il suono* (1997) is written for 104 saxophones (4 soloists and 100 others walking around the performance space); his *Il cerchio tagliato dei suoni*, of the same year, is composed for a similar arrangement of 104 flutes. David Lang's *crowd out* (2010) calls for "1,000 people yelling." None of these call for advanced technology (unless you count the amplification systems required for Branca's or Chatham's guitars), but their applications of principles of density, multiplication, and sheer weight of numbers owe much to the aesthetic ground broken by more studio-based work.

Often the motivation is quasi-sculptural: with very large numbers of similar instruments, sound can be shaped like stone or clay, with a wide range of control of density and mass that can be deployed by the composer, rather like sound within the studio. This was something learned by Xenakis in the 1950s, and although few composers today draw on his stochastic mathematical procedures, the raw architectural quality of works like *Metasteseis* and *Pithoprakta* has had an enduring influence.

Massed forces also defocus the musical detail of a work. Even if scored in unison, one hundred instrumentalists are never going to play precisely in synch or precisely in tune. The effect will always tend to be one of sound diffusing, blurring around its edges, accepting and even acquiescing to its environmental conditions. In *An Angel Moves Too Fast to See*, Chatham assembles his own band of four guitarists, one bassist, and one drummer, who act as leaders for the other hundred players. The poetry lies in the relationship of Chatham's group to the mass behind them—the contrast between the precision and the amorphous hum mirrors the dual sound of the guitar itself: pluck and ring, strike and bloom. Assembling one hundred electric guitars not only is an expression of machismo but also has the musical effect of diffusing the ego, distributing it so widely and so thickly that nearly all definition is lost.

However, there are other, less obviously musical motivations at work. Performances of pieces like *crowd out* or *Hallucination City* are marked by the particular improvised community of performers that they engender. Music made in such a mass form—echoing the giant Victorian-era performances of Handel's *Messiah*, for example—is accessible to the amateur performer. Indeed, it requires them: even if it were possible to book one hundred professional electric guitarists on the same night to perform *Hallucination City,* it would be prohibitively expensive to do so. So it is therefore necessary to include amateurs in the performance. Composing for such large-scale event formats can thus help bring the music out of the traditional new music sphere and into the public eye.

Both of Sciarrino's massed pieces mentioned above allude to the phenomenon of migration, particularly of forced movements of refugees and economic migrants. They have a distinctly theatrical dimension. In both, the four soloists are placed at the corners of the performing space and are mostly static. The one hundred "migratory" players move in predetermined paths across the performance space. In the flute piece, they take a diagonal line from the front right of the stage to the back left; once performers have exited, they run backstage to rejoin the stream once more, creating the illusion of an endless procession. Sciarrino's note to *Il cerchio tagliato del suoni* alludes to the tension between the globalizing impulse to mobility and the human instinct for stability: "But when one is taken by the fever to leave, it is not easy to resist. To him (to us): have a good journey."[45] In *La bocca, i piedi, il suono,* the movements are more complicated. The one hundred saxophones start outside the hall, and in the second half of the piece they enter one by one, as though arriving in a strange place for the first time. When creating the piece, the image of Albanian refugees fleeing war in the former Yugoslavia and arriving in Italy as foreigners was in Sciarrino's mind.[46] The sheer number of musicians is clearly symbolic, but it makes a political point too. As is typical for Sciarrino's music, individual musicians are asked to play hushed sounds, often on the edge of audibility. In other circumstances, these sounds might be lost, but as a large mass they generate a weight of their own, in the end becoming unignorable.

REACTIONS AND RESPONSES

Although many musicians embraced the possibilities of plenitude, there were those who doubted the validity of its ethic. The global financial crisis of 2008 was only the most consequential product of the twenty-first century's hubristic faith in big data; its general lesson (heeded or not) was that no amount of information removes the need for human analysis, responsibility, or intervention. Composers who turned away from the aesthetics of abundance were therefore also passing comment on such a databased, technologized culture. Mahnkopf argues that *Hommage à Thomas Pynchon* speaks against such a culture: "I decided to . . . make the work infinitely long . . . in analogy to the (not only) musical culture industry, which likewise forces itself on the whole world without asking whether this is in the recipients' interests."[47] But one must question to what extent the work really can be read as a critique and not a celebration. *Hommage à Thomas Pynchon* remains, after all, the product of an environment—the Freiburg Experimentalstudio—where such compositional extravagance is happily enabled. True excess may be Dionysian, but here it is highly circumscribed within the mechanisms and support structures of contemporary music.

Perhaps more powerful statements are made against the "culture industry" by those works that turn their own materials against themselves. Both John Oswald's (b. 1953) *Plexure* (1993) and Marko Ciciliani's (b. 1970) *Pop Wall Alphabet* (2011) take recordings of popular music as a starting point for expressions of hyperconsumption, sonic immersion and overload, and noisy excess.

Plexure is one of the most substantial statements of Oswald's "plunderphonic" style, a means of composition that relies entirely on the sampling of existing (and commercially released) recordings. It achieved notoriety with Oswald's 1989 album of the same name, a twenty-five-track compilation of cut-ups and other digital manipulations of popular artists, from Dolly Parton to Public Enemy. Following legal action from the Canadian Recording Industry Association, Oswald was forced to destroy all undistributed copies of the album. Each track used the music of one artist; often just one song. Dolly Parton featured on "Pretender," a version of her well-known hit "The Great Pretender" that begins playing at many times its intended speed (such that it sounds like an undifferentiated high-pitched wail) and gradually slows down so that Parton's voice slips slowly, psychedelically from helium-inspired falsetto to sub–Barry White bass. "Brown" is compiled entirely from samples of Public Enemy beats, many of them themselves samples of James Brown's music. Michael Jackson is featured on the album's standout track, "Dab," a remix-cum-annihilation of his hugely successful "Bad" single of 1987 that at its climax pulverizes Jackson's voice into countless grains of sound dust, somewhat like a Barry Truax composition.

Plexure takes the "plunder" aspect of Oswald's working practice a step further. Commissioned by John Zorn for release on his Avant label, it is a twenty-minute continuous suite constructed from an alleged 1,001 samples from popular music, all released between 1982 and 1992. Many of the samples are exceedingly short, some just a few milliseconds in length, but they are stitched together meticulously into an endlessly varied collage. Whereas "Dab" highlighted a self-similar sonic continuity within Jackson's song, *Plexure* highlights discontinuity and difference. The result is a high-density aural blast of popular culture, a logical conclusion to channel surfing, MTV, and accelerationism in which every snippet is—however briefly—recognizable but meaning or even flow is continually overturned.

Where *Plexure* creates excess through a high density, horizontal stream, *Pop Wall Alphabet* works vertically, compressing popular songs into "spectral freezes" that capture all the frequency and amplitude changes of a song within a single moment, as though looking at the complete song end on. The resulting sound can then be extended indefinitely, creating a thick, immersive band of particularly colored noise. There are twenty-six parts to *Pop Wall Alphabet,* lasting between six and fourteen minutes each. (The whole work may be presented as a four-and-a-half-hour installation, with accompanying videos.) Each part is built from a single pop album, with one artist representing each letter of the alphabet; for example, Abba's *Arrival* for A, Lady Gaga's *The Fame Monster* for G, and Queen's *A Night at the Opera* for Q. Each part follows the same procedure. At the start, every track of the source album is played simultaneously, overlaid with every associated spectral freeze. The freezes are gradually faded out to coincide with the ending of the shortest album track. Being of different lengths, the tracks themselves progressively end too, until only the longest is left playing. At this point, the spectral freezes start to fade back in, one at a time, in a sort of relay that mirrors the order and timing of when each track dropped out in the first half of the piece. Once all the spectral freezes have been heard, the piece ends.

Listening to *Pop Wall Alphabet* becomes a process of finding and interpreting meaning from an initially impossible density of sound. As this clarifies, as first the spectral freezes and then the individual tracks fade out, familiar elements come into focus; Ciciliani says that he chose pop recordings because of their emotive potential: "They might also represent a very specific time period in a person's history, evoking feelings of nostalgia and taking on a certain iconic quality."[48] However, the moment of perfect clarity, when one track can be heard in isolation, is just when the spectral freezes begin again, transforming what we know and recognize once more into an abstract sonic totality.

The vast expansion of possibilities that took place at the end of the twentieth century enabled composers to explore new limits, but it also presented new sets of ethical questions to which they could respond. In certain instances, the pursuit and exploitation of increasing resources—in terms not only of duration, density, and scale but also of funding, performer skills, computational power, architectural space, and audience tolerance—have been normalized in the service of music and the other arts. We can build it big, so why not? In other cases, those resources are utilized with the aim of thematizing abundance, either for the production of an ecstatic excess—the sheer pleasure that exists in indulgence—or to problematize its consequences. Faced with the dizzying opportunities of scale, still more musicians have resorted to a simplification of their means. Sometimes this may be due to a simple lack of resources, or even personal modesty; but it can also act as a way of conserving certain artistic values and attempting to halt the process of acceleration, or even, in a more radical sense, to throw a critical light on such processes.

The greatest threat of excess in artistic terms is to the concept of unity; indeed, in many cases, the use of excess may be regarded as a deliberate challenge to the validity of unity. In works such as Finnissy's *Folklore,* the music's multivalency is, at some level at least, a symptom of the disunified global reality that it seeks to reflect. Something similar may also be said of musicircus or archipelago-type

works, in which a complete experience of the work is neither possible nor anticipated, as well as of pieces like Kurtág's *Grabstein für Stephan,* whose material over-
spills their form. Works like these use excess to probe and raise questions.

Other composers have used the ideals of a unified musical language to aspire
instead to a picture of cultural homogeneity and harmony. Stockhausen's extension
in *LICHT* of the serial method into every aspect of the work may be considered one
example of such a project (and an ideology of global unity was present in his work
at least as early as *Hymnen,* 1966–7). Yet more often, such values may be found in
the work of more conservative figures, who find unity not in serialism or moment
form but in the certainties of triadic harmony and metrical rhythm. The work of
many neo-tonal composers may be considered in these terms. This is not to say that
tonality or meter necessarily signal an emphasis on unity over excess, but they can
offer a refuge and perhaps a kind of retreat. Still others, such as composers of
almost-silent music, have turned away from the very large scale to explore more
intimate kinds of music; they include Klaus Lang (b. 1971) and Jakob Ullmann, as
well as members of the Onkyo and Wandelweiser groups, mentioned elsewhere.

Reductions may also be made, paradoxically, to explore aspects of multivalency, pandimensionality, and proliferation with a greater focus, reducing the
overall canvas to pull up the greater detail within. The music of Pierluigi Billone (b.
1960) combines a radical reduction in performing materials with an extensive
examination of their remaining potential. His work differs from that of a more
minimally oriented strategy of reduction in that the musical space remains one of
seemingly endless variety and multidimensionality. Despite the limits placed on
the instrumental resources, the music may still explore at great range and in
microscopic detail the possibilities of rhythm, timbre, and articulation. Works of
this type might include the twenty-minute *Mani.De Leonardis* (2004), for four car
suspension springs and wine glass, or the hour-long *1+1 = 1* (2006), for two bass
clarinets. That this strategy is, at least on some level, a response to modernity is
clear from the titles of several of Billone's works—among them *ME.A.AN* (1994),
for voice and six instruments, and *ITI KE MI* (1995), for viola—which are translit-
erations of ancient Sumerian cuneiform. Photographs of ancient statuary and ritual objects often accompany his scores, which are written by hand and have a
rough, improvisatory, manual quality (see figure 28).

The reference to improvisation is not accidental, and Billone's practice, and the
sound of his music, shares much with that of improvisers like Malcolm Goldstein
(b. 1936), Evan Parker (b. 1944), and Ute Wassermann (b. 1960), whose music very
often begins from a rejection of all possibilities except those presented by their
instrument itself (its acoustic properties, materials, ergonomics) and continues to
construct an endlessly proliferating world. Much of the pleasure of watching a
percussionist play *Mani.De Leonardis* stems (as it does when watching a good
improviser) from seeing the sonic inventiveness unfold. This is not something an

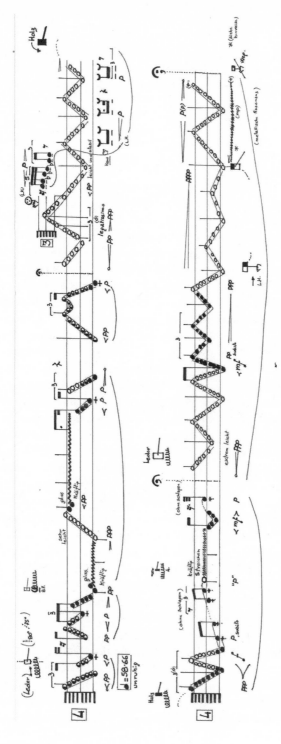

FIGURE 28. Excerpt from the score for Pierluigi Billone's *Mani.De Leonardis*, 2004. Courtesy of the composer.

orchestra or large ensemble can do; it is a function of the stripped-down nature of the piece. Rather like the unpredictable, radical mutation of a genetic code in response to its environment, the work is an expression of diversity over unity, of excess over containment.

REMAINDERS

Beyond the Pale

After the avant garde, what was left? If the decades of the 1950s, '60s, and '70s represented the peak era of musical innovation, composers seeking new resources since then have had to engage in a kind of musical fracking. As the terrain became exhausted, the best chance for invention was to dig deeper and farther to the margins. We might think of the growing compositional interest in microsounds, microtones, microrhythms, and microtimbres since the 1980s not only as a product of new possibilities and perspectives opened up by computer technology or elite new music performers but also as a consequence of a search for new sonic resources within increasingly narrow bands of unexplored territory.

Nowhere is this better shown than in the music of Helmut Lachenmann. Lachenmann's interest lies not so much in adding to the existing instrumental array (although there are plenty of examples of his doing this in the percussion parts of his orchestral pieces) as in rethinking the potential of the familiar instruments of the Western orchestra—strings, wind, brass, and keyboards. He originally called his method *musique concrète instrumentale,* although he has since sought to distance himself from the term. Recalling the *musique concrète* of tape music pioneer Pierre Schaeffer (1910–95), in which music is made from recordings made in the real world, stripped of their significance and considered only as sounds, *musique concrète instrumentale* attempts to consider musical instruments as pure sound generators, stripped of their cultural and historical baggage. The way in which those instruments are generally played and the techniques of what is considered "good" or "musical" sound production only account for a small part of their potential. In spite of a piano's size, only a small area of the instrument (the keyboard) is used to make sound, for example; and even then, the keys are only used in one particular way (they are struck by the fingers). Moreover, Lachenmann reasoned, those means of "good" sound production are deeply connected to a historical concept of music that is in turn aligned with bourgeois values, conditions of class oppression, certain market structures, and an all-around tainted system of meaning making. According to this definition, "good" (or tasteful) sound production on a clarinet, for example, minimizes squeaks, key slaps, and breath noise. Yet in order to resist habitual practices and responses—from himself, his performers, and his listeners—these are the sounds that Lachenmann brings into his music. He does not do so, it should be emphasized, for their ugliness, or in the service of a Dada-like aesthetic of trash—Lachenmann's music is frequently beautiful, even as it redefines our expectations of what musical beauty can be. The principle is less to extend existing instrumental technique—a phrasing that implies a range of sounds that are in some way supplemental or ornamental to the traditional means—as it is to step into the margins around those conventional ways of playing, indeed against which the "beauty" and "good" production of those tones are typically measured.

It is striking the degree to which Lachenmann's music has come to inspire younger composers. Like Ferneyhough's music, Lachenmann's works make considerable demands on its performers, often requiring them to rethink, break with, or even cast out years of instrumental practice. And Lachenmann's music also had to wait for a critical mass of capable and willing performers to develop before it gained international recognition and acclaim. However, since that point was reached, some time in the 1990s, Lachenmann's influence has been very great indeed. To be sure, there are additional factors to consider here, including the prestige and cultural capital a younger composer can gain from association with a now-acknowledged master. There are also direct lines of pedagogical influence too, through the postgraduate courses, summer schools, and masterclasses that Lachenmann (like Ferneyhough) teaches.

Yet there is more to it than this. The popularity of Lachenmann's music, among composers at least, indicates that his aesthetic of marginality and depletion has become as much metaphorical as it is real. Composers' capacity for inventing new sound-producing means on old instruments has not in fact diminished in recent years. If anything, it has grown. The youngest generation of composers—among them Ashley Fure (b. 1982), Clara Iannotta (b. 1983), Daniel Moreira (b. 1984), Marek Poliks (b. 1989), and Lisa Streich (b. 1985), to name just a few—remains demonstrably excited by the continuing sonic possibilities of traditional instruments and endlessly inventive in expanding them. Fure writes, "The precision of classical instruments opens avenues of transformation closed to noise in its raw state."[49] In the process, the sounds themselves, marginal and previously unloved, have become a source of sensual pleasure and a sign of humankind's enduring, even heroic, invention and capacity for beauty. In Streich's *Pietà 1* (2012), for cello, a religious tone is made explicit; small electric motors attached to the cello, which strike the strings with strips of paper, are likened to "the turning of the screws into the flesh."[50] And Iannotta's music, for all its interest in decay—of sound, explored in *D'après* (2012) in the resonance of bells; and of the body, considered in *Intent on Resurrection—Spring or Some Such Thing* (2014) in the poetry of Dorothy Molloy—directs the ear not toward processes of disintegration but to the transition of an event or object into its afterlife. Lachenmann's *Air* (1968-9) and *Kontrakadenz* (1970-71) are important precursors to these works as studies in the aftereffects of musical and instrumental energies: the air around a percussion soloist as it becomes energized by sound in *Air,* or the action of gravity on spinning metal plates and bouncing ping pong balls in *Kontrakadenz.*

The fact that many of these composers—Lachenmann and Ferneyhough included—have continued to limit themselves to sounds produced from the acoustic instruments of the Western orchestra and have not used electronics as a way of discovering new sounds (except in a limited sense for Ferneyhough, in works such as *Time and Motion Study II* and *Shadowtime*), indicates the importance of a self-defined marginality to such an aesthetic. This is music that uses limits and margins as a productive source of tension: a way of defining the edges of its canvas in order to exceed them.

Waste

In Michael Pisaro's *ricefall* (2004), sixteen performers (or multiples thereof) sit in a four-by-four grid of three-meter squares, each with a different sounding material on the floor in front of them. These materials (plastic, metal, ceramic, leaves, etc.) are specified by the composer, as is their position on the grid, although the actual items are not. So plastic may be a large sheet of bubble wrap or an array of plastic bowls. The players drop rice, or stream it in handfuls, onto each surface, following the timings indicated in the score. The quantity of rice used is substantial; the piece lasts around eighteen minutes and calls for a generally large density and volume of sound—much greater than that for Jürg Frey's *Un champ de tendresse parsemé d'adieux (4),* discussed in chapter 2, another Wandelweiser "dropping" piece, and so necessitating a much larger volume of material (see figure 29).[51] The effect of the work clearly alludes to the microsound aesthetic (in this case, the sound is literally made up of grains), explored across a parametrically differentiated timbral terrain. The potentially discomfiting tension in the piece between its refined sonic connoisseurship and the dramatic wastage of a globally traded commodity and subsistence foodstuff is mitigated by a note in the score that reads: "Performers will probably need ca. 2 to 3 pounds of rice each. Perhaps, afterward, it can be cleaned and cooked."[52]

Pisaro's piece realizes the central dynamic of superabundance: the tension between consuming and discarding. After agricultural production, the world's second largest industry is supposedly waste disposal: trash is the necessary counterpart to surplus. Faced with this reality, it is inevitable that some artists and composers would explore the expressive potential of waste materials. It is also possible to see a response to the consequences of abundance in developments in instrumental practice over the past two or three decades, such as the increased use of instruments constructed from junk or nonmusical materials and the increased playing of traditional instruments in such a way as to exploit their junk or nonmusical sounds.

Examples are too numerous to list here, but reference might be made to Judy Dunaway's (b. 1964) music for latex balloons;[53] the performances of the great

FIGURE 29. Michael Pisaro's *ricefall,* performed at Roundchapel, London, 2013. Photo by Andrej Chudý.

fences of the Australian outback made by the experimental violinist Jon Rose (b. 1951);[54] Megan Grace Beugger's (b. 1987) *Daring Doris* (2012), in which two performers gradually saw through a large cardboard sheet with violin bows (2012);[55] and James Saunders's *object network* (2012), a series of directions for movement drawn onto sheets of different materials (aluminum, corrugated card, polystyrene) that double as the music's sound source when the movements are followed across the surface of these materials.[56] Mark Applebaum's Mouseketier, one of many sound sculpture-cum-instruments built by the composer from various household objects and ironmongery, deserves particular mention for its occupation of an aesthetic space somewhere between cartoon, sculpture, and high modernism (see figure 30).

Lachenmann's term *musique concrète instrumentale* transfers the language of electronic music into the realm of acoustic instruments, yet his practice has an echo of its own in electronic music practice, in the form of the "glitch." A glitch is a technical malfunction, a breakage, an error, generally in an electronic context. Apparently it was first used as slang by US astronauts in the 1960s to signify a sudden surge of electrical current. It passed into musical use in the 1990s, in reference to the work of electronic musicians who had begun to use the sounds of digital malfunctions—coding errors, audio clipping, system crashes—as raw materials. Among the artists credited with starting the glitch aesthetic, around 1993, are

FIGURE 30. Still from a video of Mark Applebaum playing the Mouseketier, TEDxStan-ford, May 2012. www.ted.com/talks/mark_applebaum_the_mad_scientist_of_music.

Markus Popp, Sebastian Oschatz, and Franz Metzger of the German group Oval, who would use the skipping, popping sounds of deliberately damaged CDs; and the Finnish duo Panasonic (who later changed their name to Pan Sonic in defer-ence to the Japanese electronics firm's trademark lawyers), of Mika Vainio and Ilpo Väisänen, whose first CD, *Vakio* (1995), experimented with homemade equipment to create a highly abstract, stark, and hard-edged minimalist aesthetic of pops, clicks, and static.

In 2000 the sound of glitch was theorized by Kim Cascone (whose album *Blue Cube*, 1998, is a founding work in the digital glitch canon), in what has become an influential article, "The Aesthetics of Failure: 'Post-Digital' Tendencies in Contem-porary Computer Music."[57] Cascone (b. 1955) links the rise of glitch to a wider attraction across the arts to "the aesthetic of failure," which reminds us "that our control of technology is an illusion."[58] Like the negative space of Lachenmann's *musique concrète instrumentale*, glitch sounds are connected to concepts such as detritus or by-product; they are the undesired background or periphery that exists around "good" sound production, and we normally filter them out. Glitches are arrived at not just by playing the technology in a new way but by deliberately intro-ducing failure into the system.[59]

Although glitches originated in electroacoustic music, the aesthetic is not con-fined as such. Many acoustic composers have explored the possibilities of failure within a performance context, devising various ways in which to push performers beyond their physical limits. Some (even many) of these do so in ways that wit-tingly or unwittingly highlight the power imbalance between composer and performer that remains a legacy of notated music performance—Galina Ustvolskaya's Piano Sonata No. 6, discussed in chapter 1, is one such example. A gentler approach is found in the music of Charlie Sdraulig (b. 1985). Sdraulig's music, exemplified in a piece such as *close* (2012), for shakuhachi, voice, and bowed string, hovers on the border between silence and sound, which it finds productive ground for the creation of musical errors. String players are instructed to bow just slightly above the strings of their instruments, for example; the occasional squeaks of sound that are heard arise as a consequence of the natural shaking of their hands, an effect mirrored in Sdraulig's own notation, which was made in pencil, also with his hand hovering just above the page.

Sdraulig's aesthetic—in which the body's limits become a parameter—has precedents much earlier than Cascone's digital glitches. In Heinz Holliger's *Cardiophonie* (1971), for oboe and electronics, the soloist's heartbeat is used to set the tempo of the work. As this fluctuates, the oboist must play along, creating an anxiety loop that they can only escape by leaving the stage entirely. The score for La Monte Young's *Piano Piece for Terry Riley #1* (1960) instructs the performer to push a piano into (and potentially even through) a wall until they reach total exhaustion. Earliest of all is Charles Ives's *Concord Sonata* (circa 1916–19), which includes chords too large to be fully fingered by the pianist.

The difference between such pieces and work like Sdraulig's is that they seek a state of extremity, in which the body's tolerance for exhaustion, pain, speed, and so on becomes a limiting factor, resolved theatrically through a collapse or metaphorical death. The body's potential is saturated but not overcome. There is no creation of surplus, since the piece is over when the body's limit is reached. In Sdraulig's work, however, the condition is sustained, which means that its infinitesimal detail may be exposed. Like so many of the works discussed in this chapter, it is not only interested in finding the breaking point or the limit but is also intrigued and attracted by what lies on the other side, when the limit is exceeded and the damage has been done. The final counterpart to excess, then, is the ruin.

7

LOSS

Ruins, Memorials, and Documents

CROSSING THE THRESHOLD

We are in an uncertain world. It seems to be dissolving before our ears. Saxophone and clarinet players, their instruments barely speaking, sound slow scales that drip and drop onto the floor. Hesitantly, but defiantly, a soprano announces "De qui se doit / de mourir / comme ange" [By him who was the duty / to himself / to die as an angel]. The death in the text seems to be playing out almost before the music has gotten underway.

Music, whether through funeral rites, commemorations, or requiems, has for centuries served to signify and express loss. Yet recent decades have been marked by new kinds of tragedy and new means of articulating and recording losses. Modernity and postmodernity brought opportunities of all kinds, but their consequences at the turn of the century have included the destruction of habitats and communities on a globally threatening scale. The world also seems threatened by moral crises, our increasing dependence on data and technology, the pace of change and what is being left behind, and national and personal insecurities brought about by state and extrastate threats.

These millennial anxieties were captured in Gérard Grisey's *Quatre chants pour franchir le seuil* (Four songs for crossing the threshold, 1998), the opening of which I describe above. A song cycle for soprano and ensemble, its five sections (four songs and a concluding berceuse, or lullaby) address themes of personal, civilizational, global, and divine passing. The first, third, and fourth of them set, respectively, part of "The Hours of the Night," by the French poet Christian Guez-Ricord; a fragment by the ancient Greek poetess Erinna; and verses from *The*

Epic of Gilgamesh. The berceuse ends the piece softly with a final verse from Gilgamesh.

The fourth song begins with a "false interlude"—a quiet hiss of gently brushed drums—which slowly morphs into a repeating pulse, then more complex percussion patterns, and then squeaks and blarts from the other instruments, culminating in a climactic whirl across the whole ensemble. The effect—a slow drift from white noise to harmony—is a typical Grisey move, transforming timbre into harmony. This is the apocalyptic storm described in *The Epic of Gilgamesh.* Grisey's sonic transformations don't end there, however. Out of the storm's heart emerges its destruction. The whorls collapse and fade, leaving only a faint thread sustained by a solo violin and the voice: "Je regardai alentour: / Le silence régnait! / Tous les hommes étaient / Retransformés en argile / Et la plaine liquide / Semblait une terrasse." [I looked about: / Silence reigned! / All mankind had been / Returned to clay / And the flat liquid / Resembled a terrace.]

However, it is the second section, "La mort de la civilisation," that is the work's emotional core. It avoids poetry altogether and instead sets an extract from a catalog of Egyptian sarcophagi:

> 811 et 812: (presque entièrement disparus)
> 814: "Alors que tu reposes pour l'éternité . . . "
> 809: (détruit)
> 868 et 869: (presque entièrement détruits)

> [811 and 812: (almost entirely disappeared)
> 814: "Now that you rest for eternity"
> 809: (destroyed)
> 868 and 869: (almost entirely destroyed)]

This is sung over a repeated harp riff, whose softly tolling simplicity recalls the guitar-strum *objet trouvé* of Kurtág's *Grabstein für Stephan.* The soloist's line begins as single-note declamation, almost entirely without melodic or rhythmic inflection, breaking into moments of more urgent song only as glimpses of the civilization that is recorded in these fragments, writings on the sarcophagi themselves, shine through: "J'ai parcouru . . . j'ai été florissant . . . je fais une déploration . . ." [I have traveled through . . . I have been prosperous . . . I make my lamentation . . .]. The work's most chilling moment comes toward the end of the movement, with the plea "laisse-moi passer" [let me pass on].

On November 11, 1998, not long after completing *Quatre chants,* Grisey suddenly and unexpectedly died. The work's premiere in London, just weeks later, in the last year of the millennium, was a strange and somber occasion. Major works by Grisey were, at that point, rarely heard in London, and *Quatre chants* marked both an introduction and a farewell to a wider audience. Having completed perhaps his finest work, Grisey himself was lost.

RUINS

The shattered, dissolving, collapsing sounds of *Quatre chants* draw on the close relationship between modernity and ruin found also (and to different ends) in the late-century novels of W. G. Sebald and the "squeegee" paintings of Gerhard Richter. However, although the ruin has served as an icon through the art and literature of the past (one thinks back to the fanciful Roman ruins depicted in eighteenth-century Italian painting, or even further, to the *ubi sunt* poems of Old English, such as *The Wanderer, Deor,* and *The Ruin*) it has only more recently become prominent in music.

Ruined Music

Ruination is a dialogue between stasis and change. Like the journey forms discussed in chapter 4, it is a way of registering the intersection of space and time, in this case the slow passage of a fixed object through history. The ruined building is a fixed object, in which the passage of time may be read in the condition of the structure as we see it and in what we can infer of its original appearance from what remains and what we know of typical building construction. To construct a musical ruin, it is important to begin with something that is recognizable for what it is and in which the audience may have an emotional investment, and then to devise a process by which that site may be "ruined."

Like the journey form, the musical-ruin form relates to the late twentieth-century preoccupation with creating musical *states* rather than discursive *objects*. It is a development of ideas about *Werktreue*, soundtracking, fluidity, incompletion, and excess: the idea of the musical work as forever on the brink of moving on, dissolving into its surroundings, disappearing. Take, for example, Merzbow's overdriven, self-destroying noise, Pisaro's drifts from music into ambience, Reich's remixes, and Bielawa's and Packer's distributed musicalizations of sites real and virtual. As an effect, it is difficult to emulate without the existence of certain aesthetics and techniques that were developed in the second half of the century. Within the common practice era, for example, the amount of "decay" that could be inscribed on a work was limited by the rules of tonality and metrical rhythm. Composers could gradually dismantle a work in terms of its timbre or instrumentation, although works that employed this technique, such as Haydn's "Farewell" Symphony, tended to be restricted to novelties. To do the same with harmony or rhythm was much harder, since these were governed by much stricter requirements for "completeness."

With the move away from tonality and metrical rhythm in the early twentieth century, and then the development of various "procedural" musics, from serialism to minimalism, in the postwar years, those requirements were removed. Once there is a process in place and the freedom to let that process go where it will, it becomes possible to build into a work its own destruction. Like the effects of time on a ruined building, musical processes make it possible to perceive an original through its decayed form, the essential characteristic of a ruin.

A fine example of this is Gavin Bryars's haunting *The Sinking of the Titanic*, composed in its first version between 1969 and 1972. The work's inspiration is the well-known story of the ship's band playing as the liner sank. Bryars poetically imagines the band's music continuing to reverberate through the water, which he realizes sonically through echo and distortion effects that slowly transmute the Episcopalian hymn tune "Autumn" (reputed to be the last music played by the band as the ship went under) into ghostly echoes of itself. The piece itself continues to echo, like the hymn tune. The work's form is open (Bryars originally published the score as forty pages of research notes in the journal *Soundings*), and it can be reinterpreted in light of new information about the disaster. In 1990 he revisited it for a performance in Belgium and substantially expanded it, adding almost forty minutes to the length of its 1975 recording. In 2005, for a performance at the Venice Biennale, he extended it still further to seventy-two minutes.

While an approach like Bryars's is artistically successful, the risk is falling into an easy sentimentality based on nostalgic or personal associations. More recent examples of the ruin form have therefore depended less on external material and more on material that is more abstract or that is described in the course of the piece. Grisey, for example, employed simple materials such as descending scales, harmonic spectra, and the basic sound of the instruments he was using.

It is ironic that scientific discoveries contributed to the creation of the musical-ruin form. Tape recording made the gradual submersion of Bryars's *Titanic* possible, and the relationship of recorded media to forms of loss will be discussed further below. The emergence of branches of mathematics like chaos theory in the 1970s opened up new ways in which sounds and musical processes could be dissolved, dismantled, and decomposed procedurally. György Ligeti's attraction to chaos theory in the 1980s (sparked by the publication of Benoit Mandelbrot's *The Fractal Geometry of Nature*[1]) provided an extramusical justification for the broken clockworks that had been present in his music for decades, and in the three volumes of piano *Études* (1985, 1988–94, 1995–2001) that dominated his late output, he reveled in the disordered and unruly states that had now become systematically composable. In *Touches bloquées*, from the first book of *Études*, the pianist's right hand plays fast runs while her left silently depresses keys underneath. The silent keys soon become gaps as the runs pass over them, having the effect of dismantling the music brick by brick. Creation and destruction exist in a close symbiotic relationship; other composers used similar procedures—the L-systems of Poppe and Kyburz, for example[2]—but in those cases, mathematics were used to create models of proliferation and endless movement.

Ligeti dismantled a rapid stream of notes, but the development of electronic analysis of sound spectra in the late 1960s made it possible to separate sounds themselves into their constituent parts. This in turn made it possible to compose with these parts independently, just as serialism had done with pitch, duration, volume, and timbre. Yet where serialism created a multidimensional structure that placed each note at the center of its own particular geometry or unity, spectral methods decentered notes, subjecting their internal formation to constant evolution and identity deconstruction. In this way, it was possible to dismantle or disintegrate an individual sound from within, either electronically or, more interestingly, acoustically, by transcribing the separated components of the spectrum for individual performers and then playing with each line polyphonically. Again, destruction became creation. This idea is shown most clearly and most famously in Grisey's *Partiels* (1975), for eighteen musicians, in which the sound spectrum of a low trombone E is subjected to a series of progressive decompositions, from Wagnerian swell to the rustling of papers and shuffling of players' chairs—a reversal of the process in the fourth song of *Quatre chants,* written twenty-three years later. In Murail's *Désintégrations* (1982–3), for seventeen players, tape, and computer, timbres, are also separated into their individual components, but they are explored across a more complex formal terrain.

Spectralism pioneered a mode of musical dismantling that had a wide-ranging appeal, and it can be found in the work of composers as diverse as Clarence (Klarenz) Barlow (b. 1945), Donnacha Dennehy (b. 1970), Magnus Lindberg (b. 1958), Kaija Saariaho (b. 1952), Marc Sabat (b. 1965), and Helena Tulve (b. 1972). The music of Georg Friedrich Haas (b. 1953) provides a good example of the twenty-first-century evolution of this mode. The titles of many of Haas's pieces— *Blumenstück* (2000), *in vain* (2000–2002), and *natures mortes* (2003), for example—indicate the extent to which his music is haunted by loss and decay, particularly that stylized in the vanitas paintings of the sixteenth and seventeenth centuries. Other works deal in metaphysical terms with aspects of loss and/or absence, often with the addition of a stark theatricalization. The string quartet *In iij. Noct* (2001) is performed in complete darkness, with the musicians playing from memory and seated as far apart from each other as possible. In this instance, the performance circumstances, rather than dramatize decay, confront and sometimes thwart the possibility of building anything at all.

Haas's style is often compared to Grisey's and Murail's spectralism, but the resemblance is only superficial, made on the basis of a common usage of chords based on the harmonic series. Whereas in the French composers' works spectral analyses are used to decompose a sound into its constituent parts, breaking down the barriers between pitch and timbre, Haas's interest is in a perpetually renewing harmonic fluidity. Acoustic illusions like Shepard-Risset glissandi[3]— in which the sense of continuously descending pitch is created by fading in the upper partials of a descending glissando while fading out the lower ones—are a feature of *in vain,* for example. In this work and others, Haas makes extensive use of pivot notes within his harmonies so that each new chord seems to grow out of the residue of the previous one, creating potentially infinite harmonic chains without resolution.[4]

The endless flow of Haas's music reflects the claim made by Joshua Fineberg that the central principle of spectralism is that "music is ultimately sound evolving in time."[5] Haas's perpetually dissolving harmonies recall the unrooted radicant aesthetic described in chapter 4. There is no endpoint to the process, no absolute of death, just a fluid transition from one state to the next, and hypothetically further still, as dramatized in Haas's seventh opera, *Morgen und Abend* (2015), whose two scenes deal solely with the birth and dying of a North Sea fisherman. In this work, as in other pieces by Haas, the process of decomposition becomes one of continuously regenerative energy. As each chord dissolves, it creates a new center for the next. Collapses become creations; like M. C. Escher staircases, steps down become steps to nowhere. There is no conclusion here but only an immortality of movement and regeneration.

Broken Instruments, Broken Media

Of course, in the music of composers like Haas, Ligeti, or even Grisey, the decay enacted is metaphorical; it is still in the nontangible realm of timbre and harmony. However, ruin can be manifest in more concrete ways, in the form of instruments and recording media. These are subject to the same processes of decay and disintegration as any other object, but by being played in their ruined form—alongside whatever adaptations or compromises that may require—they can articulate and transmute that decay into music.

In the late twentieth century, a number of interlinked factors came together to encourage a new interest in the musical potential of the damaged and broken. Instruments have always required maintenance and eventual replacement. However, the deeper historical awareness encouraged by postmodernity gave rise to new anxieties about the permanence of the historical artifact. Counterpointed with these anxieties was a wider faith in the principle that everything could be stored, permanently and without limit. This idea was seemingly becoming real thanks to data farms and search engines, and it acquired a new name: ETEWAF (everything that ever was, available forever).[6]

Also new was the recognition that recorded media, like instruments, were themselves subject to processes of loss and decay. Magnetic tape, invented in 1928, only came into widespread use in the 1950s. By the 1980s, however, it was becoming clear that the lifespan of anything recorded on tape was limited. Over time, even if the tapes were well stored, their iron oxide coating would begin to flake off, taking the recordings with it. The countless reel-to-reel spools that are slowly rotting in libraries and studios around the world are the ruins of the recording age. Whether by physical decay like this or by the commercially mandated obsolescence designed to

FIGURE 31. Still from Bill Morrison's *Decasia*, 2001.

maintain sales of music and film back catalogs (consider the industry-driven moves from VHS video to DVD to Blu-Ray), one lesson of the late twentieth century is that no storage medium is permanent. Even digital files can degrade in the process of being transferred from one format to another, and the devices used to store them remain mortal physical objects, only more delicately engineered than their pre-digital forebears and thus more susceptible to catastrophic failure.

The phenomenon of the media ruin has been addressed in many works of music.[7] Michael Gordon's *Decasia* (2001), for large ensemble and film, meets it head-on. First performed by the Basel Sinfonietta, it was commissioned by the Europäischer Musikmonat, who asked for a musical work of symphonic scale. Filmmaker Bill Morrison was approached to supply a visual accompaniment to the piece, and he, having recently become interested in films that were showing signs of emulsion deterioration, suggested decay as a theme. Once they had agreed on the subject matter, Gordon and Morrison worked more or less independently until *Decasia*'s completion, only occasionally sharing snippets as they finished them.

Morrison's film compiles footage from early twentieth-century film stock, all of it damaged or corroded. The short clips used are often not directly related to one another, although there are common themes. Images of circling or spinning are important, for example, and the piece is framed by footage of film being spooled onto reels in a processing lab juxtaposed with scenes of a whirling Sufi dancer. Also common are images of rural life, as well as family portraits. Many clips were chosen because of the visual dialogue between the preserved image and the disin-tegrating film. In one, a boxer seems to be fighting decay itself, punching the place where the film has completely disintegrated. In another, the cars of a fairground roundabout seem to be exploding out of the film stock (see figure 31).

The music is obliquely related to the film. Although the final edit is based on the recording of music's live premiere, Morrison's cuts are not synchronized with events in Gordon's score. The music does not seek to "narrate" the images on screen or to translate them into music. The only exception may be the swirling of drumsticks around the inside rim of eight brake drums at the start of the piece, which echoes the "circles" motif in the film, as well as the circular movement of film projection itself.

Yet the film and music still clearly inhabit the same thematic territory. Where Morrison depicts decay through the actual disintegration of film stock, Gordon does so through more metaphorical devices: chords "decay" through the use of glissandi, microtonal retunings, and layers of clashing dissonances (processes related to, although distinct from, both spectral and minimalist practices); rhythms decay through similar distortions and layerings of the underlying pulse; the ensembles slide out of phase with each other. The idea is of a "decaying symphony"[8] or "a piano fallen from a great height";[9] the sound is portentous, unsettling, and noirishly thrilling.

Morrison says of his film: "It is in the end not a film about preservation. It delights in the process of decay, and deals with it not in a nostalgic way, but rather matter of factly. There is no build of decay—it exists in varying degrees from beginning to end."[10] Similarly, Gordon's rotting minimalism does not present a single process of decay or obliteration. As is typical of the composer's style, the music is structured around series of looping rhythms and nonfunctional chord progressions that switch from one configuration to another. What we therefore hear, just as we see on the film, are representations of decay, without critique or examination of its consequences.

Both film and music tread a difficult line. Although Morrison claims that there is no nostalgia in his images, their very nature—footage of bygone eras, people in old-time clothes who have long since passed away—evokes a sentimental response. Likewise, the descending lines and astringent dissonances of Gordon's music tap into long-established musical signifiers of lament.[11] Added to this, the repeating chord progressions, progressive layering of material, and amplification of the ensembles, which surround the audience on three sides, create a cumulative effect that depends on overwhelming its audience rather than calling on them to engage critically. Morrison and Gordon's work examines a site of twenty-first-century melancholy, but it risks lapsing into a sentimental stylization or even fetishization of decay that points instead to the comfort and security of life in the West, where such concerns can be reduced to aesthetics.

Incorporating the processes of physical decay—of media or instruments—into the musical realization itself is more complex, since it involves composing with materials that are by definition unstable, temporary, and unpredictable. Gordon may have wanted to compose the sound of a fallen piano, but to do so he had to carefully rebuild the sound of the orchestra. Where real decay is used, the results are typically more radical in effect.

One of the most extensive explorations of broken instruments may be that undertaken by Ross Bolleter (b. 1946). Bolleter began his *Ruined Pianos* project in 1987, locating abandoned or neglected pianos first in the Australian outback and later globally, under the auspices of the World Association for Ruined Piano Studies, formed in 1991 with Stephen Scott (b. 1944). Bolleter finds his ruined pianos in fields, on verandahs, or in barns, their mechanisms "prepared" by the effects of rain, sun, sand, plants, and even animals (see figure 32). He distinguishes them from "devastated" pianos in that they are structurally intact and may therefore be played in an upright position; a devastated piano may need to be played lying down, for example. Nevertheless, a ruined piano may be in an advanced state of disrepair, with its mechanism broken, keys stuck, wood rotting, and strings rusting or even snapped. When he finds new instruments (either by chance or via word-of-mouth tip-offs), Bolleter improvises music for them that is suitable to their condition and situation, exploiting, for instance, the rattle of broken keys and the boom of slack bass strings that can be drawn back like bowstrings. Sometimes those recordings are released in their raw state, such as the early piece *Nallan Void* (1987), recorded on a piano found at Nallan sheep station, deep in the West Australian outback, some seven hundred kilometers north of Perth. At other times, they are edited and reassembled into larger works, such as the thirty-five-minute *Secret Sandhills* (2002, rev. 2006).[12] The sound of Bolleter's improvisations echoes in the work of another Australian, Anthony Pateras (b. 1979), whose remarkable piano solo *Chasms* (2007) uses an instrument so extensively prepared with screws, bolts, coins, and other items that not a single note is unaffected, and the whole keyboard is divided into regions of variously deadened and distorted clangor. Bolleter's improvisations also recall the deliberate destruction of instruments in works such as Philip Corner's *Piano Activities* (1962) and Annea Lockwood's *Piano Transplants* (1967–71), in which pianos are destroyed; Peter Maxwell Davies's *Eight Songs for a Mad King* (1969), in which a violin is wrecked; and Ligeti's *Apparitions* (1958–9), in which a tray of crockery is shattered. However, Bolleter's interest lies not in the creation of exotic timbres or a critique of Western instrumental practice (although he notes ironically, "All that fine nineteenth-century European craftmanship [sic], all the damp and unrequited loves of Schumann, Brahms and Chopin dry out, degrading to a heap of rotten wood and rusting wire"[13]) but in marking the passage of real time on venerable instruments—in matters of process and connection rather than acts of modernist rupture. He does not ruin the pianos he plays; they are already ruined when he finds them. His improvisations articulate that ruin and highlight the distance between the pianos' present state and their origin.

FIGURE 32. Ross Bolleter playing a ruined piano at a sanctuary for ruined pianos, Wambyn Olive Farm, Western Australia. Photo by Antoinette Carrier.

Philip Jeck (b. 1952) has concerned himself with marking the passage of time on physical media, particularly vinyl records, since the early 1990s—especially in the work that made his name, *Vinyl Requiem* (1993).[14] Created in collaboration with the artist Lol Sargent, *Vinyl Requiem* was originally conceived as one-off performance, although Jeck has created further stagings of it since. Against the wall of the Union Chapel in Islington, London, 180 record players were stacked across three levels of scaffolding. Three operators, one on each level, walked back and forth across the scaffolding, cueing up scratched, aging vinyl to build up layers of noise and fragments from the history of recorded music. The record players themselves harked back to another era: they were portable Dansettes with built-in speakers, the player of choice for British teens in the 1950s and '60s. In front of the scaffold was Jeck himself, operating another six players. Against the scaffold, using the wall of record players like a film screen, Sargent projected slides and 16mm film footage, much of it also damaged.

Jeck, here and in albums such as *Loopholes* (1995) and *Stoke* (2002), is in a lineage of artists who have taken the manipulation of vinyl and turntables out of the club and street scenes of disco, house, and hip-hop and into the realm of sound art and composition. Chief among them is Christian Marclay, who began tampering with records in the late 1970s, first with *Groove* (1979), a sound collage created by placing stickers on the groove of a 7" single that cause it to skip and loop, and then with the *Recycled Records* series (1980–86), in which shards of broken records were stitched together into new discs that, when played, seemed to jump at random from one original to the next, like a sonic exquisite corpse (a game in which sentences or pictures are constructed by several players in sequence, each one only able to see the end of what the previous player had written or drawn). Oval's use of damaged CDs discussed in the previous chapter is a digital-era version of the same practice.

However, *Vinyl Requiem* was not so much a trace of the decay of its medium—like the footage in Bill Morrison's *Decasia* film—but, as its title suggests, an elegy for a medium that, in 1993 at least, seemed doomed. In the face of first CDs and then downloads and streaming, vinyl—the format of swing, rock 'n' roll, the Beatles, disco, punk, hip-hop, and techno—was passing into oblivion. The hiss and pop of Jeck's records registers the passing of time, as do Bolleter's ruined pianos. The loss expressed, however, is not on the level of individual artifacts—in any case subsumed into a literal "wall of sound" in Jeck's piece—but on that of an entire medium, even a history of music.

Vinyl Requiem and the *Ruined Pianos* project are acts of resistance as well. They counter processes of obsolescence and refute the late-capitalist ideal of permanent perfection that is enabled through the eternal upgrade. They also stand against the encroachment of digitization and ennoble the ruin as a sort of preservation. They represent gradual analog decay as opposed to the catastrophic and absolute loss of a digital ruin—a hard drive failure, for example. When an analog or real-world object, like a vinyl record or an upright piano, begins to decay, something of the original may still be traced; a ruined piano, for instance, may be coaxed back into a semblance of its previous life. A ruined laptop, however, is only so much silicon and plastic.

COMMEMORATION

So far, the losses discussed have all been of the abstract, nonhuman, or, in the case of *Quatre chants,* historically remote. However, loss can also take place on the immediate human scale. This raises the particular question of commemoration.

Human tragedies have long been marked in music, from the ritual forms of funeral music and requiems to personal memorials such as Josquin's *Nymphes des bois* (circa 1497), composed in memory of his fellow composer Jean de Ockeghem, and Berg's Violin Concerto (1935), dedicated to the memory Manon Gropius, the daughter of Alma Mahler and Walter Gropius, who died at eighteen of polio. However, the late twentieth century saw a rise in the number of works composed as spaces for public mourning (some of them commissioned as such). This development has paralleled the increasingly public nature of national or international tragedy, itself furthered by the rise of the broadcast media. Some early examples of this kind of work are Herbert Howells's *Take Him, Earth, for Cherishing*, commissioned for the memorial service for President John F. Kennedy in 1963, and Krzysztof Penderecki's *Dies irae* (1967), composed for the unveiling of the International Monument to the Victims of Fascism at Auschwitz-Birkenau. More recently, John Tavener's *A Song for Athene* was played at the funeral of Princess Diana in 1997, and although the piece was not composed for the occasion (it had actually been written four years earlier, to commemorate the death in a cycling accident of Athene Hariades, a young actress and family friend of the composer), it proved so successful that it became Tavener's most well-known and widely recorded work.

9/11

One of the most prominent disasters of the twenty-first century—in the West, at least—was the September 11, 2001, terrorist attack on New York and Washington. The years since have seen a steady stream of musical works related to the events of that day. Indeed, there are so many of these pieces that it might now be possible, were it not a little crass, to talk of a subgenre of 9/11 music. One composer, Kevin Malone (b. 1958), has written no fewer than seven such pieces.[15]

As might be expected, these works have predominantly been written by North Americans, but there are exceptions. These have come particularly from Poland and include Wojciech Kilar's *September Symphony* (2003) and Penderecki's Piano Concerto "Resurrection" (2001–2, rev. 2007). Penderecki began his concerto before 9/11 but reconceived it—and dedicated it to the victims—midway through writing it, claiming to have written the chorale that is at the work's heart immediately after the attacks. Another non-American work, *Maim* (2001–7), a three-movement work (comprising *Maim zurim maim gnuvim, the memory of water*, and *water of dissent*) by the Israeli Chaya Czernowin (b. 1957), registers the attacks with a dramatic change in expression halfway through its first movement.[16]

Performers led their own commemorations too. Notable were those of the Kronos Quartet. In addition to commissioning several works on the theme of 9/11, the group devised a special program that sought to acknowledge the post-9/11 world by bringing together its music. At its heart was Michael Gordon's *The Sad Park* (2006), around which were placed folk and classical works from around the world. Some pieces—such as *Darkness 9/11* (2002) by Osvaldo Golijov and Gustavo Santaolalla—were explicitly connected to 9/11 and its aftermath. Others were more tangentially related, like John Oswald's *Spectre* (1990), which uses overdubbing to inflate simple open string sounds into a howling wall of 1,001 string quartets, and Kronos and Paolo Prestini's arrangement of "Armenia," by the German noise group Einstürzende Neubauten (whose name translates, pertinently, as "Collapsing New

Buildings"). Still others, like the Iraqi song "Oh Mother, the Handsome Man Tortures Me," written under the Saddam regime, complicated the picture.

Perhaps the most well-known example of 9/11 music was not intended as a memorial at all. Completed before the attacks even took place, William Basinski's *Disintegration Loops* (2001) became an accidental tribute, and the work's backstory was as important to its reception as the sound of the music itself. In the early 1980s, Basinski (b. 1958), a New York-based sound artist and electronic composer, began recording broadcasts of string orchestra Muzak, which he slowed down, layered, cut, and looped using simple tape technology. These loops formed the basis of his live performances at clubs and lofts in New York, but eventually they ended up in storage. In July 2001, Basinski rediscovered them and began archiving them digitally. As he did so, he realized that the tapes themselves were disintegrating; the coating that held the magnetic information was becoming dust. He made the key decision to leave the machines running and record the unfolding process of decay. Before he had known what was going to happen to the tapes, he had added an arpeggiated pattern to the first loop (*dlp 1.1*), but the other pieces in the *Disintegration Loops* series are unadorned.[17]

Although he recognized the beauty of the recordings, he was unsure of what to do with them. That changed a few months later, on September 11. That morning, Basinski, like many other Brooklyn residents, watched from a rooftop as the Twin Towers collapsed. His recently completed recordings seemed an appropriate response to the tragedy. He played them on his apartment stereo and opened all the windows. For more than two hours, they soundtracked the plumes of smoke that were pouring over Manhattan while he and his neighbors "tried to work out what the hell was going on."[18] The conjunction was eerily right. In the evening Basinski began filming the still-smoldering buildings, and he later set the footage to the music of *dlp 1.1*. Stills from the film became the cover art for the CDs of the work, issued as four separate discs, and the film was eventually purchased by the 9/11 Memorial Museum.

The connection between *Disintegration Loops* and 9/11 may have been accidental, but the emotive power the works gained from the particular form of conjunction and documentation exemplified other commemorative works. Stephen Vitiello's *World Trade Center Recordings: Winds after Hurricane Floyd* (1999) were also created before the attacks. In 1999, Vitiello (b. 1964) was granted a six-month artistic residency on the ninety-first floor of the World Trade Center's North Tower, during which time he used contact microphones attached to the windows to record the sounds inside and outside the building. In the recordings he made during Hurricane Floyd, in September 1999, the tower can be heard creaking and twisting in the wind, revealing it as "fragile, unguarded, susceptible—if not sentient, then certainly sensitive."[19] After 9/11, Vitiello's recordings sounded eerily prescient, and they served as an anthropomorphic memorial for the towers themselves.

Their acceptance into the official canon of 9/11 was marked by their inclusion in the Whitney Museum's tenth anniversary exhibition, *September 11*.

An even more concrete piece of aural documentation is Mark Bain's *StartEnd-Time*, an audification of the seismic vibrations recorded on the East Coast during the 9/11 attacks. Sonification is defined as the more general transmission of information or data as a sound (as is done by a Geiger counter, or a clock that chimes the hour), while audification refers to the more specific process of translating data into an audio waveform (in a simple sense, this is what sonar and stethoscopes do).[20] As a sound artist, Bain (b. 1966) is principally interested in the sound of architecture. He uses seismographic equipment to collect data on the vibrations buildings make in response to their environment or to machinery and then applies audification techniques to these recordings. *StartEndTime* is a seventy-four-minute audification of data recorded by the network of seismic monitoring stations operated in the New York area by Columbia University, covering the period from shortly before American Airlines Flight 11 struck the North Tower until around ten minutes after the collapse of both towers. Bain translated the seismic vibrations represented by the data into sound waves, raised them in frequency to the range of human hearing, and then stretched them so that they unfold in real time (editing them to shorten the delay between the collision of the second plane, United Airlines Flight 175, with the South Tower and the collapses of the two towers). In gallery installations of the work, vibration machines under benches placed in the center of the room also respond to the seismic waves.

Although *StartEndTime* was created in response to 9/11, it wasn't intended as a memorial; in Bain's words, it records the global terrain becoming "a bell-like alarm denoting histories in the making."[21] Other works, however, have used 9/11 data for more straightforward commemorative purposes. One is Marty Quinn's six-minute multimedia piece *For Those Who Died* (2002), whose musical component is a sonification of a text compiled from the names of the people who died on 9/11, parts of the US Constitution, and sequences of the Human Genome Project.

Most musical responses to 9/11 sit closer to the stylistic mainstream. The public and spectacular nature of 9/11 meant that it, and its surrounding discourse, were quickly politicized and therefore controlled. Media representations and analyses of the events, their significance, and how to respond to them rapidly became absorbed into an official discourse, particularly in the United States. The power of 9/11 was such that it drew the United States, and several others, into a series of protracted (and still unresolved) conflicts in the Middle East. Most artistic responses to the attacks—including those I discuss here, I should emphasize—did not take a prowar stance. However, the mainstream discourse of commemoration, memorial, and response into which these works entered was public and institutionally determined.

The difference is highlighted if one compares the consolatory tone of the works described above—expressed through their tonal harmonies, metrical rhythms, and even timbres—to works written in response to an earlier tragedy, AIDS. Where 9/11 was a public tragedy, AIDS was, at least until the 1990s, a private one, hitting marginalized communities the hardest and being viewed more widely through the lens of popular homophobia. At a time when homosexuality was still demonized and AIDS was little understood, just showing solidarity was a political act, complicating simple commemoration with expressions of anger, defiance, and pride. Some of the earliest musical works composed to mark AIDS deaths were written for the relatively supportive but culturally marginal space of the male voice choir; the oldest piece in the Estate Project's database of classical works addressing AIDS is Craig Carnahan's *I Loved You* (1983), for men's chorus, flute, oboe, and two pianos. As discussed in chapter 3, Diamanda Galás used her music to challenge the complicity of her listeners in the deaths of AIDS sufferers and to avenge the disease's victims from beyond the grave. Yet even mainstream artists took a distinctly personal tack. John Corigliano (b. 1938) incorporated musical portraits of friends who died of AIDS into his Symphony No. 1 (1988–9), which was at the time one of the most substantial and high-profile works of concert music to address the subject. Although written within Corigliano's essentially neo-Romantic idiom, it contains some of his most confrontational music; after seeing the NAMES Project AIDS Memorial Quilt, he said, "This made me want to memorialize in music those I have lost, and reflect on those I am losing."[22] The first movement's subheading, "Of Rage and Remembrance"—which Corigliano also used for a choral work (1991) derived from the symphony's third movement—captures its expressive territory, and the first three (of four) movements are musical portraits of individuals close to the composer: a professional pianist, a music executive, and an amateur cellist. The whole symphony is full of striking personal touches, from melodies generated from pieces of text (an example of musical transcoding that is typically found in more experimental contexts), to an off-stage piano playing Leopold Godowsky's arrangement (1921) of Isaac Albéniz's *Tango*, to a fierce tarantella depicting the madness of AIDS-related encephalitis, intercutting violently between calm lucidity and agonized screams. The last movement makes use of a seventeen-part brass section, arranged in a semicircle around the back of the stage, which with outwardly fanning chords movingly embraces the fading music of the epilogue.

Commemoration or remembrance can also grant works an instrumental or purposive value. There was a sense in some quarters, particularly the Anglophone media, that contemporary music at the start of the twenty-first century had become detached from the world around it, so we might read the flood of commemorative works composed in the wake of 9/11 as an attempt to fill that void as clearly as possible. As the *Washington Post* critic Anne Midgette noted in advance of the tenth anniversary of the attacks, "Commemorative concerts represent a great opportunity for new work. Audiences that prefer traditional music over contemporary often let down their guard if the new work honors a tragedy."[23]

Steve Reich's *WTC 9/11* (2010), commissioned by the Kronos Quartet in 2009, was not initially intended as a 9/11 memorial piece. The group asked for "a piece using pre-recorded voices," and the idea of using recordings from 9/11 came to Reich several months into composing the work.[24] In terms of medium (a string quartet and recordings) and subject matter (the personal impact and legacy of massive trauma), it shares much with Reich's first Kronos commission, *Different Trains*. *WTC 9/11* continues the speech melody style Reich first used in that piece. Concrete sounds also feature in both works; in the case of *WTC 9/11*, there is the *beep-beep-beep* of a phone left off the hook, the pulse of which provides both the tempo and an underlying harmonic pedal for the work's first movement. Reich also makes use of more recent technology to timestretch some of his speech samples, transforming them into drones and bands of noise. (Gordon's *The Sad Park* applied a similar technique to the recorded voices of children who attended a kindergarten close to the World Trade Center, drawing them out into digitally inflected howls.)

The structure of *WTC 9/11* is also similar to several of Reich's other pieces that use documentary material, including the video opera *Three Tales*, which juxtaposes the *Hindenburg* airship disaster of 1937, the use of Bikini Atoll for atomic bomb tests in the 1940s and '50s, and the cloning of Dolly the sheep in 1996 (as well as the loosely related phenomenon of artificial intelligence). *Different Trains, Three Tales*, and *WTC 9/11* all feature a two-part structure that moves from representation (of a traumatic event or events) to reflection. In the case of *Different Trains*, the trauma is the Holocaust, which is prefigured in the first movement, represented in the second, and reflected on in the third. In *Three Tales*, two traumatic events are documented: the explosion of the *Hindenburg* and the removal of indigenous inhabitants from the Bikini Atoll. The third act, "Dolly," uses interviews with scientists, philosophers, and theologians to consider the phenomena of genetic engineering and artificial intelligence and, by implication, the merits and risks of technological advancement through the twentieth century, as exemplified in the two previous acts. *WTC 9/11* begins immediately in the representation phase: after the phone beep, the first recorded sounds are of NORAD air traffic controllers tracking American Airlines Flight 11, the first plane to strike the World Trade Center. They are joined by recordings from the New York City Fire Department and, in the second movement, testimonies and comments from witnesses and survivors of the attacks.[25] The third movement steps beyond reflection and into the realm of the spiritual, drawing on chants from the Psalms and the Torah as well as the voices of two Jewish women who helped sit vigil (*shmira*) over the bodies of the dead for several months before they were identified and buried.

Artists approaching the theme of 9/11 could choose either to engage with or resist the iconography of the attacks as selected and organized by the mass news media. As Robert Fink has shown,[26] the form and structure of minimalist and postminimalist music—which is based on repetition, cyclical structure, and non-teleological juxtaposition—closely matches the form and structure of television with its regular commercial breaks, self-similar rhythms, and emphasis on flow. Television news is no different; indeed, the need to fill an open-ended expanse of time with a finite (and often very small) amount of actual footage only heightens the use of repetitive structures. On September 11, 2001, itself, news channels even resorted to looping what footage they had to make it fill the large amount of time considered appropriate to such an event.[27] *WTC 9/11* leans heavily on the language and style of mass media news, selecting and editing supposedly objective field data to construct an emotional and affective narrative that gains force through repetition, sequencing, and flow.

The effect is enhanced by Reich's own editorializing. In the first movement in particular, he chose recordings that not only broadly narrate the sequence of events that took place on September 11, 2001 (planes hijacked, towers hit, emergency services scrambled, towers fall), but also allow him to articulate, by translating them into music, three layers of musical intensification: a movement from speech to noise, an increase in harmonic dissonance, and an increase in rhythmic complexity. Reich chose these layers to heighten psychological and physical tension, exploiting the relationship between certain musical devices (noise, harmony, and meter) and physical affect. In addition, there are two narratorial intensifications: the increasingly panicked words themselves (from "It came from Boston" to "I can't breathe") and a steady movement of narratorial viewpoint (from air traffic controllers remotely observing their radar screens to individuals trapped in the rubble itself).

In contrast, John Adams's *On the Transmigration of Souls* (2002), for chorus, orchestra, and electronics, begins not with the media event of 9/11 but with the intimate lives of those involved in the attacks. Nevertheless, it still uses documentary materials—although they are rather different from those in Reich's piece. The piece was commissioned by the New York Philharmonic—members of which had previously played for workers at Ground Zero and residents of the area around the World Trade Center—to open its 2002 season, one year after the attacks. In this sense, it was an "official" act of public commemoration, and Adams has spoken of the burden of what was "virtually a call to civic duty."[28] Noting that "there was no escaping the iconography of the event and its aftermath," he turned to the hand-written missing persons signs that were pasted around Ground Zero in huge numbers. He used these and obituaries published by the *New York Times* to construct a text that avoided heroic tropes and focused on the people whose lives had been lost; its use of lists of names recalls Grisey's catalog of Egyptian sarcophagi. The spoken voices were combined with New York street noise recorded late at night to create an atmospheric soundtrack that surrounded the audience while the chorus and orchestra played on stage. This enveloping effect creates a substitute reality that is a world away from the heavily mediated (and media-like) realism of Reich's piece. *On the Transmigration of Souls* uses documentary materials not to recreate a past event but to call up its ghosts.

The documentary approach was not universal, however. Corigliano renounced it entirely for his *One Sweet Morning* (2010), commissioned by the New York Philharmonic to mark the tenth anniversary of the attacks. Like Adams, he was initially opposed to the idea of creating a commemorative piece, but he finally agreed after resolving to avoid any possibility of specific recollection. In his own words, "So many in the audience of this piece will have images of the frightful day itself . . . burned into their retinas. . . . How could I instruct the audience to ignore their own memories?"[29] Unlike his personally motivated Symphony No. 1, *One Sweet Morning* contains no interjections of "outside" material. Instead it conveys, for the most part, a disturbed, dreamlike elegy that does not exceptionalize 9/11 but sees it from a decade's distance as but one day in a never-ending cycle of war and violence.

PRESERVATION

As these works suggest, our instinct in the face of loss is increasingly becoming to commemorate through documentation. Handheld recording devices that capture images, video, and sound and server farms that make it easy to store the resulting files have given us an unprecedented ability to preserve our experiences. The fact that these captured experiences may be compromised by their mediation is not a problem either; as suggested in chapter 2, our lives have become so habitually mediated anyway that the ontological distance between a recording of an occasion and our memory of it does not trouble us. Documentation, in fact, has become a sign of authenticity: we believe in the "objectivity" of the recording, although in truth there is no such thing.

Documentation is also a fight against time, against processes of loss and ruin. Vinyl LPs can be transferred to digital media (until those media themselves start to corrupt), and lives can be preserved (or reanimated) through recordings. Ruins and human tragedy may be old themes that found new expressions in music in the late twentieth century, but the newest and perhaps most significant subject of loss is that of the natural world. In this case, species and habitats that are disappearing can survive, at least in ghost form, as soundscapes.

Acoustic Ecology

The modern environmental movement can be traced to the publication in 1962 of Rachel Carson's *Silent Spring*,[30] which documented the environmental damage caused by synthetic pesticides like DDT. Selling more than two million copies, Carson's book brought the effects of human actions on the environment sharply into the public eye and led, among other things, to the formation in the United

States of the Environmental Defense Fund (1967) and the Environmental Protection Agency (1970). The creation of the first worldwide Earth Day followed in 1970; in 1971 the environmental activist organization Greenpeace was formed; and in 1972 the United Nations Conference on the Human Environment, the first government-level conference of its type, was held in Stockholm. By the 1990s, influenced by philosophies and theories such as Arne Naess's deep ecology[31] and James Lovelock and Lynn Margulis's Gaia hypothesis,[32] environmental protection had become a matter of global protection and preservation. Not least among the concerns was anthropogenic (human-caused) climate change, an issue popularized in 1989 by Bill McKibben's book *The End of Nature*.[33]

The wider environmental movement was paralleled by a musical one: acoustic ecology. In the late 1960s, in response to a rapid growth in urban noise pollution in his city of Vancouver, the composer R. Murray Schafer began teaching courses in environmental sound and what he called "soundscape studies" at Simon Fraser University. In 1969, together with a like-minded group of composers and students (Harold Broomfield, Bruce Davis, Peter Huse, Jean Reed, and Barry Truax, and joined in 1973 by Hildegard Westerkamp), he set up the World Soundscape Project (WSP) to begin work on raising public awareness of environmental noise and sound, documenting the aural environment, and establishing a practice and methodology for good soundscape design. In its first ten years, the WSP produced a number of influential publications and recordings, including field recordings made around Vancouver (e.g., *The Vancouver Soundscape*, 1973), a detailed analysis of the soundscapes of five European villages (*Five Village Soundscapes*, 1977), Truax's *Handbook for Acoustic Ecology* (1978), and, most significantly of all, *The Tuning of the World* (1977), by Schafer himself, in which he not only sets out the field of soundscape studies but also offers exercises in "ear cleaning," "soundwalking," and acoustic design, as well as examples of how to notate and analyze the acoustic environment.

Since the WSP's founding, field recording has become a significant artistic and scientific discipline. The WSP itself became less active during the 1980s as members of the original group pursued other activities. In 1993, however, it was succeeded by the much larger World Forum for Acoustic Ecology (with Westerkamp as one of its founders), a global network devoted to studying the acoustic environment.

This boom was enabled by the arrival of portable digital recorders in the mid-1990s. Because they have no moving parts, digital recorders produce none of the mechanical whirr and hiss of tape. The overall sound quality these devices can provide also makes it possible to capture more fully the very wide dynamic range that characterizes the natural world. Storage and editing are also much easier, and recordings on a hard drive can be far longer than was ever possible on tape. Microphones have similarly improved, becoming smaller, more responsive, and more directional.

As field recording became easier, it developed into an area for artistic experiment and expression. At the same time, WSP-type documentation came to be viewed with suspicion. David Dunn voiced some of the strongest criticism against field recordings as an environmental campaigning tool:

> Several recordists market their recordings as purist audio documentation of pristine natural environments with particular appeal to the armchair environmental movement. Personally I find something perverse about many of these recordings, as if the encoding of a semiotic referent in the form of an audio description of place could ever be something other than a human invention.... I can certainly understand arguments for the preservation of actual biohabitats but not as recorded sonic objects. The premise appears to be that these recordings will somehow sensitize the listener to a greater appreciation of the natural world when in fact they are more often perpetuating a 19th century vision of nature and at best merely documenting a state of affairs that will soon disappear.[34]

Dunn also criticizes the practice of some recordists of removing or not recording any manmade sounds that might be present in the environment, such as airplanes or traffic noise. Doing so, he argues, "lures people into the belief that these places still fulfill their romantic expectations."[35]

Field recording has thus come to be seen not as a way of accurately preserving or documenting an environment but as way of activating the distance between reality and representation created by recording and mediation, sometimes in pursuit of Romantic ideology. Later artists, including Annea Lockwood (b. 1939), Francisco López (b. 1964), and Toshiya Tsunoda (b. 1964), as well as Dunn, have come to use field recording in a more critical sense.

Lockwood began collecting recordings of rivers in the 1960s, but it was not until 1982 that she turned this interest into a large-scale work: *A Sound Map of the Hudson River*. The piece was an aural portrait of the American river, from its source in Lake Tear of the Clouds in the Adirondack Mountains to its mouth in the Lower New York Bay. It was followed, more than twenty years later, by two more river sound maps, of the Danube (2005) and the Housatonic (2010). All three were made in much the same way. Lockwood recorded the rivers in stages, moving downstream. She took recordings from the bank, at points that she deemed sonically interesting and that fit an overall sequence of contrasts and movements for each work as a whole. (For the later pieces, she also used a hydrophone to make recordings under the water.) The piece was thus recorded compositionally, with a final sound and structure in mind, rather than objectively; Lockwood rejected locations, for example, if they were too close to roads or presented too little of sonic interest. One may ask, of course, if strict objectivity is ever possible when the microphone is in the hands of a human decision-maker, but in this case at least, the lack of objectivity is made explicit.

Once the recordings were completed, Lockwood compiled them into a montage sequence. Compositional decisions concentrated on the selection of recordings and their respective durations and edit points. The recordings were all equalized and then stitched together with slow fade-ins and fade-outs. Finally, the complete montage was mixed for surround-sound speakers. The completed work was presented as an installation, accompanied by a map of the river that was annotated with the location, date, and time of each recording and at what point in the work they can be heard. *Hudson* included headsets playing interviews with people who live by the river; in *Danube*, interviews were mixed in with the river sounds in the main piece.

López rarely draws attention to where his recordings were made. A believer in Pierre Schaeffer's concept of "reduced listening"—a form of listening that removes all external reference from sounds and concentrates only on their abstract essence and relation to one another—López asks audiences at his concerts to wear blindfolds. He leaves his pieces untitled, and he often even chooses the sounds within them because of their obscurity and how difficult they are to identify. "The essence of sound recording," he has said, "is not that of documenting or representing a much richer or more significant world, but a way to focus on and access the inner world of sounds."[36] His seventy-minute *La Selva* (1998), named after the Costa Rican rainforest in which it was recorded, is therefore something of an exception. It shares many of the compositional processes Lockwood used in making her sound maps. It was recorded over one day in the rainy season, at different places within the forest. As in Lockwood's river pieces, the recordings are woven into a continuous sequence, in this case representing the cycle from night to day to night.

However, where Lockwood stresses the ways in which people and animals use the rivers, López is careful not to privilege any sound over another. His recordings give equal prominence to the sounds of plants, wind, water, animals, birds, and insects. His interest is in "the environment as a whole, instead of behavioural manifestations of the organisms we foresee [*sic*] as most similar to us."[37] Likewise, and in explicit opposition to the focus on preservation of many soundscape recorders, such as those associated with the WSP, he emphasizes the diversity of sounding environments (both natural and manmade). Many sections of *La Selva* are loud, even violently so, pushing back against the conservative image of the world as quiet, peaceful, and pristine.

The illusory authenticity of recording is highlighted by the work of Toshiya Tsunoda. Making dramatic use of technological intervention, Tsunoda's recordings draw attention to sound phenomena that would not otherwise be apparent. He has placed microphones where no human ear could go, such as in the mouth of a bottle or inside a water pipe (*Extract from Field Recording Archive #2: The Air Vibration inside a Hollow*, 1999), and filtered the audible spectrum to leave just the vibrating frequencies that sit below the range of human hearing (*Low Frequency*

Observed at Maguchi Bay, 2007). Like Lachenmann, he is attracted to the negative spaces around what we normally hear and to bringing forward the invisible, inaccessible, and suppressed. Most radically, in *O kokkos tis anixis* (2013), conventional field recordings become caught in little loops, eddies that cut tiny windows at right angles to the flow of documented time.

Places

Few composers have associated their work so specifically with place—an identifiable geographical location—as John Luther Adams (b. 1953).[38] Although born in Mississippi (and now a resident of Manhattan), Adams has become inextricably linked with Alaska. He first visited the state as an environmental campaigner in 1975, and he settled there three years later as executive director of the Northern Alaska Environmental Center, where he worked on the Alaska Lands Act, which passed into law in 1980. Alaska—the place—and a wider commitment to environmentalism are therefore closely linked for Adams. At first he lived in a remote cabin, cutting his own wood and carrying his own water, but in 1989 he moved in with his wife (and their son) in Fairbanks. It was around this time that he began to compose fluently in his present style—a Romantically inflected blend of minimalism and the spectral experiments of his teacher James Tenney (1934–2006)—and gain the attention of performers and record labels.

A breakthrough work was the quasi-opera *Earth and the Great Weather* (1989–93), a seventy-five-minute meditation for voices, strings, percussion, and electronics on Alaska's "sonic geography," captured in environmental field recordings, evocations of the landscape, the English and Latin names of native birds and plants, and poems in two Native American languages, Iñupiaq and Gwich'in. In line with his environmentalism, Adams has sought to render aspects of the Alaskan wilderness, drawing attention to specific places and their need for protection. Few elements of the state's environment, whether its wildlife, native peoples, light, seismic activity, climate, or geography, have not featured in his work, either as material or as organizing principle. Natural sounds were a feature of his compositions before he moved to Alaska: *songbirdsongs,* for example, which he begun in 1974 but completed after he made Alaska his home, takes the songs of different birds from rural Georgia as its material; and *Night Peace* (1977) captures the nighttime sounds of the Okefenokee Swamp on the Georgia–Florida border. However, the pieces he started in the north stand in a much more metaphysical relationship to their surroundings.

Adams's most detailed work of sonic geography is probably *The Place Where You Go to Listen* (2004–6), a sound and light installation on permanent display at the Museum of the North at the University of Alaska, Fairbanks. It is a sophisticated piece of sonification. Adams draws the basic material for this work from live datastreams of seismic and geomagnetic activity measured at sites across the state, as well as from data on the passage of the sun and moon and the amount of over-head cloud cover. That data is then used to filter or sculpt raw "pink noise."[39] The seismic activity uses low frequency noise, sounding like rumbling drums or distant thunder. The geomagnetic data uses much higher frequencies. The passage of the sun and moon are represented in mid-frequency bands. Each set of data uses a different tuning system to filter the pink noise spectrum and then moves through that spectrum in response to the data received. So the sun describes slow sweeps up and down according to its position in relation to the horizon. The bandwidth of that sweep changes according to the amount of cloud cover at any given point—less cloud cover means a broader, more expansive sweep. The sweep is further adjusted according to whether it is day or night. Related processes are used to sonify the seismic and geomagnetic data. The result is a continuous, ever-changing polyphony of the earth. The lighting effects are composed in a similar way, using the position of the sun—both in relation to the horizon and around the points of the compass—to govern the mix of colors on five specially coated glass panes.

Although the resulting sound may be generalizable, it is also specific to the installation's location. Indeed, at one point in devising the project, Adams considered the possibility of creating multiple *Places,* built to the same specifications, at different sites around the world.[40] Regarded together and severally, they would present a global sonic portrait that was both endlessly varied and profoundly interlinked, a model for the "deep ecology" that Adams sometimes espouses.[41]

Although *The Place Where You Go to Listen* is site-specific, the relationship of the work to its site is profoundly different from the site/music relationship found in earlier site-specific works like Ros Bandt's *Stargazer* (1989) or Pauline Oliveros's work with her Deep Listening Band (founded in 1988). That music was written for highly reverberant spaces—a hollow concrete cylinder in an underground Melbourne parking garage in Bandt's case and the giant Dan Harpole Cistern at Fort Worden, Washington, with its forty-five-second reverb in Oliveros's case—and enters into a sonic dialogue with them, thus creating for them a musical identity and language. Musical material is played into the space, and the space responds; in turn, the music responds back. In this way, overlooked *spaces* are reclaimed as *places,* a move that resists the increasing anonymization of public space and restores narrative and meaning to a site.[42] Taking advantage of more recently available computer and network technology, Adams's installation works in the opposite direction: he is not sounding the place, it is sounding his music. The material comes from the place; it is not as much a site for dialogue as a resource.

A parallel might be drawn by looking further back, to early nineteenth-century Romanticism. In the practice of sonification, there is an "unspoken implication of metaphysical assumptions and romantic motives" that derives from certain ideas first put forward by the early Romantics.[43] Certainly there is an attempt to capture something of nature's sublime in Adams's work.[44] Adams has spoken about moving "away from music *about* place, toward music that *is* place,"[45] an ambition that is conveyed in the massed orchestral sounds of *In the White Silence* (1998) and the Pulitzer-winning *Become Ocean* (2013) and the percussionists—up to ninety-nine of them—of *Inuksuit* (2009). *The Place*, in which data from nature itself is transmuted into a sensual, immersive spectacle of sound and light, is the most overt expression of this.

Yet there are differences between the Romantic view and Adams's perspective. Most crucial is the axis on which the composer's reconciliation of nature and music is projected. The nineteenth-century musician would work horizontally, composing a dialectic between natural forces or perhaps between nature and man. Adams composes vertically, working with the registers, scales, and harmonic spectra of his sounds. The horizontal extension of the music through time is left to the data and the movements of sun, moon, and earth and is not organized according to any dialectic program. Adams draws a link with Tenney's theorization of "ergodic form," in which "any moment of the music is statistically equivalent to any other .... An entire piece of music is conceived, composed and experienced as a single complex, evolving sonority."[46] Bernd Herzogenrath observes that "Adams privileges time-sensitive dynamics, not clear-cut states."[47] He draws a link to Deleuze's theory of "becoming," but a similar line might also be drawn to Bourriaud's radicant aesthetics; both point to a contemporary artistic focus on *conditions* rather than *objects*. Another revealing comparison might be made with Stockhausen's *LICHT* superformula. Also an attempt to capture a planetary, cosmic music, *LICHT* is discursive: it has a beginning, a middle, and an end and so constitutes an object. *The Place* has none of these: it is a state. The shift from one to the other reflects the changed aesthetic context between two compositional generations. As an ecologist, Adams's instinct is not to intervene. Not quite to, in Cage's words, "let the sounds be themselves," since the sounds have been carefully and painstakingly designed so as to create the most pleasing acoustic results,[48] but certainly to let the system run by itself. Adams talks in terms of "an ecology of music" that "can provide a sounding model for the renewal of human consciousness and culture."[49] In this ambition— and in the hypothetical global version of *The Place*—we can trace a line back to Schafer's WSP.

Adams's sonification in *The Place* presents a different prospect from the sorts of field recordings Dunn and López describe. For a start, Adams is not entering a fragile natural environment to record it; his data sources are geological and even stellar in scale and immune to human intervention. Likewise, they are not in immediate danger of disappearing. However, the accusation that uncritical field recordings present a romanticized view of nature that cannot meaningfully sensitize listeners to environmental crises and the loss of habitats could still be made about his work. Adams's installation does not problematize how it presents its data. Rather than draw attention to the translation and transcoding, it simply presents the data as an analogue of the events occurring across the Alaskan land-scape, transformed for the convenience of aesthetic pleasure and institutional presentation. For him, the beauty of the work still resides in relatively conven-tional means such as periodic rhythm, harmonic spectra, registral balance, good taste, and clarity of orchestration. Nature and ecology are heavily mediated, not to break open the gap between reality and representation but to serve aesthetic and stylistic coherency.

MIMESIS AND POIESIS

We can consider different approaches to documentation through the framework of mimesis and poiesis. Mimesis—the attempt to represent something as an unme-diated copy or imitation—has been a frequent contemporary response to loss. It may be pursued by documenting—as an act of preservation or awareness raising (as in acoustic ecology or the work of John Luther Adams)—or by commemorat-ing (as in 9/11 memorials). It may also take the form of re-enacting or reanimating the lost object itself, as in Bolleter's ruined pianos or Jeck's scratched vinyl.

Mimesis is often used to give a contemporary work authenticity. Since post-modernism has put into question the "grand narratives" of romantic and modern-ist art, the concrete world of facts has taken the place of the authority of the artist. Yet no art can be truly mimetic. Having emerged as the result of the intervention and creativity of a thinking individual, art will always have the character of some-thing "made" about it—that is, poiesis.

Advances in recording technology tempt us to believe that it is possible to accu-rately capture the sound of a place or event. But, as Westerkamp showed in 1989 on Kits Beach, a recorded sound is no more authentic or trustworthy than any other. Documentary art, such as the transcriptions of Peter Ablinger, has become aware of its own artificiality, acknowledging, testing, and absorbing the boundary between copying and creating. This lends it the possibility of critique (or, failing that, senti-mentality). Yet even then, the picture is complicated by audience expectations and understandings. López, for example, sets out to critique the mimetic approach of acoustic ecology. However, his audience's familiarity with mediated sound (which, in 1989, Westerkamp was still able to tease) means that mediation itself has become essentially transparent, and the recording he makes of La Selva becomes to all intents and purposes indistinguishable from the reality of that sonic environment.

Reich also attempts a mimetic representation in *WTC 9/11*, in this case in the name of commemoration. Although *WTC 9/11* is related to his earlier *Different Trains*, a greater mimesis appears possible in the later piece because it uses actual sound recordings from the day of the events rather than the much later testimony of survivors. Yet even those recordings are commentary on the unfolding events, as are the (albeit professionally circumscribed) reactions of air traffic controllers and emergency workers. Reich's setting, which projects a musical narrative through its layers of musical and narratorial intensification, securely positions those recordings as poietic dramatization rather than authentic mimesis. Our own memory of the events plays a part too. The recordings, and Reich's soundtracking of them, follow the climactic logic of a film score, but it is not necessary to show us the film itself because we know the images so well.

In spite of their veneer of authenticity, recordings are no less prone to sentimentality than composed sounds are. This is especially true in the twenty-first century, when mediation has become a sonic language that is as familiar to us as common practice tonality was to listeners in the eighteenth. We are all capable, depending on how a recorded sound is presented to us, of establishing information about its age, source, position in space, relationship to other sounds, and meaning.

One of the most trenchant critics of the ideology of recording fidelity is the composer Steven Kazuo Takasugi (b. 1960). His *The Jargon of Nothingness* (2007) is an electroacoustic composition made up of close-miked recordings of a range of sound sources (thirty-one in all), including various string and wind instruments, homemade percussion, and household objects such as packing tape, rice, and scissors. As in a documentary field recording, the sounds themselves are only very lightly processed; with care, nearly all of them can be identified by ear. Each is represented as a short (often very short) sample and arranged with tremendous precision. (On the CD issue of the piece, Takasugi marks each section length down to one millionth of a second.) The technique recalls the microsound compositions of Horacio Vaggione, but Takasugi's piece turns our attention not to the cumulative effect of thousands of sound grains but to the individual sounds themselves.

However, although Takasugi's work retains the "real world" identity of each of his sound samples—the scissors sound like scissors, the marbles sound like marbles—reverb effects and other postproduction techniques are used to place each one within a different acoustic space. These are arranged not only from left to right, according to the stereo field, but also from near to far and from outside to inside in virtual spaces of various dimensions and qualities of reverberation. These sudden changes, in which acoustic space is continually fragmented and deformed, make for a remarkably rich listening experience full of realized impossibilities. Takasugi's target is the uncritical use of musical space in contemporary music. Any recording, his music tells us, is a false representation of reality, whether in terms of space or time or both. Although documentation and preservation can mitigate the effects of loss, they cannot authentically close the divide between us and what we have lost.

RECOVERY

Gaps between Past and Present

UTOPIAN FUTURES, NOSTALGIC DISTANCE

Let's go back to 1989. It so happened that one of the last great works of the postwar avant garde was composed just before the fall of the Berlin Wall: Luigi Nono's *La lontananza nostalgica utopica futura* (1988–9), for violin and eight-track tape. Nono lived only one more year after completing the piece. The two great fathers of the American and European avant garde movements, John Cage and Olivier Messiaen, lived only another two years after that, both passing away in 1992. Morton Feldman had died in 1987. Many remained—among them Berio, Boulez, Carter, Ligeti, Stockhausen, and Xenakis—but an extraordinary generation was beginning to depart.[1]

Nono was the most lyrical, most politically ambitious, and least compromising of the postwar Europeans, and his music always spoke of its time. But *La lontananza* has been refracted more than most pieces by the political moment that surrounded it. A lifelong Marxist and a friend and inspiration to many composers across Eastern Europe, Nono would not have shared Francis Fukuyama's eagerness in 1989 to proclaim the end of history and the final victory of liberal democracy. Nono's avant gardism was ideologically driven: he believed that radical politics required radical art, and the ending of one meant a crisis for the other. Listening to *La lontananza* with the benefit of hindhearing, one detects that it captures an uncertain moment between the ending of one thing and the beginning of another, between nostalgic longing and utopian future.

It is certainly no ordinary violin solo. The performer's part is distributed among six music stands, which are spread around the auditorium. Several of Nono's late works refer explicitly to the notion of wandering, borrowing their titles from an inscription that he saw on the wall of a monastery near Toledo, Spain: "Caminantes, no hay caminos. Hay que caminar" (Wanderer, there is not path. Yet you must walk). These words are derived from lines of a poem by Antonio Machado (1875–1939): "Wanderer, there is no path. / Walking makes the path." They appear in the titles of three of Nono's works, *Caminantes . . . Ayachuco* (1986–7), *No hay caminos, hay que caminar . . . Andrej Tarkowskij* (1987), and *"Hay que caminar" sognando* (1989). *La lontananza* may be added to that group by virtue of its subtitle: "Madrigal for many 'wanderers' with Gidon Kremer." During the course of the piece, the soloist marks its six sections by walking from one stand to the next. Up to four more stands may be left empty. The spatialization of the work is enhanced by a tape part that is distributed to eight loudspeakers surrounding the audience.

History haunts the work in many ways. The circumstances of its creation were fraught, to say the least. Commissioned by the violinist Gidon Kremer, it was intended for the Berlin Festwochen in September 1988. A full seven months beforehand, Kremer and Nono recorded the tracks that would make up the tape part of the piece over five days of sessions at the Heinrich Strobel Foundation in Freiburg. Although Nono set to work editing and preparing the tapes, he did not begin writing Kremer's part until barely thirty-six hours before the scheduled first performance. Somehow, after a superhuman effort from Kremer to learn the fearsomely difficult music just one day before its premiere, the piece was performed, only for Nono to swiftly withdraw it afterward. He finished the second version of it in January 1989, although much in the score remains distinctly unclear.

The difficult history of the piece is captured on the tapes, which include not only Kremer's playing but also the sounds of strings being tuned, furniture being moved, and chatter between takes; these are the scars of the work's creation. This material may be freely interpreted in performance; the sound technician is free to fade the eight tracks of Nono's tape up and down more or less as she pleases, including into complete silence. The work is therefore further haunted by swathes of material that may never make it out in a given performance; indeed, all of the material is not expected to be heard in each performance, as fading up all eight tracks throughout would rather miss the point. Many realizations of the work incorporate large amounts of empty or almost silent space within the tape part. Only by hearing several different performances is it possible to gain a reasonable picture of everything that is on the tapes and therefore of what is possible within the piece.

The violinist's part is mostly fixed, in terms of what she must play, but it is also uncertain in that its context, the taped accompaniment, is to a large degree unpredictable. She must make sense of her own part in response to whatever emerges from the speakers in the moment. To help deal with this, she does have some freedom in terms of how long to make the pauses between phrases and sections, and she can of course adjust things like dynamics, tone, and phrasing in response to the tape. As she plays, the ghostly Kremer laughs, speaks, and plays back to her.

The work sits between and articulates several simultaneous folds of history: that of its creation, that of its performances, that of the specific performance taking place there and then. The violinist Aisha Orazbayeva describes it as "a piece at the end of a century, a piece at the end of a life where one is looking back all the way to the very beginning, but imagining and thinking of the future at the same time."[2] Each moment echoes the great historical fold between the 1980s and the 1990s, when Nono's utopian idealism met and was (seemingly) defeated by its greatest challenge, the liberal economic orthodoxy that arose following the fall of the Berlin Wall.

OUT OF THE GDR AND INTO THE FIRE

Nowhere did the fall of the wall mark an ending more than in the GDR—which disappeared entirely shortly thereafter. The sound engineer Eckard Rödger lived through these changes. Rödger worked at the theater at the Palast der Republik (Theater im Palast, TiP) in East Berlin and was an influential figure in East German contemporary music. As well as helping produce a number of electroacoustic works by East German composers, he oversaw a concert series at TiP dedicated to electroacoustic music that included music composed in both East and West Germany—a particular focus was the Freiburg Experimentalstudio, directed at the time by Nono, who was close to many GDR composers. Rödger's involvement with TiP ended when it closed in 1990. He vividly recalled the piles of archived materials rotting and awaiting disposal at the Palast and in the basement of the Akademie der Künste, which echoed the files of paperwork thrown from the windows of the Stasi headquarters in Leipzig after the fall of the wall:

> I was working on a piece [at the Akademie der Künste in Berlin] when [sound engineer Georg] Morawietz asked me to come, so that he could show me something. And then he led me to a room with a huge domed ceiling with a gigantic mountain of tapes in it. That was all thrown in the garbage. It was similar in the basement next to it: a pile just like it—all files. . . . All of my film music. All of my notes. After the fall of the Berlin wall, I had to start from scratch in Leipzig.[3]

In 1990, the sixteen million citizens of the former GDR changed nationality, political system, geopolitical allegiance, and economy almost overnight. In other parts of Eastern Europe, this turn to the West was only the latest link in even more complex chains of change. One thinks, for example, of cities like Wrocław, which has variously been Austrian, German, and Polish over its history,[4] and of the multiple changes in national language and even alphabet that took place in Central Asian countries such as Kazakhstan through the twentieth century. Contemporary

Eastern European novels such as Stefan Chwin's *Hanemann* (1992; published in English as *Death in Danzig* in 1995) and Andrzej Stasiuk's *Opowieści galicyjskie* (1995; published in English as *Tales of Galicia* in 2003) confronted exactly these themes of maintaining an identity in the face of an ever-changing social and political context.

The gap the fall opened up between past and present inspired a phenomenon that became known as *Ostalgie*, defined as homesickness for the products and lifestyle of the GDR. When the Berlin Wall fell, German reunification was far from many people's minds. When the *Wende* (turn, or change) did come, many citizens of the former GDR found the new status quo unsatisfactory. People were suddenly faced with the loss of the security, certainty, identity, and even pride that had accompanied their lives under the GDR, despite the regime's deep flaws, and many turned to the past for comfort. *Ostalgie* has been best presented on film, as in the movies *Sonnenallee* (1999, directed by Leander Haussmann) and *Goodbye Lenin!* (2003, directed by Wolfgang Becker).

The displacements caused by the *Wende* went further than the pop cultural longing of *Ostalgie*, however. Although the GDR was among the most oppressive of all communist states in Europe, it was home to a small school of avant-garde composers and musicians that, from the mid-1960s, had formed around the composer and teacher Paul Dessau (1894–1979).[5] Sympathetic to and motivated by the ideals of socialism, they followed Dessau's lead in writing music that reflected critically on the past, was acutely aware of history (particularly recent German history), and sought to use the most advanced technical means available. To do so was not only to gesture toward the future but also to resist the heroic, populist modes of socialist realism, as well as the truth of socialism as it existed in the GDR at the time. A key work is *Aide-mémoire* (1982–3), by Georg Katzer (b. 1935), a nightmarish collage of speeches, marches, music, and other sound recordings from the Nazi era—"acoustic fragments from the biggest garbage pile of human history."[6]

Although these composers were not completely immune to criticisms and warnings from the authorities, they were allowed relative artistic freedom under the Honecker regime in the 1970s, with its attendant relaxation in cultural policy. Their works were performed in the GDR and abroad, including in West Germany. Theaters and churches provided largely unregulated platforms where nonconformist work could be presented. Through initiatives such as Rödger's concert series at the TiP, composers could maintain contacts with colleagues in the West. Composers like Katzer and Lothar Voigtländer (b. 1943) became adept at manipulating the GDR's political system to access international travel.[7] In one respect, the GDR might even be said to have been at the musical forefront at the time: one of the world's first electronic synthesizers, the Subharchord, was developed in there in the early 1960s. Technical progress after this was slow—Katzer has said that most of his studio's equipment consisted of guitar pedals, which were illegally acquired through East German rock groups that had been allowed to play in the West[8]—but electroacoustic music gained official recognition during the 1980s, with the establishment of a studio at the Akademie der Künste (founded by Katzer in 1982, although not officially opened until 1986) and the creation in 1984 of the Association for Electroacoustic Music.[9]

The fall of the Berlin Wall ended this infrastructure of support. Composers who had been senior figures within a relatively small scene in the GDR were suddenly pushed to the fringes of a much larger, internationally connected, and prestigious scene in a united Germany. To a large extent, they were ignored or overlooked by the West German establishment. Audience interest in electroacoustic music, which had been relatively strong up to that point, evaporated abruptly: the music's forbidden appeal was gone, and the previously exotic status of the GDR had disappeared. State-owned recording companies and publishing houses were disbanded or absorbed into their western counterparts. Concert halls, orchestras, and opera houses in the east began to appoint more western figures to leadership positions. East Germany's thriving avant garde became first marginalized and then anachronistic.

As the infrastructure in the east melted away, so too did the oppositional force of its music—and hence its raison d'être. Katzer described his pre-1989 music as becoming obsolete; another composer, Rainer Bredemeyer (1929–95), noted, "The listeners don't need it any more, this type of comfort. They have completely new concerns too."[10] Loss, bitterness, and a dark nostalgia permeate many of the works these composers wrote after the *Wende*. This sense of increasing disaffection, as the realties of the new context became apparent, can be traced between two works by Katzer.[11]

Mein 1989 (1990) is a tape collage that was composed on commission for the 1990 Bourges International Festival of Experimental Music to commemorate the revolutions of 1989. It is closely related to another tape piece, *Mon 1789*, which Katzer had made the previous year. *Mon 1789* was made ostensibly to mark the two hundredth anniversary of the French Revolution, yet it serves as a critique of the ideology of the GDR as well. Katzer also draws on *Aide-mémoire* in the piece to draw a wider perspective on recent German history than was encouraged by the triumphalist rhetoric of 1989. In *Mein 1989*, the fall of the Berlin Wall is portrayed not as a unique event but as part of a longer historical cycle. The piece traces a line through the end of World War II, the rise of the GDR, the construction of the wall, the delusions of the GDR's leaders, and the demise of the country itself. It ends with the sound of the hammers and pickaxes of the souvenir-hunting *Mauerspechte* (wallpeckers, people who came to take pieces of the fallen wall) and a stuttering enunciation of the word *liberté*. As the musicologist Elaine Kelly notes, Katzer's musical statement "suggests a degree of hope but no great confidence in what the future may hold."[12]

Katzer composed *Les paysages fleurissants* (2001) just over a decade later. Its title refers to the "blooming landscapes where it is worthwhile to live and work" that were promised by the German chancellor Helmut Kohl at the moment of currency union on June 1, 1990. When those landscapes failed to materialize, Kohl's words quickly became symbolic of the divide between promise and reality in unified Germany. One of Katzer's starkest and most darkly humorous works, *Les paysages fleurissants* uses just two sound sources: the sounds of an old truck engine and of an electronically synthesized sixteen-foot organ pipe. The piece begins with the sound of the engine trying to start, the recording of which undergoes various transformations over the course of four minutes. Just as it seems to be giving up, the engine finally starts. The organ then comes in, repeatedly sounding a triumphant three notes, although its effect is undone by the continued stuttering of the engine. Eventually the engine cuts out entirely, followed by two last statements from the organ. "Distorted and descending in pitch," writes Kelly, "these speak of ironic failure."[13]

One of the most symbolically loaded of all works from this era is Bredemeyer's *Aufschwung OST* (1993), for piano, oboe, percussion, and tuba. The title alone is rich in wordplay. *Ost* means "east," but it also refers to the initials of the trio of oboe, percussion (*Schlagzeug* in German), and tuba. *Aufschwung*, meanwhile, alludes to the title of the second piece of Robert Schumann's *Fantasiestücke*, op. 12, where it refers to the "uplift" or "rapture" of the character Florestan, from Beethoven's *Fidelio*, as he indulges his passions. If *OST* refers to Bredermeyer's instrumental trio, *Aufschwung* indicates the piano part, which is creatively rearranged and adapted from Schumann's original. *Aufschwung* also refers to a stimulus or boost, of exactly the sort that was expected to benefit the former East Germany upon reunification. And there is more. As Bredemeyer's sardonic program note[14] makes clear, the choice of Schumann is not accidental: Schumann was born in Zwickau and spent most of his life in eastern Germany; shortly after moving westward to Düsseldorf, however, he descended into an illness and psychosis ("driven mad by the world there"[15]) that eventually claimed his life. Throughout the piece, Schumann's original is variously broken up, interrupted, and sabotaged by the trio, which variously parodies and attempts to synchronize with it. As with Katzer's *Les paysages fleurissants*, synthesis proves impossible, and the work ends, in fulfillment of all the dark ironies of its title, in "defiant pained resignation."[16]

NOSTALGIA

"Nostalgia inevitably reappears as a defense mechanism in a time of accelerated rhythms of life and historical upheavals."[17] So notes Svetlana Boym, in her book-length study of nostalgia in Eastern Europe and Russia since 1989. Late-century nostalgia was not confined to the former Communist bloc, however. In the more conservative areas of American and (to a lesser extent) British music, nostalgia reemerged in response to the post–identity politics arguments of the culture wars. The avant garde's radical break with tradition also inspired a nostalgic response. As I suggested in chapter 3, these two chains of cause and effect overlap to a degree.

In music, the response often takes the form of what Boym calls restorative nostalgia. Emphasizing *nostos* (home), it seeks to reconstruct a home or a past that has been lost. In the case of music, this means restoring those elements of form, harmony, and rhythm thought to have been erased by the avant garde. Very often, such a turn is accompanied by a defensive rhetorical stance that argues that the avant garde was an error, a madness that must never be repeated. Such talk began much earlier than 1989. In 1973 George Rochberg claimed that with his Third String Quartet (1971) he was "turning away from what I consider the cultural pathology of my own time toward what can only be called a *possibility:* that music can be renewed by regaining contact with the tradition and means of the past, to re-emerge as a spiritual force with reactivated powers of melodic thought, rhythmic pulse, and large-scale structure."[18] He was not alone. As more composers turned away from their youthful avant gardism through the 1980s and '90s, the argument gathered authority.

We have already encountered some examples of this. It may be found in the continuations of the symphonic tradition represented by composers such as John Corigliano, Jennifer Higdon, and Krzysztof Penderecki. (The Bartók-influenced symphonism of Chinese-American composer Bright Sheng represents a more complex case, as it speaks of nostalgia for a home that the composer never directly knew.) Restorative nostalgia attempts to step back across the historical divide, to react against changes that have already taken place. Thus, the neo-tonality of John Adams or David Del Tredici is restorative, whereas that of Laurence Crane or Peter Garland, which uses tonality against the background of modernity, is not.

Nostalgia is not necessarily conservative. Boym identifies a second mode: reflective nostalgia. This is more concerned with the sensation of longing (*algia*) itself. Rather than reconstruct what has been lost, reflective nostalgia prefers to delay the homecoming, "wistfully, ironically, desperately." It steps into the historical gap that restorative nostalgia prefers to ignore. Reconstructive nostalgia wants to recreate the past in the present; in contrast, reflective nostalgia "dwells on the ambivalences of human longing and belonging and does not shy away from the contradictions of modernity."[19]

The bleak tone of the works by Katzer and Bredemeyer mentioned above, and their use of an "advanced" musical language, make clear their reflective relationship to nostalgia. The Norwegian composer Lars-Petter Hagen (b. 1975) takes a more ambiguous approach. Hagen's music incorporates artifacts from Norway's musical past, folk elements, recordings, and, in the case of *Tveitt-Fragments* (2006), reconstructions of lost scores by Geirr Tveitt (1908–81), a controversial Norwegian nationalist. Partly as a result of his source materials, and partly as a matter of compositional choice, Hagen's music is bittersweet in tone and, on the surface at least, is extremely approachable, drawing on a range of well-worn modes of affect in its aching melodies, moments of radiant harmony, and fragile timbres.

Between the world wars, Tveitt was one of Norway's leading composers. A major figure in the national movement of the 1930s, he was deeply inspired by Norwegian folk music and, like Bartók in Hungary or Ralph Vaughan Williams in Great Britain, collected the folk tunes of his area—in this case, the Hardanger region of western Norway. These made their way into his music not only as quoted materials but also through the use of particular melodic modes and scales, and through Tveitt's allegiance to a Norwegian brand of neopaganism promoted by the philosopher Hans S. Jacobsen.

After World War II, Tveitt's nationalist—although not national socialist—aesthetic became deeply unpopular, and he increasingly isolated himself from public life. Disaster struck in 1970, when his farmhouse, containing all of his manuscripts, burned to the ground. Around 80 percent of his work was lost, although the charred fragments have been kept by the Norwegian Music Information Centre.

It is some of these remains that Hagen used as a basis for *Tveitt-Fragments*. The work is, therefore, an act of reconstruction, a revivification of ruin, and an inhabitation of the work of another composer. These are techniques and methods that have become common in music (and other arts) over the last ten to twenty years. What distinguishes *Tveitt-Fragments* is that Hagen engages with a complex and difficult moment in Norway's cultural history: the legacy of nationalism, in both its positive (ethnographical) and negative (political) dimensions.

Hagen treads a fine line between self-aware melancholy and unreflective consolation. Many of his pieces draw on clichés of musical Norwegianness: folk music, hymns, and nature. In *Norwegian Archives* (2005), the chamber orchestra, whose music is full of "folky" natural harmonics and open fifths, is accompanied by a soundtrack that adds the sounds of choral singing, orchestral recordings, and, at two points, a sheep. Yet the mediated nature of the elements is placed in the foreground. The orchestral recording is scratchy and indistinct, the choir is distant and muffled, and the sheep is too precise with its cues to be anything but a sample.

Similarly, the music's lush timbres and harmonies, which exploit the comfort and security of triadic tonality, cannot be taken for granted. Although they are superficially warm and inviting, something profoundly unresolved is running beneath. In spite of its grand swells and sweeping gestures, the music never quite coheres into a story or an argument. At some moments it sounds Romantic or nationalist; at others it sounds precociously modern. It is reluctant to side with one or the other, but equally resistant to reconciling the two.

THE END OF THE PRESENT

At the very edge of Europe, in the last days of the Soviet Union, Avet Terterian (1929–94) completed his eighth and final symphony (1989) in Baku, Armenia. Inspired by the so-called sonorism of Polish composers like Penderecki, Górecki, Bogusław Schaeffer (b. 1929), and Witold Szalonek (1927–2001), Terterian was attracted to bold juxtapositions of instrumental color with a minimum of development and an emphasis on striking aural effects. Yet whereas those Polish composers found composing in static tableaux of sound to be a means of introducing communicative expression into a late modernist musical language, Terterian ironically appears to have found the process valuable as a way to take meaning *out* of music. A process perhaps begun with Shostakovich's Symphony No. 4, in which the symphonic form becomes a carrier of meaning that is, at best, ambiguous, finds an extension in Terterian's eight symphonies, of which it might be said that the greater the sound and fury, the less it signifies.

All of Terterian's symphonies deal in extreme contrasts and static textures. The eighth begins explosively: a sustained horn blast, a fortissimo orchestral crash, and sounds on tape that resemble the noise of scaffolding being demolished. As the reverberation fades, we are left with solo high strings and the sound of two remote female voices singing a folklike lament. Successively added to these are a pianissimo string chord; a pulsing ostinato of drums and harp; the chimes of bells, celesta, and other percussion; wind solos; and, finally, heavy brass chords and pounding bass drums. The whole adds up to a gradual, harmonically static crescendo lasting a full thirteen minutes. This is abruptly curtailed by a repeat of the orchestral blast and tape noise from the opening. This is followed by a few minutes of something resembling conventional symphonic music, albeit emptied of meaning—wandering string chords, snatches of wind melody, interjections of brass and percussion. And then it is back to the beginning: a third orchestral crash, followed by the remote choir, harp ostinato, and sustained strings. One thinks of Marx's observation about history repeating first as tragedy and then as farce. The immense build of Terterian's Symphony No. 8 serves as an upbeat to almost nothing. When the upbeat returns, it plays out as a long coda. The three-note bass drum figure that accelerated the climax of the build-up returns in the second half of the piece, this time more insistently yet also more futilely, until, with a full three minutes of the work to go, it is the only thing that remains, repeating and descrescendoing slowly into silence.

Terterian's symphony rewrites a long beginning as an equally long ending, with nothing of significance in between. The historical trajectory between then and now is subsumed entirely into an eternal but directionless present. Terterian wrote the work deep in the Soviet "era of stagnation," which began in the 1970s under Brezhnev, a period when Soviet economic and social activity ground almost to a complete halt. Terterian takes Western art music's most dramatic, most narrative-driven form, the symphony, and voids it of purpose and meaning. A less nihilistic approach was taken by the Ukrainian Valentin Silvestrov (b. 1937). Everything might have been said, reflected Silvestrov, but rather than seeing that as a cause for lament, he imagined the present era as a coda, potentially endless, to the history of music. Not *the* end, but a perpetual end*ing*.

His response was the postlude. Historically, a postlude is a musical movement, rather like an epilogue or a coda, that serves as the final part of a longer piece. While preludes are common throughout music history, typically serving as a light or informal introduction to a weightier movement such as a fugue, postludes are relatively rare. Silvestrov elevated them to the center of his style, however, and between 1974 and 2005 composed seven works and movements under the title *Postlude*, as well as a number of other pieces in a similar vein. These include his archetypal work of that period, the Symphony No. 5 (1980–82). Like Terterian's Symphony No. 8, Silvestrov's piece subverts the symphony's iconic status, but instead of voicing empty despair it turns itself back toward that tradition as a coda to it, "a postlude of a culture."[20]

Silvestrov addressed his motives for the postlude style in the early 1990s: "I wanted to write something not so much beginning, as responding to something already uttered . . . The postlude is like a collection of echoes, a form assuming the existence of a certain text that does not really enter into the given text, but is connected to it."[21] In 2010 he expanded on this idea, noting, "The postlude is an answer to a text, musical or historical. It is an echo."[22]

Although Silvestrov developed the postlude style in response to the economic situation of the late Soviet era, after 1989 he remained interested in composing music that in some way stood to one side of what it seemed to be about. He came to call this style "metamusic," a term he also used as the title of a large-scale work for piano and orchestra he composed in 1992. In his metamusic pieces, "one is, in effect, experiencing the future of an event long gone."[23] Silvestrov describes *Post Scriptum* (1991), for violin and piano, as "a postscript to Mozart and the whole classical tradition."[24]

Unlike his much earlier *Classical Sonata* (1963, rev. 1974), an exuberant and cheeky pastiche of the classical Viennese style, *Post Scriptum* is an elegiac work. Nostalgically stepping into the divide between past and present, it does not attempt to drive futilely into the future or to drag the past into the present day. Instead, it reconciles itself to existing in the gap, choosing to decorate it rather than escape it. "The text has already been written," Silvestrov explains. "We simply add our annotations, thoughts, questions, consternation, astonishment and regret."[25]

The music contains hints of Mozart in how phrases or melodies are shaped. But these little idiosyncrasies are reduced to faint echoes, dissociated from one another, disconnected by frequent pauses and breaks in the music's flow. However, the fragmentary first movement might barely make sense at all were it not held together by that point of historical reference. Listening to the piece is a little like flicking between the chapters of a book, between Silvestrov and Mozart. Musical continuity is elusive, but the listener creates it as the mind travels back and forth, from past to present. It is as though what we actually hear is not the form of the work itself but its components, which we must reconstruct against the Mozart background we hold within us. The three movements are progressively shorter. While the second is a relatively unified slow movement that stretches a continuous violin melody over broken piano chords, the third returns to the material of the first, reducing it still further until Silvestrov's Mozart is little more than a few alternating piano notes and col legno clicks of the violin bow.

While Silvestrov might be accused of acquiescing to an eternal coda of reinscription and commentary, other composers have emphasized the tension between past and present. The music of Giya Kancheli (b. 1935) draws extensively on nostalgic elements—in particular elements of tonal harmony, Romantic orchestration, and Georgian folk music—but reflectively points to their problematic nature as much as their comfort and reassurance. These elements always appear in fragmentary form, often barely emerging from their surrounding silence, yet prone at any moment to invasion by colossal boulders of orchestral sound, as in Kancheli's *Lament* (1994), for violin, soprano, and orchestra.

Nostalgia, like ruins and journeys, conflates movements in time with those in space: back *then* I lived *there; now* I live *here.* The particular form of nostalgia in Kancheli's music is the conflicted longing of an exile. In 1991, at the time of the dissolution of the Soviet Union and the civil war that followed Georgian independence, Kancheli, who was born in Tbilisi, accepted a DAAD scholarship to work in Berlin for a year. Unwilling to return to his stricken homeland, he stayed in Western Europe, settling in Antwerp. His personal history is reflected in the title of one of his most substantial works of the 1990s, *Exil* (1994), for soprano, ensemble, and tape.

Kancheli's aesthetic derives from this dislocation and disjoining of body and memory, inhabiting and emphasizing the distance between past and present. Like Stefan Prins's work, Kancheli's music effects a kind of disembodying, but one that takes place across time rather than space, through the medium of memory rather than electronic circuitry. Elements of traditional Georgian music—modal melodies, drones, sharp dynamic contrasts, phrases of great harmonic richness that end in sudden unisons—appear throughout his post-1991 music, but they are often heavily distorted. Traditional ornaments are dilated beyond recognition, dynamic contrasts pushed to almost absurd extremes, melodies abstracted and placed in discomfiting contexts. What seems concrete is destabilized, either through fuzziness or extreme contrast. With these distortions, Kancheli emphasizes the mediating effect of his own compositional process—poiesis rather than mimesis—and, hence, the distance that exists between his present and his past.

Franghiz Ali-Zadeh (b. 1947) makes still more overt use of traditional materials to trace the intersection of memory and place. Born in Azerbaijan, she draws on the traditional Azerbaijani *mugam*, a complex set of modes (scales) and rhythmic and structural rules for using them. Unlike Kancheli, however, she is not an exile, and she divides her time between Baku and Berlin (she was a DAAD recipient in 1999). While her music does not express the same profound melancholy arising from a sense of displacement as Kancheli's, it nevertheless identifies a similar space between past and present, traditional and contemporary, and Asian and Western. In the string quartet *Mugam Sayagi* (1993), *mugam*-style melodies are presented polyphonically (instead of in their traditional single-line form) and with the accompaniment of contemporary percussion and (briefly) electronics. Modern and postmodern gestures are present throughout. Yet the quartet is also edged closer toward a traditional *mugam* sound through imitations of the Azerbaijani *daf* (a type of drum) and *tār* (a type of plucked string instrument). By foregrounding the liminal space implicit in Kancheli's music, Ali-Zadeh creates a space for dramatic and playful juxtapositions, in which difference is simply acknowledged, without anxiety.

Because it exists in gaps—deliberately not fixed to anything—the music of Ali-Zadeh, Kancheli, and other composers of the former Soviet Union has proved able to slip between stylistic boundaries and is hence susceptible, like spiritual minimalism, to mediation through a number of channels, including folk, mystical, avant-garde, jazz, and world. *Mugam Sayagi* was commissioned for the Kronos Quartet and recorded by them for Nonesuch Records. Kronos have also recorded an arrangement of Kancheli's *Night Prayers* (1992, arr. 1994), which was among the first pieces he wrote having left Georgia. The same piece—in an arrangement for string orchestra and soprano saxophone—has been recorded for ECM as well, featuring the jazz saxophonist Jan Garbarek in the solo role. ECM also recorded Kancheli's *Lament*, "funeral music" for Luigi Nono, featuring Gidon Kremer, Nono's inspiration for *La lontananza* and an ECM favorite. Kancheli even dedicated *Exil* to ECM's producer Manfred Eicher, who introduced the composer to the poems of Paul Celan and Hans Sahl that feature in this piece and in others he composed after 1991. Ali-Zadeh, meanwhile, has written for the Silk Road Ensemble, another product of the interest in Central Asian culture that arose following the end of the Soviet Union.

Nostalgia, then, can become mediated as a site for exoticism, or even for modish New Ageism. If one takes the most cynical view, it could be considered a form of postcolonial titillation. Yet to acknowledge this is not to diminish the psychological complexity behind the best nostalgic works. Fundamentally, Ali-Zadeh, Kancheli, Silvestrov, and Terterian (many of whose works incorporate traditional Armenian melodies and instruments) are attempting a multidimensional reconciliation of here and there, past and present. In some cases, this takes the form of acquiescence (Silvestrov) or reconciliation (Ali-Zadeh); in others, it manifests itself as defiance (Kancheli and Terterian).

ANXIETY FREE

While many composers have been unable to escape their pasts, or have at least felt an uneasy responsibility toward them, others have enjoyed freedom from their backgrounds. There is a significant generational shift between composers who came of age during the postwar decades and those who reached adulthood toward the end of the century, and this is palpable in the different approaches the two groups take to the use of historical materials.

There are few composers who convey this shift more clearly than Thomas Adès. Born in London in 1971, Adès turned eighteen in the year *La lontananza* premiered and the Berlin Wall fell. A prodigious talent, he soon exhibited a familiarity and facility with music history that ran from the early English Renaissance to contemporary pop. Moreover, like many of his peers who came of age during the 1990s, on the cusp of the Internet era and ETEWAF culture, he has no anxieties about selecting materials from that past, and he has done so without showing concern for historical dialectics, undue respect, or aesthetic hang-ups. For Adès, the past is not so much a foreign country as an out-of-town supermarket.

This goes beyond postmodernism. In Adès's music, we can hear clearly a post-postmodern or even altermodern approach to history. His is an entirely postdialectical music, in which "the tension between tradition and modernism is simply not an issue."[26] He is not alone in this: we hear similar freedoms in the comic theater of Richard Ayres (b. 1965), the knowingly clever art songs of Julia Holter, and the hyperactive polystylism of Andrew Norman (b. 1979), as well as in other music discussed in previous chapters.

Adès's output includes arrangements of pop songs (for example, *Cardiac Arrest,* 1995, after the song of the same name by English two-tone band Madness) and irreverent portraits of the great composers of the past (such as *Brahms,* 2001). A revealing early work is *Darknesse Visible* (1992), a "recomposition" of *In Darknesse Let Me Dwell,* by the seventeenth-century English composer John Dowland. Similar to how Stravinsky treated the madrigals of Carlo Gesualdo, Adès does little more than orchestrate the original, adding no new notes (and, in fact, leaving some out).[27] Yet Adès's approach reflects a later aesthetic position. Where Stravinsky draws an almost didactic connection between Gesualdo's highly chromatic harmonic language and his own mid-twentieth-century idiom, Adès pursues a now-familiar set of late-century tropes that have to do with erasure and transformation, explicitly acting *on* the music rather than *with* it. His transcription opens up gaps within Dowland's music, as though with a crowbar. Adès makes use of the particular timbres of the very high and very low registers, which not only pulls the music to the extreme edges of the piano but also stretches Dowland's melodic and harmonic logic to breaking point. (Adès calls it an "explosion."[28]) Stravinsky co-opts Gesualdo, enlisting him to his own neoclassical program; Adès writes himself more thoroughly over Dowland, pushing the original music to its limits.

Because his music seems at first to work with the grain of tradition rather than against it, Adès has been embraced by a musical establishment that is desperate for a successor to the line of Beethoven, Brahms, and Bartók. In the United Kingdom, where such a need was felt acutely by a generally conservative critical establish-ment, he has been compared since his teens to another great B, Benjamin Britten. Yet Adès employs a logic of excess in his music that engages the past, not to align with it but to burst it apart. In Adès's music, quotations or allusions to the familiar are not sources of certainty but opportunities, starting points. A neoromantic or antimodernist might seek stillness or unity in idioms of the past; Adès uses them to turn outward, to exceed their associations. Like a positive ruin, Adès shows us the original and its construction so that we can follow where he has taken it, and in the process he destabilizes that object's original meanings and associations. Tonal underpinnings are removed, rhythms displaced, timbres and registers shifted, and expected developments interrupted. In the fourth movement of *Asyla* (1997), Adès makes an allusion to Bartók's *Bluebeard's Castle* but removes its underlying harmonic logic. In the third movement of his string quartet *Arcadiana* (1994), he transforms the harmonic and rhythmic stability of Schubert's *Auf dem Wasser zu singen* into gloopy drips and pools.[29] The Piano Quintet (2000) is per-haps his most radical step into the past. Its first movement is a strict A–B–A sonata form, of the kind used throughout the eighteenth and nineteenth centuries, but the music is constantly looking for ways to undo itself, from the start cutting a Brahmsian three-chord motif into a quasi-minimalistic loop.

RESTORATION

Where Adès prizes open the historical distance between past and present, others have sought ways to close it, through forms of restoration and recomposition. "Restoration" is a term more often applied to art than to music: as physical objects, works of art are more obviously subject to processes of decay and damage and are therefore more suitable for acts of restoration. In her discussion of restorative nos-talgia, Svetlana Boym draws extensively on the modern restoration of the frescoes of the Sistine Chapel, begun in 1979 and completed in 1999. One of the most substantial restoration projects of its type, it also proved to be one of the most controversial. In seeking to remove all traces of the passage of time—cracks, soot, brush hairs, and other marks and detritus—from Michaelangelo's paintings, the late-twentieth-century restorers inadvertently raised a key question: "What is more authentic: the original image of Michaelangelo not preserved through time, or a historical image that aged through centuries?"[30] By virtue of being susceptible to decay, works of visual art can enter more easily into this sort of dialogue about what is a more or a less true representation.

Yet as Hagen's *Tveitt-Fragments* suggests, music may also be restored, in a fashion at least. Further to the examples of musical ruin described in the previous chapter, a work of music, as a once-fixed object, may become damaged in one of two ways. The first is that the sole copies can be damaged, either by accident (such as in a fire, in the case of Tveitt's work) or the passage of time (such as, say, a medieval motet that has only survived as a fragment). Exceptions like *Tveitt-Fragments* aside, restorations of music damaged in this way are typically confined to the academic sphere of historical musicology and manuscript studies, where scholars intervene creatively at an absolute minimum, presenting as objectively as possible what material actually survives and making few, if any, prescriptions for what may be missing. The second way a work can be damaged is in a more metaphysical sense: a piece of music may become "damaged" as knowledge if its performance practice falls out of circulation, meaning that any performance seeking to be faithful to the original must involve a mix of historical reconstruction, creative guesswork, and straightforward compromise. Here, performers have taken the lead, through what has become known as historically informed performance. This philosophy of performance practice, which originated in the 1950s and gained traction in the 1970s and '80s, attempts to be sensitive to the original performing context of a work—its instrumentation, performing style, venue, and so on.

More common is a form of musical reconstruction that is applied to works that have been completed posthumously. Three historical instances are Mozart's *Requiem* (completed by Franz Xaver Süssmayr), Puccini's *Turandot* (finished by Franco Alfano), and Mahler's Symphony No. 10 (concluded by Deryck Cooke, among others). An important contemporary example is Anthony Payne's completion of Elgar's Symphony No. 3 (1993–7), reconstructed from fragments and sketches (1932–3) left by the composer.

Payne's reconstruction is notable not only for its remarkable success (it was performed in fifteen countries within its first two years and has been recorded five times), but also for the high level of creative input it required. Payne is unusual among musical restorers in that he is an established composer in his own right, and the Symphony No. 3 is unusual in that it is often credited to both him and Elgar. Whereas Cooke had a more or less finalized piano reduction to work from when completing Mahler's Symphony No. 10, Payne had only sketches of Elgar's Symphony No. 3, with no overall plan, and large sections—including much of the fourth and final movement—where no material existed at all. Completion of the work from such means required a composer of considerable ability and ambition.[31]

Payne's completion was scrupulous in its attention to what Elgar might have intended, right down to the bowing indications for the violins. Those who engage in acts of musical restoration are not always so willing to defer to the original composer, however. Of all postwar composers, Luciano Berio (1925–2003) had perhaps the most complex relationship with musical history. In the famous third movement of his *Sinfonia* (1968–9), he creates a fantastical tapestry of quotations from Bach to Stockhausen, stitched together by a thread derived from the third movement of Mahler's Symphony No. 2. Yet while *Sinfonia* is his tour de force, many of Berio's other pieces, particularly later in his life, draw extensively on musical works of the past.

Borrowings from, transcriptions of, and variations on earlier works—by other composers or by himself—recur throughout Berio's output, but starting the 1980s, he began to more frequently produce "recompositions," that is, pieces that go beyond quotation to enter wholly into the world of another work. Among them are *Opus 120 No. 1* (1986), a transcription for clarinet and orchestra of Brahms's clarinet sonata of 1894 that effectively created a hitherto nonexistent Brahms clarinet concerto; *8 Romanze* (1991), transcriptions for tenor and orchestra of eight short songs by Verdi that are part authentic reconstruction and part historical commentary; and a new final scene (2001) for Puccini's *Turandot*, meant to replace Franco Alfano's version of 1925.

Berio's most successful recomposition, however, has been *Rendering* (1989), for orchestra, a completion of Schubert's Symphony No. 10, which otherwise exists only in the form of preparatory sketches. As with Elgar's Symphony No. 3, these sketches are fragmentary and thus leave the restorer much to do. Berio takes a much more liberal approach to his reconstruction than Payne, however, retaining the discontinuities in the extant Schubert and filling in the gaps with original music of his own. The result is an interweaving of two quite distinct musical styles: Schubert's nascent Romanticism and Berio's (post)modernism.

Schubert has proved to be a popular subject for acts of creative restoration and appropriation. As well as the pieces by Berio and Adès already mentioned is Hans Zender's *Winterreise* (1993), a dramatic reimagining of Schubert's 1828 song cycle on poems by Wilhelm Müller. It is one of a series of "composed interpretations," as Zender (b. 1936) calls them, which he began in 1986 with *Schubert-Chöre* and continued with interpretations of music by Debussy (*5 préludes*, 1991), Schumann (*Schumann-Phantasie*, 1997), and Beethoven (*33 Veränderungen über 33 Veränderungen*, 2010–11). In *Winterreise*, Zender leaves the vocal part untouched but enlarges Schubert's piano accompaniment, arranging it for chamber orchestra and expanding or making more graphic much of what was implicit in the original. The shuffling steps of the approaching narrator in the first song, "Gute Nacht," are transformed from the gentle plod of Schubert's piano accompaniment into an extended, largely unpitched introduction, in which a steady pulse is passed around the full orchestra before Schubert's music itself comes gradually into focus. Later in the same song, Zender turns the irony implicit in Müller's verse "Love loves to wander / My dearest, good night! / From one to the other / My dearest, good night!" into bitter sarcasm by employing dissonant percussion that recalls the tone of Kurt Weill's Weimar-era cabaret.

Whereas Zender remains in large part faithful to Schubert's original, Wolfgang Mitterer (b. 1958) reinvents the Schubert lied for the remix era. *Im Sturm* (2004, rev. 2007), for baritone, prepared piano, and electronics, combines a distinctly Schubertian vocal line, consisting of melodies and texts cut and pasted from the corpus of Schubert lieder, with a whirl of breakbeats, digital glitches, jazz, and new music instrumental licks—the storm (*Sturm*) of the work's title—all drawn from Mitterer's personal sample library, compiled over many years. Characteristic of the fluid aesthetics of the digital era, Mitterer has used the same library in creating many of his other works, thus shapeshifting echoes of other pieces—*Sopop* (2008), *Coloured Noise* (2005), the Piano Concerto (2001), and more—can be heard bleeding into the nineteenth-century quasi-Schubert world of lyrical voice and nostalgic piano chords. In explaining his thinking behind *Im Sturm*, Mitterer has written, "I wanted to drag this ancient form of song with piano accompaniment down from the attics of the 19th century wipe off the dust & prejudice and find out whether the old splendor can be polished up again whether the old lyrical element and the music of missile defense systems of bugging devices and large sewage plants of high-speed trains & feelings can be connected interlocked & overturned."[32]

David Lang takes yet a different approach to working with Schubert's music. The five songs of his *death speaks* (2012) set all the lines from Schubert's songs that speak in the voice of death, which Lang translated into English and reordered into poems of their own. Schubert's words—"I am your pale companion . . . Listen to me."—are wrapped in the eerily comforting blanket of Lang's music. The music, although reminiscent of Schubert in its delicate poise, is written for an updated ensemble of indie musicians and composers—Shara Worden (vocals), Bryce Dessner (guitar), Owen Pallett (violin), and Nico Muhly (piano)—as Lang identifies a link between the nineteenth-century lied and contemporary pop.

Rather than attempting such a wholesale reinvention of Schubert's aesthetic, Berio enters into a cautious dialogue with the older composer's materials. His interpolations in *Rendering* have a dream-like quality, as though entering the music from another world. Each is signaled by a celesta, and in contrast to Schubert's clear-sightedness, they are indecisive, amorphous, and reticent, played at a subdued dynamic and often fading to the edge of nothing.

Although reception for *Rendering* has generally been warm, the piece has not been immune from criticism. Friedemann Sallis questioned Berio's claim to legitimacy: while composers may be entitled to resist the attempts of musicologists to restore or complete unfinished or damaged manuscripts on the grounds of bureaucratic and inartistic interference, he notes, this does not automatically give them the right "to do whatever they please with the working documents of their colleagues."[33]

Trying to understand what Berio has done through the usual terms of music history may be missing the point, however, as are, to an extent, comparisons with art restoration. Architecture, of which Berio was an informed admirer, provides a better model of practice. Sallis's objections rest on the persistent notion of *Werktreue*. Judging a compositional reconstruction or completion according to its faithfulness presupposes an autonomous and sacrosanct original, just as a historically informed performance practice must have in mind a "correct" way to play a given piece of music based on upholding the integrity of the score.

To a large degree, this is what Payne achieved on behalf of Elgar, by setting out to realize as credibly as possible what his Symphony No. 3 would have sounded like had he finished it. There is no sense, however, that *Rendering* is remotely what Schubert would have written had he lived a little longer. Large sections—around two-thirds of the piece, in fact—are early nineteenth-century Schubert, to be sure, but the rest is very definitely late twentieth-century Berio.

When restoring a work of art, one must think of what extent to maintain faithfulness to the original, what to do with gaps and areas of irreparable damage, to what degree the history of the object should be incorporated into its restoration, and how the voices of author and restorer should be balanced and combined. These questions are more easily resolved when dealing with works of architecture than with works of music. The concept of *Werktreue* is less significant, for example, as buildings already track the course of time. They are adapted for different purposes, extended, renovated, and refitted; they fall into disrepair and even ruin. At any given moment, a building reveals its whole history. Attempts are still sometimes made to preserve historical buildings in as close to their original state as possible, but it is more widely recognized that buildings are fluid.

Rendering sits closer to this fluid model—and perhaps even to the architectural notion of adaptive reuse, in which disused buildings are converted as a way of combating urban sprawl and minimizing the environmental impact of new construction. Fruitful comparisons can be made with such buildings as Jean Nouvel's Opéra Nouvel in Lyon (1985–93), an up-to-date opera house built within the shell of the existing nineteenth-century building, and Peter Zumthor's Kolumba Museum in Cologne (2003–7), built around the ruins of the Romanesque Church of St. Columba (see figure 33). In *Rendering*, Schubert's glimpses of a new, nineteenth-century symphonism are repurposed as commentary on late twentieth-century fragmentation and decay and the impossibility of true restoration. Like these buildings, Berio's piece brings contrasting styles into sympathetic and productive dialogue with one another.

FIGURE 33. Window frame at the Kolumba Museum,
Cologne, designed by Peter Zumthor, 2003–7. Photo by Esther
Westerveld, www.flickr.com/photos/westher/5287846364/,
licensed under CC Attribution 2.0.

RECOMPOSITION

Berio and Payne were dealing with incomplete originals. In other cases, however, composers have acted on finished works by their predecessors. This practice has been around for a long time, typically in the form of transcription. However, the interest in cultural heritage that accompanied the boom in art and architectural restoration and reconstruction from the 1980s on—as well as a revival in practices of transcription itself—appears to have prompted a revaluation of the possibilities of musical recomposition.

British composers have been particularly attracted to this manner of using the past. The extensive engagement of Sir Peter Maxwell Davies (1934–2016), a leader of British musical modernism during the 1960s and '70s, with arranging and adapting Renaissance music has undoubtedly been an influence, as may have been Britten's similar practices before him. Adès has already been mentioned, as has Finnissy (see chapter 5). In his *Arianna* (1995), Alexander Goehr reconstructed a lost Monteverdi opera from the libretto and a sole remaining lament. George Benjamin (b. 1960), Oliver Knussen (b. 1952), Steve Martland (1959–2013), and Colin Matthews (b. 1946) are among those to have made transcriptions of Purcell.

One of the most curious and most ambitious examples of recomposition is Robin Holloway's *Gilded Goldbergs* (1992–7). Although a student of Goehr's and a longtime lecturer at Cambridge University (where he taught Adès, among many others), Holloway (b. 1943) has worked for most of his career somewhat at the margins of the British new musical establishment. Many of his works, including the two operas *Clarissa* (1976) and *Boys and Girls Come Out to Play* (1991–5, as yet unstaged), have been composed without commission; his music has received little scholarly attention; and only a small proportion of his substantial output has been recorded. This may be due, in part, to Holloway's own neoromantic leanings, which place him at odds with the more modernist inclinations of the United Kingdom's new music mainstream. Yet it must be said that he remains, perhaps because of a determined refusal to bend to external pressures, one of the country's most singular and intriguing voices.

The *Gilded Goldbergs* began as a transcription exercise. Bach's original aria and thirty variations were written for a harpsichord with two keyboards (manuals). Performing the pieces on a piano is very difficult, since Bach's intricate part-writing involves a great deal of crossing of hands. While it is not too bad on two keyboards, it is much harder on one. Holloway therefore set out to transcribe the whole work for two pianos and so bring it into the range of the typical pianist.[34]

However, as his diary of the work's composition attests, Holloway quickly ventured beyond straight transcription.[35] Already with the third variation he completed, variation 20, he had added material to the end (a "burst of Scarlatti-clashing"), as well as thickened the texture considerably. The fifth transcription, variation 11, began to make associative connections outside the world of Bach, drawing in references to both Brahms and Schubert (incorporating a phrase from the latter's A major Rondo, D. 951). Within two months of having begun, and with ten or so of Bach's variations transcribed, Holloway was departing far from the originals, altering modes and key relationships, changing the order of events, and interpolating an increasing range of external influences.

We can compare Holloway's approach to history with that of Adès. Both compress the space between past and present, but whereas Adès fractures the old against the grid of the new, Holloway draws outward, beginning with Bach and passing, according to his own tastes, through musical history, from the late Baroque to the early twentieth century. Although very different in aesthetic, Holloway's piece shares with Boulez's *sur Incises* a desire to explore the boundaries of an existing musical object, to elaborate (i.e., "gild") its internal implications. Of course, the same impulse underlies Bach's own variations: thirty recompositions of the same tune that run the gamut of technical possibilities available at the time and inventing a few new ones along the way. Holloway pushes these limits, however, with a knowledge of all the musical history that has come since, which enables him to far exceed the limits of Bach's own practice. Nevertheless, Holloway's variations are just as unified as Bach's, something he accomplished through the use of continuities of voice-leading technique, timbre, register, and balance that find their origin in Bach's own music.

Where Holloway is capricious, the German composer Isabel Mundry (b. 1963) is considered. She was a student with Zender at the same time he was composing *Winterreise*. While Zender's interests lie in the great composers of the German Classical-Romantic era, Mundry is more interested in the composers of the fifteenth and sixteenth centuries. Inspirations from these periods may be found in her work as early as *Spiegel Bilder* (1996), for clarinet and accordion. However, *Dufay-Bearbeitungen* (Dufay Arrangements, 2003–4) marks the first time she worked directly on music by an older composer. This was followed by two sets of pieces based on harpsichord music by Louis Couperin, *Non mésuré—mit Louis Couperin I/II* (2008–9) and the large-scale cycle *Schwankende Zeit* (Fluctuating time, 2007–9); and *Scandello-Verwehungen* (Scandello drifts, 2010), based on a mass by the mid-sixteenth-century Italian composer Antonio Scandello.

Dufay-Bearbeitungen is based on seven chansons by the leading fifteenth-century Franco-Flemish composer Guillaume Du Fay. Originally composed for three voices, Mundry arranged Du Fay's songs for an ensemble of violin, viola, cello, flute, oboe, clarinet, piano, and percussion. The seven pieces are divided into three sets—the first set includes chansons 1–3, the second contains 4–6, and the third is made up of only chanson 7—which may be interpolated with other works. The staging suggests a discontinuous presentation, and each set requires a slightly different arrangement. In the first, all eight instruments are on stage. Piano and percussion are at the back, and the three winds and three strings sit on either side. For the second set, the piano and percussion stay where they are, but the viola moves to center stage, and the other instruments encircle the audience. For the last chanson, the piano and percussion again stay in place, but all six melody instruments move into the hall. They are still arranged in two groups of three, but this time they flank the audience on either side. The overall movement is from the stage into the auditorium, from a unified sound-space to a divided one.

Mundry does not change the melodic or harmonic material of her source. Apart from short additions at the start of each set of chansons, her interventions are entirely on the level of instrumentation and timbre. The three voice parts of the original chansons are distributed between the three winds and three strings. The winds generally play with a clean, "Renaissance-sounding" tone, but the string parts are sometimes modified with various playing techniques. The piano and percussion add further augmentations and distortions of tone: even when the piano is used melodically (although it more often provides percussive clunks), it is played with a sheet of cardboard running between the strings to produce an indistinct fuzzy sound.

Sometimes the groups alternate, sometimes they play together, and at other times they interlink in various ways. In this way, Du Fay's originals are broken up to reveal cracks and discontinuities. Furthermore, each chanson is heard a total of three times, each time in a different realization, and each time changing the various spatial and timbral relationships within the piece, duplicating the shape-shifting effect on a higher level. Combined with the three-fold transformation in the spatial arrangement of the players across the whole piece, we hear a complex and multilayered exploration of identity as Du Fay's music is continually redistributed and reconceived around the space.

Dufay-Bearbeitungen is clearly a reflective approach to the past. Mundry does not subtract from or even alter Du Fay but instead adds layers, dirtying the original like the patina of soot and dust particles that had accumulated on the Sistine Chapel ceiling. Each repeat shows us the same fresco, the same past, through a different present; nothing about either should be taken for granted. Rather than compress the passage of time, like Holloway, she emphasizes distance.

Methods may differ, but the motives behind artistic and architectural restorations and reconstructions are usually clear. Education, research, prestige, ownership, and utility all play a part. In the case of buildings, repurposing and adaptation are also driven by social, economic, and environmental factors. The fact that these motives often correspond closely to the present-day priorities of funding bodies such as museums, cities, and other institutions accounts in large part for the rise in popularity of such buildings over the past three decades.

The motives behind musical reconstructions are not always as clear. There are elements of education, historical research, and perhaps prestige involved in Payne's faithful reconstruction of Elgar, but Berio's adaptation of Schubert is too free to be considered in a similar light, as are works by Holloway, Mundry, and others. Perhaps a case could be made that these works are a sort of repurposing, analogous to the conversion of Bankside power station into the Tate Modern gallery, although this doesn't accommodate the fact that both original and recomposition are functionally present in the new work. Bach's music is still very much there in the *Gilded Goldbergs,* whereas the oil-fired generators have long gone from the Tate. Yet the increase in artistic and architectural restoration work has no doubt contributed to the creation of an aesthetic of restoration that has fed into the production of musical works that don't necessarily share the same motives.

A final motive of reconstruction is commercial value. This does not apply so much to works of art or architecture, but it does apply to recorded music, where there is a sales component. In the West, the past has proved to be a useful commodity, point of orientation, and even branding strategy. Combined with the trappings of modernity, it satisfies both the search for novelty and the acquisition of cultural capital.

The commercial value of the past has encouraged an artistically exploitable tension between the modern and the historical, and this is where institutional actors begin to play a role. Transcriptions, for example, are often motivated in this way. On a pragmatic level, they may be requested so as to create a more accessible version of an existing piece. This is what prompted Holloway to begin *Gilded Goldbergs*, although he made the decision to do so privately, and the piece was not commissioned by a publisher. They may also be commissioned to meet the demands of a particular occasion. This is the background of the Purcell transcriptions by Benjamin, Knussen, and Matthews referred to above, which Knussen commissioned as artistic director of the Aldeburgh Festival to mark the three hundredth anniversary of Purcell's death, and which together are known as *A Purcell Garland* (1995). Another collaborative Purcell-based piece, *Bright Cecilia* (2002), comprised a set of variations by seven composers[36] written to mark the tenth anniversary of *BBC Music Magazine* and performed at the Last Night of the BBC Proms. The Freiburg-based ensemble recherche is one group that combines contemporary and early music in its repertory[37] and also works closely with composers like Mundry, Gérard Pesson (b. 1958), and Brice Pauset (b. 1965), who frequently incorporate elements of early and Classical-Romantic era music into their work. One ongoing project is the creation of a collection of "In nomines," contemporary additions to the sixteenth-century English tradition of composing instrumental music based on a particular piece of plainchant, the antiphon *Gloria tibi Trinitas*. The series was initiated by recherche's founding member, cellist Lucas Fels, to mark the tenth anniversary, in 1999, of Harry Vogt's direction of the Wittener Tage für Neue Kammermusik. The collection has grown ever since, today numbering more than forty pieces by almost as many composers.

Record labels have also been tempted to bring together past and present. With its *Recomposed* series, discussed in chapter 3, Deutsche Grammophon sought to close another gap, that between existing and new markets. The press materials for Max Richter's soft-edged, postminimalist recomposition of Vivaldi's *The Four Seasons* make the connection explicit: "Max Richter . . . has brought Antonio Vivaldi's masterpiece *The Four Seasons* into the present for *Recomposed*, opening up the work to an entirely new listenership. At the same time, his respect for the original and its performance history mean that seasoned classical music lovers will also find plenty to enjoy in this recomposition."[38]

ECM Records also frequently combines early and contemporary music on its releases and seeks out music that includes elements of both. However, unlike Deutsche Grammophon, whose *Recomposed* is an overtly commercial move intended to

FIGURE 34. CD cover for Jan Garbarek and the Hilliard Ensemble's *Officium*, 1994. ECM 1525.

draw new listeners to the label's core catalogue, ECM's strategy has grown more organically, built on the enormous success of its Arvo Pärt discs in the late 1980s and early 1990s. ECM is something of a pioneer in defining the market for such music, although it is not always easy to say to what extent it has responded to the kind of music that is being written or driving its production. Certainly there are instances when the label has innovated crossovers of its own. The most notable is *Officium* (1994), a collaboration between saxophonist Jan Garbarek and the Hilliard Ensemble, in which Garbarek improvised over sacred medieval and Renaissance vocal music. There are several echoes between *Officium* and the Pärt album *Tabula rasa*. First is the way that Manfred Eicher has drawn two regular ECM artists together, as he also did when he brought Keith Jarrett in to record *Fratres* with Gidon Kremer, and Garbarek to record Kancheli's *Night Prayers*. Second is the combination of sacred music with spiritually inclined jazz, which can also be traced back to Jarrett. A detail of the *Tabula rasa* CD was the concept behind *Officium*. Third are similarities in presentation of both releases, including the use of a resonant acoustic for recording, the design of the CD sleeves (see figure 34), and the common ECM trick of including more than one version of the same piece on a disc—*Officium* features several takes on Cristóbal de Morales's *Parce mihi Domine*, whose combination of stately vocal chords and saxophone flights became the album's signature.

POSTPRODUCTION

"Postproduction" is a term used in film and TV to refer to all the stages of production that take place after the primary material has been recorded. These include editing, adding a soundtrack and sound effects, and creating special effects. In large part, this is where the final film or episode is actually made, whereas what happens on set is, to an extent, a process of collecting raw material. The fact that so much of the final product is created after the moment of its realization, as it were, is also what sets film and TV apart as artistic forms. In a theater, for example, the actors' delivery of their lines is the endpoint in the creation of the play, the moment when the respective visions of writer and director reach fruition. In a film, the point when a line is delivered is still very early in the process; there are still many stages of postproduction to go through before it becomes part of the film.

As mediation has played an increasingly important role in the arts, so postproduction has become an increasingly important part of the artistic process. A painting, for example, has no elements of postproduction, unless one includes the context and manner in which it is hung. A play requires a much larger apparatus of actors, directors, designers, and technicians, but their role is to realize and enhance the author's work; once the lines are spoken and the play is brought to life, there are no further stages of adaptation. The same is true of live music.[39]

Move into a more modern media age, however, and postproduction starts to play a larger role. A book requires editors, typesetters, and designers to work on the author's raw material. In general, their role—like that of the painting's hangers—is to enhance and illuminate the work, intervening as little as possible. Nevertheless, the fact that a single text can exist in multiple editions and translations (consider the case of James Joyce's *Ulysses,* or even the Bible) points to the presence of distinct phases of production (by the author) and postproduction (by the publisher).

With the advent of photography, film, and sound recording, the creative balance began to shift more fully into the realm of postproduction. This was true from early on, with the work that went on in the darkroom or the editing suite. With the rise in the use of digital means of recording and production, however, the range of tasks that can be done in postproduction has increased greatly, and the balance of work done before and after the click of the shutter, the delivery of a line, or the singing of a note has shifted accordingly. When you experience a film today, you may be seeing a background that wasn't there when the camera was rolling, events that didn't happen in the order you are watching them in, colors that weren't the same as in the original footage, and actors who weren't on set together, as well as hearing sounds that weren't made on location, dialogue that was recorded many months later, and music that was produced entirely separately.

As film, TV, photography, and popular music—the chief media in which post-production techniques are used—have come to dominate the cultural landscape, so has postproduction become adopted by artists and composers. Bourriaud notes that, "since the early nineties, an ever increasing number of artworks have been created on the basis of preexisting works; more and more artists interpret, repro-duce, re-exhibit, or use works made by others or available cultural products."[40] Bourriaud groups these artistic practices under the heading of "postproduction," although his use of the term—and the manner in which I use it in the following pages—is slightly adapted from its application in the film industry. When Bourri-aud refers to postproduction, he is talking about a way of creating artworks on the basis of already existing works rather than from materials, such as film footage, that are still in a raw state. The analogy with the postproduction process in film relies on the distinction of a pre- and post- relationship between the new artwork (or finished film) and the already existing artwork (or raw footage) that is sus-tained through the application of a technical, or mechanical, studio-based proce-dure that transforms one into the other.

Postproduction opens yet another gap between the work and its source, this one created not by time or space but by method or technique. This points to a fundamental shift in creative priority, from what is made to what is done *to* what is made. This is significant. As with Peter Ablinger's *Voices and Piano,* a quintes-sential work of postproductive composition, our attention is shifted from the source material to what the composer has subsequently done to it. When meaning stops residing in the object itself, it starts to reside in the actions made on it—as is the case with the ruin or the journey, the transcription or the reconstruction.

There has long been a postproduction element to the composition of Western art music, exemplified in the transcriptions and arrangements that composers have made over the years of one another's work. For this reason, I use "postpro-duction" in a more specialized sense than Bourriaud, to refer to works of music that not only use other music but also do so at a level beyond that of score-based transcription. That is, they go beyond the means available to composers before approximately the 1980s. Very often, this will involve a degree of technological mediation. Sometimes the results will themselves be technologically mediated, as recordings, for example, but more often they will be presented in the form of scores, another, older form of mediation.

68SFTD (2008), by Seth Kim-Cohen, is an unusual example of the postproduc-tion aesthetic in that, although it is based on a recording and adapts a technologi-cal paradigm of looping and time-stretching, it in fact uses no technological mediation at all. It is constructed on a simple premise: a rock band plays the

Rolling Stones' song "Sympathy for the Devil," but with the twist that each four-bar section is played twelve times before moving on to the next. In this way, the original song is blown up to a sixty-eight-minute marathon, a test to destruction of one of rock 'n' roll's catchiest grooves.

68SFTD draws on the semantic content of its source material: the fact that the material is recognizable and that the process applied to it is identifiable is essential to its interpretation. It may be an experimental work, but Kim-Cohen highlights the political and historical import of the material he is distorting:

> If you're searching for the zeitgeist of 1968, you could do worse than Sympathy For The Devil's intimations (and imitations) of the Prague Spring, the events of Paris in May, the Chicago 7 protests at the Democratic National Convention, the My Lai Massacre, the assassinations of Martin Luther King Jr. and Robert Kennedy. The music of '68 announces the death of values like progress, resolution, and authority—replacing them with repetition, extreme duration, and the downplaying of virtuosity in the minimalism of Philip Glass and Steve Reich; the circularity of Can and the Velvet Underground; the extended grooves of James Brown and Miles Davis. Like a demon accountant calculating the tenor of the times, Sympathy for the Devil tallies the spirit of 1968. Forty years later, we take the measure of the geist of our own zeit. History repeats itself like a groove.[41]

Postproductive strategies are not confined to experimental works like this. *Clouds and sky* (2010), for example, by Johannes Schöllhorn (b. 1962), presents a time-stretched orchestration of a piano nocturne by Gabriel Fauré that extends Fauré's dreamy miniature to a full twenty-four minutes, but without stepping outside a familiar early twenty-first-century orchestral idiom. Marko Nikodijevic (b. 1980) uses a similar strategy, working from digital stretches and compressions of whole pieces by other composers. The truly harrowing *cvetić, kućica . . . /la lugubre gondola* (2009) takes Liszt's late piano piece *La lugubre gondola* as its underlying data. The choice is not arbitrary and relates to the first part of the title. *Cvetić, kućica* (little flower, little house) describes a drawing found in the hands of a Kosovo-Albanian girl, whose drowned body was discovered inside a container lorry thrown into the Danube in 1999 by Serbian police. Thus the girl in her waterborne coffin is memorialized in the work just as the stately funeral procession of Wagner's body through the canals of Venice was supposedly prefigured in Liszt's piece, the first version of which was composed just weeks before Wagner's death in Venice in February 1883. Nikodijevic's queasily beautiful distortion adds layers of melancholy and the grotesque.

A very different approach is taken by Bernhard Lang (b. 1957). Like Bourriaud, Lang has been influenced by the philosophical work of Deleuze and Guattari, and since 1998 almost all of his output has been devoted to two cycles of works concerned with extrapolating their ideas: *Differenz und Wiederholung* (Difference and repetition, 1998–) and *Monadologies* (2007–).

There are now more than thirty *Monadologies*. Each is composed according to the same process, and each, until the most recent works in the series, uses as its starting point fragments of music by others. The compositional process is almost wholly automated. First, Lang chooses an existing piece. This might be a piece of popular or art music, and Lang has used, among others, works by Bob Dylan, John Coltrane, Richard Strauss, and Joseph Haydn. Next he extracts a small number of "cells," each just a few seconds long, or shorter. These are processed algorithmically by computer to create indefinitely long self-generative sequences of music by applying a small number of rules, such as compressing or expanding pitch and duration relationships, to create endless iterations of the original cell. Lang's inspiration is Stephen Wolfram's *A New Kind of Science*,[42] which argues that understanding simple computational programs, such as cellular automata, is key to understanding how complexity in the natural world derives from the implementation of simple initial rules. However, the link between Wolfram's work and Lang's music is once again the shift from material to process. The actual nature of a cell within one of Wolfram's systems is less significant than the rules by which it must operate. In Lang's compositional process, he is free to adjust the software's parameters before starting a piece, but the underlying rules are the same for every work in the series: once the computer has generated the music, Lang orchestrates it, intervening only to correct any moments of awkward or nonidiomatic instrumental writing.

We have seen other examples of algorithmic compositions, in particular works by Enno Poppe. Where Lang differs, and what highlights the postproductive nature of what he is doing, is that where Poppe uses self-composed and musically neutral materials in his initial cell, Lang derives his from works in the historical canon. Moreover, the pieces Lang chooses are often from well-known and semantically loaded pieces. The extracts used in *Monadologie XIVA* and *XIVB*, for example, are from Puccini's *Madame Butterfly*, and *Monadologie XVIII* "Moving Architecture*" uses the music of Bob Dylan's "Like a Rolling Stone." Others draw on fragments from Mozart's *Don Giovanni* and Schoenberg's Chamber Symphony No. 2, and with *Monadologies XX* ". . . for Franz," *XXI* ". . . for Franz II*," and *XXXI* "*The Cold Trip Pt. 1*," Lang joins those composers who have drawn on Schubert, extracting his cells from Piano Trio No. 1 in B♭, op. 99; Piano Trio No. 2 in E♭, op. 100; and *Winterreise*, respectively. The fact that so much of the source material is well known matters strangely little because of the minimal impact it has on the final piece. The movements of *Monadologie XI* "*The Anatomy of Disaster*" may each begin with a more or less recognizable fragment of Haydn's string quartet *Die seiben letzten Worte unseres Erlösers am Kreuze*, altered only in terms of register and timbre, but any echo of the contemplative mood of Haydn's original is quickly subsumed by Lang's processes and their dizzying, machine-like results.

AFTERNESS

It begins with exhalation. An expiration of air from the lungs, yes, but also the energy drop of bows landing on strings. Then a film, grainy and projected onto a scrim across the front of the stage. At first it is indistinct and out of focus. Light through trees perhaps? We are in a car, driving through an unnamed city.[43] Our way is continually interrupted by traffic, road junctions, and pedestrians, as well as cuts in camera shot and footage that take us back to a row of poplars. The music is full of similar breaks in flow: the sounds of winds and strings being stopped, distorted, split. They are more than notes—we feel them being played, particularly as different forms of abrasion and pressure: air pushing against dilating lips, bow hairs sliding against strings, fingertips plucking and sliding. Sometimes the sounds are smooth; sometimes they catch and break. The musical space is articulated not by continuities of melody, rhythm, or harmony but, like the car ride in the film, by relative degrees of resistance and obstruction.

Many of the works discussed in this chapter—indeed in this book—have been concerned with the historical break that occurred around 1989. However, *Pnima . . . ins innere* (1998–9), this large-scale work of music theater by Chaya Czernowin (b. 1957), addresses an older, deeper rupture. There are two characters: an old man and a boy. The man is a Holocaust survivor; the boy is trying to understand the trauma his grandfather will not discuss. Like the boy, Czernowin is of a generation born and brought up in Israel—the "second generation" of Holocaust survivors. As described in David Grossman's novel *See Under: Love* (1989), on which *Pnima* is loosely based, it is a generation of Israelis who grew up knowing something terrible had happened in their parents' past but who were only ever shown glimpses of it. This profound discontinuity is expressed in the piece by the language of friction and disruption outlined in the opening film and music. These discontinuities carry through into the dramaturgy. Although the work is ostensibly an opera, neither the boy nor the man sing or speak on stage to each other or to the audience. Instead they are represented by two pairs of off-stage voices and small instrumental groupings—which express not only the space between the characters but also their conflicted, complex, and fragmented internal states—rather than an external (and hence unified) projection.

In her next major work, *Maim zurim maim gnuvim* (2001–2), for five soloists, orchestra, and electronics, Czernowin returned to the theme of communication, although on more optimistic terms. In particular, she was interested in the gap that exists between what is said and how it is said—what she describes as the difference between a gesture (an act of direct communication) and a dance (a mode of expression distinct from communication itself).[44] Her model was water and its various states as droplets, streams, vapor, and ice, each a different expression of the same element.

However, as noted in the previous chapter, the work's composition was deeply affected by news of the Second Intifada and 9/11. The impact this had on Czernowin's compositional approach can be heard almost exactly midway through: a thunderous percussion stroke shakes the piece; it is paired with a breath glissando involving almost all the wind and brass that descends through a wide arc, as though tracing the fall of the drummer's arm. Until this point, the piece has been composed as tiny pricks of sound, subject to endless changes as each droplet is smeared across one parameter or another—pitch, rhythmic placement, timbre. Now, for the first time, the allusive dance of actions and aftereffects coheres into a single, shocking gesture. There is no turning back. Fragile, abstract beauty has become infected by the horror of the world outside: "strange water" (*maim zarim*) is now "stolen water" (*maim gnuvim*). As one step in a multipart commissioning process, *Maim zurim maim gnuvim* became the first movement of a three-movement work, *Maim* (2001–7), one of the most significant orchestral works of the new century. The remaining movements try (with an inbuilt risk of failure) to heal the "wound" opened up in the first, between the point of the droplet and the line of the smear, or, as Czernowin puts it, between "What you see is only a hint," and "What you see is what you get."[45]

· · ·

Czernowin's words echo—perhaps surprisingly, given her work's particular aesthetic—Frank Stella's famous remark about minimalism: "What you see is what you see."[46] If, as Lang's *Monadologies* suggest, canonic materials can be so easily rinsed clean of all significance, then why use them as a ground at all? Why not act on the most basic, most neutral elements one can? The materials of 1960s' minimalism, both musical and sculptural, were often devoid of significatory content and, like Donald Judd's boxes or Carl Andre's bricks, stressed only their nature as *material*. There were limits of course—one thinks of Reich's tape piece *Come Out*, which carries an unavoidable political charge because of its use of speech samples from a young black victim of police brutality, Daniel Hamm. However, such pieces were the exception that proved the rule.

Unlike sculptural or pictorial minimalism, however, musical minimalism did not typically emphasize stasis but rather activity and change. Reich's 1968 manifesto was, after all, titled "Music as a Gradual Process," not "Music as a Static Object." Minimalism's origins (if not its aesthetic) lay in serialism, and Reich's original complaint was not that serialism used procedures but rather that those procedures were not audible. By making them audible, he and other process music composers—Glass, Riley, Lucier, Tenney, Oliveros, Nyman, Bryars, Parsons, and so on—were able to transform musical material from an object into a state, from a noun into a verb.

At much the same time, others—among them Ferneyhough, Lachenmann, and the French spectralists—were reaching very different musical conclusions from somewhat similar premises: that musical materials contain within them the energies and implications necessary for their own development as music. The simplified equation might look like: *object* (i.e., musical material) + *energy* = *action or state*. This suggests a temporal division between musical material and its realization as *music*. Between the various musical schools—minimalism, complexity, *musique concrète instrumentale*, and spectralism—that emerged during the late 1960s and early '70s and had the most significant influence on the following decades, we might therefore identify a common approach, what we might call a general poetics of "afterness."

A recurring image throughout this book has been of gaps: between global cultures (Tarek Atoui, Liza Lim, the Silk Road Ensemble), between global economies (Johannes Kreidler, Alan Hilario), between audiences (Bang on a Can, Warp Works, *Recomposed*), between recordings and live sound (Hildegard Westerkamp, Steven Kazuo Takasugi), between mimesis and poiesis (Francisco López, Steve Reich, John Luther Adams), between material and resonances (György Kurtág, Claus-Steffen Mahnkopf, Bernhard Lang), and between stories and their telling (Olga Neuwirth, Diamanda Galás, Pamela Z). Afterness rearranges this spatial metaphor for the time-based medium of music, whether in the transcriptions of Peter Ablinger and Michael Finnissy, the displacements and disruptions of Aaron Cassidy and Stefan Prins, the mediations of John Oswald and ECM records, the journey forms of Jennifer Walshe and Enno Poppe, and the passage of time in the recompositions and nostalgias of Isabel Mundry and Giya Kancheli.

Rather than beginnings, afterness is about consequences. Like Czernowin's or Ustvolskaya's sonic traumas, it shifts our focus away from the object and toward its aftermath. Afterness restores the age-old binary of figure and ground, but over time rather than in space. It is less interested in presenting objects as they are than in asking, "what happens when . . . ?" It sees things not as indicators of or signs toward the future but as consequences of the past. A scar is not the thing itself but the mark of something that has happened.

What unites composers as disparate as those discussed in this book is not just that the past or the Other has entered their work—this has been a feature of music for centuries—but also that the way in which that past or that Other is processed has become a part of the musical discourse. Understanding or appreciating new music's use of the past is no longer just a question of technique, of reading the skill in which, say, a chant melody has been incorporated into a polyphonic texture, but is now also a matter of reading the relationship that is created between the work and its source. That is, a musical concept that presents not only the Z of a completed piece but also the X and Y of source and process that came before it. This is not only a legacy of earlier twentieth-century movements but also a function of, response to, reflection on, and even celebration of the wider social and political forces of our time.

At the start of this book I identified six developments in global society, economics, politics, and technology that enabled or inspired the development of contemporary composition since 1989: social liberalization, globalization, digitization, the Internet, late capitalist economics, and the green movement. As these intersected with the musical legacies of the 1960s and '70s—experimentalism, spectralism, complexity, *musique concrète instrumentale,* and minimalism—they gave rise to a number of formal types and thematic preoccupations: the journey, the ruin, and the transcription; modes of nostalgia and displacement; forms of excess and reduction; preoccupations with the body and the audience; and (qualified) returns to tonality and meter.

Afterness can take many different forms. Some of its manifestations have been enabled by developments in technology (spectral analysis or multimedia, for example) or by trends in the other arts (such as conceptualism). Others have been inspired by outside developments: the various types of ruin and journey form that I have discussed were inspired by technology and globalization. Still others followed the historical ruptures surrounding 1989.

Searching for or describing unities in the present age, which is usually described as fragmentary, may be foolhardy. But as economic, political, and technological forces conspire to create a world that is more homogenous and interconnected, it should not be a surprise to find composers responding—albeit in very different ways—to common sets of questions. As our world is reconfigured in terms of flows (and resistances), perhaps the way past this fragmentation is to turn things on their sides, to seek out the continuities across relationships and networks at the same time as we relish the differences between individuals.

APPENDIX ONE

RECOMMENDED LISTENING

The following list is just a starting point. Where possible, I have given suggested recordings for all the works discussed at length in the book, as well as additional items and links that may be useful. All entries are for CD releases unless otherwise stated.

Aa, Michel van der

Spaces of Blank; Mask; Imprint. Christianne Stotijn, Royal Concertgebouw Orchestra, ASKO|Schönberg Ensemble, Freiburg Baroque Orchestra, Ed Spanjaard, Otto Tausk, Gottfried von der Goltz. Disquiet Media DQM01, 2010.
One. Barbara Hannigan. Disquiet Media DQM03, 2011. DVD.
Up-close. Sol Gabetta, Amsterdam Sinfonietta. Disquiet Media DQM04, 2012. DVD.
The Book of Sand. Kate Miller-Heidke, MaNOj Kamps, Nederlands Kamerkoor. www.thebookofsand.net. 2015. Digital, interactive song cycle.

Ablinger, Peter

Der Regen, Das Glas, Das Lachen; Ohne Titel; Quadraturen IV ("Selbstportrait mit Berlin"). Sylvain Cambreling, Klangforum Wien. KAIROS 0012192KAI, 2000.
Weiss/Weisslich. Various artists. Maria de Alvear World Edition 0008, 2002.
Voices and Piano. Nicolas Hodges. KAIROS 0013082KAI, 2009.

Adams, John

Violin Concerto; Shaker Loops. Gidon Kremer, Orchestra of St. Luke's. Nonesuch 79360-2, 1996.
On the Transmigration of Souls. Preben Antonson, Philip Smith, Lorin Maazel, Brooklyn Youth Chorus Academy, New York Choral Artists, New York Philharmonic. Nonesuch 7559-79816-2, 2004.

Nixon in China. Russell Braun, James Maddalena, Janis Kelly, Richard Paul Fink, Robert Brubaker, Kathleen Kim, Metropolitan Opera Orchestra, Chorus and Ballet. Nonesuch 7559–9796088, 2011. DVD.

Adams, John Luther

Earth and the Great Weather. Various artists. New World Records 80459–2, 1994.
In the White Silence. Oberlin Contemporary Music Ensemble, Tim Weiss. New World Records 80600–2, 2003.
Inuksuit. Various artists. Cantaloupe CA21096, 2013.
Become Ocean. Seattle Symphony, Ludovic Morlot. Cataloupe CA21101, 2014.

Adès, Thomas

Life Story. Various artists. EMI 7243 5 69699 2, 1997. [Includes *Darknesse Visible.*]
Asyla. City of Birmingham Symphony Orchestra, Birmingham Contemporary Music Group, Simon Rattle, Thomas Adès. EMI 7243 5 56818 2 9, 1999.
Adès: Anthology. Various artists. EMI 50999 0 88560 2 9, 2011. [Includes *Concert Paraphrase on Powder Her Face; Arcadiana;* Piano Quintet; *Living Toys.*]

Ali-Zadeh, Franghiz

Mugam Sayagi. Kronos Quartet. Nonesuch 79804–2, 2005.

Applebaum, Mark

Mousetrap Music. innova 511, 1996.
The Bible without God. Various artists. innova 649, 2006.

Arfmann, Matthias

Recomposed. Deutsche Grammophon 00289 477 5579, 2005.

Atoui, Tarek

Morte aux vaches. Staalplaat, 2008.
The Ruptured Sessions Volume 2. Various artists. Ruptured RPTD 030, 2010. [Includes *Undrum 3: The Semantic Scanning Microscope.*]

Bandt, Ros

Stargazer. Move Records MD3075, 1989.

Bang on a Can

Brian Eno: Music for Airports. Point Music 536 847–2, 1998.
Classics. Cantaloupe CA21010, 2002.

Barrett, Richard

Chamber Works. ELISION. Etcetera KTC 1167, 1993. [Includes *EARTH; Negatives.*]
Opening of the Mouth. ELISION. ABC Classics 465268–2, 1999.

transmission. ELISION. NMC D117, 2008. [Includes *Interference.*]
DARK MATTER. ELISION, Cikada Ensemble, Christian Eggen. NMC D183, 2012.

Basinski, William
Disintegration Loops. Temporary Residence TRR 194, 2012.

Beaudoin, Richard
Microtimings. Mark Knoop, Kreutzer Quartet. New Focus Recordings fcr125, 2012. [Includes *Études d'un prélude.*]

Berio, Luciano
Rendering. London Symphony Orchestra, Luciano Berio. RCA Victor 09026-68894-2, 1998.

Beuger, Antoine
calme étendue (spinoza). Edition Wandelweiser Records EWR0107, 2001.
Silent Harmonies in Discrete Continuity. Edition Wandelweiser Records EWR 0402, 2004.
Cantor Quartets. Jürg Frey. Another Timbre at62x2, 2013.

Beugger, Megan Grace
Daring Doris. Crossfire Percussion Duo. Performance, June 2012. www.youtube.com/watch?v=WUwH9GMeFJg.

Bielawa, Lisa
Chance Encounter. Susan Narucki, The Knights. Orange Mountain Music 7004, 2011.

Billone, Pierluigi
ME A AN; ITI KE MI. ensemble recherche. Stradivarius STR 33716, 2005.
1+1 = 1. Heinz-Peter Linshalm, Petra Stump. KAIROS 0012602KAI, 2006.
Mani. Adam Weisman. Ein Klang ekr 044, 2010. [Includes *Mani.De Leonardis.*]

Bolleter, Ross
Secret Sandhills and Satellites. Emanem 4128, 2006.

Boulez, Pierre
sur Incises; Messagesquisse; Anthèmes II. Ensemble Intercontemporain, Pierre Boulez. Deutsche Grammophon 00289 477 6351, 2000.

Branca, Glenn
Symphony No. 6 (Devil Choirs at the Gates of Heaven). Blast First BFFP 39, 1989.
Symphony No. 3 (Gloria). Atavistic ALP008, 1993.

Braxton, Tyondai
Central Market. Warp WARPCD184, 2009.

Brittelle, William

Mohair Time Warp. New Amsterdam NWAM007, 2008.

Bryars, Gavin

The Sinking of the Titanic. Gavin Bryars Ensemble. Les Disques du Crepuscule TWI 922–2, 1990.

Cage, John

Europeras 3 and 4. Long Beach Opera, Andrew Culver. Mode 38/39, 1995.

Cascone, Kim

Blue Cube. Rastermusic cdr 014, 1998.

Cassidy, Aaron

Transference. ELISION. Huddersfield Contemporary Records HCR02, 2010. [Includes *And the scream, Bacon's scream, is the operation through which the entire body escapes through the mouth.*]
Donaueschinger Musiktage 2010. JACK Quartet. NEOS 11114–7, 2011. [Includes *Second String Quartet.*]
The Crutch of Memory. ELISION. NEOS 11201, 2012. [Includes *The Crutch of Memory; What then renders these forces visible is a strange smile; Metallic Dust.*]
Exposure. EXAUDI. Huddersfield Contemporary Records HCR06, 2013. [Includes *A painter of figures in rooms.*]

Chambers, Wendy Mae

A Mass for Trombones. Various artists. Centaur CRC 2263, 1996.

Chatham, Rhys

An Angel Moves Too Fast to See. Radium TOE-CD-802, 2006.
A Crimson Grail. Table of the Elements TOE-CD-106, 2006.

Chin, Unsuk

Akrostichon-Wortspiel. Ensemble Intercontemporain. Deutsche Grammophon 00289 477 5118, 2005.
sprechgesänge. Musikfabrik. Wergo WER6851–2, 2010. [Includes *Cantatrix Sopranica.*]

Ciciliani, Marko

Composer's Soundcloud page, www.soundcloud.com/ciciliani.

Corigliano, John

Of Rage and Remembrance. National Symphony Orchestra, Leonard Slatkin. RCA Victor 09026–68450–2, 1996. [Includes Symphony No. 1.]
One Sweet Morning. Stephanie Blythe, New York Philharmonic, Alan Gilbert. New York Philharmonic, NYP 20120101, 2011. MP3 download.

Craig, Carl, and Moritz von Oswald
Recomposed. Deutsche Grammophon 00289 476 6912, 2008.

Crane, Laurence
Solo Piano Pieces. Michael Finnissy. Métier MSV28506, 2008.
Chamber Works 1992–2009. Apartment House. Another Timbre at74x2, 2014. [Includes *Sparling* and *Come Back to the Old Specimen Cabinet John Vigani, John Vigani Part 1.*]

Curran, Alvin
Crystal Psalms. Various artists. New Albion NA 067, 1994.
Maritime Rites. Various artists. New World Records 80625-2, 2004.

Czernowin, Chaya
Pnima . . . ins innere. Various artists. Mode 169, 2006. DVD.
Maim. Rico Gubler, Peter Veale, John Mark Harris, Seth Josel, Mary Oliver, Konzerthausorchester Berlin, Johannes Kalitzke. Mode 219, 2010.
Shifting Gravity. Various artists. Wergo WER6726-2, 2011. [Includes *Anea Crystal.*]

Del Tredici, David
Gotham Glory: Complete Piano Works Vol. 1. Marc Peloquin. Naxos 8.559680, 2012.

Duckworth, William
Cathedral. www.monroestreet.com/Cathedral/main.html. Online composition.

Dunn, David
Four Electroacoustic Compositions. Pogus Productions P21026-2, 2002.
The Sound of Light in Trees. Earth Ear ee0513, 2006.

Einaudi, Ludovico
Le Onde. BMG 74321397022, 1996.

ELISION
Transference. Huddersfield Contemporary Records HCR02, 2010.
Strange Forces. Huddersfield Contemporary Records HCR03, 2010.

ensemble recherche
In Nomine: The Witten In Nomine Broken Consort Book. Kairos 0012442KAI, 2004.

Feiler, Dror
Point Blank. Various artists. Phono Suecia PSCD 155, 2006.

Ferneyhough, Brian
Fourth String Quartet; Kurze Schatten II; Trittico per G. S.; Terrain. Irvine Arditti, Brenda Mitchell, Arditti Quartet, Magnus Andersson, Stefan Scodanibbio, ASKO|Schönberg Ensemble. Montaigne MO 782169, 1996.

Shadowtime. Nicolas Hodges, Mats Scheidegger, Jurjen Hempel, Neue Vocalisten Stuttgart, Nieuw Ensemble. NMC D123, 2006.
Terrain; No Time (at all); La chute d'Icare; Incipits; Les froissements d'ailes de Gabriel. ELI-SION Ensemble. Kairos 0013072KAI, 2010.

Finnissy, Michael

Folklore. Ian Pace. Métier MSV 92010, 1998. [Includes *Folklore II.*]
Verdi Transcriptions. Ian Pace. Métier 92027, 2001.
Etched Bright with Sunlight. Nicolas Hodges. Metronome Recordings MET 1058, 2002. [Includes *Wenn wir in höchsten Nöthen sind.*]
The History of Photography in Sound. Ian Pace. Métier 77501, 2013.

Frey, Jürg

String Quartets. Bozzini Quartet. Wandelweiser 0410, 2006.
Piano Music. Andrew Lee. Irritable Hedgehog IHM006, 2012.
Wandelweiser und so weiter. Various artists. Another Timbre at56x6, 2012. [Includes *Un champ de tendresse parsemé d'adieux.*]

Fullman, Ellen

The Long String Instrument. Apollo Records AR 118501, 1985. LP.
Body Music. Experimental Intermedia Foundation XI 109, 1993.
Change of Direction. New Albion NA 102, 1998.

Fure, Ashley

Recordings posted to composer's website, www.ashleyfure.net/multimedia-1.

Galás, Diamanda

Masque of the Red Death. Mute GALAS 1, CDSTUMM 33, and CDSTUMM 46, 1988. Box set comprising *The Divine Punishment, Saint of the Pit,* and *You Must Be Certain of the Devil.*
Plague Mass. Mute CDSTUMM 83, 1991.

Garbarek, Jan, and the Hilliard Ensemble

Officium. ECM 1525, 1994.

Glass, Philip

1,000 Airplanes on the Roof. Philip Glass Ensemble. Virgin 7 91065-2, 1989.
"Heroes" and "Low" Symphonies. American Composers Orchestra, Brooklyn Philharmonic Orchestra, Dennis Russell Davies. Philips 475 075-2, 2003.
The Voyage. Bruckner Orchestra Linz, Landestheater Linz, Dennis Russell Davies. Orange Mountain Music 0017, 2006.

Gordon, Michael

Decasia. Basel Sinfonietta. Cantaloupe CA21008, 2002.
The Sad Park. Kronos Quartet. Cantaloupe CA21078, 2011.

Górecki, Henryk

Symphony No. 3. Dawn Upshaw, London Sinfonietta, David Zinman. Nonesuch 7559 792822, 1992.

Greenwood, Jonny

The Jerwood Series 2. London Sinfonietta. London Sinfonietta SINF CD2, 2006. [Includes *smear.*]

Krzysztof Penderecki/Johnny Greenwood. Aukso Orchestra, Krzysztof Penderecki, Marek Moś. Nonesuch 530223–2, 2012. [Includes *48 Responses to Polymorphia; Popcorn Superhet Receiver.*]

Grisey, Gérard

Vortex temporum. ensemble recherche. Accord 206352, 1997.

Quatre chants pour franchir le seuil. Catherine Dubosc, Klangforum Wien, Sylvain Cambreling. KAIROS 0012252KAI, 2001.

Haas, Georg Friedrich

in vain. Klangforum Wien, Sylvain Cambreling. KAIROS 0012332KAI, 2003.

Donaueschinger Musiktage 2003. Various artists. col legno WWE 2CD 20230, 2005. [Includes *natures mortes.*]

Hagen, Lars Petter

Norwegian Archives; The Artist's Despair before the Grandeur of Ancients Ruins; Tveitt-Fragments; Funeral March over Edvard Grieg; To Zeitblom. Gjermund Larsen, Oslo Philharmonic Orchestra, Rolf Gupta. Aurora ACD 5074, 2013.

Herbert, Matthew

Bodily Functions. Studio !K7 !K7097CD, 2001.

Plat du jour. Accidental AC19CD, 2004.

Recomposed. Deutsche Grammophon 006025 273 4438 6, 2010.

Hilario, Alan

Donaueschinger Musiktage 2002. Various artists. col legno 20229, 2004. [Includes *phonautograph.*]

Holloway, Robin

Gilded Goldbergs. Micallef-Inanga Piano Duo. Hyperion CDA67360, 2002.

Iannotta, Clara

Composer's Soundcloud page, www.soundcloud.com/claraiannotta.

A Failed Entertainment. Various artists. edition rz 10023 DAAD, 2016. [Includes *D'après; Intent on Resurrection—Spring or Some Such Thing.*]

Ikeda, Ryoji

Test Pattern. Raster-Noton R-N 093, 2008.

Dataphonics. Dis Voir 13393, 2010.

James, Richard

ICCT Hedral. Arranged by Philip Glass. Warp WAP 63, 1995.

26 Remixes for Cash. Warp WARPCD102, 2003. [Includes *The Sinking of the Titanic* (remix); *Heroes Symphony* (remix).]

Jeck, Philip

Loopholes. Touch TO:26, 1995.

Stoke. Touch TO:56, 2002.

Jenkins, Karl

Songs of Sanctuary. Adiemus. Venture CDVE 925, 1995.

Kancheli, Giya

Exil. Various artists. ECM Records ECM 1535, 1995.

Lament. Gidon Kremer, Maacha Deubner, Tbilisi Symphony Orchestra, Jansug Kakhidze. ECM Records ECM 1656, 1999.

Katzer, Georg

Musik in Deutschland 1950–2000, 17, Elektroakustische Musik. Various artists. RCA Red Seal 73668, 2008. [Includes *Mon 1789; Mein 1989*]

Kim-Cohen, Seth

68SFTD. Various artists. Performance at the Institute of Contemporary Arts, London, July 16, 2008. www.youtube.com/watch?v=kEthBrny2ek. Video.

Kreidler, Johannes

Scanner Studies. www.youtube.com/watch?v=HiyB_zN95xU. Video.

Kronos Quartet

25 Years. Nonesuch 79504–2, 1998.

Kurtág, György

Song-Cycles. Various artists. Sony Classical SK 53 290, 1993. [Includes . . . *quasi una fantasia . . .*]

Grabstein für Stephan; Stele. Berlin Philharmonic, Claudio Abbado. Deutsche Grammophon 447 761–2, 1996.

Signs, Games, and Messages. Various artists. ECM Records ECM 1730, 2003.

Kafka-Fragmente. Julianne Banse, András Keller. ECM Records ECM 1965, 2006.

Játékok. Gábor Csalog, Márta Kurtág, György Kurtág. Budapest Music Center BMC CD 123, 2006.

Kyburz, Hanspeter

New Saxophone Chamber Music. Johannes Ernst, Ensemble UnitedBerlin, Peter Hirsch. col legno WWE 1CD 31890, 1996. [Includes *Cells.*]

Lang, David

world to come. Maya Beiser. Koch International Classics KIC-CD-7556, 2003.
Death Speaks. Various artists. Cantaloupe CA21092, 2013.

Lehto, Lassi

Recomposed. Deutsche Grammophon 00289 476 5676, 2006.

Lely, John

The Harmonics of Real Strings. Anton Lukoszevieze. Another Timbre at80, 2014.

Ligeti, György

Études, Books 1–3. Thomas Hell. Wergo WER67632, 2012.

Lim, Liza

The Intertwining—The Chasm (Brisbane: Institute of Modern Art, 1998). Book accompanied by CD of improvisations performed by ELISION. [Includes extracts from *Bardo'i-thos-grol.*]
The Tongue of the Invisible. Uri Caine, Omar Ebrahim, Musikfabrik, André de Ridder. Wergo WER68592, 2013.
Solitude. Séverine Ballon. Aeon AECD 1647, 2015. [Includes *Invisibility.*]

Lockwood, Annea

A Sound Map of the Hudson River. Lovely Music LCD 2081, 1989.
A Sound Map of the Danube. Lovely Music LCD 2083, 2008.

López, Francisco

La Selva. V2_Archief V228, 1998. LP.

Mahnkopf, Claus-Steffen

Angelus Novus Cycle. Ensemble SurPlus, James Avery. NEOS 11211-12, 2012.
Pynchon Cycle. Ensemble SurPlus, James Avery. NEOS 11036, 2011.

Malone, Kevin

The Music of 9/11. New World Ensemble, Manchester Sinfonia, Richard Howarth. Métier MSV CD92106, 2014.

Martland, Steve

Crossing the Border. Various artists. Factory Facd 09026 62670 2, 1992.

Masonna

Frequency L.S.D. Alien8 Recordings ALIENCD007, 1998.

Merzbow

Cloud Cock OO Grand. ZSF Produkt MERZ CD-01, 1990.

Venereology. Release Entertainment RR 6910–2, 1994.
Bloody Sea. Vivo VIVO2006022CD, 2006.

Miller, Cassandra

Composer's Soundcloud page, www.soundcloud.com/cassandra-miller-composer.

Mitterer, Wolfgang

Im Sturm. Georg Nigl, Wolfgang Mitterer. col legno WWE 1CD 20278, 2008.
Sopop. Various artists. col legno WWE 1CD 20901, 2008.

Mundry, Isabel

Dufay-Bearbeitungen; Traces des Moments; Sandschleifen. ensemble recherche. KAIROS 001642KAI, 2007.

Nikodijevic, Marko

dark/rooms. Various artists. col legno WWE 1CD 40408, 2013. [Includes *cvetić, kućica . . . / la lugubre gondola.*]

Nono, Luigi

La lontananza nostalgica utopica futura. Gidon Kremer, Hans Peter Haller, Luigi Nono. Deutsche Grammophon 435870–2, 1992.
La lontananza nostalgica utopica futura. Clemens Merkel, Wolfgang Heiniger. Edition Wandelweiser Records EWR0102, 2001.

Norman, Andrew

Play. Boston Modern Orchestra Project, Gil Rose. BMOP/sound 1040, 2015.

Neuwirth, Olga

Lost Highway. Vincent Crowly, Constance Hauman, Georg Nigl, David Moss, Andrew Watts, Jodi Melnick, Grayson Millwood, Lukas Rössner, Rodolfo Seas-Araya, Gavin Webber, Kai Wessel, Klangforum Wien, Johannes Kalitzke. KAIROS 0012542KAI, 2006.

Nyman, Michael

The Cook, the Thief, His Wife and Her Lover. Michael Nyman Band. Venture CDVE 53, 1989.
The Piano Concerto. Kathryn Stott, Royal Liverpool Philharmonic, Michael Nyman. Argo 443382–2, 1994.

Oliveros, Pauline

Deep Listening. Pauline Oliveros, Stuart Dempster, Panaiotis. New Albion NA 022CD, 1989.

Oswald, John

Plunderphonic, self-released CDr, 1989. Withdrawn in 1989, but available as MP3 downloads at www.plunderphonics.com/xhtml/xunavailable.html.
Plexure. Avant AVAN016, 1993.
Short Stories. Kronos Quartet. Elektra 9 79310–2, 1993. [Includes *Spectre.*]

Pan Sonic

Vakio. Blast First BFFP118CD, 1995.

Pärt, Arvo

Tabula rasa. Various artists. ECM 1275 817 864–1, 1984.
Litany. Various artists. ECM 1592, 1996.

Pateras, Anthony

Chasms. Anthony Pateras. Sirr 0030, 2007.

Payne, Anthony

Elgar: Symphony No. 3. Sir Colin Davis, London Symphony Orchestra. LSO Live LSO0019, 2002.

Penderecki, Krzysztof

Piano Concerto "Resurrection." Barry Douglas, Warsaw Philharmonic Orchestra, Antoni Wit. Naxos 8.572696, 2013.
The Complete Symphonies. Various artists. Dux DUX0947, 2013.

Pisaro, Michael

Transparent City (Volumes 1 and 2). Edition Wandelweiser Records EWR 0706/7, 2007.
Fields Have Ears. Philip Thomas, edges ensemble. Another Timbre at37, 2010. [Includes *Fade.*]
ricefall (2). Greg Stuart. Gravity Wave gw 001, 2010.

Poliks, Marek

Composer's Soundcloud page, www.soundcloud.com/marek-poliks.

Poppe, Enno

Interzone. Omar Ebrahim, Neue Vocalsolisten, Ensemble Mosaik, Jonathan Stockhammer. KAIROS 0012552KAI, 2004.
Chamber Music. Various artists. col legno WWE 1CD 20237, 2005.
Holz–Knochen–Öl. Klangforum Wien, Stefan Asbury. Wergo WER6564–2, 2006.

Prins, Stefan

Composer's video channel, www.vimeo.com/stefanprins. [Includes *Generation Kill.*]
Fremdkörper. Various artists. Sub Rosa SR352, 2012. [Includes *Fremdkörper 1–3; Not I.*]

Reich, Steve

Different Trains. Kronos Quartet. Elektra Nonesuch 79176–2, 1989.
The Cave. Various artists. Nonesuch 79327–2, 1995.
Reich Remixed. Various artists. Nonesuch 79552–2, 1999.
Three Tales. Various artists. Nonesuch 79662–2, 2003.
WTC 9/11. Kronos Quartet. Elektra Nonesuch 528236–2, 2011.
Radio Rewrite. Alarm Will Sound. Nonesuch 79457–0, 2014.

Richter, Max

Recomposed. Daniel Hope, Konzerthaus Kammerorchester Berlin, André de Ridder. Deutsche Grammophon 476 5040, 2012.

Roden, Steve

Forms of Paper. Line LINE_007, 2001.

Saunders, James

#[unassigned]. Anton Lukoszevieze, Andrew Sparling. Confront 15, 2007.
Divisions that could be autonomous but that comprise the whole. Various artists. Another Timbre at44, 2011.

Sciarrino, Salvatore

La bocca i piedi il suono. Lost Cloud Quartet. col legno WWE 1CD/DVD 20701, 2004.

Sheng, Bright

H'un. New York Chamber Symphony, Gerard Schwarz. New World 80407–2, 1991.

Shepard, Craig

On Foot. Edition Wandelweiser Records EWR1101, 2011.

Shim, Kunsu

LOVE. Greg Stuart, Nick Hennies. Senufo Editions 38, 2013.

Shlomowitz, Matthew

Popular Contexts. Mark Knoop. Sub Rosa SR382, 2013.

Silvestrov, Valentin

Post Scriptum. Gidon Kremer, Vadim Sacharov. Teldec 4509–99206–2, 1996.

Skempton, Howard

Lento. BBC Symphony Orchestra, Mark Wigglesworth. NMC D005, 1992.

Steen-Andersen, Simon

Run-Time Error. Edition·S, 2009. www.edition-s.dk/media/run-time-error. Video installation.
Pretty Sound. Aasamisamasa. Dacapo 8.226523, 2011.

Stockhausen, Karlheinz

WELT-PARLAMENT vom MITTWOCH aus LICHT. Südfunk-Chor Stuttgart. Stockhausen 51, 1996.
ORCHESTER-FINALISTEN vom MITTWOCH aus LICHT. ASKO|Schönberg Ensemble. Stockhausen 52, 1997.
HELIKOPTER-STREICHQUARTETT. Arditti String Quartet. Stockhausen 53A–B, 1999.
MITTWOCHS-GRUSS. Stockhausen 66, 2003.

Stone, Carl
Mom's. New Albion NA 049, 1992. [Includes *Shing Kee.*]
Al-Noor. In-Tone Music ITO/CD 10, 2007. [Includes *Jitlada.*]

Takasugi, Steven Kazuo
Recordings posted to composer's website, www.steventakasugi.com/music. [Includes *Jargon of Nothingness.*]

Tavener, John
The Protecting Veil. Steven Isserlis, London Symphony Orchestra, Gennadi Rozhdestvensky. Virgin 0777 7590522 9, 1992.
A Song for Athene, Syvati and Other Choral Works. Choir of St. John's College, Cambridge; Christopher Robinson. Naxos 8.555256, 2000. [Includes *Two Hymns to the Mother of God.*]

Terterian, Avet
Symphonies 7 and 8. Ural Philharmonic Orchestra, Dmitri Liss. Megadisc Classics MDC 7826, 2000.

Torke, Michael
Color Music. Baltimore Symphony Orchestra, David Zinman. Argo 433 071–2, 1991. [Includes *Ash; Bright Blue Music.*]

Truax, Barry
Digital Soundscapes. Wergo WER 2017–50, 1988. [Includes *Riverrun.*]
Beauty and the Beast. Cambridge Street Records CSR-CD 9601, 1989.
Pacific. Cambridge Street Records CSR-CD 9101, 1990.

Tsunoda, Toshiya
Extract from Field Recording Archive #2: The Air Vibration inside a Hollow. Häpna H.01, 1999.
O kokkos tis anixis. edition.t e.04, 2013.

Turnage, Mark Anthony
Greek. Various artists. Arthaus Musik 102105, 1998. DVD.
Some Days; Your Rockaby; Night Dances; Dispelling of Fears; Blood on the Floor. Various artists. Decca 468 814–2, 2001.

Ustvolskaya, Galina
Piano Sonatas. Oleg Malov. Megadisc Classics MDC 7876, 1994.

Vaggione, Horacio
Musique pour piano et électroacoustique. Le Chant du Monde LDC 2781102, 1995. [Includes *Schall.*]

Walshe, Jennifer

Nature Data. Interval Recordings IL05, 2010.

Wandelweiser

Edition Wandelweiser Records catalog, www.wandelweiser.de/_e-w-records/_ewr-catalogue.

Wandelweiser und so weiter. Various artists. Another Timbre at56x6, 2012.

Warp Records and London Sinfonietta

Warp Works and Twentieth-Century Masters. London Sinfonietta. Warp WARPCD144, 2006.

Werder, Manfred

Wandelweiser und so weiter. Various artists. Another Timbre at56x6, 2012. [Includes *zwei ausführende.*]

2005I. Various realizations. Another Timbre, 2012. www.anothertimbre.com/werder2005(1).html.

stück 1998 (seiten 676 bis 683). Christián Alvear. Irritable Hedgehog IHM018, 2015.

Westerkamp, Hildegard

Électro Clips. Empreintes DIGITALes IMED 9604, 1996. [Includes *Breathing Room.*]

Transformations. Empreintes DIGITALes IMED 9631, 1996. [Includes *Kits Beach Soundwalk.*]

Z, Pamela

A Delay Is Better. Starkland ST-213, 2004.

Zender, Hans

Winterreise. Hans Peter Blochwitz, Ensemble Modern, Hans Zender. BMG Classics 09026–68067–2, 1995.

Zorn, John

Naked City: The Complete Studio Recordings. Tzadik TZ 7344–5, 2005. [Includes *Naked City; Radio.*]

FURTHER READING

Where possible, I have included some reading for every composer or theme discussed at length in the book, although I have omitted studies of composers that cover little or none of their work since 1989. Many items have also been cited in the text.

There are four lists: collections of writings and interviews by and with composers, items on individual composers and composer collectives, regional surveys, and thematic topics. Some items will appear on more than one list. With a few exceptions, I have chosen texts written in English or translated to English.

ABBREVIATIONS

ARCEM	James Saunders, ed., *The Ashgate Research Companion to Experimental Music* (Farnham, England: Ashgate, 2009).
ARCMPM	Keith Potter, Kyle Gann, and Pwyll ap Siôn, eds., *The Ashgate Research Companion to Minimalist and Postminimalist Music* (Farnham, Surrey: Ashgate, 2013).
CMR	*Contemporary Music Review*
MT	*Musical Times*
NMA	Claus-Steffen Mahnkopf, Frank Cox, and Wolfram Schurig, eds., *New Music and Aesthetics in the 21st Century* (Hofheim: Wolke Verlag, 2002–).
OS	*Organised Sound*
PNM	*Perspectives of New Music*
WE	John Lely and James Saunders, eds., *Word Events: Perspectives on Verbal Notation* (London: Continuum, 2012).

COLLECTIONS

Beyer, Anders. *The Voice of Music: Conversations with Composers of Our Time.* Aldershot: Ashgate, 2000.

Böhme-Mehner, Tanya, ed. "Creating Sound behind the Wall: Electroacoustic Music in the GDR." Special issue, *CMR* 30, no. 1 (2011).

Duckworth, William. *Talking Music: Conversations with John Cage, Philip Glass, Laurie Anderson and Five Generations of American Experimental Composers.* New York: Da Capo Press, 1999.

Ford, Andrew. *Composer to Composer: Conversations about Contemporary Music.* Sydney: Hale and Iremonger, 1993.

Lely, John, and James Saunders, eds. *Word Events: Perspectives on Verbal Notation.* London: Continuum, 2012.

Palmer, Andrew. *Encounters with British Composers.* Woodbridge: Boydell Press, 2015.

Palmer, John. *Conversations.* N.p.: Vision Edition, 2015.

Rodgers, Tara. *Pink Noises: Women on Electronic Music and Sound.* Durham, NC: Duke University Press, 2010.

Saunders, James, ed. *The Ashgate Research Companion to Experimental Music.* Farnham, England: Ashgate, 2009.

Varga, Bálint András. *Three Questions for Sixty-Five Composers.* Rochester, NY: University of Rochester Press, 2011.

Zorn, John, ed. *Arcana: Musicians on Music.* Vols. 1–7. New York: Hips Road, 2001–14.

COMPOSERS AND COLLECTIVES
Aa, Michel van der

www.vanderaa.net. Composer's official website.
www.disquietmedia.net. Disquiet multimedia label.
Novak, Jelena. *Postopera: Reinventing the Voice-Body.* Aldershot: Ashgate, 2015.

Ablinger, Peter

http://ablinger.mur.at. Composer's official website.

Barrett, G. Douglas. "Between Noise and Language: The Sound Installations and Music of Peter Ablinger." December 1, 2009. http://ablinger.mur.at/docs/barrett_between.pdf.

———. "Window Piece: Seeing and Hearing the Music of Peter Ablinger." May 22, 2010. http://ablinger.mur.at/docs/barrett_window_piece.doc.

Blomberg, Katja, Chico Mello, Christian Scheib, Trond Reinholdtsen, and Peter Ablinger. *HÖREN hören.* Heidelberg: Kehrer, 2008.

Mendez, Matthew. "'It Is Always the OTHER That Creates Ourself': On Peter Ablinger's Vocal Automatons." *Colony* 1 (2014). Available at www.academia.edu/6250329/_It_Is_Always_the_OTHER_that_Creates_Ourself_On_Peter_Ablingers_Vocal_Automatons.

Adams, John

www.earbox.com. Composer's official website.
Adams, John. *Hallelujah Junction.* New York: Picador, 2008.
May, Thomas, ed. *The John Adams Reader.* Portland: Amadeus, 2006.

Adams, John Luther

www.johnlutheradams.net. Composer's official website.

Adams, John Luther. *Winter Music: Composing the North.* Middletown, CT: Wesleyan University Press, 2004.

———. *The Place Where You Go to Listen.* Middletown, CT: Wesleyan University Press, 2009.

Herzogenrath, Bernd, ed. *The Farthest Place.* Boston: Northeastern University Press, 2012.

Kinnear, Tyler. "Voicing Nature in John Luther Adams' *The Place Where You Go to Listen.*" *OS* 17, no. 3 (2012): 230–39.

Adès, Thomas

www.thomasades.com. Composer's official website.

Fox, Christopher. "Tempestuous Times: The Recent Music of Thomas Adès." *MT* 145 (2004): 41–56.

Roeder, John. "Co-Operating Continuities in the Music of Thomas Adès." *Music Analysis* 25, nos. 1–2 (2006): 121–54.

Service, Tom. *Thomas Adès: Full of Noises.* London: Faber, 2012.

Venn, Edward. "'Asylum Gained'? Aspects of Meaning in Thomas Adès' *Asyla.*" *Music Analysis* 25, nos. 1–2 (2006): 89–120.

Wells, Dominic. "Plural Styles, Personal Style: The Music of Thomas Adès." *Tempo* 66, no. 260 (2012): 2–14.

Andriessen, Louis

Trochimczyk, Maja. *The Music of Louis Andriessen.* New York: Routledge, 2002.

Applebaum, Mark

Applebaum, Mark. "Progress Report: The State of the Art after Sixteen Years of Designing and Playing Electroacoustic Sound-Sculptures." In *NMA*, vol. 4, *Electronics in New Music,* 9–35. Hofheim: Wolke Verlag, 2006.

Bang on a Can

www.bangonacan.org. Ensemble's official website.

www.redpoppymusic.com. Red Poppy Music publishing company.

www.cantaloupemusic.com. Cantaloupe Music record label.

Wolfe, Julia. "Embracing the Clash." PhD diss., Princeton University, 2012.

Barrett, Richard

www.richardbarrettmusic.com. Composer's official website.

Barrett, Richard. "*NO*—Programme Note and Interview." 2005. www.richardbarrettmusic.com/NOinterview.html.

———. "Construction of *CONSTRUCTION.*" 2011. www.richardbarrettmusic.com/CONSTRUCTIONessay.pdf.

Deforce, Arne, and Richard Barrett. "The Resonant Box with Four Strings." 2000. https://issuu.com/arnedeforce/docs/the_resonant_box_with_four_strings.

Whittall, Arnold. "Resistance and Reflection: Richard Barrett in the 21st Century." *MT* 146 (2005): 57–70.

Basinski, William

Doran, John. "Time Becomes a Loop: William Basinski Interviewed," *Quietus*, November 15, 2012. www.thequietus.com/articles/10680-william-basinski-disintegration-loops-interview.

Beaudoin, Richard

www.richardbeaudoin.com. Composer's official website.
Beaudoin, Richard. "You're There and You're Not There: Musical Borrowing and Cavell's 'Way.'" *Journal of Music Theory* 54, no. 1 (2010): 91–105.
Beaudoin, Richard, and Andrew Kania. "A Musical Photograph?" *Journal of Aesthetics and Art Criticism* 70, no. 1 (2012): 115–27.
Trottier, Danick. "Conceiving Musical Photorealism." *PNM* 51, no. 1 (2013): 174–95.

Berio, Luciano

Berio, Luciano. *Remembering the Future*. Cambridge, MA: Harvard University Press, 2006.
Mehinovic, Vedran. "Two Late Orchestral Works of Luciano Berio." *Tempo* 67, no. 273 (2015): 20–29.
Metzer, David. "Musical Decay: Luciano Berio's 'Rendering' and John Cage's 'Europera 5.'" *Journal of the Royal Musical Association* 125, no. 1 (2000): 93–114.

Beuger, Antoine

www.wandelweiser.de/_antoine-beuger/texts.html. Writings by Beuger, hosted on the Edition Wandelweiser website.
Saunders, James. Interview with Antoine Beuger. In *ARCEM*, 231–42.
Saunders, James. "Commentary: *one tone. rather short. very quiet.*" In *WE*, 106–8.

Bielawa, Lisa

www.lisabielawa.net. Composer's official website.

Billone, Pierluigi

www.pierluigibillone.com/en/home. Composer's official website.

Bolleter, Ross

www.corms30.wix.com/warpsmusic. World Association for Ruined Piano Studies.
Kouvaras, Linda Ionna. "The Nostalgic: The Dawning of the Altermodern (1)." In *Loading the Silence: Australian Sound Art in the Post-Digital Age*, 193–6. Farnham, Surrey: Ashgate, 2013.

Boulez, Pierre

Coult, Tom. "Pierre Boulez's 'Sur Incises': Refraction, Crystallisation and the Absent Idea(l)." *Tempo* 67, no. 264 (2013): 2–21.

Branca, Glenn

www.glennbranca.com. Composer's official website.

Duckworth, William. "Glenn Branca." In *Talking Music*, 418–43. New York: Da Capo Press, 1999.

Cassidy, Aaron

www.aaroncassidy.com. Composer's official website.

Cassidy, Aaron. "Physicality and Choreography as Morphological Determinants." In *NMA*, vol. 2, *Musical Morphology*, 34–51. Hofheim: Wolke Verlag, 2004.

——. "Constraint Schemata, Multi-Axis Movement Modeling, and Unified, Multi-Parametric Notation for Strings and Voices." *Search*, no. 10 (2013). www.searchnewmusic. org/cassidy.pdf.

Kanno, Mieko. "Prescriptive Notation: Limits and Challenges." *CMR* 26, no. 2 (2007): 231–54.

Rutherford-Johnson, Tim. "A Journey to Aaron Cassidy's Second String Quartet." *NewMusicBox*, February 9, 2011. www.newmusicbox.org/articles/A-Journey-to-Aaron-Cassidys-Second-String-Quartet.

Chatham, Rhys

www.rhyschatham.net. Composer's official website.

Young, Rob. "Zelig Complex." *Wire*, no. 182 (1999): 50–52.

Chin, Unsuk

Whittall, Arnold. "Unsuk Chin in Focus: Meditations and Mechanics." *MT* 141 (2000): 21ff.

Ciciliani, Marko

Ciciliani, Marko. "Molding the Pop Ghost: Noise and Immersion." In *Noise in and as Music*, edited by Aaron Cassidy and Aaron Einbond, 191–208. Huddersfield: University of Huddersfield Press, 2013.

Corigliano, John

www.johncorigliano.com. Composer's official website.

Bergman, Elizabeth. "*Of Rage and Remembrance*, Music and Memory: The Work of Mourning in John Corigliano's Symphony No. 1 and Choral Chaconne." *American Music* 31, no. 3 (2013): 340–61.

Oteri, Frank J. "The Gospel According to John Corigliano." *NewMusicBox*, February 1, 2005. www.newmusicbox.org/articles/the-gospel-according-to-john-at-home-with-john-corigliano-john-corigliano.

Crane, Laurence

Reynell, Simon. "Interview with Laurence Crane." Another Timbre, accessed December 24, 2014. www.anothertimbre.com/craneinterview.html.

Saunders, James. Interview with Laurence Crane. In *ARCEM*, 243–52.

——. "Commentary: *Only*." In *WE*, 320–27.

Thomas, Philip. "The Music of Laurence Crane and a Post-Experimental Performance Practice." *Tempo* 70, no. 275 (2016): 5–21.

Curran, Alvin

www.alvincurran.com. Composer's official website.

Czernowin, Chaya

www.chayaczernowin.com. Composer's official website.
Czernowin, Chaya. "A Few Examples from MAIM (Water, 2001/2, 2005, 2006/7): How This Music Thinks." In *NMA*, vol. 6, *Facets of the Second Modernity*, 99–134. Hofheim: Wolke Verlag, 2008.

Del Tredici, David

www.daviddeltredici.com. Composer's official website.

Duckworth, William

Duckworth, William. "Making Music on the Web." *Leonardo Music Journal* 9 (1999): 15–18.
———. "*Cathedral*: A Case Study in Time." In *Virtual Music: How the Web Got Wired for Sound*, 89–101. New York: Routledge, 2013.

Dunn, David

www.davidddunn.com/~david. Composer's official website.
Dunn, David. "Nature, Sound Art, and the Sacred." In *The Book of Music and Nature*, edited by David Rothenburg and Marta Ulvaeus, 95–107. Middletown, CT: Wesleyan University Press, 2001.
England, Phil. "David Dunn," *Wire*, no. 357 (2013): 36–43.
Lampert, Michael R. "Environment, Consciousness, and Magic: An Interview with David Dunn." *PNM* 27, no. 1 (1989): 94–105.

ELISION

www.elision.org.au. Ensemble's official website.
Hewes, Michael. "Conducting Space: An Analysis-Based Approach to Spatial Sound Design in Contemporary Chamber Music Performance." PhD diss., RMIT University, 2013.

Ferneyhough, Brian

Feller, Ross. "Resistant Strains of Postmodernism: the Music of Helmut Lachenmann and Brian Ferneyhough." In *Postmodern Music/Postmodern Thought*, edited by Judy Lochhead and Joseph Auner, 249–62. London: Routledge, 2002.
Ferneyhough, Brian. *Collected Writings*. Edited by James Boros and Richard Toop. Amsteldijk: Harwood Academic Publishers, 1995.
Fitch, Lois. *Brian Ferneyhough*. Bristol: Intellect, 2014.
———. "Brian Ferneyhough, 'Postmodern Modernist.'" In *The Modernist Legacy: Essays on New Music*, edited by Björn Heile, 159–76. Aldershot: Ashgate, 2009.
Fitch, Lois, and John Hails. "Failed Time, Successful Time, Shadowtime: An Interview with Brian Ferneyhough." In *Contemporary Music: Theoretical and Philosophical Perspectives*, edited by Max Paddison and Irène Deliège, 319–30. Aldershot: Ashgate, 2010.
Whittall, Arnold. "Connections and Constellations." *MT* 144 (Summer 2003): 23–32.

Finnissy, Michael

Composer's official website. www.michaelfinnissy.info.

Beaudoin, Richard, and Joseph Moore. "Conceiving Musical Transdialection." *Journal of Aesthetics and Art Criticism* 68, no. 2 (2010): 105–17.

Brougham, Henrietta, Christopher Fox, and Ian Pace, eds. *Uncommon Ground: The Music of Michael Finnissy*. Aldershot: Ashgate, 1997.

Finnissy, Michael. "Biting the Hand That Feeds You." *CMR* 21, no. 1 (2002): 71–9.

Fox, Christopher. "Michael Finnissy's *History of Photography in Sound*: Under the Lens." *MT* 143, no. 1879 (2002): 26–35.

Fujieda, Mamoru

Fujieda, Mamoru. "Tuning 'Patterns of Plants.'" In *Arcana*, vol. 4, edited by John Zorn, 140–50. New York: Hips Road, 2009.

Fullman, Ellen

Fullman, Ellen. "A Compositional Approach Derived from Material and Ephemeral Elements." *Leonardo Music Journal* 22 (2012): 3–10.

———. "The Long String Instrument." *Musicworks* 85 (2003): 20–8.

Galás, Diamanda

Jarman-Ivens, Freya. "Diamanda Galás: One Long Mad Scene." In *Queer Voices: Technologies, Vocalities, and the Musical Flaw,*127–60. Basingstoke: Palgrave Macmillan, 2011.

Penman, Ian. "Matters of Life and Death." *Wire*, nos. 190–91 (2000): 58–65.

Schwarz, David. "Lamentation, Abjection, and the Music of Diamanda Galás." In *Listening Subjects: Music, Psychoanalysis, Culture*, 133–64. Durham, NC: Duke University Press, 1997.

Glass, Philip

www.philipglass.com. Composer's official website.

Glass, Philip. *Words without Music: A Memoir*. New York: Liveright, 2015.

Grimshaw, Jeremy. "High, 'Low,' and Plastic Arts: Philip Glass and the Symphony in the Age of Postproduction." *Musical Quarterly* 86 no. 3 (2002): 472–507.

Liao, Ping-hui. "From the Multicultural to Creole Subjects: David Henry Hwang's Collaborative Works With Philip Glass." In *The Creolization of Theory*, edited by Francoise Lionnet and Shu-mei Shih, 142–55. Durham: Duke University Press, 2011.

Maycock, Robert. *Glass: A Portrait*. London: Sanctuary Publishing, 2002.

Novak, Jelena. *Postopera: Reinventing the Voice-Body*. Aldershot: Ashgate, 2015.

Gordon, Michael

www.michaelgordonmusic.com. Composer's official website.

Grisey, Gérard

Grisey, Gérard. "Did You Say Spectral?" *CMR* 19, no. 3 (2000): 1–3.

Haas, Georg Friedrich

Hasegawa, Robert. "Clashing Harmonic Systems in Haas's *Blumenstück* and *in vain.*" *Music Theory Spectrum* 37, no. 2 (2015): 204–23.

Hagen, Lars Petter

www.lphagen.no. Composer's official website.

Hilario, Alan

Fricke, Stefan. "Objections to the Status Quo: On the Music of Alan Hilario." *World New Music Magazine* 16 (2006): 49–52.

Holloway, Robin

Bye, Anthony. "Acts of Possession." *MT* 134 (October 1993): 567–8, 570.
Hewett, Ivan. "Composer in Interview: Robin Holloway." *Tempo* 57, no. 226 (2003): 11–20.
Whittall, Arnold. "Connections and Constellations." *MT* 144 (Summer 2003): 23–32.

Hübler, Klaus K.

Hübler, Klaus K. "Expanding String Technique." In *NMA*, vol. 1, *Polyphony and Complexity*, 233–44. Hofheim: Wolke Verlag, 2002.

Jeck, Philip

www.philipjeck.com. Composer's official website.
Bell, Clive. "Vinyl Redemption." *Wire*, no. 221 (2002): 28–31.
Saunders, James. Interview with Philip Jeck. In *ARCEM*, 293–304.

JLIAT

www.jliat.com. Composer's official website.
JLIAT. "Un-Sounding Music: Noise Is Not Sound." In *Noise in and as Music*, edited by Aaron Cassidy and Aaron Einbond, 11–30. Huddersfield: Huddersfield University Press, 2013.

Kancheli, Giya

Trigg, Dylan. "Giya Kancheli and the Aesthetics of Nostalgia." In *Azimute: Critical Essays on Deleuze and Guattari*, edited by Robert Lort, 327–39. London, Canada: Enigmatic Ink, 2011.
———. "The Space of Absence in the Music of Giya Kancheli." In *Azimute: Critical Essays on Deleuze and Guattari*, edited by Robert Lort, 319–26. London, Canada: Enigmatic Ink, 2011.
Wilson, Samuel John. "An Aesthetic of Past-Present Relations in the Experience of Late 20th- and Early 21st-Century Music." PhD diss., Royal Holloway University, 2013.

Katzer, Georg

Böhme-Mehner, Tatjana. "Interview with Georg Katzer, 18th October, 2009, Leipzig." *CMR* 30, no. 1 (2011): 101–9.

Kelly, Elaine. "Reflective Nostalgia and Diasporic Memory: Composing East Germany after 1989." In *Remembering and Rethinking the GDR: Multiple Perspectives and Plural Authenticities*, edited by Anna Saunders and Debbie Pinfold, 130–45. Basingstoke: Palgrave Macmillan, 2013.

Kim-Cohen, Seth
www.kim-cohen.com. Composer's official website.

Kreidler, Johannes
www.kreidler-net.de. Composer's official website.
Iddon, Martin. "Outsourcing Progress: On Conceptual Music." *Tempo* 70, no. 275 (2016): 36–49.
Interview with Johannes Kreidler. *Neural*, no. 36 (2010): 29–31.

Kurtág, György
Toop, Richard. "*Stele*—a Gravestone as End or Beginning? György Kurtág's Long March Towards the Orchestra." *CMR* 20, nos. 2–3 (2001): 129–49.
Williams, Alan E. "Kurtág, Modernity, Modernisms." *CMR* 20, nos. 2–3 (2001): 51–69.

Lachenmann, Helmut
Albertson, Dan, ed. "Helmut Lachenmann." Special issue, pts. 1 and 2, *CMR* 23, nos. 3–4 (2004); 24, no. 1 (2004).
Feller, Ross. "Resistant Strains of Postmodernism: the Music of Helmut Lachenmann and Brian Ferneyhough." In *Postmodern Music/Postmodern Thought*, edited by Judy Lochhead and Joseph Auner, 249–62. London: Routledge, 2002.
Heathcote, Abigail. "Sound Structures, Transformations, and Broken Magic: An Interview With Helmut Lachenmann." In *Contemporary Music: Theoretical and Philosophical Perspectives*, edited by Max Paddison and Irène Deliège, 331–48. Farnham: Ashgate, 2010.
Lachenmann, Helmut. *Musik als existentielle Erfahrung*. Wiesbaden: Breitkopf und Härtel, 1996.
Pace, Ian. "Positive or Negative." Pts. 1 and 2. *MT* 139, no. 1859 (January 1998): 9–17; 139, no. 1860 (Februay 1998): 4–15.
Tsao, Ming. "Helmut Lachenmann's 'Sound Types.'" *PNM* 52, no. 1 (2014): 217–38.

Lang, Bernhard
http://members.chello.at/bernhard.lang. Composer's official website.
Dysers, Christine. "Re-Writing History: Bernhard Lang's *Monadologie* Series." *Tempo* 69, no. 271 (2015): 36–47.
Redhead, Lauren. "Quotation, Psychogeography, and the 'Journey Form' in the Music Theatre of Bernhard Lang and Chico Mello." *CMR* 33, no. 2 (2014): 148–66.

Lang, David
www.davidlangmusic.com. Composer's official website.

Ligeti, György

Bauer, Amy. "The Cosmopolitan Absurdity of Ligeti's Late Works." *CMR* 31, nos. 1–2 (2012): 163–76.

Steinitz, Richard. *György Ligeti: Music of the Imagination.* London: Faber, 2003.

Lim, Liza

Clarke, Eric, Mark Doffman, and Liza Lim. "Distributed Creativity and Ecological Dynamics: A Case Study of Liza Lim's 'Tongue of the Invisible.'" *Music and Letters,* 94 (2013): 628–63.

Lim, Liza. "Staging an Aesthetics of Presence." *Search,* no. 6 (2009). www.searchnewmusic.org/index6.html.

Rutherford-Johnson, Tim. "Patterns of Shimmer: Liza Lim's Compositional Ethnography." *Tempo* 65, no. 258 (2011): 2–9.

López, Francisco

Bailey, Thomas Bey Willam. "Francisco López: The Big Blur Theory." In *MicroBionic: Radical Electronic Music and Sound Art in the 21st Century,* 2nd ed., 242–63. London: Belson Books, 2012.

López, Francisco. "Profound Listening and Environmental Sound Matter." In *Audio Culture: Readings in Modern Music,* edited by Christoph Cox and Daniel Warner, 82–7. London: Continuum, 2004.

Machover, Tod

Duckworth, William. "The *Brain Opera*: A Case Study in Space." In *Virtual Music: How the Web Got Wired for Sound,* 45–58. New York: Routledge, 2013.

Mahnkopf, Claus-Steffen

Mahnkopf, Claus-Steffen. "*The Courier's Tragedy*: Strategies for a Deconstructive Morphology." In *NMA,* vol. 2, *Musical Morphology,* 147–61. Hofheim: Wolke Verlag, 2004.

———. "Hommage à Thomas Pynchon." In *NMA,* vol. 4, *Electronics in New Music,* 100–39. Hofheim: Wolke Verlag, 2006.

———. "*Medusa*: Concerning Conception, Poetics, and Technique." In *NMA,* vol. 1, *Polphony and Complexity,* 245–65. Hofheim: Wolke Verlag, 2002.

Zehentreiter, Ferdinand, ed. *Die Musik von Claus-Steffen Mahnkopf.* Hofheim: Wolke Verlag, 2012.

Mason, Benedict

Mason, Benedict. *Outside Sight Unseen and Opened.* Saarbrücken: Pfau-Verlag, 2002.

Merzbow

Pouncey, Edwin. "Consumed by Noise." *Wire,* no. 198 (2000): 26–33.

Miller, Cassandra

www.cassandramiller.wordpress.com. Composer's official website.

Weeks, James. "Along the Grain: The Music of Cassandra Miller." *Tempo* 68, no. 269 (2014): 50–64.

Mundry, Isabel

Taddy, Ulrich, ed. *Isabel Mundry.* Musik-Konzepte Sonderband, no. 12. Munich: Edition Text + Kritik, 2011.

Murail, Tristan

Fineberg, Joshua, and Pierre Michel, eds. "Models and Artifice: The Collected Writings of Tristan Murail." Special issue, *CMR* 24, nos. 2–3 (2005).

Murail, Tristan. "After-Thoughts." *CMR* 19, no. 3 (2000): 5–9.

Neuwirth, Olga

Metzer, David. "Sonic Flux." In *Musical Modernism at the Turn of the Twenty-First Century,* 221–36. Cambridge: Cambridge University Press, 2009.

New Amsterdam

www.newamrecords.com. Composer's official website.

Nicolai, Carsten

Collis, Adam. "Sounds of the System: The Emancipation of Noise in the Music of Carsten Nicolai." *OS* 13, no. 1 (2008): 31–9.

Pesch, Martin. "Transfer and Transformation: Strategies in the Oeuvre of Carsten Nicolai." *Parachute* 107 (2002): 80–93.

Nonclassical

www.nonclassical.co.uk. Label's official website.

Andrewes, Thom, and Dimitri Djuric *We Break Strings.* London: Hackney Classical Press, 2014.

Nono, Luigi

Davismoon, Stephen, ed. "Luigi Nono." Special issue, *CMR* 18, nos. 1–2 (1999).

Onkyo

Novak, David. "Playing Off Site: The Untranslation of Onkyō." *Asian Music,* 41, no. 1 (2010): 36–59.

Oswald, John

www.plunderphonics.com. Composer's official website.

Cutler, Chris. "Plunderphonics." In *Music, Electronic Media and Culture,* edited by Simon Emmerson, 87–114. Aldershot: Ashgate, 2000.

Keenan, David. "Undoing Time." *Wire,* no. 219 (2002): 42–9.

Metzer, David. "Sampling and Thievery." In *Quotation and Cultural Meaning in Twentieth-Century Music,* 160–87. Cambridge: Cambridge University Press, 2003.

Oswald, John. "Plunderstanding Ecophonomics." In *Arcana,* vol. 1, edited by John Zorn, 9–17. New York: Hips Road, 2000.

Packer, Randall

Packer, Randall. "Composing with Media: Zero in Time and Space." *CMR* 24, no. 6 (2005): 509–25.

Pärt, Arvo

Hillier, Paul. *Arvo Pärt.* Oxford: Oxford University Press, 1997.
Shenton, Andrew, ed. *The Cambridge Companion to Arvo Pärt.* Cambridge: Cambridge University Press, 2012.
Skipp, Benjamin. "Out of Place in the 20th Century: Thoughts on Arvo Pärt's Tintinnabuli Style." *Tempo* 63, no. 249 (2009): 2–11.

Payne, Anthony

Payne, Anthony. *Elgar's Third Symphony: The Story of the Reconstruction.* London: Faber, 1998.

Pisaro, Michael

Pisaro, Michael. "Eleven Theses on the State of New Music." October 2004; revised December 2006. www.timescraper.de/_michael-pisaro/11theses-12–06.pdf.

Prins, Stefan

www.stefanprins.be/eng/index.html. Composer's official website.

Reich, Steve

Cumming, Naomi. "The Horrors of Identification: Reich's 'Different Trains.'" *PNM* 35, no. 1 (1997): 129–52.
Fox, Christopher. "Steve Reich's 'Different Trains.'" *Tempo*, no. 172 (1990): 2–8.
Hillier, Paul. "'Some More Lemon? . . .' A Conversation with Steve Reich." *CMR* 12, no. 2 (1995): 65–75.
Novak, Jelena. *Postopera: Reinventing the Voice-Body.* Aldershot: Ashgate, 2015.
Stier, Oren Baruch. "Different Trains: Holocaust Artifacts and the Ideologies of Remembrance." *Holocaust and Genocide Studies* 19, no. 1 (2005): 81–106.
Wlodarski, Amy Lynn. "The Testimonial Aesthetics of *Different Trains*." *Journal of the American Musicological Society* 63, no. 1 (2010): 99–141.

Richter, Max

Stone-Davis, Férdia J. "*Vivaldi Recomposed*: An Interview with Max Richter." *CMR* 34, no. 1 (2015): 44–53.

Roden, Steve

LaBelle, Brandon, and Steve Roden. *Site of Sound: Of Architecture and the Ear.* Los Angeles: Errant Bodies, 2009.
Roden, Steve. "On Lowercase Affinities and Forms of Paper." 2001. www.lineimprint.com/pressreleases/line_053_essay.pdf.

Saunders, James

www.james-saunders.com. Composer's official website.
Saunders, James. "Modular Music." *PNM* 46, no. 1 (2008): 152–93.

Sheng, Bright

Chang, Peter. "Bright Sheng's Music: An Expression of Cross-Cultural Experience—Illustrated through the Motivic, Contrapuntal and Tonal Treatment of the Chinese Folk Song *The Stream Flows*." *CMR* 26, nos. 5–6 (2007): 619–33.
Sheng, Bright. "H'un (Lacerations): In Memoriam 1966–1976 for Orchestra." *PNM* 33, nos. 1–2 (1995): 560–603.

Shim, Kunsu

www.kunsu-shim.de. Composer's official website.

Shlomowitz, Matthew

www.shlom.com. Composer's official website.
Shlomowitz, Matthew. "Music without Borders." Lecture for Darmstadt Summer Course, 2012. www.shlom.com/?p=mwb.

Silk Road Ensemble

www.silkroadproject.org. Silk Road Project's official website.
Cuno, James, and Yo-Yo Ma. "The Silk Road and Beyond." *Art Institute of Chicago Museum Studies* 33, no. 1 (2007): 20–29.
Yang, Mina. "East Meets West in the Concert Hall: Asians and Classical Music in the Century of Imperialism, Post-Colonialism, and Multiculturalism." *Asian Music* 38, no. 1 (2007): 1–30.

Silvestrov, Valentin

Savenko, Svetlana. "Valentin Silvestrov's Lyrical Universe." In *Ex-Oriente II: Nine Composers from the Former USSR*, edited by Valeria Tsenova, 97. Berlin: Ernst Kuhn, 2003.
Schmelz, Peter. "Valentin Silvestrov and the Echoes of Music History." *Journal of Musicology* 31, no. 2 (2014): 231–71.
Wilson, Samuel John. "An Aesthetic of Past-Present Relations in the Experience of Late 20th- and Early 21st-Century Music." PhD diss., Royal Holloway University, 2013.

Skempton, Howard

Fallas, John. "Conditions of Immediacy: Howard Skempton in Interview." *Tempo* 66, no. 262 (2012): 13–28.
Müller, Hermann-Christoph. "Emanzipation der Konsonanz: Howard Skemptons Orchesterstück *Lento*," *MusikTexte*, no. 75 (August 1998): 77–81.

Sonami, Laetitia

Rodgers, Tara. "Laetitia Sonami." In *Pink Noises: Women on Electronic Music and Sound*, 226–34. Durham, NC: Duke University Press, 2010.

Steen-Andersen, Simon

www.simonsteenandersen.dk. Composer's official website.

Stockhausen, Karlheinz

www.karlheinzstockhausen.org. Composer's official website.

Maconie, Robin. "Divine Comedy: Stockhausen's 'MITTWOCH' in Birmingham." *Tempo* 67, no. 263 (2013): 2–18.

———. "Facing the Music: Stockhausen's Wizard of Oz." *Tempo* 64, no. 251 (2010): 2–7.

———. *Other Planets: The Music of Karlheinz Stockhausen.* Lanham, MD: Scarecrow Press, 2005.

Stone, Carl

www.rlsto.net/Nooz. Composer's official website.

Oteri, Frank J. "Carl Stone: Intellectual Property, Artistic License and Free Acces to Information in the Age of Sample-Based Music and the Internet." *NewMusicBox*, November 1, 2000. www.newmusicbox.org/articles/carl-stone-intellectual-property-artistic-license-and-free-access-to-information-in-the-age-of-samplebased-music-and-the-internet.

Takasugi, Steven Kazuo

Takasugi, Steven Kazuo. "Vers une myopie musicale." In *NMA*, vol. 1, *Polphony and Complexity*, 291–302. Hofheim: Wolke Verlag, 2002.

Tsao, Ming. "Between the Lines of Steven Kazuo Takasugi's Recent Work 'The Jargon of Nothingness.'" *Music und Ästhetik*, no. 3 (2004): 63–83.

Tavener, John

Haydon, Geoffrey. *Glimpses of Paradise.* London: Gollancz, 1995.

Tavener, John. *The Music of Silence: A Composer's Testament.* London: Faber and Faber, 1999.

———. "The Sacred in Art." *CMR* 12, no. 2 (1995): 49–54.

Torke, Michael

Bernard, Jonathan W. "Minimalism, Postminimalism, and the Resurgence of Tonality in Recent American Music." *American Music* 21, no. 1 (2003): 112–33.

Murray, David. "Michael Torke." *Tempo*, no. 180 (1992): 2–5.

Tsunoda, Toshiya

Pisaro, Michael. "Membrane—Window—Membrane (The Folded Worlds of Toshiya Tsunoda)." *surround*, no. 3 (February 2015). http://surround.noquam.com/membrane-window-mirror.

Turnage, Mark Anthony

Clements, Andrew. *Mark-Anthony Turnage.* London: Faber, 2000.

Pettit, Stephen. "Mark-Anthony Turnage and 'Greek.'" *MT* 129, no. 1746 (1988): 397–400.

Ustvolskaya, Galina

Cizmic, Maria. "Hammering Hands: Galina Ustvolskaya's Piano Sonata No. 6 and a Hermeneutic of Pain." In *Performing Pain: Music and Trauma in Eastern Europe*, 67–96. Oxford: Oxford University Press, 2012.

Taddy, Ulrich, ed. *Galina Ustvolskaya*. Musik-Konzepte, no. 143. Munich: Edition Text + Kritik, 2009.

Vaggione, Horacio

Solomos, Makis, ed. "Horacio Vaggione: Composition Theory." Special issue, *CMR* 24, no. 4–5 (2005).

Vitiello, Stephen

Kim-Cohen, Seth. "Stephen Vitiello: The Lost Voice." *Art Review*, May 2005. www.kim-cohen.com/Assets/Texts/Kim-Cohen_Stephen%20Vitiello%20(2005).pdf.

Weidenbaum, Marc. "In the Echo of No Towers," *Disquiet* (blog), September 8, 2011. www.disquiet.com/2011/09/08/stephen-vitiello-wtc-911-floyd.

Walshe, Jennifer

Clark, Philip. "Misshapen Identities." *Wire*, no. 321 (2010): 44–9.

Saunders, James. Interview with Jennifer Walshe. In *ARCEM*, 343–52.

———. "Commentary: *dirty white fields.*" *WE*, 372–6.

Wandelweiser

See also entries for individual composers belonging to the Wandelweiser Group.

www.wandelweiser.de. Label and publishing company's website.

Houben, Eva-Maria, and Burkhard Schlothauer, eds. *MusikDenken: Texte der Wandelweiser Komponisten.* Zurich: Edition Howeg, 2008.

Johnson, Tom. "Almost Nothing." *Focus* (blog), *Journal of Music*, December 1, 2009. www.journalofmusic.com/focus/almost-nothing.

Melia, Nicholas, and James Saunders, eds. "Wandelweiser." Special issue, *CMR* 30, no. 6 (2011).

Pisaro, Michael. "Wandelweiser." *erstwords* (blog), September 23, 2009. www.erstwords.blogspot.co.uk/2009/09/wandelweiser.html.

Warburton, Dan. "The Sound of Silence." Paris Transatlantic, July 2006. www.paristransatlantic.com/magazine/monthly2006/07jul_text.html.

Werder, Manfred

Lely, John. "Commentary: *2005¹.*" *WE*, 382–6.

Montgomery, Will. "Five Ways of Looking at Manfred Werder." *Wolf Notes*, no. 3 (2012): 14–16.

Saunders, James. Interview with Manfred Werder. In *ARCEM*, 353–8.

Westerkamp, Hildegard

Kolber, David. "Hildegard Westerkamp's Kits Beach Soundwalk: Shifting Perspectives in Real World Music." *OS* 7, no. 1 (2002): 41–3.

McCartney, Andra. "Sounding Places: Situated Conversations through the Soundscape Compositions of Hildegard Westerkamp." PhD diss., York University, Toronto, 1999.

McCartney, Andra, and Marta McCarthy. "Choral, Public and Private Listener Responses to Hildegard Westerkamp's *École Polytechnique.*" *Music and Arts in Action* 4, no. 1 (2012): 56–72.

Westerkamp, Hildegard. "Soundwalking." Originally published in *Sound Heritage* 3, no. 4 (1974): 18–27. Revised 2001. Available online at www.sfu.ca/~westerka/writings%20 page/articles%20pages/soundwalking.html.

Wolfe, Julia

www.juliawolfemusic.com. Composer's official website.

Wolman, Amnon

www.amnonwolman.org. Composer's official website.
Wolman, Amnon. "Statement." *WE*, 420–22.

Z, Pamela

www.pamelaz.com. Composer's official website.
Hassan, Salah M., and Cheryl Finley, eds. *Diaspora Memory Place.* Munich: Prestel, 2008.
Rodgers, Tara. "Pamela Z." In *Pink Noises: Women on Electronic Music and Sound*, 216–25. Durham, NC: Duke University Press, 2010.

Zaven, Cynthia

www.cynthiazaven.com. Composer's official website.

Zender, Hans

Gruhn, Wilfried. "Wider der ästhetische Routine: Hans Zenders Version von Schuberts 'Winterreise.'" *Neue Zeitschrift für Musik* 158, no. 1(1997): 42–7.
"Hans Zender." Special issue, *Neue Zeitschrift für Musik*, no. 192 (2011).
Hasegawa, Robert. "*Gegenstrebige Harmonik* in the Music of Hans Zender." *PNM* 49, no. 1 (2011): 207–30.

Zorn, John

Duckworth, William. "John Zorn." In *Talking Music*, 444–76. New York: Da Capo Press, 1999.)

REGIONAL SURVEYS (BY REGION, COUNTRY, OR CITY)
Australia

Kouvaras, Linda Ioanna. *Loading the Silence: Australian Sound Art in the Post-Digital Age.* Farnham, Surrey: Ashgate, 2013.
McCombe, Christine, ed. "Musical Hybrids—Sonic Intermedia in Australia." Special issue, *CMR* 25, no. 4 (2006).

China

Green, Edward, ed. "China and the West: The Birth of a New Music." Special issue, *CMR* 26 nos. 5–6 (2007).

Lau, Frederick. "Fusion or Fission: The Paradox and Politics of Contemporary Chinese Avant-Garde Music." In *Locating East Asia in Western Art Music,* edited by Frederick Lau and Yayoi Uno Everett, 22–39. Middletown, CT: Wesleyan University Press, 2004.

———. "Voice, Culture, and Ethnicity in Contemporary Chinese Compositions." In *Vocal Music and Contemporary Identities: Unlimited Voices in East Asia and the West,* edited by Christian Utz and Frederick Lau, 99–115. New York: Routledge, 2013.

East Asia

Lau, Frederick, and Yayoi Uno Everett, eds. *Locating East Asia in Western Art Music.* Middletown, CT: Wesleyan University Press, 2004.

Utz, Christian, and Frederick Lau, eds. *Vocal Music and Contemporary Identities: Unlimited Voices in East Asia and the West.* New York: Routledge, 2013.

Yoshihara, Mari. *Musicians from a Different Shore: Asians and Asian Americans in Classical Music.* Philadelphia: Temple University Press, 2007.

Former GDR

Böhme-Mehner, Tanya, ed. "Creating Sound behind the Wall: Electroacoustic Music in the GDR." Special issue, *CMR* 30, no. 1 (2011).

Kelly, Elaine. "Reflective Nostalgia and Diasporic Memory: Composing East Germany after 1989." In *Remembering and Rethinking the GDR: Multiple Perspectives and Plural Authenticities,* edited by Anna Saunders and Debbie Pinfold, 130–45. Basingstoke: Palgrave Macmillan, 2013.

Mayer, Günter. "Advanced Composition and Critical (Political) Ambition." In *NMA,* vol. 5, *Critical Composition Today,* 171–84. Hofheim: Wolke Verlag, 2006.

Nauck, Gisela. "Ferment and New Departures: The Last Generation of East German Composers." *CMR* 12, no. 1 (1995): 41–75.

Schneider, Frank. "New Music from the Old GDR." *CMR* 12, no. 1 (1995): 25–40.

Former Soviet Union

Tsenova, Valeria, ed. *Underground Music from the Former USSR.* New York: Routledge, 1998.

Germany (West and Unified)

Beins, Burkhard, Christian Kesten, Gisela Nauck, and Andrea Neumann, eds. *Echtzeitmusik Berlin: Self-Defining a Scene.* Hofheim: Wolke Verlag, 2011.

Hinz, Klaus-Michael, ed. "New Developments in Contemporary German Music." Special issue, *CMR* 12, no. 1 (1995).

Warnaby, John. 1995: "A New Left-Wing Radicalism in Contemporary German Music?" *Tempo,* no. 193 (1995): 18–26.

Williams, Alistair. *Music in Germany Since 1968.* Cambridge: Cambridge University Press, 2013.

Great Britain

Palmer, Andrew. *Encounters with British Composers*. Woodbridge: Boydell and Brewer, 2015.

Ireland

Dervan, Michael, ed. *The Invisible Art: A Century of Music in Ireland 1916–2016*. Woodbridge: Boydell and Brewer, 2015.

Israel

Gluck, Robert J. "Fifty Years of Electronic Music in Israel." *OS* 10, no. 2 (2005): 163–80.

Japan

Long, Stephen. "Japanese Composers of the Post-Takemitsu Generation." *Tempo* 58, no. 228 (2004): 14–22.

Novak, David. *Japanoise*. Durham, NC: Duke University Press, 2013.

Wade, Bonnie C. *Composing Japanese Musical Modernity*. Chicago: University of Chicago Press, 2013.

Korea

Killich, Andrew. *Hwang Byungki: Traditional Music and the Contemporary Composer in the Republic of Korea*. Aldershot: Ashgate, 2013.

Lee, Heekyung. "Reconsidering Traditional Vocal Practices in Contemporary Korean Music." In *Vocal Music and Contemporary Identities: Unlimited Voices in East Asia and the West*, edited by Christian Utz and Frederick Lau, 133–57. New York: Routledge, 2013.

Lebanon

Asmar, Sami W. "Challenging the Status Quo in War-Torn Lebanon: Ziad Rahbani, the Avant-Garde Heir to Musical Tradition." In *The Arab Avant-Garde: Music, Politics, Modernity*, edited by Thomas Burkhalter, Kay Dickinson, and Benjamin J. Harbert, 145–64. Middletown, CT: Wesleyan University Press, 2013.

Burkhalter, Thomas. *Local Music Scenes and Globalization: Transnational Platforms in Beirut*. New York: Routledge, 2013.

———. "Multisited Avant-Gardes or World Music 2.0? Musicians from Beirut and Beyond between Local Production and Euro-American Reception." In *The Arab Avant-Garde: Music, Politics, Modernity*, edited by Thomas Burkhalter, Kay Dickinson, and Benjamin J. Harbert, 89–118. Middletown, CT: Wesleyan University Press, 2013.

Peterson, Marina. "Sonic Cosmopolitanisms: Experimental Improvised Music and a Lebanese–American Cultural Exchange." In *The Arab Avant-Garde: Music, Politics, Modernity*, edited by Thomas Burkhalter, Kay Dickinson, and Benjamin J. Harbert, 185–208. Middletown, CT: Wesleyan University Press, 2013.

London

Andrewes, Thom, and Dimitri Djuric. *We Break Strings*. London: Hackney Classical Press, 2014.

New York

Gann, Kyle. *Music Downtown: Writings from the Village Voice.* Berkeley, CA: University of California Press, 2006.

New Zealand

Russell, Bruce, and Richard Francis, eds. *Erewhon Calling: Experimental Sound in New Zealand.* Auckland: Audio Foundation, 2012.

Palestine

Shaked, Yuval. "On Contemporary Palestinian Music." *Search,* no. 8 (2011). www.search-newmusic.org/shaked.pdf.

South America

Dal Farra, Ricardo. "Something Lost, Something Hidden, Something Found: Electroacoustic Music by Latin American Composers." *OS* 13, no. 2 (2006): 131–42.

Latin American Electroacoustic Music Collection. La fondation Daneil Langlois pour l'art, la science et la technologie. www.fondation-langlois.org/html/e/page.php?NumPage=556.

Syria

Silverstein, Shayna. "Transforming Space: The Production of Contemporary Syrian Art Music." In *The Arab Avant-Garde: Music, Politics, Modernity,* edited by Thomas Burkhalter, Kay Dickinson, and Benjamin J. Harbert, 37–73. Middletown, CT: Wesleyan University Press, 2013.

THEMATIC TOPICS
Acoustic Ecology

www.wfae.net. World Forum for Acoustic Ecology.

Dunn, David. "Acoustic Ecology and the Experimental Music Tradition." *NewMusicBox,* January 9, 2008. www.newmusicbox.org/articles/Acoustic-Ecology-and-the-Experimental-Music-Tradition.

———. "Nature, Sound Art, and the Sacred." In *The Book of Music and Nature,* edited by David Rothenburg and Mart Ulvaeus, 95–107. Middletown, CT: Wesleyan University Press, 2001.

Schafer, R. Murray. *The Soundscape: Our Sonic Environment and the Tuning of the World.* Rochester, VT: Destiny Books, 1994.

Soundscape: The Journal of Acoustic Ecology, 2000–. www.wfae.net/journal.

Truax, Barry. *Handbook for Acoustic Ecology.* Vancouver: ARC Publications, 1978.

———. "Soundscape, Acoustic Communication and Environmental Sound Composition." *CMR* 15, nos. 1–2 (1996): 49–65.

The Body

Craenen, Paul, and Helen White. *Composing under the Skin: The Music-Making Body at the Composer's Desk.* Leuven: Leuven University Press, 2014.

Fink, Robert. *Repeating Ourselves: American Minimal Music as Cultural Practice.* Berkeley, CA: University of California Press, 2005.

McClary, Susan. "Getting Down Off the Beanstalk: The Presence of a Woman's Voice in Janike Vandervelde's *Genesis II.*" In *Feminine Endings: Music, Gender, and Sexuality,* 112–31. Minnesota: University of Minnesota Press, 1991.

Schroeder, Franziska, ed. "Bodily Instruments and Instrumental Bodies." Special issue, *CMR* 25, nos. 1–2 (2006).

Thompson, Marie, and Ian Biddle, eds. *Sound Music Affect: Theorizing Sonic Experience.* New York: Bloomsbury, 2013.

Complexity/Complexism

Boros, James, ed. "Complexity Forum." Special issue, *PNM* 31 (1993).

Duncan, Stuart Paul. "Re-Complexifying the Function(s) of Notation in the Music of Brian Ferneyhough and the "New Complexity."' *PNM* 48 (2010): 136–72.

———. "To Infinity and Beyond: A Reflection on Notation, 1980s Darmstadt, and Interpretational Approaches to the Music of New Complexity." *Search,* no. 7 (2010). www.search-newmusic.org/index7.html.

Morgan, Tom, ed. "Aspects of Complexity in Recent British Music." Special issue, *CMR* 13, no. 1 (1995).

NMA, esp. vol. 1, *Polyphony and Complexity.*

Toop, Richard. "Against a Theory of Musical (New) Complexity." In *Contemporary Music: Theoretical and Philosophical Perspectives,* edited by Max Paddison and Irène Deliège, 89–97. (Farnham: Ashgate, 2010.

———. "Four Facets of the New Complexity." *Contact,* no. 32 (1988): 4–50.

Conceptual Music

Iddon, Martin. "Outsourcing Progress: On Conceptual Music." *Tempo* 70, no. 275 (2016): 36–49.

Kreidler, Johannes. "New Conceptualism in Music." Lecture given at the Darmstadter Ferienkürse für Neue Musik, Darmstadt, Germany, July 27, 2012. www.youtube.com/watch?v=T-kEs_RIiiE.

Rainer Nonnenmann, ed. "Umfrage zum Thema '(Neuer) Konzeptualismus." *MusikTexte,* no. 145 (May 2015): 41–90.

Straebel, Volker. "Aspects of Conceptual Composing." *Open Space Magazine,* no. 10 (2008): 69–78.

Cross-Cultural Exchange and Interaction

Gluck, Robert. "Between, within and across Cultures." *OS* 13, no. 2 (2008): 141–52.

Kiwan, Nadia, and Ulrike Anna Meinhof, eds. "Music and Migration: A Transnational Approach." Special issue, *Music and Arts in Action,* 3, no. 3 (2011).

Koay, Kheng K., and Mikel LeDee. "Crossed Boundaries in Musical Culture between Asia and the West." *CLCWeb: Comparative Literature and Culture* 15, no. 2 (2013). www.dx.doi.org/10.7771/1481-4374.2229.

Liao, Ping-hui. "From Multicultural to Creole Subjects: David Henry Hwang's Collaborative Works with Philip Glass." In *The Creolization of Theory*, edited by Françoise Lionnet and Shu-Mei Shih, 142–55. Durham, NC: Duke University Press, 2011.

Winzenburg, John. "Heteroglossia and Traditional Vocal Genres in Chinese–Western Fusion Concertos." *PNM* 51, no. 2 (2013): 101–40.

Yang, Mina. "East Meets West in the Concert Hall: Asians and Classical Music in the Century of Imperialism, Post-Colonialism, and Multiculturalism." *Asian Music* 38, no. 1 (2007): 1–30.

Data and Sonification

Hermann, Thomas, Andy Hunt, and John G. Neuhoff, eds. *The Sonification Handbook*. Berlin: Logos Publishing House, 2011.

Jevbratt, Lisa. "The Prospect of the Sublime in Data Visualizations." *Ylem* 24, no. 8 (2004): 4–8.

Manovich, Lev. "The Anti-Sublime Ideal in Data Art." August 2002. http://virus.meetopia.net/pdf-ps_db/LManovich_data_art.pdf.

Polli, Andrea. "*Atmospherics/Weather Works*: A Spatialized Meteorological Data Project." *Leonardo Music Journal* 38, no. 1 (2005): 31–6.

Schedel, Margaret, and David R. Worrall, eds. "Sonification." Special issue, *OS* 19, no. 1 (2014).

Digitization

Lehmann, Harry. "Digitization and Concept: A Thought Experiment Concerning New Music." *Search*, no. 7 (2010). www.searchnewmusic.org/lehmann.pdf.

DIY Instruments

Applebaum, Mark. "Progress Report: The State of the Art after Sixteen Years of Designing and Playing Electroacoustic Sound-Sculptures." In *NMA*, vol. 4, *Electronics in New Music*, 9–35. Hofheim: Wolke Verlag, 2006.

Collins, Nicholas. *Handmade Electronic Music: The Art of Hardware Hacking*. New York: Routledge, 2006.

Shapiro, Peter. "Deck Wreckers: The Turntable as Instrument." In *Undercurrents: The Hidden Wiring of Modern Music*, 163–80. London: Continuum, 2002.

Electronic Music

Borchert, Gavin. "American Women in Electronic Music, 1984–94." *CMR* 16, nos. 1–2 (1997): 89–97.

Collins, Nick. *Introduction to Computer Music*. Hoboken: Wiley and Sons, 2010.

Collins, Nick, and Julio d'Escrivan, eds. *The Cambridge Companion to Electronic Music*. Cambridge: Cambridge University Press, 2007.

Demers, Joanna. *Listening through the Noise: The Aesthetics of Experimental Electronic Music*. Oxford: Oxford University Press, 2010.

Duckworth, William. *Virtual Music: How the Web Got Wired for Sound*. New York: Routledge, 2013.

Emmerson, Simon, ed. *The Language of Electroacoustic Music.* Basingstoke: Macmillan, 1986.
———. *Living Electronic Music.* Aldershot: Ashgate, 2007.
———, ed. *Music, Electronic Media and Culture.* Farnham: Ashgate, 2000.
Holmes, Thom. *Electronic and Experimental Music: Technology, Music, and Culture.* 4th ed. New York: Routledge, 2012.
Manning, Peter. *Electronic and Computer Music.* 4th ed. New York: Oxford University Press, 2013.
Nelson, Peter, ed. "Live Electronics," Special issue, *CMR* 6, no. 1 (1991).
Roads, Curtis. *Microsound.* Cambridge, MA: MIT Press, 2001.

Experimental Music

ARCEM
Gottschalk, Jennie. *Experimental Music since 1970.* London: Bloomsbury, 2016.
Priest, Eldritch. *Boring Formless Nonsense: Experimental Music and the Aesthetics of Failure.* New York: Bloomsbury, 2013.
Weiss, Allen S., ed. *Experimental Sound and Radio.* Cambridge, MA: MIT Press, 2001.

Field Recording

Anderson, Casey. "Faithfully Re-Presenting the Outside World." *NewMusicBox,* June 12, 2013. www.newmusicbox.org/articles/faithfully-re-presenting-the-outside-world.
Lane, Cathy, and Angus Carlyle. *In the Field: The Art of Field Recording.* Axminster, Devon: Uniformbooks, 2013.
López, Francisco. "Profound Listening and Environmental Sound Matter." In *Audio Culture: Readings in Modern Music,* edited by Christoph Cox and Daniel Warner, 82–7. London: Continuum, 2004.
Montgomery, Will. "Beyond the Soundscape: Art and Nature in Contemporary Phonography." In *ARCEM,* 145–61.
Pisaro, Michael. "Ten Framing Considerations of the Field (Working Notes for Making Field Recordings)." *Experimental Yearbook,* October/November 2010. www.experimentalmusicyearbook.com/ten-framing-considerations-of-the-field.

Glitch and Failure

Cascone, Kim. "The Aesthetics of Failure: 'Post-Digital' Tendencies in Contemporary Computer Music." *Computer Music Journal* 24, no. 4 (2000): 12–18.
Kelly, Caleb. *Cracked Media: The Sound of Malfunction.* Cambridge, MA: MIT Press, 2009.
Priest, Eldritch. *Boring Formless Nonsense: Experimental Music and the Aesthetics of Failure.* New York: Bloomsbury, 2013.
Vanhanen, Janne. "Virtual Sound: Examining Glitch and Production." *CMR* 22, no. 4 (2003): 45–52.
Young, Rob. "Worship the Glitch: Digital Music, Electronic Disturbance." In *Undercurrents: The Hidden Wiring of Modern Music,* 45–58. London: Continuum, 2002.

Globalization

Böhme-Mehner, Tanya. "Sound and Musics in the *Global Village:* On Landscapes in Sound and Soundscapes in Culture." *OS* 13, no. 2 (2008): 153–60.

Burkhalter, Thomas. *Local Music Scenes and Globalization: Transnational Platforms in Beirut.* New York: Routledge, 2013.

Denyer, Frank. "Finding a Voice in an Age of Migration." *CMR* 15, nos. 3–4 (1996): 77–80.

Feld, Steven. "A Sweet Lullaby for World Music." In *Globalization,* edited by Arjun Appadurai, 189–216. Durham, NC: Duke University Press, 2001.

Taylor, Timothy D. *Beyond Exoticism: Western Music and the World.* Durham, NC: Duke University Press, 2007.

Utz, Christian, and Frederick Lau, eds. *Vocal Music and Contemporary Identities: Unlimited Voices in East Asia and the West.* New York: Routledge, 2013.

White, Bob W., ed. *Music and Globalization: Critical Encounters.* Indiana: Indiana University Press, 2011.

Wishart, Trevor. "Globally Speaking." *OS* 13, no. 2 (2008): 137–40.

Yang, Mina. "East Meets West in the Concert Hall: Asians and Classical Music in the Century of Imperialism, Post-Colonialism, and Multiculturalism." *Asian Music* 38, no. 1 (2007): 1–30.

Improvisation

Blazanovic, Marta. "Berlin Reductionism: An Extreme Approach to Improvisation Developed in the Berlin *Echtzeitmusik*-Scene." Paper presented at the International Musicological Conference, *Beyond the Centres: Musical Avant-Gardes Since 1950,* Thessaloniki Archaeological Museum, Thessaloniki, Greece, July 1–3, 2010. www.btc.web.auth.gr/proceedings.html.

Keep, Andy. "Instrumentalizing: Approaches to Improvising with Sounding Objects in Experimental Music." In *ARCEM,* 113–29.

Lewis, George. *A Power Stronger Than Itself: The AACM and American Experimental Music.* Chicago: University of Chicago Press, 2008.

Prévost, Eddie. *No Sound Is Innocent: AMM and the Practice of Self-invention.* Matching Tye, Essex: Copula, 1995.

Toop, David. "Frames of Freedom: Improvisation, Otherness and the Limits of Spontaneity." In *Undercurrents: The Hidden Wiring of Modern Music,* 233–48. London: Continuum, 2002.

Uitti, Frances-Marie, ed. "Improvisation." Special issue, *CMR* 25, nos. 5–6 (2006).

Watson, Ben. *Derek Bailey and the Story of Free Improvisation.* London: Verso, 2013.

Listening

Burt, Warren. "Ways of Listening." *Warren Burt* (blog), 2009. www.warrenburt.com/ways_of_listening.

Carlyle, Angus, and Cathy Lane, eds. *On Listening.* Axminster, Devon: Uniformbooks, 2013.

Chaves, Rui, and Pedro Rebelo. "Evocative Listening: Mediated Practices in Everyday Life." *OS* 17, no. 3 (2012): 216–22.

Clarke, Eric F. "The Impact of Recording on Listening," *Twentieth-Century Music* 4, no. 1 (2007): 47–70.

Dunn, David. *Purposeful Listening in Complex States of Time.* 1997–8. www.warrenburt.com/storage/ways_of_listening/Plicsot.pdf.

Norman, Katherine, ed. "Sound, Listening and Place I." Special issue, *OS* 16, no. 3 (2011).

———, ed. "Sound, Listening and Place II." Special issue, *OS* 17, no. 3 (2012).

Novak, David. "2.5 × 6 Metres of Space: Japanese Music Coffeehouses and Experimental Practices of Listening." *Popular Music* 27, no. 1 (2007): 15–34.

Schwarz, David. "Listening Subjects: Semiotics, Psychoanalysis, and the Music of John Adams and Steve Reich." In *Keeping Score: Music, Disciplinarity, Culture*, edited by David Schwarz, Anahid Kassabian, and Lawrence Siegel, 275–98. Charlottesville: University Press of Virginia, 1997.

Thompson, Marie, and Ian Biddle, eds. *Sound, Music, Affect: Theorizing Sonic Experience.* New York: Bloomsbury, 2013.

Truax, Barry. *Acoustic Communication.* 2nd ed. Westport, CT: Ablex, 2001.

Voegelin, Salome. *Listening to Noise and Silence.* London: Continuum, 2010.

Marketing

Carboni, Marius. "Marketing Strategies in the UK Classical Music Business: An Examination into Changes in the Classical Music Business since 1989." PhD diss., University of Hertfordshire, 2011.

Dolp, Laura. "Pärt in the Marketplace." In *The Cambridge Companion to Arvo Pärt*, edited by Andrew Shenton, 177–92. Cambridge: Cambridge University Press, 2012.

Downie, Gordon. "Aesthetic Necrophilia: Reification, New Music, and the Commodification of Affectivity." *PNM* 42, no. 2 (2004): 264–75.

Jarman, Freya. "Relax, Feel Good, Chill Out: The Affective Distribution of Classical Music." In *Sound, Music, Affect: Theorizing Sonic Experience*, edited by Marie Thompson and Ian Biddle, 183–204. New York: Bloomsbury, 2013.

Stanbridge, Alan. "The Tradition of All the Dead Generations: Music and Cultural Policy." *International Journal of Cultural Policy* 13, no. 3 (2007): 255–71.

Memory

Cox, Geoffrey. "A Return to the Future or Forward to the Past?" *CMR* 29, no. 3 (2010): 251–64.

Lane, Cathy, and Nye Parry, eds. "Sound, History and Memory." Special issue, *OS* 11, no. 1 (2006).

Stier, Oren Baruch. "Different Trains: Holocaust Artifacts and the Ideologies of Remembrance." *Holocaust and Genocide Studies* 19, no. 1 (2005): 81–106.

Wlodarski, Amy Lynn. "The Testimonial Aesthetics of *Different Trains.*" *Journal of the American Musicological Society* 63, no. 1 (2010): 99–141.

Microsound

Demers, Joanna. "Minimal Objects in Microsound." In *Listening through the Noise: The Aesthetics of Experimental Electronic Music*, 69–89. Oxford: Oxford University Press, 2010.

Phillips, Thomas. "Composed Silence: Microsound and the Quiet Shock of Listening." *PNM* 44, no. 2 (2006): 232–48.

Roads, Curtis. *Microsound.* Cambridge, MA: MIT Press, 2001.

Turner, Jeremy. "The Microsound Scene: An Interview with Kim Cascone." *CTheory*, December 4, 2001. www.ctheory.net/articles.aspx?id=322.

Whitelaw, Michael. "Sound Particles and Microsonic Materialism." *CMR* 22, no. 4 (2003): 93–101.

Minimalism and Postminimalism

ARCMPM

Ashby, Arved. "Minimalist Opera." In *Twentieth-Century Opera*, edited by Mervyn Cooke, 244–66. Cambridge: Cambridge University Press, 2005.

Beirens, Maarten. "The Identity of European Minimalist Music." PhD diss., University of Leuven, 2005.

Bernard, Jonathan W. "Minimalism, Postminimalism, and the Resurgence of Tonality in Recent American Music." *American Music* 21, no. 1 (2003): 112–33.

Fink, *Repeating Ourselves: American Minimal Music as Cultural Practice* (Berkeley, CA: University of California Press, 2005).

Johnson, Tom. "Almost Nothing," *Focus* (blog), *Journal of Music*, December 1, 2009. www.journalofmusic.com/focus/almost-nothing.

McClary, Susan. "Rap, Minimalism, and Structures of Time in Late Twentieth-Century Culture." In *Audio Culture: Readings in Modern Music*, edited by Christoph Cox and Daniel Warner, 289–98. London: Continuum, 2008.

Mobile Music

Ashby, Arved. *Absolute Music, Mechanical Reproduction*. Berkeley, CA: University of California Press, 2010.

Bull, Michael. "No Dead Air! The iPod and the Culture of Mobile Listening." *Leisure Studies* 24, no. 4 (2005): 343–55.

———. *Sound Moves: iPod Culture and Urban Experience*. New York: Routledge, 2007.

Gopinath, Sumanth S., and Jason Stanyek, eds. *Oxford Handbook of Mobile Music Studies*. 2 vols. Oxford: Oxford University Press, 2014.

Hosokawa, Shuhei. "The Walkman Effect." *Popular Music* 4 (1984): 165–80.

Multimedia

Cook, Nicholas. *Analysing Musical Multimedia*. Oxford: Oxford University Press, 2000.

Packer, Randall, and Ken Jordan, eds. *Multimedia: From Wagner to Virtual Reality*. New York: Norton, 2001.

Networked Music

https://ccrma.stanford.edu/groups/soundwire/publications. Publications of the Sound-WIRE research group at the Center for Computer Research in Music and Acoustics, Stanford University.

Ayers, Michael D., ed. *Cybersounds: Essays on Virtual Music Culture*. New York: Peter Lang, 2006.

Barbosa, Á. "Displaced Soundscapes: A Survey of Network Systems for Music and Sonic Art Creation." *Leonardo Music Journal* 13 (2003): 53–9.

Duckworth, William. *Virtual Music: How the Web Got Wired for Sound*. New York: Routledge, 2005.

Hugill, Andrew, ed. "Internet Music." Special issue, *CMR* 24, no. 6 (2005).

Lévy, Pierre. "The Art and Architecture of Cyberspace." In *Multimedia: From Wagner to Virtual Reality*, ed. Randall Packer and Ken Jordan, 335–44. New York: Norton, 2001.

Rebelo, Pedro, ed. "Network Performance." Special issue, *CMR* 28, nos. 4–5 (2009).

Reddell, Trace. "Laptopia: The Spatial Poetics of Networked Laptop Performance." *CMR* 22, no. 4 (2003): 11–23.

Whalley, Ian, and Ken Fields, eds. "Networked Electroacoustic Music." Special issue, *OS* 17, no. 1 (2012).

Noise

Attali, Jacques. *Noise: The Political Economy of Music*. Minneapolis: University of Minnesota Press, 1985.

Cassidy, Aaron, and Aaron Einbond, eds. *Noise in and as Music*. Huddersfield: University of Huddersfield Press, 2013.

Goddard, Michael, Benjamin Halligan, and Paul Hegarty, eds. *Reverberations*. London: Continuum, 2012.

Hegarty, Paul. *Noise/Music: A History*. London: Continuum, 2007.

Keenan, David. "The Primer: Noise." *Wire*, no. 246 (2004): 36–43.

Novak, David. *Japanoise: Music at the Edge of Circulation*. Durham, NC: Duke University Press, 2013.

Smith, Nick. "The Splinter in Your Ear: Noise as the Semblance of Critique." *Culture, Theory and Critique* 46, no. 1 (2005): 43–59.

Nostalgia

Cox, Geoffrey. "A Return to the Future or Forward to the Past?" *CMR* 29, no. 3 (2010): 251–64.

Trigg, Dylan. "Giya Kancheli and the Aesthetics of Nostalgia." In *Azimute: Critical Essays on Deleuze and Guattari*, edited by Robert Lort, 327–39. London, Canada: Enigmatic Ink, 2011.

Wilson, Samuel John. "An Aesthetic of Past-Present Relations in the Experience of Late 20th- and Early 21st-Century Music." PhD diss., Royal Holloway University, 2013.

Notation

Barrett, Richard. "Notation as Liberation." *Tempo* 68, no 268 (2014): 61–71.

Duncan, Stuart Paul. "Re-Complexifying the Function(s) of Notation in the Music of Brian Ferneyhough and the "New Complexity."" *PNM* 48 (2010): 136–72.

———. "To Infinity and Beyond: A Reflection on Notation, 1980s Darmstadt, and Interpretational Approaches to the Music of New Complexity." *Search*, no. 7 (2010). www.searchnewmusic.org/duncan.pdf.

Fox, Christopher. "Opening Offer or Contractual Obligation? On the Prescriptive Function of Notation Today." *Tempo*, 68, no. 269 (2014): 6–19.

Kanno, Mieko. "Prescriptive Notation: Limits and Challenges." *CMR* 26, no. 2 (2007): 231–54.

Pisaro, Michael. "Writing, Music." In *ARCEM*, 27–76.

WE

Performance

Harle, John. "Performing Minimalist Music." In *ARCMPM*, 381–4.

Schick, Steven. "Developing an Interpretive Context: Learning Brian Ferneyhough's *Bone Alphabet*." *PNM* 32, no. 1 (1994): 132–53.

Thomas, Philip. "The Music of Laurence Crane and a Post-Experimental Performance Practice." *Tempo* 70, no. 275 (2016): 5–21.

Polyworks

Hoban, Wieland. "On the Methodology and Aesthetics of Form Polyphony." In *NMA*, vol. 3, *The Foundations of Contemporary Composing*, 85–117. Hofheim: Wolke Verlag, 2004.

Popular music

Bernard, Jonathan W. "Minimalism and Pop: Influence, Reaction, Consequences." In *ARCMPM*, 337–56.

Rutherford-Johnson, Tim. "The Influence Engine: Steve Reich and Pop Music." *NewMusicBox*, March 27, 2013. www.newmusicbox.org/articles/the-influence-engine-steve-reich-and-pop-music.

Witts, Richard, and Rob Young. "Stockhausen vs. the 'Technocrats.'" *Wire*, no. 141 (November 1995): 32–5.

Prestige

Downie, Gordon. "Aesthetic Necrophilia: Reification, New Music, and the Commodification of Affectivity." *PNM* 42, no. 2 (2004): 264–75.

McClary, Susan. "Terminal Prestige: The Case of Avant-Garde Music Composition." *Cultural Critique* 12 (1989): 57–81.

Pace, Ian. "Verbal Discourse as Aesthetic Arbitrator in Contemporary Music." In *The Modernist Legacy: Essays on New Music*, edited by Björn Heile, 81–100. Aldershot: Ashgate, 2009.

Recording

Ashby, Arved. *Absolute Music, Mechanical Reproduction*. Berkeley, CA: University of California Press, 2010.

Clarke, Eric F. "The Impact of Recording on Listening." *Twentieth-Century Music* 4, no. 1 (2007): 47–70.

Sampling

Gann, Kyle. "Plundering for Art: Sampling." In *Music Downtown*, 73–7. Berkeley, CA: University of California Press, 2006.

Oswald, John. "Plunderphonics, or Audio Piracy as a Compositional Prerogative." *Musicworks* 34 (1986): 5–8.

Oteri, Frank J. "Carl Stone: Intellectual Property, Artistic License and Free Acces to Information in the Age of Sample-Based Music and the Internet." *NewMusicBox*, November 1, 2000. www.newmusicbox.org/articles/carl-stone-intellectual-property-artistic-license-and-free-access-to-information-in-the-age-of-samplebased-music-and-the-internet.

Silence

Phillips, Thomas. "Composed Silence: Microsound and the Quiet Shock of Listening." *PNM* 44, no. 2 (2006): 232–48.

Sound Art

Kim-Cohen, Seth. *In the Blink of an Ear: Toward a Non-Cochlear Sound Art.* New York: Bloomsbury, 2009.

LaBelle, Brandon. *Background Noise: Perspectives on Sound Art.* London: Continuum, 2006.

Rudi, Jøran. ed. "Sound Art." Special issue, *OS* 14, no. 1 (2009).

Toop, David. *Sonic Boom: The Art of Sound.* London: Hayward Gallery, 2000.

Voegelin, Salome. *Listening to Noise and Silence.* London: Continuum, 2010.

Weiss, Allen S., ed. *Experimental Sound and Radio.* Cambridge, MA: MIT Press, 2001.

Space/Place

Burtner, Matthew. "Ecoacoustic and Shamanic Technologies for Multimedia Composition and Performance." *OS* 10, no. 1 (2005): 3–19.

Drever, John Levack. "Soundwalking: Aural Excursions into the Everyday." In *ARCEM*, 163–92.

Gandy, Matthew, and B. J. Nilsen. *The Acoustic City.* Berlin: Jovis Verlag, 2015.

Grant, M. J. "Series and Place." *CMR* 30, no. 6 (2011): 525–42.

LaBelle, Brandon. *Acoustic Territories: Sound Culture and Everyday Life.* New York: Bloomsbury, 2010.

Norman, Katherine, ed. "Sound, Listening and Place I." Special issue, *OS* 16, no. 3 (2011).

———, ed. "Sound, Listening and Place II." Special issue, *OS* 17, no. 3 (2012).

Rudi, Jøran, ed. "Sound Art." Special issue, *OS* 14, no. 1 (2009).

Spectral Music

Drott, Eric. "Spectralism, Politics and the Post-Industrial Imagination." In *The Modernist Legacy: Essays on New Music,* edited by Björn Heile, 39–60. (Aldershot: Ashgate, 2009.

Fineberg, Joshua, ed. "Spectral Music." Special issue, *CMR* 19, nos. 2–3 (2000).

"Spiritual" or "Holy" Minimalism

Clarke, David. "Parting Glances." *MT* 134 (1993): 680–84.

Dies, David. "Defining 'Spiritual Minimalism.'" In *ARCMPM*, 315–35.

Dolp, Laura. "Pärt in the Marketplace." In *The Cambridge Companion to Arvo Pärt,* edited by Andrew Shenton, 177–92. Cambridge: Cambridge University Press, 2012.

Howard, Luke. "'Laying the Foundation': The Reception of Górecki's Third Symphony, 1977–1991." *Polish Music Journal* 6, no. 2 (2003). www.usc.edu/dept/polish_music/PMJ/issue/6.2.03/Howard.html.

———. "Motherhood, 'Billboard,' and the Holocaust: Perceptions and Receptions of Górecki's Symphony No. 3." *Musical Quarterly* 82, no. 1 (1998): 131–59.

———. "Production vs. Reception in Postmodernism: The Górecki Case." In *Postmodern Music/Postmodern Thought,* edited by Judy Lochhead and Joseph Auner, 195–206. New York: Routledge, 2002.

Maimets-Volt, Kaire. "Mediating the 'Idea of One': Arvo Pärt's Pre-Existing Music on Film." PhD diss., Estonian Academy of Music and Theatre, 2009. http://tagg.org/xpdfs/MaimetsVolt%20PhD.pdf.

Sholl, Robert, and Sander van Maas, eds. *Contemporary Music and Spirituality*. New York: Routledge, 2016.

Studios

www.ircam.fr. Institut de Recherche et Coordination Acoustique/Musique.

http://opera.media.mit.edu. Opera of the Future.

www.steim.org. STudio for Electro-Instrumental Music.

Cont, Arshia. ed. "Musical Research at IRCAM." Special issue, *CMR* 32, no. 1 (2013).

Landy, Leigh, ed. "Groupe de Recherches Musicales: Musique Concrète." Special issue, *OS* 12, no. 3 (2007).

——, ed. "ZKM—20 Years." Special issue, *OS* 14, no. 3 (2009).

Vinet, Hughes. "Recent Research and Development at IRCAM." *Computer Music Journal* 23, no. 3 (1999): 9–17.

Tonality

Bernard, Jonathan W. "Minimalism, Postminimalism, and the Resurgence of Tonality in Recent American Music." *American Music* 21, no. 1 (2003): 112–33.

Boros, James. "A New Totality?" *PNM* 33, nos. 1–2 (1995): 538–53.

Fox, Christopher. ed. "Temperaments, Tonalities and Microtonalities." Special issue, *CMR* 22, nos. 1–2 (2003).

Lerdahl, Fred. "Tonality and Paranoia: A Reply to Boros." *PNM* 34, no. 1 (Winter 1996): 242–51.

Moravec, Paul, and Robert Beaser, eds. "New Tonality." Special issue, *CMR* 6, no. 2 (1993).

Transcription

Beaudoin, Richard, and Joseph Moore. "Conceiving Musical Transdialection." *Journal of Aesthetics and Art Criticism* 68, no. 2 (2010): 105–17.

Trauma

Cizmic, Maria. *Performing Pain: Music and Trauma in Eastern Europe*. Oxford: Oxford University Press, 2012.

Cumming, Naomi. "The Horrors of Identification: Reich's 'Different Trains.'" *PNM* 35, no. 1 (1997): 129–52.

Stier, Oren Baruch. "Different Trains: Holocaust Artifacts and the Ideologies of Remembrance." *Holocaust and Genocide Studies* 19, no. 1 (2005): 81–106.

Wlodarski, Amy Lynn. "The Testimonial Aesthetics of *Different Trains*." *Journal of the American Musicological Society* 63, no. 1 (2010): 99–141.

NOTES

CHAPTER 1

1. Among these histories I include Joseph Auner, *Music in the Twentieth and Twenty-First Centuries* (New York: W. W. Norton, 2013); Paul Griffiths, *Modern Music and After*, 3rd ed. (Oxford: Oxford University Press, 2010); Alex Ross, *The Rest Is Noise* (New York: Farrar, Straus and Giroux, 2007); Richard Taruskin, *The Oxford History of Western Music*, vol. 5, *Late Twentieth Century* (Oxford: Oxford University Press, 2005); and Arnold Whittall, *Musical Composition in the Twentieth Century* (Oxford: Oxford University Press, 1999).

2. These include Robert Adlington, *Composing Dissent: Avant-Garde Music in 1960s Amsterdam* (Oxford: Oxford University Press, 2013); Adlington, ed., *Sound Commitments: Avant-Garde Music and the Sixties* (Oxford: Oxford University Press, 2009); Beate Kutschke and Barley Norton, eds., *Music and Protest in 1968* (Cambridge: Cambridge University Press, 2013); and Alastair Williams, *Music in Germany since 1968* (Cambridge: Cambridge University Press, 2013).

3. For a complete exposition of this argument, see Christian Caryl, *Strange Rebels: 1979 and the Birth of the 21st Century* (New York: Basic Books, 2013). David Metzer chooses 1980 as a cutoff, although for exclusively musical reasons. See David Metzer, *Musical Modernism at the Turn of the Twenty-First Century* (Cambridge: Cambridge University Press, 2009).

4. Archived at www.w3.org/History/1989/proposal.html.

5. Mark Weiser, "Ubiquitous Computing," March 17, 1996, www.ubiq.com/hypertext/weiser/UbiHome.html.

6. Steve Reich, liner notes for *Different Trains*, Elektra Nonesuch, 7759–79176–2, 1989.

7. See Richard Henderson, "Out of This World," *Wire*, no. 231 (2003): 30–35.

8. Christopher Fox, "Steve Reich's 'Different Trains,'" *Tempo*, no. 172 (1990): 2.

9. See Maria Cizmic, *Performing Pain: Music and Trauma in Eastern Europe* (Oxford: Oxford University Press, 2012), chapter 2.

10. Ibid., 90.

11. For an understandably partial Merzbow discography, see http://en.wikipedia.org/wiki/Merzbow_discography; for an alternative list running up to 2011, see www.ifitmoveskissit.net/oppositerecords/artists/merzdiscog.html.

12. This does not mean that those who have written about his work aren't drawn to certain records over others. Among those albums that have attracted more attention are *Noisembryo* (1994), *Venereology* (1994), *Merzbuddha* (2005), *Bloody Sea* (2006), and *Turmeric* (2006). And then there is the fifty-CD *Merzbox* (1999), which exerts a gravity all its own.

13. David Novak, *Japanoise: Music at the Edge of Circulation* (Durham, NC: Duke University Press, 2013).

14. For a detailed discussion of the techniques and aesthetics of mastering for noise records, see ibid., 51–8.

15. Paul Hegarty, *Noise/Music: A History* (London: Continuum, 2007), 158.

16. Ibid., 134.

17. Hildegard Westerkamp, "Soundwalking," originally published in *Sound Heritage* 3, no. 4 (1974), revised 2001, available online at www.sfu.ca/~westerka/writings%20page/articles%20pages/soundwalking.html.

18. Hildegard Westerkamp, composer's note, *Kits Beach Soundwalk*, accessed August 24, 2015, www.electrocd.com/en/select/piste/?id=imed_1031-1.3.

19. Hildegard Westerkamp, "Listening and Soundmaking: A Study of Music as Environment" (master's thesis, Simon Fraser University, 1988), 3.

20. In this context it is worth noting the striking contrast between the spoken voices used in *A Walk in the City* and *Kits Beach Soundwalk*, both imaginative soundscape collages of Vancouver. They form a pair of a sort (a city walk and a beach walk), with Ruebsaat's hard, masculine declamation contrasting sharply with Westerkamp's soft and sharing intimacy.

21. Bright Sheng, "H'un (Lacerations): In Memoriam 1966–1976 for Orchestra," *Perspectives of New Music* 33, nos. 1–2 (1995): 561.

22. Ibid., 596.

23. Douglas Murphy, *The Architecture of Failure* (Winchester, UK: Zero Books, 2012), 119–30.

24. Ibid., 121.

25. Ibid., 122.

26. In more recent Merzbow releases, such as *Bloody Sea* (2006), which is ostensibly a protest against Japanese whaling, this relationship becomes more complex. See Hegarty, *Noise/Music*, 161–5.

CHAPTER 2

1. Timothy Garton Ash, *History of the Present* (New York: Vintage, 2000), xiii.

2. Other coinages—such as "spectralism," New Complexity, and "postminimalism"—featured prominently in the 1990s and 2000s, but on the whole they were terms that applied to older repertories. Other terms, like "alt-," "indie classical," and Kyle Gann's "totalism," emerged later but didn't stick. The terms "holy minimalism" and "spiritual minimalism,"

however, have crossed over from critical shorthand into musicological discourse. See, for example, David Dies, "Defining 'Spiritual Minimalism,'" in *The Ashgate Research Companion to Minimalist and Postminimalist Music*, ed. Keith Potter, Kyle Gann, and Pwyll ap Siôn (Farnham, Surrey: Ashgate, 2013), 315–35.

3. See Dies, "Spiritual Minimalism."

4. Norman Lebrecht, *When the Music Stops: Managers, Maestros and the Corporate Murder of Classical Music* (London: Simon and Schuster, 1996), 291.

5. Quoted in Luke Howard, "Motherhood, 'Billboard,' and the Holocaust: Perceptions and Receptions of Górecki's Symphony No. 3," *Musical Quarterly* 82, no. 1 (1998): 139.

6. Bob Hurwitz, "Recording Górecki's Third Symphony in London, May 1991," *Journal* (blog), *Nonesuch*, June 18, 2008, www.nonesuch.com/journal/recording-gorecki-third-symphony-in-london-may-1991.

7. Luke B. Howard, "'Laying the Foundation': The Reception of Górecki's Third Symphony, 1977–1991," *Polish Music Journal* 6, no. 2 (2003), www.usc.edu/dept/polish_music/PMJ/issue/6.2.03/Howard.html.

8. Paul Jamrozy, "The Inner Sleeve," *Wire*, no. 361 (2014): 74.

9. See Howard, "Laying the Foundation."

10. At its start, the Mercury Music Prize, awarded for the best album of the year, was avowedly eclectic in its shortlists. After 1992, nominations were included for Gavin Bryars's *Jesus' Blood Never Failed Me Yet* (in 1993), Michael Nyman's *The Piano Concerto* (in 1994), James MacMillan's *Seven Last Words from the Cross* (in 1995), Peter Maxwell Davies's *The Beltane Fire/Caroline Mathilde* (in 1996), Tavener's *Syvati* and Mark-Anthony Turnage's *Your Rockaby* (in 1997), and Nicholas Maw's *Violin Concerto* (in 2000). At the time of publication, *Play* (nominated in 2002), by the pianist Joanna MacGregor, was the most recent classical album to be nominated.

11. Quoted in Geoffrey Haydon, *John Tavener: Glimpses of Paradise* (London: Indigo, 1998), 229.

12. ECM Records, "Manfred Eicher in Conversation: Arvo Pärt's 'Tabula rasa,' (ECM Podcast Vol. 1)," November 26, 2014, www.youtube.com/watch?v=eyAR3votpZw.

13. For the original and most complete formulation of classical music as a "museum culture," see Lydia Goehr, *The Imaginary Museum of Musical Works*, rev. ed. (Oxford: Oxford University Press, 2007). For some later elaborations, see Richard Taruskin, "The Pastness of the Present and the Presence of the Past," in *Text and Act: Essays on Music and Performance* (Oxford: Oxford University Press, 1995), 90–154; and Taruskin, *The Oxford History of Western Music* (Oxford: Oxford University Press, 2004), vol. 2, chapter 11, and vol. 3, chapter 13.

14. Quoted in Laura Dolp, "Pärt in the Marketplace," in *The Cambridge Companion to Arvo Pärt*, ed. Andrew Shenton (Cambridge: Cambridge University Press, 2012), 184.

15. Howard, "Motherhood, 'Billboard,' and the Holocaust," 150.

16. Ibid., 152.

17. Bradley Bamberger, "Retail Eagerly Awaits ECM's Arvo Pärt Set," *Billboard* 108, no. 36 (September 7, 1996): 1, 119–20.

18. Wilfrid Mellers, review of *Te Deum, Silouan's Song, Magnificat*, and *Berliner Messe*, by Arvo Pärt, performed by the Estonian Philharmonic Chamber Choir, Tallinn Chamber Orchestra, and Tonu Kaljuste (ECM 1505 439162-2), *Musical Times* 134, no. 1810 (1993): 714.

312 NOTES TO PAGES 34-44

19. For a particularly strong criticism of this function, see David Clarke, "Parting Glances," *Musical Times* 134, no. 1810 (1993): 680–84.

20. Howard suggests this may even have been Pierre Boulez, although this is unsubstantiated. Luke Howard, "Production vs. Reception in Postmodernism: The Górecki Case," in *Postmodern Music/Postmodern Thought*, ed. Judy Lochhead and Joseph Auner (New York: Routledge, 2002), 196.

21. Quoted in Mark Pappenheim, "Master of the Circus," *Independent* (London), November 19, 1993.

22. For uses of Pärt's music in film, see Kaire Maimets-Volt, "Mediating the 'Idea of One': Arvo Pärt's Pre-Existing Music on Film" (PhD diss., Estonian Academy of Music and Theatre, 2009), http://tagg.org/xpdfs/MaimetsVolt%20PhD.pdf; as well as Dolp, "Pärt in the Marketplace."

23. Arved Ashby, *Absolute Music, Mechanical Reproduction* (Berkeley, CA: University of California Press, 2010).

24. Shuhei Hosokawa, "The Walkman Effect," *Popular Music* 4 (1984): 165–80.

25. Ibid., 169–71.

26. Michael Bull, "No Dead Air! The iPod and the Culture of Mobile Listening," *Leisure Studies* 24, no. 4 (2005): 345.

27. Ibid., 344.

28. Brandon LaBelle, *Acoustic Territories: Sound Culture and Everyday Life* (New York and London: Bloomsbury, 2010), 93ff.

29. I am currently the editor of Michel van der Aa's website.

30. The two most prominent channels of this kind are incipitsify and Score Follower; since 2015 these have both been managed by the Massachusetts-based composer Dan Tramte. See http://scorefollower.com.

31. The project's website can be found at www.digitalconcerthall.com/en/home.

32. Marathons vary in length; the longest was given in 2007 and ran for twenty-seven hours.

33. "Bang on a Can Marathon," Bang on a Can, accessed June 20, 2015, www.bangona-can.org/bang_on_a_can_marathon.

34. Julia Wolfe, "Embracing the Clash" (PhD diss., Princeton University, 2012), 3–4.

35. Ibid., 9.

36. Examples include the Elysian String Quartet, the Juice Vocal Ensemble, and percussionist Joby Talbot's ensemble Powerplant.

37. Michael Hewes, "Conducting Space: An Analysis-Based Approach to Spatial Sound Design in Contemporary Chamber Music Performance" (PhD diss., RMIT University, 2013).

38. A second performance, at the Midland Railway Workshops in Perth in 1995, used slightly different timings to correspond with sunset on the first day and sunrise on the last.

39. Domenico de Clario, "Bardo'i-thos-grol," in *The Intertwining—The Chasm: Installation-Performance Works 1994–96*, Domenico de Clario and Liza Lim (Brisbane: Institute of Modern Art, 1998), 39.

40. See "Text Pieces," Amnon Wolman official website, accessed January 9, 2015, www.amnonwolman.org/text-pieces; and John Lely and James Saunders, eds., *Word Events: Perspectives on Verbal Notation* (London: Continuum, 2012), 418–22.

41. Michael Pisaro, Wandelweiser," *erstwords* (blog), September 23, 2009, www.erst-words.blogspot.co.uk/2009/09/wandelweiser.html. See also Richard Barrett, "Construction of *CONSTRUCTION*," 2011, www.richardbarrettmusic.com/CONSTRUCTIONessay.pdf, 451.

42. Unlike some of these other labels, however, Edition Wandelweiser does not make its recordings available through major channels, like Amazon, but exclusively through independent distributors.

43. One exception, and the product of a similarly enduring composer collective, is the music released on Bang on a Can's label, Cantaloupe.

44. Pisaro, "Wandelweiser."

45. Ibid.

46. Joanna Demers, *Listening through the Noise: The Aesthetics of Experimental Electronic Music* (Oxford: Oxford University Press, 2010).

CHAPTER 3

1. Paul Revoir, "Anna Nicole Smith Family May Sue Royal Opera House as Father of Her Daughter Blasts 'Sleazy' Opera," *Daily Mail*, February 18, 2011, www.dailymail.co.uk/tvshowbiz/article-1358034/Anna-Nicole-Smith-family-sue-Royal-Opera-House-father-daughter-blasts-sleazy-opera.html.

2. Attempts have been made, however. See, for example, Ihab Hassan, *The Dismemberment of Orpheus* (Oxford: Oxford University Press, 1971); Charles Jencks, *The Language of Post-Modern Architecture* (New York: Rizzoli, 1977); Jean-François Lyotard, *La condition postmoderne: Rapport sur le savoir* (Paris: Les Éditions de minuit, 1979); and Brian McHale, *Postmodernist Fiction* (London: Methuen, 1987). Specific to music, the best short summary is Jonathan D. Kramer, "The Nature and Origins of Musical Postmodernism," in *Postmodern Music/Postmodern Thought*, ed. Judy Lochhead and Joseph Auner (New York: Routledge, 2002), 13–26.

3. Kramer, "Musical Postmodernism," 17.

4. Rhys Chatham, "Composer's Notebook 1990: Toward a Musical Agenda for the Nineties," Kalvos and Damian: Chronicle of the NonPop Revolution, accessed January 24, 2015, http://kalvos.org/chatess1.html.

5. Other notable contributions include Richard Leppert, *The Sight of Sound: Music, Representation and the History of the Body* (Berkeley, CA: University of California Press, 1993); Philip Brett, Elizabeth Wood, and Gary C. Thomas, eds., *Queering the Pitch: The New Gay and Lesbian Musicology* (New York: Routledge, 1994); and Nicholas Cook, *Beyond the Score: Music as Performance* (New York: Oxford University Press, 2013).

6. It must be noted that McClary's point overlooks the sonic sensuality of Boulez's music, the overt theatre of Stockhausen's, and the sheerly pragmatic fact that most of Cage's early output was written for dance.

7. See Susan McClary, "Terminal Prestige: The Case of Avant-Garde Music Composition," *Cultural Critique*, no. 12 (1989): 57–81.

8. Susan McClary, "Rap, Minimalism, and Structures of Time in Late Twentieth-Century Culture," in *Audio Culture: Readings in Modern Music*, ed. Christoph Cox and Daniel Warner (London: Continuum, 2004), 295.

9. Susan McClary, "Getting Down Off the Beanstalk: The Presence of a Woman's Voice in Janike Vandervelde's *Genesis II*," in *Feminine Endings: Music, Gender, and Sexuality* (Minnesota: University of Minnesota Press, 1991), 113.

10. Robert Fink, *Repeating Ourselves: American Minimal Music as Cultural Practice* (Berkeley, CA: University of California Press, 2005), chapter 1.

11. Freya Jarman, "Relax, Feel Good, Chill Out: The Affective Distribution of Classical Music," in *Sound, Music, Affect: Theorizing Sonic Experience,* ed. Ian Biddle and Marie Thompson (New York: Bloomsbury, 2013), 183–204.

12. See Marius Carboni, "Marketing Strategies in the UK Classical Music Business: An Examination into Changes in the Classical Music Business since 1989" (PhD diss., University of Hertfordshire, 2011).

13. McClary, "Rap, Minimalism, and Structures of Time."

14. Griffiths, *Modern Music and After,* 365.

15. Jonathan D. Kramer, "Bernard Rands's . . . *Body and Shadow* . . . : Modernist, Postmodernist, or Antimodernist," *Contemporary Music Review* 20, no. 4 (2001): 29–43.

16. *Grove Music Online,* s.v. "Neue Einfachheit," by Christopher Fox, accessed September 22, 2015, www.oxfordmusiconline.com.

17. Although minimalism, at least at first, did not draw on past idioms, its development was motivated by a similar desire for expressive directness. See, for example, Steve Reich, "Music as a Gradual Process," in *Writings about Music* (Halifax, NS: Press of Nova Scotia College of Art and Design, 1974), 9–11.

18. Jonathan W. Bernard, "Minimalism, Postminimalism, and the Resurgence of Tonality in Recent American Music," *American Music* 21, no. 1 (2003): 131.

19. The examples are drawn from Bernard, "Minimalism, Postminimalism."

20. Ibid., 118.

21. John Adams, "John Adams on the Chamber Symphony," June 1994, www.earbox.com/chamber-symphony.

22. For a summary and an analysis of serialism's perceived stranglehold, see Joseph N. Straus, "The Myth of Serial 'Tyranny' in the 1950s and 1960s," *Music Quarterly* 83, no. 3 (1999): 301–43.

23. The two clear exceptions are Henry Brant's *Ice Field* for one hundred spatially distributed musicians (2002 prizewinner) and Ornette Coleman's free jazz album *Sound Grammar* (2007 prizewinner, awarded after the prize responded to criticism and broadened its scope beyond European-style art music in 2004). Cases may also be made for a small number of other works, including John Luther Adams's *Become Ocean* (2014 prizewinner), although this piece stretches conventional notions of triadic tonality to the breaking point.

24. These were Joan Tower, for *Silver Ladders* (1986); John Corigliano, for Symphony No. 1 (1989); John Adams, for Violin Concerto (1993); Aaron Jay Kernis for *Colored Field* (1994); George Tsontakis, for Violin Concerto No. 2 (2003); Sebastian Currier, for *Static* (2003); and Peter Lieberson, for *Neruda Songs* (2005). The first Grawemeyer Award was given in 1985, to Witold Lutosławski for his Symphony No. 3 (1981–3).

25. Paul Moravec and Robert Beaser, "Issue Editors' Introduction," *Contemporary Music Review* 6, no. 2 (1992): 3.

26. George Rochberg, "Guston and Me: Digression and Return," *Contemporary Music Review* 6, no. 2 (1992): 7.

27. John Anthony Lennon, "The Daedalian Factor: Tonality, Atonality, or Musicality," *Contemporary Music Review* 6, no. 2 (1992): 24.

28. James Boros, "A 'New Tonality'?" *Perspectives of New Music* 33, nos. 1-2 (1995): 547.

29. Between 1991 and 1995, Garland lived itinerantly. He documented his prolonged round-the-world trip in the two volumes of *Gone Walkabout* (Lebanon, NH: Frog Peak Music, 2004).

30. An example of the Plantron in action can be viewed at https://vimeo.com/41195144.

31. Mamoru Fujieda, "Tuning 'Patterns of Plants,'" in *Arcana*, vol. 4, ed. John Zorn (New York: Hips Road, 2009), 145.

32. See Simon Reynell, "Interview with Laurence Crane," Another Timbre, accessed December 24, 2014, www.anothertimbre.com/craneinterview.html.

33. Michael Pisaro, "Less Than Normal," Another Timbre, December 2013/February 2014, www.anothertimbre.com/laurencecrane.html.

34. This divide is similar to the one the linguist Ferdinand de Saussure draws between *langue* (the rules of a language) and *parole* (the individual, concrete uses of those rules; language as it is actually spoken). See Ferdinand de Saussure, *Course in General Linguistics*, trans. Roy Harris (La Salle, IL: Open Court, 1983).

35. Philip Thomas, "The Music of Laurence Crane and a Post-Experimental Performance Practice," *Tempo* 70, no. 275 (2016): 13.

36. Nick Smith, "The Splinter in Your Ear: Noise as the Semblance of Critique," *Culture, Theory and Critique* 46, no. 1 (2005): 43-59; Novak, *Japanoise*, 134-6. See also Hegarty: *Noise/Music*, 157-8.

37. Marie Thompson, "Music for Cyborgs: The Affect and Ethics of Noise Music," in *Reverberations: The Philosophy, Aesthetics and Politics of Noise*, ed. Michael Goddard, Benjamin Halligan, and Paul Hegarty (London: Continuum, 2012), 211.

38. Aaron Cassidy, "Noise and the Voice: Exploring the Thresholds of Vocal Transgression," in *Noise in and as Music*, ed. Aaron Cassidy and Aaron Einbond (Huddersfield: University of Huddersfield Press, 2013), 33-53.

39. Quoted in Ian Penman, "Matters of Life and Death," *Wire*, nos. 190-91 (2000): 63.

40. Gail Holst-Warhaft, *Dangerous Voices: Women's Laments and Greek Literature* (London: Routledge, 1992), 43.

41. The version recorded to CD omits two parts due to space restrictions and lasts seventy-two minutes. Diamanda Galás, *Plague Mass*, Mute CDSTUMM 83, 1991.

42. Quoted in Dan Warburton, "The Sound of Silence: The Music and Aesthetics of the Wandelweiser Group," Paris Transatlantic, July 2006, www.paristransatlantic.com/magazine/monthly2006/07jul_text.html.

43. The score of *Metamusica* can be downloaded from Sergei Letov's Moscow Conceptualism website at www.conceptualism.letov.ru/sergei-zagny/Scores/008-Metamusica.pdf.

44. Günter Mayer, "Advanced Composition and Critical (Political) Ambition," in *New Music and Aesthetics in the 21st Century*, vol. 5, *Critical Composition Today*, ed. Claus-Steffen Mahnkopf (Hofheim: Wolke Verlag, 2006), 182.

45. http://ablinger.mur.at.

46. Peter Ablinger, "STÜHLE / CHAIRS," note on the chair pieces, last modified August 19, 2007, http://ablinger.mur.at/docu01.html.

47. Warren Burt, "Ways of Listening," *Warren Burt* (blog), 2009, www.warrenburt.com/ways_of_listening.

48. David Dunn, *Purposeful Listening in Complex States of Time*, 1997–8, www.warrenburt.com/storage/ways_of_listening/Plicsot.pdf, preface to score.

49. Westerkamp, "Soundwalking."

50. The term is from David Dunn, "The Sound of Light in Trees: The Acoustic Ecology of Pinyon Pines," Acoustic Ecology Institute, accessed August 24, 2015, www.acousticecology.org/dunn/solitsounds.html. This webpage also hosts some of the source sounds Dunn used.

51. Dunn, *Purposeful Listening*.

52. David Graeber, "Of Flying Cars and the Declining Rate of Profit," *Baffler*, no. 19 (2012), www.thebaffler.com/salvos/of-flying-cars-and-the-declining-rate-of-profit.

53. Richard Witts and Rob Young, "Stockhausen vs. the 'Technocrats,'" *Wire*, no. 141 (November 1995): 32–5.

54. Aphex Twin, "Raising the Titanic (Big Drum Mix)," Point Music PRO-1187, 1995.

55. Aphex Twin, "Heroes Remix," Point Music SADP-5, 1997.

56. Björk has also performed a cover of *Gotham Lullaby*, by the minimalist composer and vocalist Meredith Monk (b. 1942). A joint interview with both women, conducted by the pianist Sarah Cahill, may be found at "Radical Connections: Meredith Monk and Björk," *NewMusicBox*, March 16, 2007, www.newmusicbox.org/articles/radical-connections-meredith-monk-and-bjork.

57. Reich had in fact intended to write for Radiohead before this, with *2x5* (2009), but the idea proved unworkable, and he revisited it as a piece for the Bang on a Can All-Stars instead.

58. Simon Reynolds, "Shaking the Rock Narcotic," *Wire*, no. 123 (1994): 28–35.

59. "About," New Amsterdam Records, accessed February 14, 2016, www.newamrecords.com/about.

60. David K. Israel, "How to Start a Record Label, with New Amsterdam Records," mental_floss, May 5, 2009, www.mentalfloss.com/article/21631/how-start-record-label-new-amsterdam-records.

61. Burkhard Beins, Christian Kesten, Gisela Nauck, and Andrea Neumann, eds., *Echtzeitmusik Berlin: Self-Defining a Scene* (Hofheim: Wolke Verlag, 2011).

62. The exact relationship of influence between popular music and minimalism is complex, however. Undoubtedly there are many popular artists, from The Who ("Baba O'Riley," 1971), to David Bowie ("Weeping Wall," 1977), to Orbital ("Kein Trink Wasser," 1994), who have directly and indirectly made references to minimalist sounds and techniques. However, minimalism's roots lie equally in 1960s jazz and blues, and later composers, including Louis Andriessen, the Bang on a Can trio, Rhys Chatham, Elodie Lauten (1950–2014), Graham Fitkin (b. 1963), and Tristan Perich (b. 1982), have themselves drawn equally on contemporary popular styles of funk, rock, and electronica. For more on this chain of connections, see Jonathan W. Bernard, "Minimalism and Pop: Influence, Reaction, Consequences," in *The Ashgate Research Companion to Minimalist and Postminimalist Music*, ed. Keith Potter, Kyle Gann, and Pwyll ap Siôn (Farnham, Surrey: Ashgate, 2013), 337–56; and Tim Rutherford-Johnson, "The Influence Engine: Steve Reich and Pop Music," *NewMusicBox*, March 27, 2013, www.newmusicbox.org/articles/the-influence-engine-steve-reich-and-pop-music.

63. See Madvillain's "America's Most Blunted" (2004); Nero's "Choices" (2008); Tortoise's "Djed (Bruise Blood Mix)" (1996); and Yokota's "Gekkoh" (2000).

64. In this paragraph and those that follow, I am deliberately (if anachronistically) limiting my discussion to composers of music primarily conceived for the concert hall. Many composers working more in the fields of sound art or recorded media have also had their work remixed, but in those fields the concept of *Werktreue* is less important, and often almost irrelevant, and the number of possible examples is so long as to make the practice trivial.

65. Jimi Tenor, "Deutsche Grammophon Recomposed: Track by Track with Jimi Tenor," accessed September 8, 2016, www.jimitenor.com/recomposed_tbt.html.

66. Examples include Murcof and DJ Spooky.

67. For more on this work, see chapter 6.

68. Max Nyffeler, "Robert HP Platz," publisher's profile, G. Ricordi und Co. Bühnen- und Musikverlag, accessed August 24, 2015, http://www.ricordi.de/~/media/Files/PDF/Ricordi/Background%20Information/Platz/Website_Portrait_Platz_englisch.pdf.

CHAPTER 4

1. This does not mean that such claims aren't sometimes made. Mathias Spahlinger's *Farben der Frühe* (2005), for seven pianos, supposedly contains a quotation from Chopin composed of a single, low Db.

2. CD quality sound, for example, has 44,100 samples per second.

3. It also exemplifies the mediated nature of much contemporary music. Although conceived as a live performance work, *Up-close* perhaps works best in its recording for DVD, as no other live stage will quite match that used in the work's filmed segments and hence be able to fully articulate the visual echo that is inherent in the work.

4. Among the more involved examples of such work is Gerhard E. Winkler's interactive opera *Heptameron* (2002), composed using video tracking and sensor technology developed at the IMA to generate score, lighting, and scenic projections in real time from movements on stage.

5. The website's usefulness is reflected in the title of the very first of the *Popular Contexts* pieces, *Free Sound* (2010), for piano and sampler.

6. Bauman's bibliography is vast, but see in particular *Liquid Modernity* (Cambridge: Polity, 2000), *Liquid Life* (Cambridge: Polity, 2005), and *Culture in a Liquid Modern World* (Cambridge: Polity, 2011).

7. Bauman, *Liquid Life*, 8.

8. Bourriaud outlines this aesthetic most fully in *The Radicant* (New York: Lukas and Sternberg, 2009), building on his earlier studies *Relational Aesthetics* (Dijon: Les presses du réel, 2002) and *Post-Production* (New York: Lukas and Sternberg, 2002). *The Radicant* itself may be seen as a step toward a wider-reaching theory of post-postmodern artistic production, which Bourriaud termed the "altermodern" and expanded as the theme of the 2009 Tate Triennial exhibition.

9. Bourriaud, *Radicant*, 133–4.

10. These documentaries are available to watch online: "Rolf Borch Learning to Skateboard," February 18, 2010, www.vimeo.com/9565336; and "Øyvind Skarbø Learning to Skateboard," January 28, 2011, www.vimeo.com/19314102.

11. Richard Beaudoin and Joseph Moore, "Conceiving Musical Transdialection," *Journal of Aesthetics and Art Criticism* 68, no. 2 (2010): 105–17.

12. The LARA software is available for free download at www.hslu.ch/musik/m-forschung-entwicklung/m-forschung-lara.htm.

13. Some of Kilchenmann and Senn's analysis of the Argerich recording has been published as "Expressive Timing: Martha Argerich Plays Chopin's Prelude Op. 28/4 in E Minor," in *Proceedings of the International Symposium on Performance Science*, ed. A. Williamson, S. Pretty, and R. Buck (Utrecht: European Association of Conservatoires, 2009).

14. Danick Trottier, "Conceiving Musical Photorealism: An Interview with Richard Beaudoin," *Perspectives of New Music* 51, no. 1 (2013): 180.

15. For an extended analysis of Neuwirth's opera, see David Metzer, *Musical Modernism at the Turn of the Twenty-First Century* (Cambridge: Cambridge University Press, 2009), 221–36.

16. I am grateful to Richard Barrett for this insight.

17. Aaron Cassidy, program note for *The Crutch of Memory* (2004), accessed December 5, 2015, www.aaroncassidy.com/music/crutchofmemory.htm.

18. Stefan Prins, program note for *Generation Kill* (2012), accessed February 3, 2016, www.stefanprins.be/eng/composesChrono/comp_2012_03.html.

19. Quoted in Stefan Prins, program note for *Generation Kill, Donaueschinger Muskitage 2012*, NEOS 11303–05, 2013, p. 39.

20. Frank J. Oteri, interview by Carl Stone, *NewMusicBox*, November 1, 2000, www.newmusicbox.org/articles/carl-stone-intellectual-property-artistic-license-and-free-access-to-information-in-the-age-of-samplebased-music-and-the-internet.

21. Kyle Gann, "Plundering for Art: Sampling," in *Music Downtown: Writings from the Village Voice* (Berkeley, CA: University of California Press, 2006), 73.

22. This is a slight simplification. In fact, Stone has divided his source into eight sections, which he overlaps at staggered time intervals.

23. David Henry Hwang, quoted in Ping-hui Liao, "From Multicultural to Creole Subjects: David Henry Hwang's Collaborative Works with Philip Glass," in *The Creolization of Theory*, ed. Françoise Lionnet and Shu-Mei Shih (Durham, NC: Duke University Press, 2011), 143.

24. Another notable composer working in this way was Paul Panhuysen (1934–2015).

25. Bauman, *Liquid Life*, 82.

CHAPTER 5

1. Novak, *Japanoise*.

2. Richard A. Rogers, "From Cultural Exchange to Transculturation: A Review and Reconceptualization of Cultural Appropriation," *Communication Theory* 16, no. 4 (2006): 474–503.

3. See Bourriaud, *Radicant*; Okwui Enwezor, "History Lessons," *Artforum* 46, no. 1 (2007): 382; Tim Griffin, "Worlds Apart: Contemporary Art, Globalization, and the Rise of Biennials," in *Contemporary Art: 1989 to the Present*, ed. Alexander Dumbadze and Suzanne Hudson (Chichester, West Sussex: Wiley and Sons, 2013), 7–14; and Peter Weibel, "Globalization and Contemporary Art," in *The Global Contemporary and the Rise of New Art Worlds*, ed. Hans Belting, Andrea Buddensieg, and Peter Weibel (Karlsruhe: ZKM Center for Art and Media, 2013), 20–26.

4. Nicolas Bourriaud, *Relational Aesthetics*, trans. Simon Pleasance and Fronza Woods (Dijon: Les presses du réel, 2002).

5. Silk Road Project, accessed June 22, 2015, www.silkroadproject.org.

6. Ibid.

7. Alex Ross, "Yo-Yo Ma: The Rest Is Noise Interview," *The Rest is Noise* (blog), September 20, 2007, www.therestisnoise.com/2007/09/yo-yo-ma-the-re.html.

8. Rogers, "Cultural Exchange," 479.

9. Mari Yoshihara, *Musicians from a Different Shore: Asians and Asian Americans in Classical Music* (Philadelphia: Temple University Press, 2007), 16.

10. Ibid., 18.

11. Ibid., 33.

12. East Asian instrument manufacturing—particularly of pianos, by firms such as Yamaha—also helped switch this flow. See ibid., 33–4.

13. Quoted in Thomas Burkhalter, *Local Music Scenes and Globalization: Transnational Platforms in Beirut* (New York: Routledge, 2013), 5.

14. Thomas Burkhalter, "Multisited Avant-Gardes or World Music 2.0? Musicians from Beirut and Beyond between Local Production and Euro-American Reception," in *The Arab Avant-Garde: Music, Politics, Modernity*, ed. Thomas Burkhalter, Kay Dickinson, and Benjamin J. Harbert (Middletown, CT: Wesleyan University Press, 2013), 96.

15. Quoted in Nana Asfour, "Tarek Atoui: Visiting Tarab," *New Yorker*, November 4, 2011.

16. Juan A. Gaitán, *8. Berlin-Biennale für Zeitgenössische Kunst* (Ostfildern: Hatje/Cantz, 2014), 78.

17. A significant exception is the concerto for sheng, a Chinese mouth organ, *Šu* (2009).

18. "Unsuk Chin Interview: Daring to Cross Many Boundaries," *US Asians* (blog), accessed September 22, 2015, http://usasians-articles.tripod.com/unsuk-chin-music-compositions.html.

19. Yoshihara, *Different Shore*, 219.

20. Laura Battle, "Music Is Music," *Financial Times*, August 1, 2009.

21. Hee Yun Kim, "The Act of Singing: A Study of Unsuk Chin's "Cantatrix Sopranica" for Two Sopranos, Countertenor, and Ensemble" (PhD diss., University of Illinois at Urbana-Champaign, 2008), 6.

22. Shayna Silverstein, "Transforming Space: The Production of Contemporary Syrian Art Music," in Burkhalter, Dickinson, Harbert, *Arab Avant-Garde*, 37–73.

23. Ricardo Dal Farra, "Something Lost, Something Hidden, Something Found: Electroacoustic Music by Latin American Composers," *Organised Sound* 11, no 2 (2006): 131–42.

24. Miwon Kwon, *One Place after Another: Site-Specific Art and Locational Identity* (Cambridge, MA: MIT Press, 2004), 46.

25. See Marina Peterson, "Sonic Cosmopolitanisms: Experimental Improvised Music and a Lebanese-American Cultural Exchange," in Burkhalter, Dickinson, and Harbert, *Arab Avant-Garde*, 185–6.

26. Burkhalter, "Multisited Avant-Gardes," 99. See also Peterson, "Sonic Cosmopolitanisms."

27. Kwon, *One Place*, 31.

28. George Lewis compares Z's work to that of the West African griot, a sort of oral historian, musician, poet, and storyteller, whose practice of "signification" is an ancestor of

all these musics. Lewis, "The Virtual Discourses of Pamela Z," in *Diaspora Memory Place*, ed. Salah M. Hassan and Cheryl Finley (Munich: Prestel, 2008), 268. See also Henry Louis Gates Jr., *The Signifying Monkey* (Oxford: Oxford University Press, 1988); and Dick Hebdige *Cut 'n' Mix* (London: Methuen, 1987).

29. We might also read in it a racial critique, in which intersections between location and property rights take on a whole new set of meanings within the history of slavery.

30. Remarkably, however, *Interference is* being taken up by a slowly growing number of clarinetists, including Richard Haynes, another ELISION alumnus.

31. Nicholas Cook, *Beyond the Score: Music as Performance* (Oxford: Oxford University Press, 2013), chapter 8, 273ff.

32. Richard Barrett and Arne Deforce, "The Resonant Box with Four Strings: Interview on the Musical Esthetics of Richard Barrett and the Genesis of his Music for Cello," September 2000–February 2001, www.issuu.com/arnedeforce/docs/the_resonant_box_with_four_strings.

33. Barrett, quoted in liner notes for Richard Toop, *Negatives*, NMC D143, 2009.

34. *CONSTRUCTION* has had just one performance, at the 2011 Huddersfield Contemporary Music Festival; no others were projected at the time of writing (2016).

35. Richard Barrett, "Construction of *CONSTRUCTION*," 2011, www.richardbarrettmusic.com/CONSTRUCTIONessay.pdf.

36. Ibid.

37. Alvin Curran, "Nineteen Eighty Five—A Piece for Peace," accessed June 22, 2015, www.alvincurran.com/writings/1985.html.

38. Ibid.

39. Á. Barbosa, "Displaced Soundscapes: A Survey of Network Systems for Music and Sonic Art Creation," *Leonardo Music Journal* 13 (2003): 53–9.

40. Randall Packer, "Composing with Media: Zero in Time and Space," *Contemporary Music Review* 24, no. 6 (2005): 513.

41. See Pierre Lévy, "The Art and Architecture of Cyberspace: Collective Intelligence," in *Multimedia: From Wagner to Virtual Reality*, ed. R. Packer and K. Jordan (New York: Norton, 2001), 370–79.

42. Packer, "Composing with Media," 524.

43. This exchange, and extracts from the first performance, is documented at "Fremdarbeit—by Johannes Kreidler Doku," November 26, 2009, www.youtube.com/watch?v=L72d_ozIToc.

44. See Martin Iddon, "Outsourcing Progress: On Conceptual Music," *Tempo* 70, no. 275 (2015): 36–49.

45. Ibid., 48.

46. Alan Hilario, composer's program note (my translation) for *phonautograph* (2002), October 2, 2002, www.swr.de/swr2/festivals/donaueschingen/programme/2002/werke/hilario-alan-phonautograph/-/id=2136806/did=3329804/nid=2136806/1bfzfyv/index.html.

47. A Korean equivalent to Turkmani may be Hwang Byungki, another contemporary composer to work in a wholly traditional idiom—in this case the Korean instrumental genre of *kayagŭm sanjo*. See Andrew Killich, *Hwang Byungki: Traditional Music and the Contemporary Composer in the Republic of Korea* (Aldershot: Ashgate, 2013).

48. Quoted in Tim Griffin, "Worlds Apart: Contemporary Art, Globalization, and the Rise of Biennials," in Dumbadze and Hudson, *Contemporary Art*, 11.

49. Described in Griffin, "Worlds Apart," 11–13.

50. Philip Clark, "Manufacturing Dissent," *Wire*, no. 220 (2002): 34.

51. Werder has repeated this model in his performer series (1999) of works for one to nine performers, each consisting of four thousand pages of music.

52. This list can be found at www.stuck1998.blogspot.co.uk.

53. After the series was completed, in 2009, Saunders went on to create fixed versions of some iterations of the piece under the title *assigned*.

54. Seth Kim-Cohen, *Brevity Is a Sol LeWitt*, score, 2007, www.kim-cohen.com/Assets/Texts/Kim-Cohen_Brevity%20Is%20A%20Sol%20LeWitt%20(2007).pdf.

55. Lim's first three operas are *The Oresteia* (1991–3), *Yuè Lìng Jié* (Moon Spirit Feasting, 1991–9), and *The Navigator* (2008). She is married to ELISION's artistic director, Daryl Buckley.

56. Liza Lim, "A Mycelial Model for Understanding Distributed Creativity: Collaborative Partnership in the Making of *Axis Mundi* (2013) for Solo Bassoon," CMPCP Performance Studies Network Second International Conference, Cambridge, UK, April 4–7, 2013, p. 12.

57. Howard Morphy, *Ancestral Connections: Art and an Aboriginal System of Knowledge* (Chicago: University of Chicago Press, 1991).

58. Ibid., 194.

59. Liza Lim, interview by the author, Paris, December 9, 2009.

60. Christopher Alexander, Murray Silverstein, and Sara Ishikawa, *A Pattern Language* (Oxford: Oxford University Press, 1977). See also www.patternlanguage.com.

61. Lim, interview, 2009.

62. Liza Lim, *Invisibility* (Munich: Ricordi, 2009), preface.

63. See Finnissy's website: www.michaelfinnissy.info.

64. Christopher Fox, "Michael Finnissy's *History of Photography in Sound*: Under the Lens," *Musical Times* 143, no. 1879 (2002): 27.

65. The borrowed melody is from "My Bonny Boy." The same tune is used in the second movement of Ralph Vaughan Williams's *English Folk Song Suite* (1923).

66. Quoted in Richard Beaudoin and Joseph Moore, "Conceiving Musical Transdialection," *Journal of Aesthetics and Art Criticism* 68, no. 2 (2010): 110.

67. The alternative term "musical transdialection" has been suggested by analogy with dialectical translations of religious texts into contemporary language. Beaudoin and Moore, "Musical Transdialection."

68. Ian Pace, "The Piano Music," in *Uncommon Ground: The Music of Michael Finnissy*, ed. Henrietta Brougham, Christopher Fox, and Ian Pace (Aldershot: Ashgate, 1997), 94.

69. Beaudoin and Moore, "Musical Transdialection."

70. Pace, "Piano Music," 80.

71. In his preface to the score, Finnissy refers to "a 'respectable' Victorian mantleshelf, spineless and domesticated."

72. Maarten Beirens, "Archaeology of the Self: Michael Finnissy's 'Folklore,'" *Tempo* 57, no. 223 (2003): 48.

73. The architect Rem Koolhaas has referred to a similar concept, which he terms the "bigness" of a building. Rem Koolhaas, "Bigness (or the Problem of Large)," in *S, M, L, XL* (New York: Monacelli Press, 1994), 494–516.

74. Compare Feldman's remark about very long pieces of music: "Up to one hour you think about form, but after an hour and a half it's scale. Form is easy—just the division of things into parts. But scale is another matter." Quoted in Griffiths, *Modern Music and After*, 280.

75. Koolhaas, "Bigness."

CHAPTER 6

1. These requirements are dwarfed by those of multiseries TV blockbusters.

2. Robin Maconie, *Other Planets: The Music of Karlheinz Stockhausen* (Lanham, MD: Scarecrow Press, 2005), 516.

3. Ashley has likened this to "a TV series without a name." Quoted in Thom Holmes, "Built for Speed," *Wire*, no. 234 (2003): 30.

4. Nicolas Bourriaud, *Relational Aesthetics*.

5. Anthon Vidler, "'Building in Empty Space': Daniel Libeskind's Museum of the Voice," in *Daniel Libeskind: The Space of Encounter*, by Daniel Libeskind (London: Thames and Hudson), 222.

6. "Kinsale Arts Week 2007," press release, June 25, 2007, www.corkgigs.com/news/2007/06/kinsale-arts-week-2007.

7. Olivia Kelleher, "Arts Festival's Tribute to Brave Fishermen Who Perished at Sea," *Independent* (Dublin), July 9, 2007.

8. Few of these works have been conducted on the same scale as *Maritime Rites*.

9. Thames Festival website, accessed February 25, 2014, www.thamesfestival.org/about.

10. "Tempelhof Broadcast: What's the Music? Part 1," January 14, 2014, www.vimeo.com/57372658.

11. B. Joseph Pine II and James H. Gilmore, *The Experience Economy: Work Is Theater and Every Business a Stage* (Boston: Harvard Business School Press, 1999). See also Jennifer Radbourne, Hilary Glow, and Katya Johnson, eds., *The Audience Experience: A Critical Analysis of Audiences in the Performing Arts* (Bristol: Intellect, 2013).

12. Herman Sabbe, "A Philosophy of Tonality," in *Contemporary Music*, ed. Max Paddison and Irène Deliege (Farnham: Ashgate, 2010), 175.

13. Tom Coult, "Pierre Boulez's 'Sur Incises': Refraction, Crystallisation and the Absent Idea(l)," *Tempo* 67, no. 264 (2013): 7. Coult's article details Boulez's various other methods of expansion, which include pitch rotations and harmonic multiplication.

14. See Wolfgang Fink, "Metamorphoses of Solo Music in Three Works by Pierre Boulez," liner notes for *Boulez: Sur Incises*, Deutsche Grammophon, DG CD 463 475-2, 2000.

15. Quoted in Coult, "Pierre Boulez's 'Sur Incises,'" 5.

16. Alan E. Williams, "Kurtág, Modernity, Modernisms," *Contemporary Music Review* 20, nos. 2–3 (2001): 67.

17. Ferneyhough's long list of students includes: Toshio Hosokawa, Klaus K. Hübler, Roger Redgate, and Kaija Saariaho at Freiburg; Mark Applebaum, Chaya Czernowin, and

Franklin Cox at San Diego; and Ching-Wen Chao, Kristian Ireland, Timothy McCormack, and Matthew Shlomowitz at Stanford. For an appraisal of Ferneyhough's methods, see Roger Redgate, "Ferneyhough as Teacher," *Contemporary Music Review* 13, no. 1 (1995): 19–21.

18. Richard Toop, "Four Facets of the New Complexity," *Contact*, no. 32 (1988): 4–50.

19. Brian Ferneyhough, "Incipits (1996)," composer's note, accessed February 16, 2016, www.editionpeters.com/resources/0001/stock/pdf/incipits.pdf.

20. Ferneyhough, quoted in Richard Toop, liner notes for Brian Ferneyhough, *Terrain*, ELISION Ensemble, KAIROS 0013072KAI, 2010.

21. Evan Johnson, composer's program note for *vo mesurando* (2012), accessed November 29, 2015, www.evanjohnson.info/multiple-voices-choral-works.

22. Claus-Steffen Mahnkopf, "Hommage à Thomas Pynchon," in *New Music and Aesthetics in the 21st Century*, vol. 4, *Electronics in New Music*, ed. Claus-Steffen Mahnkopf, Franklin Cox, and Wolfram Schurig (Hofheim: Wolke Verlag, 2006), 101.

23. Ibid.

24. Ibid.

25. Ibid., 138.

26. Mahnkopf has himself written about the construction of the work at more length in Mahnkopf, "Hommage à Thomas Pynchon." See also Claus-Steffen Mahnkopf, "*The Courier's Tragedy*: Strategies for a Deconstructive Morphology," in *New Music and Aesthetics in the 21st Century*, vol. 2, *Musical Morphology*, ed. Claus-Steffen Mahnkopf, Franklin Cox, and Wolfram Schurig (Hofheim: Wolke Verlag, 2004), 146–61; and Claus-Steffen Mahnkopf, "Technik und moderne Musik," in *Musik–Technik–Philosophie: Fragen und Positionen*, ed. Christoph Lütge and Torsten L. Meyer (Freiburg: Alber, 2005).

27. An extensive critique of this period can be found in Georgina Born, *Rationalizing Culture: IRCAM, Boulez, and the Institutionalization of the Musical Avant-Garde* (Berkeley, CA: University of California Press, 1995).

28. Louis Ferdinand, "Review: IRCAM, les années 90," *Computer Music Journal* 23, no. 3 (1999): 104–6.

29. A collection of interviews with artists who use Max/MSP can be found at www.cycling74.com/category/interview.

30. Johannes Goebel, "The ZKM Institute for Music and Acoustics up to 2002: Politics, Context and Foundations," *Organised Sound* 14, no. 3 (2009): 238.

31. Tara Rodgers, "Laetitia Sonami," in *Pink Noises* (Durham, NC: Duke University Press, 2010), 226–34.

32. Bauman, *Liquid Life*, 84.

33. JLIAT, "Un-Sounding Music: Noise Is Not Sound," in *Noise in and as Music*, ed. Aaron Cassidy and Aaron Einbond (Huddersfield: Huddersfield University Press, 2013), 28.

34. JLIAT, "All Possible CDs," accessed July 29, 2015, www.jliat.com/APCDS/index.html.

35. The "quantum of time," the amount of time it would take a proton to travel the distance of a Planck length at light speed, is the shortest possible distance of length.

36. JLIAT, "The Shortest Piece of Music," February 2014, www.jliat.com/TSPM.pdf.

37. JLIAT, "1 TB Noise," accessed July 28, 2015, www.jliat.com/n1tb.

38. See Martin Pesch, "Transfer and Transformation: Strategies in the Oeuvre of Carsten Nicolai," *Parachute*, no. 107 (2002): 80–93.

39. Curtis Roads, "The Art of Articulation: The Electroacoustic Music of Horacio Vaggione," *Contemporary Music Review* 24, nos. 4–5 (2005): 301.

40. Curtis Roads, *Microsound* (Cambridge, MA: MIT Press, 2001).

41. Roads, "Art of Articulation," 323.

42. Ibid., 303.

43. This was the title of a 2007 documentary about the piece made by cellist Neil Heyde, composer Paul Archibold, and filmmaker Colin Still.

44. David Lang, "Concerto (*world to come*) (2003)," composer's note, accessed February 12, 2016, www.musicsalesclassical.com/composer/work/44270.

45. Salvatore Sciarrino, "Nota dell'autore" (program note, author's translation), accessed July 29, 2015, www.salvatoresciarrino.eu/Data/Catalogo/Il_cerchio_tagliato_dei_suoni.html.

46. Cited in Tom Service, "Sax It Up," *Guardian* (London), August 19, 2004.

47. Mahnkopf, "Hommage à Thomas Pynchon," 101.

48. Marko Ciciliani, "Molding the Pop Ghost: Noise and Immersion," in *Noise in and as Music*, ed. Aaron Cassidy and Aaron Einbond (Huddersfield: University of Huddersfield Press, 2013), 195.

49. Ashley Fure, composer's statement, accessed February 24, 2016, www.ashleyfure.net.

50. Lisa Streich, composer's program note for *Pietà 1*, accessed February 24, 2016, www.lisastreich.se.

51. A second version of the piece, *ricefall (2)*, uses sixty-four recorded tracks of rice falling to create a dense and immersive sonic atmosphere.

52. I am grateful to Jennie Gottschalk for this observation.

53. These pieces are showcased on Judy Dunaway, *Ballon Music*, Composers Recordings, CD778, 1998; and Dunaway, *Mother of Balloon Music*, innova, 648, 2006.

54. These performances are documented under "Great Fences" at www.jonroseweb.com/f_projects_great_fences.html.

55. A video of this piece, performed by Jason Bauers and Robert Fullex, can be viewed at www.youtube.com/watch?v=WUwH9GMeFJg.

56. See "*object network* (2012)," accessed August 2, 2015, www.james-saunders.com/composing-2/object-network-2012.

57. Kim Cascone, "The Aesthetics of Failure: 'Post-Digital' Tendencies in Contemporary Computer Music," *Computer Music Journal* 24, no. 4 (2000): 12–18.

58. Ibid., 13.

59. See Caleb Kelly, *Cracked Media: The Sound of Malfunction* (Cambridge, MA: MIT Press, 2009).

CHAPTER 7

1. Benoit Mandelbrot, *The Fractal Geometry of Nature* (San Francisco: W. H. Freeman, 1982).

2. See also Bernhard Lang's *Monadologies*, discussed in chapter 8.

3. An aural effect analogous to a rotating barber's pole in which a sense of continuously descending pitch is created by fading in the upper partials of a descending glissando while fading out the lower ones.

4. Robert Hasegawa, "Clashing Harmonic Systems in Haas's *Blumenstück* and *in vain*," *Music Theory Spectrum* 37, no. 2 (2015): 204–23.

5. Joshua Fineberg, "Spectral Music," *Contemporary Music Review* 19, no. 2 (2000): 2.

6. The term was coined by the comedian Patton Oswalt. See Patton Oswalt, "Wake Up, Geek Culture. Time to Die," *Wired*, December 27, 2010, www.wired.com/2010/12/ff_angrynerd_geekculture.

7. The media ruin is an even more prominent topic within popular music, where the recording medium is a more central part of the creative process. "Lo-fi" music and "hauntology" are just two trends that might be understood within this framework.

8. Quoted in Dave Heaton, "Portrait of Decay: Bill Morrison on *Decasia*," *erasing clouds*, no. 13 (2003), www.erasingclouds.com/02april.html.

9. "Michael Gordon: *Decasia*," Bang on a Can, accessed August 9, 2014, www.bangona-can.org/store/music/decasia.

10. Quoted in Heaton, "Portrait of Decay."

11. See David Metzer, *Musical Modernism at the Turn of the Twenty-First Century* (Cambridge: Cambridge University Press, 2009), chapter 4; and Richard Steinitz, *György Ligeti: Music of the Imagination* (London: Faber, 2003), 294–9.

12. This work features six ruined pianos, from the Alice Springs and Murchison areas; coincidentally, one of them is the same piano featured in *Nallan Void*.

13. Quoted in Linda Ioanna Kouvaras, *Loading the Silence: Australian Sound Art in the Post-Digital Age* (Farnham, Surrey: Ashgate, 2013), 195.

14. Jeck also featured as a turntablist in the 2005 performance of Gavin Bryars's *The Sinking of the Titanic*.

15. The best of these is probably *Requiem 77* (2012), for cello (or alto saxophone) and recording.

16. I discuss this piece in more depth in chapter 8.

17. John Doran, "Time Becomes a Loop: William Basinski Interviewed," *Quietus*, November 15, 2012, www.thequietus.com/articles/10680-william-basinski-disintegration-loops-interview.

18. Ibid.

19. Marc Weidenbaum, "In the Echo of No Towers," *Disquiet* (blog), accessed May 31, 2014, www.disquiet.com/2011/09/08/stephen-vitiello-wtc-911-floyd.

20. For more on audification, see Florian Dombois and Gerhard Eckel, "Audification," in *The Sonification Handbook*, ed. Thomas Hermann, Andy Hunt, and John G. Neuhoff (Berlin: Logos Publishing House, 2011), 301–24.

21. Mark Bain, "StartEndTime: The sound of the ground vibrations during the collapse of the World Trade Center," September 11, 2011, www.archive.org/details/Startendtime-the-SoundOfTheGroundVibrationsDuringTheCollapseOfThe.

22. John Corigliano, composer's program note for Symphony No. 1 (1988), accessed September 21, 2016, www.johncorigliano.com/index.php?p=item2&sub=cat&item=13.

23. Anne Midgette, "9/11 Commemorative Music Should Do More Than Comfort," *Washington Post*, August 27, 2011.

24. "Steve Reich—WTC 9/11: About Project," Kronos Quartet, accessed February 26, 2016, www.kronosquartet.org/projects/detail/steve_reich_new_work.

25. Among them is the composer David Lang, a resident of lower Manhattan, whose words "world to come" became the title of a piece of his own; see chapter 6.

26. Robert Fink, "Going with the Flow: Minimalism as Cultural Practice in the USA since 1945," in *The Ashgate Research Companion to Minimalist and Postminimalist Music*, ed. Keith Potter, Kyle Gann, and Pwyll ap Siôn (Farnham, Surrey: Ashgate, 2013), 201–18.

27. There is a striking parallel here with Brian Ferneyhough's thoughts on the relationship between material and form; see chapter 6.

28. John Adams, *Hallelujah Junction* (New York: Farrar, Straus, and Giroux, 2008), 260.

29. John Corigliano, composer's program note for *One Sweet Morning* (2010), accessed May 1, 2014, www.johncorigliano.com/index.php?p=item2&sub=cat&item=120.

30. Carson's book has been commemorated musically in Steven Stucky's symphonic poem *Silent Spring* (2011), which was composed to mark the book's fiftieth anniversary.

31. The concept of deep ecology was first formulated in Arne Naess, "The Shallow and the Deep, Long-Range Ecology Movement," *Inquiry* 16 (1973): 95–100.

32. The Gaia hypothesis was first formulated in James E. Lovelock and Lynn Margulis, "Atmospheric Homeostasis by and for the Biosphere: The Gaia Hypothesis," *Tellus* 26, nos. 1–2 (1974): 2–10.

33. Bill McKibben, *The End of Nature* (New York: Random House, 1989).

34. David Dunn, "Nature, Sound Art, and the Sacred," in *The Book of Music and Nature*, ed. David Rothenburg and Marta Ulvaeus (Middletown, CT: Wesleyan University Press, 2001), 103.

35. Quoted in Francisco López, "Blind Listening," in *The Book of Music and Nature*, ed. David Rothenburg and Marta Ulvaeus (Middletown, CT: Wesleyan University Press, 2001), 166.

36. Francisco López, "Environmental Sound Matter," liner notes for *La Selva: Sound Environments from a Neotropical Rain Forest*, V2_Archief V228, 1998. Also available at www.franciscolopez.net/env.html (accessed February 12, 2016).

37. Ibid.

38. Kyle Gann has said that Adams "may be one of the most self-consciously regional musicians." See Kyle Gann, "John Luther Adams: Music as a Geography of the Spiritual," in *Winter Music: Composing the North*, by John Luther Adams (Middletown, CT: Wesleyan University Press, 2004), xiii.

39. Pink noise is similar to white noise, but its higher frequencies are progressively reduced in volume so that they sound more evenly across the whole audible spectrum. It sounds more "natural" to the ear than true white noise—more like the sea than the hiss of an untuned television.

40. John Luther Adams, "A Composer's Journal Part II—Studio Notes," in *The Place Where You Go to Listen* (Middletown, CT: Wesleyan, 2009): 31, 37–8; and Adams, "Afterword," in *The Place Where You Go to Listen*, 141–2. Adams's work was to have been called *Sila: The Breath of the World*, a title he in fact used in 2014 for a work for sixteen to eighty musicians, which premiered at Lincoln Center in New York.

41. Had it been realized, this would have been an unusual example of a telematic installation of the sort discussed in chapter 5, in which the connections between sites were not made by communications technology but by changes in the Earth's plate tectonics, magnetic field, and climate.

42. See Marc Augé, *Non-Places: An Introduction to Supermodernity* (London: Verso, 2008), 66–7.

43. Volker Straebel, "The Sonification Metaphor in Instrumental Music and Sonification's Romantic Implications," in *Proceedings of the 16th International Conference on Auditory Display* (Washington, DC: International Community for Auditory Display, 2010), www.straebel.de/praxis/text/pdf_Straebel-Sonification%20Metaphor.pdf.

44. See Robert Carl, "Place and Space: The Vision of John Luther Adams in the Ultramodernist Tradition," in *The Farthest Place: The Music of John Luther Adams*, ed. Bernd Herzogenrath (Boston, MA: Northeastern University Press, 2012), 206–18; and Bernd Herzogenrath, "The Weather of Music: Sounding Nature in the Twentieth and Twenty-First Centuries," in Herzogenrath, *Farthest Place*, 219–34.

45. John Luther Adams, "Resonance of Place: Confessions of an Out-of-Town Composer," in *Winter Music*, 15.

46. Adams cited in Carl, "Place and Space," 211.

47. Herzogenrath, "Weather of Music," 229.

48. Detailed in Adams's project diaries. See John Luther Adams, *The Place Where You Go to Listen* (Middletown, CT: Wesleyan University Press, 2009), 11–100.

49. Ibid., 1.

CHAPTER 8

1. By the time I completed this book, in 2016, all of the composers listed had passed away.

2. Aisha Orazbayeva, email correspondence with the author, April 2012.

3. Quoted in Tanya Böhme-Mehner, "Interview with Eckard Rödger, 16 March 2010, Leipzig," *Contemporary Music Review* 30, no. 1 (2011): 30.

4. See Norman Davies and Roger Moorhouse, *Microcosm: Portrait of a Central European City* (London: Jonathan Cape, 2002).

5. See Günter Mayer, "Advanced Composition and Critical (Political) Ambition," in *New Music and Aesthetics in the 21st Century*, vol. 5, *Critical Composition Today*, ed. Claus-Steffen Mahnkopf (Hofheim: Wolke Verlag, 2006), 171–84.

6. Georg Katzer, liner notes for *Six Classical Concrète, Electroacoustic and Electronic Works, 1970–1990*, ReR CMCD, 2004.

7. See Tatjana Böhme-Mehner, "Interview with Georg Katzer, 18th October, 2009, Leipzig," *Contemporary Music Review* 30, no. 1 (2011): 101–9; and Böhme-Mehner, "Interview with Lothar Voigtländer, 5 December 2009, Berlin," *Contemporary Music Review* 30, no. 1 (2011): 111–17.

8. Achim Heidenrich, "'Shaping Electronic Sounds Like Clay': The Historical Situation and Aesthetic Position of Electroacoustic Music at the ZKM | Institute for Music and Acoustics," *Organised Sound* 14, no. 3 (2009): 248.

9. For an account of the history of electronic music during the last years of the GDR, see Tatjana Böhme-Mehner, "Liberalization and Discovery," *Contemporary Music Review* 30, no. 1 (2011): 91–6.

10. Katzer and Bredemeyer cited in Elaine Kelly, "Reflective Nostalgia and Diasporic Memory: Composing East Germany after 1989," in *Remembering and Rethinking the GDR:*

Multiple Perspectives and Plural Authenticities, ed. Anna Saunders and Debbie Pinfold (Basingstoke: Palgrave Macmillan, 2013), 135.

11. My descriptions in the following paragraphs are based on those given in E. Kelly, "Reflective Nostalgia."

12. Ibid., 138.

13. Ibid., 142.

14. Quoted in Mayer, "Advanced Composition," 182.

15. Ibid.

16. Günter Olias quoted in E. Kelly, "Reflective Nostalgia," 141.

17. Svetlana Boym, *The Future of Nostalgia* (New York: Basic Books, 2001), xiv.

18. Quoted in Richard Taruskin, *The Oxford History of Western Music,* vol. 5, *Music in the Late Twentieth Century* (Oxford: Oxford University Press, 2005), 433.

19. Boym, *Future of Nostalgia,* xviii.

20. Svetlana Savenko, "Valentin Silvestrov's Lyrical Universe," in *Ex-Oriente II: Nine Composers from the Former USSR,* ed. Valeria Tsenova (Berlin: Ernst Kuhn, 2003), 97.

21. Quoted in Peter Schmelz, "Valentin Silvestrov and the Echoes of Music History," *Journal of Musicology* 31, no. 2 (2014): 241.

22. Quoted in ibid., 240.

23. *Grove Music Online,* s.v. "Sil'vestrov, Valentyn Vasil'yovych," by Virko Baley, accessed August 22, 2015, www.oxfordmusiconline.com.

24. Quoted in Tatiana Frumkis, description of Valentin Silvestrov's *Post Scriptum* (1991), sonata for violin and piano, Schott Music website, accessed September 21, 2016, https://en.schott-music.com/shop/post-scriptum.html.

25. Ibid.

26. Dominic Wells, "Plural Styles, Personal Style: The Music of Thomas Adès," *Tempo* 66, no. 260 (2012): 6.

27. Ibid., 4.

28. Thomas Adès, program note for *Darknesse Visible* (1992), Faber Music website, accessed August 20, 2015, www.fabermusic.com/repertoire/darknesse-visible-2461.

29. Samuel Adams, "Following the Prophecies of Song: Schubert Lieder in Thomas Adès's 'Arcadiana,'" *Perspectives of New Music* 48, no. 1 (2010): 200–207.

30. Boym, *Future of Nostalgia,* 46.

31. *Grove Music Online,* s.v. "Elgar, Sir Edward," by Diana McVeagh, accessed August 17, 2015, www.oxfordmusiconline.com.

32. Quoted in Eberhard Petschinka, liner notes for *Im Sturm,* col legno WWE1CD 20287, 2008, p. 40. Punctuation as in original.

33. Friedemann Sallis, *Music Sketches* (Cambridge: Cambridge University Press, 2015), 192.

34. At this stage, Holloway was unaware that Josef Rheinberger had already published a transcription of the *Goldberg Variations* for two pianos in 1883.

35. See Robin Holloway, liner notes for *Gilded Goldbergs,* performed by the Micallef-Inanga Piano Duo, Hyperion CDA67360, 2002.

36. Magnus Lindberg, Colin Matthews, Anthony Payne, Poul Ruders, David Sawer, Michael Torke, and Judith Weir.

37. Other such groups are the Hilliard Ensemble vocal quartet and the EXAUDI vocal ensemble.

38. "Recomposed Series," Recomposed by Max Richter, accessed September 21, 2016, www.recomposed.net.

39. I am not taking into account here the impact of sound design on both music and theater.

40. Nicolas Bourriaud, *Postproduction* (New York: Lukas and Sternberg, 2002), 13.

41. Seth Kim-Cohen, program note for *68SFTD* (2008), accessed May 12, 2015, www.kim-cohen.com/projects/68SFTD_home.html.

42. Exemplified by John Horton Conway's *Game of Life.*

43. However, there are enough clues in the film to guess that the city is Munich.

44. There is a remote echo here of Pamela Z's griot-like storytelling. See chapter 5.

45. Chaya Czernowin, "A Few Examples from MAIM (Water, 2001/2, 2005, 2006/7): How This Music Thinks," in *New Music and Aesthetics in the 21st Century*, vol. 6, *Facets of the Second Modernity*, ed. Claus-Steffen Mahnkopf, Frank Cox, and Wolfram Schurig (Hofheim: Wolke Verlag, 2008), 99–134.

46. Bruce Glaser, "Questions to Stella and Judd," in *Minimal Art: A Critical Anthology*, ed. Gregory Battcock (Berkeley, CA: University of California Press, 1995), 158.

INDEX

Page numbers in italic refer to figures.

Aa, Michel van der, 38, 39, 265, 280; *After Life,* 91; and multimedia spectacle, 91–92; *Up-close,* 90–91, *91*, 94, 102, 317n3

Abba, *Arrival,* 197

Abbado, Claudio, 173

Abbey of Santa Domingo de Silos, *Chant,* 34

Abercrombie, Alexander, 157

Ablinger, Peter, 69, 70, 102, 230, 262, 265, 280; *Kleines Klavierstück, 70, 71; A Letter From Schoenberg,* 70; *Listening Pieces,* 70–71, *72; Piano and Record,* 99–100, 119; *Quadraturen* series, 100; *Seeing and Hearing* pieces, 70; *Voices and Piano* series, 100–101, 257

Abou-Khalil, Rabih, 125

acoustic ecology, 13, 224, 297. *See also* documentation; field recording

ACTUEL REMIX (Xavier Garcia and Guy Villerd), 84

ACT UP (AIDS Coalition to Unleash Power), 67

Adams, John, 56, 238, 265–266, 280; Chamber Symphony, 60; *Hellmouth* (blog), 38; *Nixon in China,* 33; *On the Transmigration of Souls,* 222–223; Violin Concerto, 314n24

Adams, John Luther, 227–230, 262, 266, 281, 326n38; *Earth and the Great Weather,* 227; *Night Peace,* 227; *The Place Where You Go to Listen,* 227–228, 229–230, 326n39–41; *songbirdsongs,* 227

Adès, Thomas, 251, 266, 281; *Arcadiana,* 245; *Asyla,* 245; *Darknesse Visible,* 244–245; Piano Quintet, 245; *Powder Her Face,* 52–53

affect and pleasure, 55–57, 73

African American spirituals, 160; "Deep River," 159

afterness, poetics of, 261–263

Age of Consent, "Heartbreak," 52

AIDS commemorations, 67–68, 219–220

Akademie der Künste, 236

Akademie Schloss Solitude, 131

Alaska, 227

Albéniz, Isaac, *Tango,* 220

Alexander, Christopher, 155

Alfano, Franco, 246, 247

algorithmic compositions, 259

Ali-Zadeh, Franghiz, 125, 243–244, 266; *Mugam Sayagi,* 243

Alter Ego (ensemble), 83

alternate tunings, 58, 61–62

Amacher, Maryanne, *City-Links* series, 143, 144

ambient music, 33

American Composers Forum, 48

American Composers Orchestra, 168

Anderson, Laurie, 137

Andre, Carl, 261

Andriessen, Louis, 40, 187, 281, 316n62; *De Staat,* 60; *De Tijd,* 60; *Hoketus,* 60 antimodernism, 58–59

Apartment House (ensemble), 63

Aphex Twin: "Donkey Rhubarb," 77; *Drukqs*, 78; "ICCT Hedral," 77; *26 Mixes for Cash*, 78. *See also* James, Richard

Applebaum, Mark, 203, *204*, 266, 281, 322–323n17

Arab music, 128–130, 138, 149–150

Arab Spring, 109

Arcade Fire, 80

archipelago concept, 150–152, 170, 175

architecture, 155, 161, 166, 218–219, 250, 322n73; adaptive reuse, 249, *250*, 253; deconstructivist, 17, 18, *18*, 104. *See also* visual arts

Arfmann, Matthias, 84, 266

Argerich, Martha, 101

Asano, Koji, *Quoted Landscape*, 115

Ashley, Robert, 322n3; *Atalanta*, 163; *Now Eleanor's Idea*, 163; *Perfect Lives*, 163

Asphalt Orchestra, 40

Asphodel Records, 84

al-Assad, Bashar, 134

Association for Electroacoustic Music, 236

Atlas Ensemble, 127

Atoui, Tarek, 81, *129*, 138, 139, 149, 187, 262, 266; *Dahlem Sessions*, 130; *Un-drum*, 129–130; *Visiting Tarab*, 130

audience: barrier between performers and, 41, 42–44; crossovers as idiom and, 75; loss of, 31–32, 61; new, 9–10, 38, 122–123; and opera, 52; and spectacle as experience, 165–166, 170; spiritual minimalism and, 32, 33

audification, 219

Australia, 139, 294; Yolngu culture, 154, 155

Avant (record label), 196

avant garde: in Australia, 139; and cultural signification, 135; and electronic dance music, 75, 77–78; in GDR, 235–236; innovation in the wake of, 200; in Lebanon, 81; in Middle East, 81, 128–129; passing of, 232; restorative nostalgia and turn from, 238; spiritual minimalism and the new, 34–35; support during Cold War, 32; vestiges of, 10

Avraamov, Arseny, 96

Ayres, Richard, 244

Azerbaijani *mugam*, 243

Babbit, Milton, "Who Cares If You Listen," 176

Bach, Johann Sebastian, 11, 89, 112, 173, 247, 251–252, 253; deathbed chorale, 157–158

Bacon, Francis, 104, 105, 106

Badreddin, Shafi, 134

Bain, Mark, *StartEnd-Time*, 219

Ballon, Séverine, 140, 154

Balter, Marcos, 81

Bandcamp, 39

Bandt, Ros, 266; *Stargazer*, 228

Bang on a Can, 40, 262, 266, 281, 316n62; All-Stars, 40, 76, 316n57; Marathon (music festival), 40–41, *41*, 312n32; record label (Cantaloupe), 40, 85, 313n43; Summer Institute, 40

Barlow, Clarence (Klarenz), 184, 210

baroque music, 60, 76

Barrett, Richard, 85–86, 104, 173–174, 176, 266–267, 281–282; *Another heavenly day*, 140; *Codex* series, 21; *Coïgitum*, 140; *CONSTRUCTION*, 142–143, 320n34; *DARK MATTER*, 42, 142; *EARTH*, 142; *Interference*, 141, 320n30; *ne songe plus à fuir*, 142; *ON*, 142–143; *Opening of the Mouth*, 42, 142; *world-line*, 140–141

Bartók, Béla, 4, 238, 239; *Bluebeard's Castle*, 245; *Mikrokosmos*, 173

Basinski, William, 267, 282; *Disintegration Loops*, 218

Bauman, Zygmunt, 94–95, 109, 188, 317n6

Bayle, Laurent, 183, 184

BBC: Concert Orchestra, 79; Proms, 44, 53, 254; Radio 3, 37–38, 53; and Tavener, 29, 32–33

BEAST (Birmingham Electroacoustic Sound Theatre), 135

Beaudoin, Richard, 101–102, 267, 282; *Études d'un prélude*, 101

Beck, 84

Beethoven, Ludwig van, 59, 96, 99, 111, 132, 245, 247; *Fidelio*, 237; Piano Sonata No. 26, 173

Beirut, Lebanon, 81, 129

The Beloved, "The Sun Rising," 34

Benjamin, George, *A Purcell Garland*, 251, 254

Berg, Alban, Violin Concerto (1935), 158, 216

Berio, Luciano, 103, 232, 247, 253, 267, 282; *Rendering*, 247, 248–249; *Sinfonia*, 247

Berkowicz, Filip, 79

Berlin Artists-in-Residence program, 130–131

Berlin Biennale, 130

Berlin Festwochen, 233

Berlin Philharmonic, 31, 40, 84, 173

Berlin Wall, fall of, 7, 24, 168, 184, 232, 234–237. *See also* Soviet Union

Berne, Alexander, *Self-Referentials Volumes I and II*, 48

Bernstein, Leonard, 16